California Perfo.
Test Workbook

California Performance Test Workbook

Preparation for the Bar Exam

SECOND EDITION

MARY BASICK

TINA SCHINDLER

Wolters Kluwer

Published by Wolters Kluwer in New York.

Wolters Kluwer Legal & Regulatory U.S. serves customers worldwide with CCH, Aspen Publishers, and Kluwer Law International products. (www.WKLegaledu.com)

To contact Customer Service, e-mail customer.service@wolterskluwer.com, call 1-800-234-1660, fax 1-800-901-9075, or mail correspondence to:

> Wolters Kluwer
> Attn: Order Department
> PO Box 990
> Frederick, MD 21705

Printed in the United States of America.

2 3 4 5 6 7 8 9 0

ISBN 978-1-5438-1351-7

Library of Congress Cataloging-in-Publication Data

Names: Basick, Mary, author. | Schindler, Tina, author.
Title: California performance test workbook : preparation for the bar exam
  / Mary Basick, Tina Schindler.
Description: Second edition. | New York : Wolters Kluwer, 2019. | Summary:
  "The California Performance Test Workbook's instruction, strategy, and
  actual California Bar Performance Test exam questions train law students
  to write appropriate Performance Test answers within the exam's
  proscribed timetable. The Workbook includes explanations of each
  component of the Performance Test and its timetable; a step-by-step
  method and strategy for approaching the exam; advice for creating a
  Performance Test study plan; troubleshooting tips to improve
  performance; practice California Performance Tests; and sample answers
  with analysis"—Provided by publisher.
Identifiers: LCCN 2019039433 | ISBN 9781543813517 (paperback) |
  ISBN 9781543816723 (ebook)
Subjects: LCSH: Bar examinations—California—Examinations, questions, etc. |
  Practice of law—California—Examinations, questions, etc. | Bar
  examinations—California—Study guides. | LCGFT: Study guides.
Classification: LCC KFC76 .B378 2019 | DDC 349.794/076—dc23
LC record available at https://lccn.loc.gov/2019039433

About Wolters Kluwer Legal & Regulatory U.S.

Wolters Kluwer Legal & Regulatory U.S. delivers expert content and solutions in the areas of law, corporate compliance, health compliance, reimbursement, and legal education. Its practical solutions help customers successfully navigate the demands of a changing environment to drive their daily activities, enhance decision quality, and inspire confident outcomes.

Serving customers worldwide, its legal and regulatory portfolio includes products under the Aspen Publishers, CCH Incorporated, Kluwer Law International, ftwilliam.com, and MediRegs names. They are regarded as exceptional and trusted resources for general legal and practice-specific knowledge, compliance and risk management, dynamic workflow solutions, and expert commentary.

Summary of Contents

Contents

Preface

Dear Bar Taker,

This book includes everything you need to know to write a passing performance test answer for the California bar exam. After much experience working with potential bar takers and extensive analysis of the released 90-minute California performance exams, we have created this book to be a condensed, yet thorough review of how to approach a performance test, including step-by-step instructions and annotated demonstrations, real sample questions, and realistic answers.

The introduction covers the skills involved in successfully writing a passing California performance test. In particular, this section includes valuable information on how to successfully organize and write a passing answer within the allotted time frame.

Practice performance tests and sample passing answers are included for each performance test. We also include our assessment grid for each performance test to help you quickly identify any missing issues, rules, facts, or organizational challenges. In addition, there is an Extra Practice Appendix section with guidance on getting extra practice on critical skills using Performance Test task and library files.

We wish you the best of luck on the upcoming bar exam!

Mary Basick and Tina Schindler

August 2019

Acknowledgments

We have many people to thank who made this book possible. First, we must thank our wonderful families for their love and support. Tina has the encouragement of Jim, Madilyn, and J.C. Schindler. Mary has the support of Mark, Abby, Tara, and Blake Ribisi and Zachary Basick. We are also grateful for the support of Barbara Lasoff, Sarah Hains, and the rest of the entire team at Wolters Kluwer.

PART I ## PREPARING FOR THE CALIFORNIA PERFORMANCE TEST

INTRODUCTION

This book includes everything needed to write passing performance tests. Use our step-by-step approach and timetable to ensure you can craft an effective passing answer within timed conditions.

PERFORMANCE TEST BASICS

The performance test provides California bar exam applicants with a role-play exercise involving a mock real-life task that a beginning lawyer should be able to accomplish. The test assesses two things about you: First, do you act and think like a lawyer? And second, do you have the minimal competence expected of a beginning lawyer?

Applicants must role-play to solve the hypothetical client's factual problem by following directions, analyzing law, assessing facts, and writing a comprehensive, well-organized response under timed conditions. The performance test closely resembles a real-life legal experience and should feel similar to legal writing or pretrial litigation class exercises or to a clerking experience. Your job as a bar exam applicant is to think and act like a lawyer, to role-play to solve the client's problem, and to communicate effectively in writing. Unlike a real-life scenario, however, the performance test occurs in a closed universe that provides all information needed to solve the problem without doing any of the research you ordinarily would do. The problem will include a client file containing documents with factual information about the task assigned and about the client's case. It will also supply a library of all the law needed to complete the assigned task, but it will leave to applicants the obligation to be mindful of potential ethical issues.

During the afternoon bar exam session on Tuesday, two one-hour essay questions and one 90-minute performance test will be administered. The performance test (PT) is important because while it is allotted 90 minutes, it has the point value of two one-hour essays and is worth 14 percent of your overall bar score. Scoring 65 out of 100 is the target to ensure a passing score. Since the PT counts double, it is important that you do well on it. The good news is that everyone can write a passing PT with enough practice.

> *Bar Passing Tip:* The PT and the expected PR essay combined are worth 43 percent of your *written score* on the California bar exam (the remaining four essays are where the other 57 percent come from, but those could be from any subject). Both are easily passable with enough practice, so be strategic in your bar studies. Issue spot a PR essay each day, and practice PTs until you are comfortable with the format. Some students will pick it up quicker than others, but with enough practice, everyone can pass the PT, so practice as many as you need to ensure you will pass.

COMPONENTS OF THE PERFORMANCE TEST PACKET

Each PT consists of two components. The first is the "Instructions and File"; the second is the "Library."

Instructions and File

The instructions and the file section include a table of contents, the instructions, the task memo, possibly a format internal firm memo, and the remainder of the client file.

- **File table of contents:** This is the first page of the packet. It will have a listing of which documents are included in the client file and the order in which they appear. You can also glean the length of the file contents here.
- **Instructions:** This document is always the first page of the file. It summarizes the bar examiners' instructions to the applicant. Instructions for most PTs are almost always nearly identical.
- **The task memo:** This document immediately follows the instructions. It addresses the applicant as a beginning lawyer and is written as if from the lawyer's boss. The memo assigns the lawyer the specific task(s) to be completed in the PT. Any documents specifically referred to in the task memo are of particular importance. The memo may also contain case facts.
- **The format internal memo:** Not every PT has a format internal memo, but if it does, it is the document immediately after the task memo. This document is typically on firm letterhead and explains how the assigned document should be written and what the format of the finished product should look like. Often a sample will be provided.
- **Client file:** The client file can consist of a variety of documents and the length can vary. The client file provides the facts that will be used to solve the problem.

Library

The library section consists of the library table of contents and a set of legal materials. Very rarely does a PT not include a library.

- **Library table of contents:** The first page of the library packet will list all of the statutes and/or cases included in the library and their order. You can glean the length of the library here, too.
- **Library:** The library includes statutes and/or cases of varying length. The library provides the law to be used to solve the problem.

STEP-BY-STEP APPROACH AND STRATEGY

APPROACH AND TIMETABLE FOR PERFORMANCE TESTS

Your approach to the performance test should be the same, regardless of the task presented. Every PT is different. Often students see a "new" task that they didn't practice during bar preparation and panic. Don't panic! Plan to approach every single performance test in the same way, regardless of the specific task assigned. While the finished product might look different, the familiar process that leads you there will always be the same.

Since time management is key to success, the first part of the process is employing a timetable guideline to appropriately allocate the limited time you have. You will spend approximately half of your time reading the materials and organizing your answer, and the other half of your time writing your response. You need to actively engage with the materials since there is insufficient time to read passively through all the materials and then circle back for a more thorough re-read. Rather, you need to decide actively what information you need to know and read with the purpose to find that information in the materials provided. As you go through the materials, you will actively be partially crafting your answer as you go or creating your own roadmap that you will then use to craft your answer.

PT Approach and Timetable		
Task	**Roadmap** on paper (in minutes)	**Roadmap** on computer (in minutes)
Scan instructions and the client file and library tables of contents	1	1
Start your roadmap: • Read the task memo • Identify the macrostructure for the answer • Read the format memo (if any)	5–7	7–10
Skim the client file (add to roadmap if possible)	2	2
Read the library and synthesize rules (add to roadmap)	15–20	20–30
Read the file (add to roadmap)	10–15	15–20
Reread task memo and refine roadmap to solve the problem	5	5
Write the answer	About 45	22–30
Note: The time required will vary slightly based on the length of the file and the size of the library, whether the bulk of the organization and structure comes from the file or the library, and how much content you include in your answer as you are organizing.		

There are many ways to tackle a PT, and it is important that you find a strategy that works for you. The approach we describe below has been shown to be very effective with all of the many varieties of tasks you might see in a PT. Keep in mind, however, that each PT is different, so the process is fluid and the time estimates are guidelines, not hard and fast rules.

We have created a step-by-step guide to enable you to master each of the many different tasks needed to successfully complete a performance test. This allows you to focus on each piece of the puzzle independently, which is needed for mastery. Unfortunately, this may provide the misleading impression that this process is linear and sequential. It isn't always. In practice, many of the steps will blend together. Once you get the hang of it, this process will flow smoothly and fluidly, but to get started, we will specify in detail what you should do at each step in the approach outlined above.

Step 1.   **Scan the instructions, the file table of contents, and the library table of contents (1 minute)**

What Are You Looking For?

Although the instructions are almost always the same, you should scan them to make sure. You are looking for three important pieces of information:

1. The jurisdiction
2. The contents of the PT packet
3. Task weighting information, if provided

Jurisdiction

Look for the jurisdiction the case is in, since that information will be essential as you read the library and determine the authority of the cases. The jurisdiction information is usually found in paragraph two. If the task is in state court, you will likely be told that you are in the fictional State of Columbia. (*Note:* If you practice with MPT materials, they will likely be set in the fictional State of Franklin.)

Packet Contents

The instructions will also identify, typically in paragraph three, the information provided, which is almost always a file and library. We mention this because very occasionally a performance test will only include a file, so at this point you should double-check to see if something seems amiss with your packet.

- **Task weighting:** This is not often present, but if more than one task is assigned, you may also find in the instructions an allocation of point value (for example, 50/50 or 30/70 between two tasks). If provided, this information usually appears after the final paragraph; make a note at the top of your scratch paper and allocate your time accordingly.
- **File and library tables of contents:** A one-page table of contents will precede the client file and another will accompany the library. Take a quick look at each to get a feel for what materials the PT contains and the relative length of each section.

Step 2.   **Read the task and format memos, and identify the macrostructure for your answer (5–7 minutes on paper or 7–10 minutes on computer)**

In Step 2 you begin gathering key information. This step is intertwined with the process of creating your roadmap, which is noting this key information in an organized and accessible manner from which to efficiently draft your response. The process of creating a roadmap is covered with specificity in Step 3, but keep in mind that this process actually begins here.

The Task Memo

Begin with the task memo, which immediately follows the instructions page. **The task memo is the most important document in the packet.** The PT is a role-play exercise, and the task memo is the pretend memo from your boss asking you to complete a task and providing specific directions for you to follow. You must *carefully and slowly* read the task memo and then use this information to start your roadmap (see Step 3 below). Following directions exactly is essential to passing the PT, so slow down here. Then, carefully read the accompanying format memo (if one is provided, it will usually be referenced in the task memo and will usually be the document immediately following the task memo). If the task memo specifically references another document, that document is important, so carefully read that document also.

PT Tip: The importance of the task memo cannot be overstated. A passing score on the PT can be won or lost right here, even though you are only 10 minutes into the exam. Be certain you understand what is being asked of you before you proceed. To double-check your understanding, imagine explaining the task to another associate. If you can articulate the task, you likely understand what is being asked of you. Misinterpreting the task memo is the primary reason students fail the PT. For extra practice deconstructing task memos, see the Appendix in this book.

What Are You Looking For?

You are looking for three key pieces of information:

1. Specific details about your client and the task assigned;
2. A macro-organizational structure for your answer; and
3. Specific directions about how your response is to be formatted, *if* you are provided with formatting directions or a format memo.

1. Client details and task assigned. The task memo is the first document after the instructions addressed to "applicant." It is typically less than one page.

Your goal is to gain clarity on the task details and to identify your answer's macrostructure so that as you go through the rest of the file and the library you can annotate the roadmap with the pertinent rules and facts that will solve the problem and place them in the appropriate section of your planned answer. Slow down here and read carefully.

Failure to follow to the letter the specific directions in the task memo is akin to running a race facing in the wrong direction: doomed to fail. It is worth the extra time at this point to be absolutely sure you are crystal clear on the instructions.

The task memo should provide the following key information, which should be noted at the top of your roadmap:

- **Task assigned:** The task memo sets out the nuts and bolts of the assignment and of the task you are being asked to do.
- **Your role:** The task memo will identify your role in the task, for example, junior associate.
- **Your client:** From the task memo you should be able to identify your client and the opposing party.
- **Client's legal issue and goal:** The client's legal issue and goal should also be identified. (Sometimes the client's goals aren't identified here but in the transcripts or interviews within the file documents, so if the task memo doesn't identify the client's goals, you will know you need to look for them in the file.) Other key client facts may also be included.
- **Tone and intended audience:** For each task assigned, if there are more than one, determine if your responses should be objective or persuasive. Also, identify the intended audience for the document you are writing, the level of formality required, and the appropriate vocabulary. Vocabulary used for court will be formal, whereas vocabulary used with another lawyer may be slightly less formal. Avoid using legal jargon when addressing a layperson, client, or a jury.
- **Any specific instructions:** Make a special note of anything you are told to exclude from your document (such as a statement of facts). Follow these instructions exactly.

PT Tip: Although the bar examiners assign a variety of tasks, the most frequently assigned are an Objective Memorandum and a Persuasive Brief/Memorandum of Points and Authorities. If you are assigned an unusual, unfamiliar task, be sure to follow the directions and use common sense. See the Examples section in this book for guidance on an appropriate format for some of the more unusual performance test formats and tasks that have been assigned.

2. Macro-organizational structure for your answer.   It is important to identify how you will organize your answer using a skeletal outline of the issues, which you can then annotate as you go through the steps, outlined below, of gathering applicable law from the library and legally significant facts from the client file. A typical PT will have two to four major issues or sections that provide the macro-organizational structure for your document. This structure can come from legal theories, causes of action, defenses, a client's goal or questions, etc. The organizational information is provided three ways:

- **The task memo:** The task memo typically provides the information on how your answer should be organized. At some point, the memo will provide a list of issues or point headings around which you can start to organize and build your answer. Often the task memo will directly list the issues presented. For example, you may be told that the client wants you to answer three questions. This information should be transferred to your roadmap, since that means you will have three major point headings in your answer that match the client's three questions. It is a good idea to use a separate piece of paper to "roadmap" each point heading. Other task memos may be less clear on the issues presented, but they will reference a document in the client file or a theory of law that provides a clue on where you can find the organizational structure for your answer in the client file or library (see below).

- **The client file:** The task memo may give you a hint about where you can find the organizing information by directly mentioning a document in the client file. If the structure is not obvious from the task memo, you should take a moment to try to locate that information before you move forward. First, look at any document specifically mentioned in the task memo. If it isn't there, look at any document providing insight into the client, such as a letter from the client or a client-interview transcript. (You can quickly identify such a document by looking at the file table of contents.) Sometimes, the task memo will mention the client's goals from their interview or deposition; if so, look there for the structure. If the task memo mentions the opposing counsel's complaint, look there. Once you have found the list of issues, you have found the macrostructure for your answer.

- **The library:** Sometimes the task memo will be more vague and only refer to a theory of law under which the client may or may not recover. If you can't find the organizational structure in the task memo or from a quick look in the file, keep an eye out for that information while you move forward. It will likely come from the rules themselves. Often when the task memo mentions specific causes of action, the structure will be based on the law or elements for that particular cause of action, which will be found in the library.

> **PT Tip:** The reason finding the organizational structure is so important is that it will help you match your answer to the grading rubric. The PT authors have embedded clues on the structure into the file or library, and you need to find them to match your answer to the grading rubric, thus making it easy for the grader to give you a passing score.

3. Format directions.   If you are given information on the format your answer should follow, you must follow the directions exactly. Although a separate format memo is not usually provided, if one is provided it will appear immediately after the task memo, and the task memo will reference it directly. For example, you may be directed in the task memo to draft a document "in accordance with the firm guidelines"; if so, those firm guidelines will be included in another memo in the file, immediately following the task memo. A format internal memo should be read very carefully.

Format internal memos are usually very specific and may provide an example. If so, deconstruct the example, much like you would deconstruct a rule, to determine the format's key components. Follow the directions and any example model exactly. Look for information about what the document should look like visually (underlining, using bold, spacing, columns, etc.), the proper tone of the document, and the expected contents: what the document should include, and what it should exclude. Follow these directions exactly. If no format memo is included to provide guidance, use common sense to create the structure for your answer.

Step 3. **Start roadmap (time included in steps 2-7)**

What Is a Roadmap?

Your "roadmap" is nothing more than notes you write to yourself to jog your memory of key information you plan to use when writing your answer. The goal of the roadmap is to provide the big picture of the organizational structure of the task including enough detail so you don't have to keep flipping around referring to the source documents in the packet. Since time is of a premium, it is essential to passing that you are extremely efficient with your use of time, and a roadmap allows you to efficiently craft a well-organized and responsive answer.

The key to passing a PT is following directions, and the roadmap consolidates all critical information in one place. It is a working document. After you have identified the preliminary information and the structure of the task from going through the task memo and format memo (if any), proactively go through the file and library and systematically pull out the key law and facts you will need in your response and place them where they go within the organizational structure you have outlined. You will then use your notes to craft an answer that solves the problem posed.

How Do You Create a Roadmap?

The good news is there is no particular format you need to use for your roadmap, so you'll want to experiment a little and find a system that works for you. You can make a roadmap on paper or on your computer. Either method, or a hybrid method, works fine, and we suggest you try different approaches until you find the one that works best for you. We alternate between the two approaches in our step-by-step demonstrations in this book.

- **Roadmap mostly on scratch paper:** If you make a roadmap mostly on scratch paper, you will spend roughly the first 45 minutes of your time going through all the materials and organizing your answer. Then you will spend about 45 minutes using your roadmap to write your answer. Many students use a piece (or more) of paper laid horizontally. We recommend using a separate piece of paper for each section of your answer to help keep your concepts organized.
- **Roadmap mostly on the computer:** You will want to spend at least the first 60 minutes of your time going through all of the materials, organizing your answer, and inputting key information directly into your answer in the section where it belongs as you go. You can start with a section for the introduction, the section headings (once you can identify them), and a conclusion. As you gather additional information, input it directly where it belongs in your answer. Then, you will spend your remaining minutes (which will vary depending on how completely you already input your rules, analysis, etc. while organizing) crafting the information you've compiled into a composed answer. You will probably also want to have a scratch paper skeletal roadmap that includes key information and a bullet point type listing of your task organizational structure to help keep you on track. This will also give you some peace of mind in case there are any technical problems.

What Goes in the Roadmap?

Your roadmap should include all key instructions for the assigned task and should identify the organizational structure you plan to use in your answer. Make a note of all critical task information at the top of your roadmap for easy reference, because it can be easy to lose track of essential details while you are immersed in the task. Identify the parties, which party is your client, the legal issue presented, and your client's goal. You should also identify the task document(s) you are crafting (for example, a memorandum or letter), note if the task is objective or persuasive, the intended audience (such as lay person, lawyer, or judge), the appropriate tone and vocabulary for the document (for example, layman's terms for a client or a formal tone for a judge), and any specific instructions (such as sections you've been instructed to include or exclude from a brief).

This may seem unnecessary, but it is much more efficient to look at your own notes for this information than to try to dig through the file to find it later when you are in the middle of the task and the clock is running out. Further, going through this step will force you to be clear on the task, the client's goal, the tone, and the intended audience for your response so you can more easily stay focused along the way and not run your fastest in the wrong direction. If you've been assigned more than one task you may be told how the tasks will be weighted. If so, make a note. Lastly, note at the top of your roadmap the time at which you need to start writing so you can manage your time appropriately.

Sample:

π Δ	Start writing at _____
_____ v. _____	Task:
	Objective/Persuasive:
Client:	Audience:
Issue:	Include:
Goal:	Exclude:

Step 4.   Skim the client file/facts (2 minutes)

Why do you skim the client file first? It is human nature to want to know the "story" of the client's case. Given the tight time frame, however, it is inefficient to spend time reading the client's facts before you have identified the rules that apply to solving the problem because you won't be able to determine which facts are legally significant until you understand the law. Skimming the client's facts will help because it usually takes less than two minutes, satisfies your curiosity, provides a general idea of what facts are contained in the client file and where they are located, and gives you enough of the client's story to provide context for the rules you will obtain from the library.

The types of documents that may be included in the client file range from letters, depositions, and interview transcripts to newspaper articles, contracts, reports, arrest records, wills, and other documents. A good method for skimming is to **read the heading** of each letter or paper in the file (who wrote it and to whom it's addressed) and to **read the first and last sentence of each paragraph** for all documents. If a transcript is included, do a more general skim.

Step 5.   Actively read the library and synthesize rules (15–20 minutes on paper or 20–30 minutes on computer)

After you have the macro structure identified on your roadmap and you have the gist of the facts, you need to turn to the library.

First, take note of the type of law you have to work with.

- **Statutes:** Although the statutes will appear first in the library, **read the cases first** since often they will interpret the statute(s).
  - **Legislative history:** Legislative notes (footnotes) may accompany the statutes; if so, you should pay attention to them, since the PT authors will often drop a clue in a footnote.
  - **Do you use them all?** If you have been provided with one to four statutes or regulations, they will all most likely be important, especially if they are not sequential. If, instead, you are given a long list of sequential statutes, they may have been provided for reference, so you need to discern which will be important to cite.
- **Cases:** Every case is provided for a purpose. As you read the cases, your goal is to find law that you can *use* to write your answer. Cite every case in the library in your answer, including any cases within a case. Also note whether each case is binding or persuasive authority.

Common Rule Structures

On California PTs, look for rules to start generally and then narrow. The starting point in the first case or statute will usually be a general rule, followed by cases that further define elements or terms in the rule. These will be followed by a case (or cases or a case within a case) that applies the narrowed rule to a fact situation. Typically, the cases are presented in the same order as any elements contained in the general rule, so if you are in doubt, use the cases sequentially. Similarly, if there is a factor test, the rule will start with the whole factor test, and the cases will then narrow down to elaborate on some of the factors. Provide a similar structure in your answer and avoid jumping straight to the narrow rule. It is a good idea to use subheadings for the narrower rule or element or the individual factors.

Book Brief the Cases

Read the cases with the purpose of identifying what you can do with the case in light of solving the problem posed and to determine how they fit in the macrostructure you've identified. Although the cases are edited specifically for the PT, you will not have time to do a thorough and exhaustive review and brief of each. It is important to read the cases actively. Use a pen and underline the holdings and make notes on the cases in the margins. You can use highlighters in the exam room on the written portion of the California bar exam, so it may be helpful to create a system where you highlight each part of the case in different colors (i.e., rules in blue, analysis in pink, holdings in yellow, etc.). The idea is to annotate your cases so you can easily find information later when you are writing.

- **Rules:** Extract a rule or rules from the case.
- **Facts:** Note all key legally significant facts by underlining, circling, or highlighting them, since you may need to apply and/or distinguish them with your client's facts.
- **Holding:** Note the court's reasoning and make note of any dicta.
- **Case within a case:** Treat a case within a case as its own case.
- **Footnotes:** Footnotes often contain clues that will make your job easier, so pay attention to them.
- **Does the case help or hurt?** Make a note at the top of the case, such as a + or −, or a happy/ unhappy face.
- **Is the case binding?** Make a note at the top of each case if it is binding or persuasive. If a case hurts your client, you may want to argue that it is nonbinding, so pay special attention to the jurisdiction.

Use the Law to Solve the Problem

Your goal is to *use* the law and sound like a lawyer, not to give a treatise like a law student. If the library presents binding cases with differing results, focus on the factual differences. If there is a jurisdictional split, look for the underlying policies that explain the result and note if either case is controlling. You want to avoid writing summaries of a case as you would for class; rather, you want to *use* the law provided to problem-solve and discover how the law has treated other clients with similar issues and then to compare the law and facts to your client's situation to predict how your client will be treated. To that end, determine why each case is given, clearly identify the rules, emphasize the outcome-determinative facts, and focus on using good headings to guide your reader.

What if you aren't sure how to use a case?   If a case is not obviously applicable, or is causing you difficulty, make a note and continue with your reading to see if the following case or cases provide context. Be alert for cases that seem familiar but that have been altered. Since you won't have time to write extensive briefs, be proactive and precise.

> *PT Timing Tip:* Applicants who run out of time on the PT often do so because they spend too much time on the library. If you haven't been book briefing your own cases to prepare for class, you should brush up on this key skill. See the Appendix in this book for targeted library practice on book briefing.

Weight of authority.   Pay attention to the weight of authority for the cases and which are controlling. You will likely be in the fictional State of Columbia, in the fictitious Fifteenth Circuit. If you practice with an MPT, you will be in the State of Franklin. By way of analogy, in California the court hierarchy is the State Supreme Court at the top, then the Court of Appeals, followed by the Superior Court at the lowest level. In federal court, the hierarchy moves from the U.S. Supreme Court at the top, followed in descending order by the Circuit Court or Court of Appeal for the X Circuit and then the District Court. It may be important to identify if the precedential weight is mandatory or persuasive, or if the case has dicta.

Citation.   Cite every case and most statutes (see above for guidelines). You can use the first name of the case, instead of a full cite. Underline the case name in your answer, instead of using italics, because under-lining catches the eye more readily and will be easier for the grader to spot. Refrain from using id. when referring to a case; repeat the case name, which will make it easier for the grader to see at a glance if you have included the right case in the right section.

What do you do with the information from the library?   Sometimes you will only pluck a rule from a case (for example, when a case repeats a general rule, such as the elements for fraud), but more often you will need to deconstruct a rule, synthesize the cases, and/or write a rule explanation.

- **Rule deconstruction:** Distill a rule down into its elements or factors. Read word by word and phrase by phrase, while paying special attention to the important structural signals, such as *and, either/or, unless, except, shall, may,* etc.
- **Rule synthesis:** Develop a complete depiction of a rule by pulling together pieces from various cases and reconciling any discrepancies among the cases.
- **Rule explanation:** Any time you need to explain *why* the holding from a case applies to your fact situation, you need to write a rule explanation. This is a quick explanation of why the case turned out as it did and includes the key facts in the underlying case and the holding. The rule explanation sets up your analysis paragraph, in which you will either analogize how your case facts are like the case facts in the underlying case, and thus your case should result in the same outcome, or explain that your facts are distinguishable, such that your case should result in a different outcome.

> *PT Timing Tip:* Every sentence you can pull from a case and use (appropriately) in your answer is one less sentence you have to create from scratch. Keep an eye out as you go through each case for language you can "borrow" and use in your introduction, topic sentences, and transitions.

What do you do with negative authority?   As happens in real life, you may get a case holding that is bad for your client. Be sure that your answer addresses and handles any contrary authority. How you handle it will depend on your task: is it objective or persuasive?

- **Objective analysis:** Analyze the case matter-of-factly. Acknowledge the difficulty for the client that the authority poses.
- **Persuasive argument:** Try to minimize the impact of the negative authority by arguing that it is not binding authority (assuming this is arguable) or by distinguishing your case facts and leading with your strongest argument first. Do not fail to address the negative authority.

A word of caution about the rules.   All of the rules you need to solve the problem are included in the library; *however,* you are expected to bring your knowledge of Professional Responsibility rules.

- **Professional Responsibility:** Be especially cautious of potential Professional Responsibility issues if your client is a lawyer. Be mindful of the rules of confidentiality, especially if you have access to client information the client would not want shared or that could hurt the client. Do not do anything, or suggest anything, unethical.
- **No specialized knowledge:** Do not rely on any special knowledge you may have of the rules in the PT subject area. The cases have been edited especially for the PT and may not line up with the real rules. The cases may seem familiar, but they have been edited, so don't make any assumptions about the rules.

Add the Information from the Library to Your Roadmap

As you study the cases in the library and determine their significance, add them to your roadmap. Add the cases and/or statutes under the issues they pertain to and note any key facts. Once you have added the rules to your roadmap, including rule explanations or a note reminding yourself where you can find that key information quickly, go back to the client file and review the facts to see how they fit the legal rules.

If you are organizing on your computer as you go, type in statutes, key holdings, and case information directly into your computer as you go, but be sure to understand and absorb each case before you start typing so you don't waste time typing in information you don't end up using. Since you haven't yet ascertained the legally significant facts from your file, you may want to wait to write the rule explanation since it might not be clear how much explanation you need until you look at your case facts.

> *PT Timing Tip:* If you need to explain *why* a case holding applies to your situation, you need a rule explanation. However, the graders will likely take a closer look at your analysis, since that is where you will show them how you can use that law to solve the problem posed. Strategically, if you are short on time, the rule explanation is a good place for brevity, since it is probably worth fewer points than the analysis.

| Step 6. | **Actively read the client file/facts (10–15 minutes on paper or 15–20 minutes on computer)** |

Actively look for legally significant facts. Once you have identified the key rules from the library that correspond to each section of your answer, you need to go through the client file and find the pertinent legally significant facts to support your legal arguments. Separate the relevant facts from the irrelevant ones. The pertinent facts then need to be marshaled and matched to the appropriate law and transferred to the roadmap.

The client file factual analysis will be one of two types:

- If **factual analysis** is the primary focus of the task, focus on the overall legal theory or rule and the facts that correspond to the factors or rule elements that prove or disprove each element or factor. You will also want to focus on your opponent's weaknesses in credibility and any potential evidentiary problems. Use critical thinking to assess the consistency and reliability of the facts and respond accordingly.
- If **fact gathering** is the primary focus of the task, identify the additional facts needed and the various types of discovery tools that may be useful to obtain that information. It may be helpful to find the ultimate fact, divide it into elements or factors, and then gather facts for each element or factor. Use common sense. Don't overlook common sense solutions, such as directly questioning a non-hostile party. Don't waste time explaining why a fact needs to be gathered. Also, your answer should still use paragraphs and complete sentences, rather than bulleted lists. Don't concern yourself with admissibility issues unless you are instructed to do so.

If you are organizing on your computer as you go, make note of the key facts in the appropriate section.

| Step 7. | **Reread the task memo and refine your roadmap to solve the problem posed (5 minutes)** |

Rereading the task memo and refining your roadmap are key to writing a passing answer. We know—you are pressed for time by now and are likely feeling pressure to write. If you don't stop and make sure you are solving the problem posed, however, you risk spending the next 30 to 45 minutes writing an answer to a different problem than the one you were asked to solve: that will ensure a failing score.

It is easy to get lost in the sea of rules and client facts and lose focus on your assigned task. So before you rush to write your answer, take some time to think your answer through.

- **Be certain your planned answer solves the problem posed.** Role-play, look at the big picture, and refocus on what, precisely, is at issue given your client's goals. Don't overlook commonsense considerations. For example, a client may win a case against her brother-in-law, but the holidays will be difficult thereafter.

- **Review your boss's instructions in the task memo** and format internal memo, if provided. Consciously limit your discussion to only what is at issue. Be clear on the appropriate tone and vocabulary to use in the answer.
- **Use an effective overall organizational structure for the answer.** Make sure your answer will be easy to read and your logic easy to follow. Use headings and subheadings that make sense for the task and that will guide the grader. For example, perhaps a section would be clearer if you included subheadings; if so, refine your outline as necessary.
- **Decide how you should apportion your writing time.** Lastly, review your roadmap, plan to apportion your time appropriately, and add those writing timetable goals to your roadmap. For example, if you have four sections to write in 45 minutes and two require more in-depth treatment than the others, you may want to apportion five minutes each to the easier sections and 15 minutes each to the difficult sections; that will leave you five minutes to deal with unforeseen difficulties.
- **Spend your time proportionately where the points are located.** Usually, the point-rich areas are those in which the issues, rules, and facts are most complex. Be precise and do not waste any time analyzing a problem you weren't asked to solve: it will be worth zero points on the grading rubric. If you've been assigned more than one task, you may or may not be told how the tasks will be weighted. Spend your time in accordance with the relative importance of the tasks.

| Step 8. | **Write an answer that solves the problem posed (about 45 minutes on paper or 22–30 minutes on computer)** |

Once you have a completed roadmap and have followed the steps above, you are ready to write your answer. If you've been organizing on paper, you should have about 45 minutes to convert your notes into an answer. If you've been inputting information directly into your answer as you go, you have about 22 to 30 minutes to edit your notes into a responsive answer; the precise time left will depend on how much information you input directly into your answer as you organized.

Basic Structure of the Answer

All answers should start with a **brief introduction** and end with a **conclusion**. The general body of your answer should consist of the following structure, repeated for each separate issue:

- **Heading** for Issue 1
- **Issue statement** (objective task) or **conclusion/persuasive point heading** regarding issue (persuasive task)
- **Rule** (from the library case or statute)
- **Rule explanation** (if needed to explain the library case facts and why the holding turned out as it did)
- **Analysis** (prediction of what will happen when the holding from the library case is applied to the key facts in our client's case and **why** our case is similar or dissimilar to the library case)
  - **Analogize:** Use when the case facts are similar to the underlying case facts and you want (or predict that) the outcome will be the same in your case as in the underlying case.
  - **Distinguish:** Use when the case facts are dissimilar to the underlying case facts and you want (or predict that) the outcome will be different in your case than in the underlying case.
- **Conclusion** on Issue 1

This structure is fluid and can be modified depending on the task assigned and the development of the body of law available to solve the problem. For example, you may have several cases that apply to an issue and therefore several rule explanations and analysis sections in treating that one section.

Content of the Answer

The writing should be clear and concise and should make all necessary points briefly.

Use headings. Headings make your answer easy to follow and, consequently, easy to grade. Use headings to guide your grader, even if you are writing a letter, a closing argument, or another document in which headings aren't typically used. Use subheadings if appropriate and helpful.

Visual appearance of the answer. Your answer should look like the document it purports to be and should comply with the mandates of any format memo. Include an introduction, even if brief, setting up who you are and what issue you are addressing. It should look organized and follow all instructions. Use plenty of white space to make your answer visually appealing and easy to read.

Use an appropriate tone and vocabulary. Be mindful of the vocabulary that is appropriate for your audience (legal shorthand for a lawyer or judge and layman's terms for a client); the task (formal or less formal); and the tone. If the task is objective, provide an even-handed analysis. If the task is persuasive, craft an argument that persuades and puts your best foot forward while still addressing and distinguishing contrary authority.

Role-play. Don't ignore problematic areas. Rather, address them appropriately as you would in real life. Address both favorable and unfavorable facts appropriately. Note appropriately any facts that are potentially unreliable, such as when it appears your client is not telling the truth.

Produce a complete document. Make certain your finished answer looks finished. Include a conclusion or signature block where appropriate (be sure to sign it "applicant" and never use your real name). Failure to complete the task will ensure a failing score. If you are running out of time, it is better to make a point briefly than to leave it out of your answer.

PT Timing Tip: Write the conclusion or signature block when you start writing. That way, if you run out of time, you don't risk being so obvious about it to the grader.

STUDYING FOR THE PERFORMANCE TEST

Everyone would pass the PT if given two hours to complete it. The trick is writing a minimally competent answer in 90 minutes, which is not enough time. That takes practice. How much practice you need depends on you. Some students get the timing figured out after completing a few PTs, while others need to do more than a dozen. Do as many as you need to comfortably get passing scores. That should leave you going into the bar exam feeling confident, and confidence is essential to passing the bar.

Many students make the mistake of spending too little time studying for the performance test. Since there is no law to memorize and one must devote 90 minutes to taking a practice PT and then at least another 30 minutes analyzing the answer, practicing PTs can easily fall to the bottom of the "to do" list in favor of tasks that feel more pressing during the busy bar prep season. Time spent mastering the PT is time well spent, however, since one PT counts as much as two essays. Further, you don't have to memorize any rules to do well on a PT. You just need to practice until you get the hang of it: a doable proposition for any bar taker.

PERFORMANCE TEST STUDY PLAN

How much time and energy you should devote to studying for the performance test will vary according to your individual circumstances. If you have had clerking experience, the tasks assigned in the performance test will probably feel familiar, but it will still be important to practice using old performance tests to become familiar with the exam timing. Try to do one exam a week during your bar studies until you feel comfortable with the format and are managing your time effectively. Do a self-assessment of each PT to identify your strengths and weaknesses. (See the self-assessment section below.)

Once you feel comfortable with the PT timing and format, you may want to organize (without writing the answer) a practice PT each week to increase your familiarity with the various types of tasks that are tested. If you are struggling with the format and timing of the PT you should incorporate more practice into your bar studies; if you feel comfortable with the format you can do fewer practice tests and may wish to focus your time on an area of weakness, such as essay writing or MBE.

PT Tip: The most common areas of difficulty on a PT are:

1. Not following the directions of the task memo closely enough.
2. Inefficiency in the library, by either taking too much time to brief cases or struggling to extract the necessary rules/holdings from the cases.

For that reason, the Appendix provides a convenient way to do some targeted practice in these two problem areas without having to spend the time to complete an entire practice PT. You can also use MPTs, which are available on the NCBE website for extra practice.

SELF-ASSESSMENT

Improving your PT skills requires assessing how you perform on practice PTs. As you do practice PTs, keep track of the time you spend on each step. This record will help you to identify which parts of the process cause you trouble.

Step	Minutes Spent
Scan instructions, tables of contents	
Read the task memo and format memo	
Skim the client file (facts)	
Read the library and synthesize rules	
Read the client file	
Reread the task memo and solve the problem	
Write the answer	

SELF-ASSESSMENT ON YOUR PROCESS AND ANSWER

ROADMAPPING AND TIMING

____How long did you spend on each step of the PT process?
____Did you spend too much time on any of the steps?
____Did you create your roadmap on paper or computer or both?
____Did your roadmapping strategy work?
____Did you properly allocate your time given the relative importance of the issues?
____Did you complete the PT in the time provided?
____What could you have done differently to use your time more efficiently?

FORMAT

____Does your organization match the sample answer?
____Did you use the proper format for the task? (Your response looks like the memo, letter, brief, etc., called for.)
____Is the tone appropriate (objective or persuasive)?
____Is the vocabulary appropriate for the audience (legal/layperson, formality level)?
____Did you include a brief introductory paragraph?
____Does your answer look finished?

CONTENT

HEADINGS

____Did you have similar headings (in structure and number) to the sample answer?
____Are your headings formatted appropriately for the task?

ISSUES

____Did you address all issues? If not, why do think that happened?

____Misunderstood task memo
____Missed the legal significance of fact(s)
____Did not pull a rule from a case properly
____Misunderstood how to use a rule

RULES

____Did you use and cite all cases/statutes from the library?
____Did you use the cases/statutes to analyze the correct issue/sub-issue?
____Did you present the rule before the analysis?
____Did you deconstruct the rule(s) properly?
____Did you synthesize the rules (where necessary)?
____Did you use a rule explanation where needed?
____Did you analogize/distinguish cases as needed to solve the problem?

FACTS AND ANALYSIS

____Did you use all legally significant facts?
____Did you explain how/why your reasoning led to the result?

CONCLUSION

____Did you conclude as to each issue?
____Did you provide a summary that "solves the problem"?

TROUBLESHOOTING TIPS TO IMPROVE PERFORMANCE

If you are not properly organizing your performance tests and continue to miss key facts, rules, etc., then writing out ten performance tests before the bar exam will not help you pass. You need to think quality over quantity. While exposure to the different types of performance tests is helpful, the key to success lies in having a workable approach on which you can rely, not in what particular task a given PT asks you to address.

- **Misunderstanding the task assigned:** Misunderstanding the task is responsible for at least half of the failing PT scores, and this result has most often already happened before you are ten minutes into the PT. This common, but fixable mistake almost always results from failing to read slowly and critically to ensure you understand the task assigned before proceeding with the rest of the PT.

> ***Extra Practice Tip:*** If you need targeted practice on deconstructing the task assigned by the task memo, see the Appendix for targeted work on this skill.

- **Issue spotting:** If you had a problem spotting an issue that was required, you should pay attention to where the information came from that raised the issue. Reread all parts of the task memo to see if you missed something that referred to the issue(s) or where you could find the issue. It is possible that you just quickly overlooked something (such as an "and" in the task memo that would have indicated to you that there was more than one issue) or that you didn't carefully read some other document referred to in the task memo. Going forward, be sure to handle each distinct issue in a separate section.
- **Missing rules:** If you omitted key rules, reread the cases or statutes to see where you went wrong. Did your book brief note the missing rule? You may have missed it by reading too quickly, or you may not have understood that it was a rule. Either way, you need to determine what you missed and why so you can make changes going forward to help avoid missing rules. For example, if you read too quickly and missed a rule altogether, discipline yourself to read more slowly and/or try to review cases quickly after reading them once to ensure you didn't miss anything. On the other hand, if you had it briefed and/or in your roadmap but just accidentally left it out of your answer, you should try highlighting or checking off the various parts of your roadmap as you incorporate them into your actual answer to ensure you don't overlook something important. The key is to change your practice techniques to avoid making the same mistakes in the future.

> ***Extra Practice Tip:*** If you struggle to pull the correct rules out of the cases or to properly deconstruct a rule or if you spend too much time book briefing the cases, see the Appendix for targeted work on these skills.

- **Missing or misused facts:** The same process and principles apply to missing or misused facts. If you missed them, identify where they came from. See if you used them at all and, if not, determine why you missed them. Did you quickly glance over the file before going into the library and then come back and thoroughly read them? Did you add them to your roadmap as you read them? Make sure to figure out why you omitted them and that you change your practice techniques to avoid missing others in the future. Consider highlighting key facts as you use them so you can easily see which facts you haven't used.
- **Timing:** It is essential that you finish the assigned task(s). If you are struggling with finishing within the allotted time, you may need to try varying your approach to shave off some time. Pay attention to your timing and try to identify where the time drain is occurring: in the organization phase or in the writing phase? If the organization phase is the problem, practice book briefing the cases or try using a more skeletal roadmap, focusing only on key words. If the writing phase is the problem, practice more PTs; this will help the language to flow more easily. Another strategy to help stay on track is to apportion your time by each section of your answer. If organizing on paper, and that isn't working for you, try organizing on your computer to see if that helps your timing, and vice versa if you are organizing on the computer.

Carefully assess your practice PTs and take time to reflect on the completeness and quality of your answers and how you can improve. If you do, you will see improvement with each PT you write, helping you to avoid wasting precious study time. Practice smart!

EXAMPLES

PERFORMANCE TEST BUILDING BLOCKS

While the essay portion of the California bar exam always requires that answers use the IRAC format, the PT may require a variety of formats in addition to, or in place of, IRAC. The format needed to solve the problem for any assigned task should be identifiable from the client file. Typically, it will be an IRREAC (objective) or CRREAC (persuasive) format, as illustrated in Step 8 above.

Below are some common building blocks used in a typical PT answer.

PT Format	
Objective: IRREAC	**Persuasive: CRREAC**
• Headings: Objective • Issue Statement • Rule • Rule Explanation • Analysis • Conclusion	• Headings: Persuasive • Conclusion as to Issue • Rule • Rule Explanation • Analysis • Conclusion
PT Tone	
• Objective • Even-handed assessment	• Persuasive • Emphasize strengths • Minimize (but address) weaknesses

- **Introduction:** Always start your answer with a brief statement of who you are (if needed) and the issue you intend to address. You may also wish to include a quick summary of your findings.

> Pursuant to your request in the case referenced above, I have prepared an objective memorandum assessing whether the state government violated the establishment clause when it provided free computers to religious schools. In sum, the provision of computers does not violate the establishment clause because there is no excessive government entanglement.

- **Headings:** Each issue and sub-issue needs a heading. Headings guide the reader and allow the grader to easily give you points. Sometimes with slight modification you can use the language straight from the assignment in the task memo.
  - **Objective headings:** The heading can be phrased as a statement or as a question. If you were not provided with a specific format, use the following formula to include all key components:

    Law + legally significant fact

    - Phrased as a statement:

    > The State Government May Have Violated the Establishment Clause When It Provided Free Computers to Religious Schools

- Phrased as a question:

> Did the State Government Violate the Establishment Clause When It Provided Free Computers to Religious Schools?

- **Persuasive headings:** If you were not provided with a specific format, use the following formula to include all key components:

Result + legally significant fact + law + why

> The State Government Did Not Violate the Establishment Clause When It Provided Free Computers to Private Religious Schools Because It Did Not Endorse or Encourage Any Religion.

Issue Statements

An issue statement can be an introductory sentence in a letter or memorandum.

- Objective:

> The issue is whether the state government violated the Establishment Clause when it provided free computers to religious schools in Columbia.

- Persuasive:

> The court should hold that the state did not violate the Establishment Clause when it provided free computers to private religious schools, because the practice does not unconstitutionally aid, encourage, or endorse religion as measured by the Lemon test.

Rule

> Under the Establishment Clause, governments are prohibited from endorsing, aiding, or encouraging religion, and potential violations are measured using the Lemon test: the government law must have a secular purpose, the primary effect of the law must neither advance nor inhibit religion, and the law must not involve excessive government entanglement. Lemon.

Rule Explanation

Use the following formula to include all key components:

Library case holding + library case key facts + the case reasoning (how/why)

> In Lemon, the court explained that government salary stipends to private Catholic high school teachers violated the Lemon test because the ongoing nature of teaching would necessitate prolonged monitoring by the government to ensure the stipends were only used for secular teaching, thus requiring excessive government entanglement in religion.

Analysis

Use the following formula to include all key components:

Facts (our case) + rule (library case) + how/why (apply or distinguish library case) = result

> In this case, the provision of free government computers to private religious schools is not like the salary stipends in <u>Lemon</u> because the government would not have to constantly monitor computer use, as the government had to do in <u>Lemon</u> in order to ensure that the salary stipends were used only for secular teaching. The monitoring process inherent in the stipend scheme is what produced the excessive government influence on religious teachers in <u>Lemon</u>, but there is no similar excessive government entanglement present in this case since there will be no need for ongoing monitoring with a one-time provision of free government computers, as contemplated here.

Conclusion

> Therefore, the provision of free government computers to the private religious school does not violate the Establishment Clause.

PERFORMANCE TEST FORMATS

Objective or Bench Memorandum

> To: (usually to your boss from the task memo)
>
> From: Applicant
>
> Re: Client's name
>
> Date: Exam date
>
> Introduction: If you are drafting the task for your boss, introduce the document to put it in context, such as "Pursuant to your request, . . . ," identify the issues presented, and perhaps include a brief summary of your findings.
>
> Label body of document "Discussion"
>
> Use objective headings
>
> Use IRREAC format
>
> Conclusion

Persuasive Brief or Memorandum

> To: (usually to your boss from the task memo)
>
> From: Applicant
>
> Re: Client's name
>
> Date: Exam date
>
> Introduction: If you are drafting the task for your boss, introduce the document to put it in context, such as "Pursuant to your request, . . .," identify the issues presented, and perhaps include a brief summary of your findings.
>
> Label body of document "Argument"
>
> Use persuasive point headings
>
> Use CRREAC format
>
> Conclusion

Letter to Client

> Address block
>
> Dear Client's name,
>
> Introduce yourself if new to the client (role-play)
>
> Introductory paragraph stating the purpose of the letter
>
> Identify alternatives and the pros/cons of each choice (including legal and personal considerations where appropriate)
>
> Use headings for each alternative/issue (even though you might not normally do this in a letter)
>
> Use lay language, unless the client is an attorney; explain legal terms and simplify rules/theories
>
> Objective tone
>
> Signature line (sign your name as "Applicant")

Opening or Closing Argument

> Introduction: "Ladies and gentlemen of the jury . . ."
>
> Use headings to organize the issues/sub-issues
>
> Opening: Introduce each witness and the evidence the witness will present: "X will testify that . . ."
>
> Closing: Explain why your client has met the burden of proof based on the evidence and witness credibility
>
> Use a persuasive tone and lay vocabulary

Discovery Plan

For each element/fact in dispute, list the types of evidence you want to obtain, state briefly why you want to obtain that evidence, and indicate the potential source of the information

- Be creative and use common sense
- Include informal and formal methods of discovery
  - *Informal:* Talk to witnesses, examine records, collect data, perform tests, etc.
  - *Formal:* Depositions, interrogatories, requests for production of documents, admissions, subpoenas, requests for exams, etc.

Affidavit

Identify the witness

Qualify the witness; personal knowledge of the witness is key, so establish it first

Use numbered paragraphs and include only one fact per paragraph

Be concise when stating the facts

Be strategic about the facts and witnesses you include and exclude

Use a persuasive, best-foot-forward tone to accentuate the positive for your client, without lying

Witness Examination

Anticipate questions and objections

Be specific and concise

Determine the goals for each witness

Organize questions in chronological or issue order

Settlement Proposal

Suggest a compromise solution, but still be persuasive

Focus on convincing the opposition of how the settlement will benefit them

Include language stating that the client does not admit liability or waive any rights

Use law that will bolster your argument and encourage the opposition to settle

Analysis of or Redrafting a Document

Examples: analyzing or redrafting a statute, ordinance, contract, will/trust, regulation, policy

Focus on the changes that will best serve your client's goals but are permissible pursuant to the legal authority

Edit language to benefit the client

Comport with the legal authorities given

Use an objective tone, but address your audience in a way that furthers your client's goals

If you can properly organize the five full PTs contained in this book, as well as the additional task memos in the Appendix, you should be well on your way to passing the PT portion of the exam. For additional practice, MPTs (the PT version used in other states) are available on the NCBE website. Remember to practice smart and to believe in yourself.

DEMONSTRATION 1

HAYNES v. NATIONAL BANK OF COLUMBIA

California
Bar
Examination

SAMPLE 90-MINUTE

Performance Test

INSTRUCTIONS AND FILE

HAYNES v. NATIONAL BANK OF COLUMBIA

1

HAYNES v. NATIONAL BANK OF COLUMBIA

INSTRUCTIONS

1.   This performance test is designed to evaluate your ability to handle a select number of legal authorities in the context of a factual problem involving a client.

2.   The problem is set in the fictional State of Columbia, one of the United States.

3.   You will have two sets of materials with which to work: a File and a Library.

4.   The File contains factual materials about your case. The first document is a memorandum containing the instructions for the tasks you are to complete.

5.   The Library contains the legal authorities needed to complete the tasks. The case reports may be real, modified, or written solely for the purpose of this performance test. If the cases appear familiar to you, do not assume that they are precisely the same as you have read before. Read each thoroughly, as if it were new to you. You should assume that cases were decided in the jurisdictions and on the dates shown. In citing cases from the Library, you may use abbreviations and omit page citations.

6.   You should concentrate on the materials provided, but you should also bring to bear on the problem your general knowledge of the law. What you have learned in law school and elsewhere provides the general background for analyzing the problem; the File and Library provide the specific materials with which you must work.

7.   This performance test is designed to be completed in 90 minutes. Although there are no parameters on how to apportion that 90 minutes, you should allow yourself sufficient time to thoroughly review the materials and organize your planned response. Since the time allotted for this session of the examination includes two (2) essay questions in addition to this performance test, time management is essential.

8.   Your response will be graded on its compliance with instructions and on its content, thoroughness, and organization.

PAGER MONT AND WHITE

Attorneys at Law

3216 Morningside Drive

Roslyn, Columbia

www.PagerMont.com

TO: Applicant

FROM: Susan Mont, Senior Partner

DATE: July 28, 2015

SUBJECT: Conrad Haynes Case

Conrad Haynes was referred to our firm by the Columbia Bar Association Pro Bono Project and we have agreed to represent him in an administrative appeal of the denial of his claim for unemployment compensation. His former employer, the National Bank of Columbia, opposes his claim, alleging that he voluntarily left his job as a bank teller and thus is ineligible for benefits.

Unemployment compensation appeals are decided by an administrative law judge (ALJ) in the Office of Administrative Appeals (OAA) on the record before the claims examiner -- in this case, the interviews of Mr. Haynes and that of Sandra Bennett, a bank employee.

Prepare an argument to include in our appeal brief. Be sure to argue both that Haynes' resignation should be construed as involuntary and that, if voluntary, it was for good cause. We will need to convince the ALJ that the circumstances that led our client to resign do not disqualify him from receiving benefits. We will have to marshal facts effectively to persuade the ALJ that Haynes should not be disqualified. Make sure to assert arguments in his favor and to rebut potential arguments against this conclusion.

Do not prepare a separate statement of facts. Your draft should relate specific facts to the legal tests and conclude how your analysis would establish that the client should prevail.

3

DEPARTMENT OF EMPLOYMENT SERVICES

SUBJECT: Intake Interview of Conrad Haynes

FROM: Jane Epstein, Claims Examiner

DATE: May 11, 2015

Conrad Haynes is a 28-year-old father of two who quit his job at the National Bank of Columbia (NBC), Frog Hollow Branch, 6 weeks ago. He expected at the time that he resigned that, with his experience and abilities, he would be able to find a new job quickly. Because of the number of bank failures and mergers, he has not gotten an interview.

Haynes worked for NBC for a total of 3 years, but had been at the Frog Hollow Branch for the last 6 months of his employment. Before going to Frog Hollow, he worked as a "Roving Teller," substituting in branches all through the city and suburbs of San Carlos as needed in any particular week. While working as a Roving Teller for the region, Haynes took evening courses at Central Community College, taking advantage of NBC's tuition payment program; he ultimately got the degree of Associate in Business. His hope, he said, was to advance beyond the lowest level teller job and get into a management position at the bank.

In September 2014, Haynes was temporarily assigned to Frog Hollow to fill in for a teller who was on leave due to a medical issue. He got along well with Sandy Bennett, the branch manager there. She told him that she was impressed with the fact that he was able to perform many aspects of the teller job that were "above his pay grade." Because he had worked in so many branches, filling in for people in various jobs, he had learned to do the work at each of the three levels of teller as well as that of "Customer Service Representative." Bennett noticed that he was a hard worker, that he took initiative, and that he got along well with customers.

Even while serving as a fill-in, he was able to form relationships with customers that enabled him to sell other bank services. On at least three occasions that he could

4

remember, "his" customers opened brokerage accounts upon his suggestion and two took out loans to purchase new cars. These are examples of work normally done by a "Customer Service Representative." Haynes said that Bennett was very pleased with each of these occurrences and praised his ability to connect the customers with the bank's other products.

Bennett invited him to apply for an opening at her branch as a Customer Service Representative (CSR) and he gladly did so. He saw it as a stepping stone to management positions at the bank. He said that he very much liked the kind of customer contact that the job entailed and that he welcomed the opportunity for higher level training about the banking business. Getting the job would also result in an increase in pay of at least $5,000 per year because the pay grade for the job is higher than any teller position.

Haynes was interviewed by a committee of three people for the CSR job and one week later was told by Bennett that he had the job and that she would arrange a transfer from the city-wide Roving Teller position to the Frog Hollow Branch and that he would start one week later, on the first of November 2014.

When Haynes reported for work on what was to have been his first day in the new job, Bennett called him in and said that the CSR job "had not been authorized" by senior management and that she was sorry. She said that she did not know when the authorization might come through. Instead, she said, he could continue to work as a teller and "be patient" until something changed. Haynes said he was very disappointed by this news but felt he had no choice but to do his job well and strive to get ahead.

Haynes believed he had been offered and accepted a position as CSR at Frog Hollow. When he got his paycheck he found himself in the lowest level teller position, which paid the lowest salary. He explained that there are three levels of teller: Teller, Senior Teller, and Teller Manager. After he started at Frog Hollow, his supervisors often asked him to take on some of the tasks that Senior Tellers and Teller Managers were supposed to do. Bennett also asked him to train and mentor other tellers "because the other tellers didn't like doing it." He was not paid more for this extra

5

responsibility.

Haynes thought that it was unfair that he wasn't paid for it or given the formal recognition that he felt he deserved. About four months ago he asked Bennett for at least a promotion in the teller ranks, but she said that he needed more time on the job. When he said it wasn't fair to do the job of the more senior tellers without being paid for it, she told him that if he was dissatisfied with his work, he should quit.

After that, Haynes spoke with Bennett every two weeks to ask when the CSR job would be his. Each time, Bennett stalled him and advised patience.

Haynes said that on March 25, 2015 he received a written performance appraisal that was positive but that said that he "wasn't a team player." He suspected that this comment was the result of his complaints to Bennett about his promised job.

The next day, Haynes once more talked to Bennett about the CSR job and pointed out that in his performance appraisal the things that were listed as his strengths were all the things that would make him an excellent customer service representative. Bennett responded that, "It just isn't going to happen." She told Haynes that NBC had been bought by a large nationwide bank, that there was a new senior management team in place, that there was attrition going on in the total number of employees the bank would employ, and that no one's job was secure. She said, "My boss thinks you aren't ready for promotion. And you should know that you have no future at this bank."

Haynes said, "I felt completely defeated, misled about the job I had been promised, so I quit." The next day Haynes resigned and gave two weeks' notice. Bennett told him that the policy of the bank was that when someone quit, the employment ended immediately, and thus the last day of his employment was right then.

Haynes applied for unemployment benefits, stating that he left because "I had no choice when I learned that they lied to me about my position." I informed Haynes that I would interview a representative of the bank and that he would get my decision in the mail.

6

STATE OF COLUMBIA

DEPARTMENT OF EMPLOYMENT SERVICES

ADJUDICATION BRANCH

196 Magnolia Street
Celiana, Columbia

JUNE 22, 2015

CLAIMANT:

CONRAD HAYNES
17 BEMBE ROAD
ROSLYN, COLUMBIA

EMPLOYER:

NATIONAL BANK OF COLUMBIA
FROG HOLLOW BRANCH
2173 WILLOW STREET
ROSLYN, COLUMBIA

DETERMINATION BY CLAIMS EXAMINER

The Columbia Unemployment Compensation Act provides that an individual shall be disqualified from receiving benefits if it is found that he/she voluntarily left his/her most recent work without good cause connected with the work. (*Col. Unemployment Comp. Code, section 110.*)

Per the statement you, Conrad Haynes, provided to the Department of Employment Services, you left your most recent employment on March 27, 2015 because of general dissatisfaction with your job. You said that you resigned from your position with the National Bank of Columbia immediately after you were told that you were not getting a promotion that you believed had been promised to you.

Sandra Bennett, the branch manager of the bank, was your supervisor. She

7

stated you were not yet ready for a promotion.   She also said that you had often expressed dissatisfaction with your work, despite being given opportunities to work as a permanent teller.   She said that you left your job of your own volition.

Accordingly, it is determined that you voluntarily left available employment and that your employer did not force you to leave.   It is also determined that you did not have good cause connected with your work to quit your position and that you left because of general unhappiness with your job.

For these reasons, you are disqualified from receiving benefits.

_____*JANE EPSTEIN*_____

Jane Epstein
Claims Examiner

8

California Bar Examination

SAMPLE 90-MINUTE

Performance Test

LIBRARY

HAYNES v. NATIONAL BANK OF COLUMBIA

LIBRARY

1

Columbia Association of Accountants v. Columbia Department of Employment Services

Columbia Supreme Court (1991)

In this claim for unemployment compensation benefits, an administrative law judge (ALJ) reversed the decision of a claims examiner of the Department of Employment Services (DOES) who had ruled that Lindsey Schultz was ineligible for unemployment compensation because she had voluntarily left her employment. The ALJ concluded that Schultz's resignation was coerced and thus involuntary and that she is entitled to unemployment benefits. The Columbia Association of Accountants (CAA) appealed.

An individual who leaves his or her most recent work involuntarily or with good cause connected with the work shall be eligible for unemployment compensation benefits. *Columbia Unemployment Compensation Code, section 110.* Whether an individual leaves voluntarily or involuntarily is determined in accordance with the totality of the circumstances. Whether an individual leaves with or without good cause is determined in accordance with the test: "What would a reasonable and prudent person in the labor market do in the same circumstances?"

Schultz was employed by the Cincinnati (Ohio) Chapter of the CAA until January 1989, when she joined the Columbia Chapter as Executive Vice President. After seven months, Arnold Prince, president of the Columbia Chapter, asked Schultz to stay after an Executive Committee meeting. Schultz testified that Prince gave no indication that anything was wrong or that she should be concerned. The day before the meeting, Schultz called the secretary of the chapter, William Hansen, to ask what he could tell her about the meeting. Schultz said Hansen told her that "there was some dissatisfaction and some anger" on both sides of the employment relationship and that "we need to talk some things over."

After the meeting, five of the Committee members met with Schultz. Prince told

2

her that "we have no choice but to ask for your resignation." Hansen then gave Schultz a draft letter of resignation to which a positive letter of recommendation was attached. The resignation letter provided for an additional six months of salary and health benefits upon termination of employment, as well as a "suitable positive employment reference." The letter also contained extensive waiver provisions absolving the CAA of liability attributable to Schultz's leaving her job.

Schultz testified before the ALJ that: "I was absolutely and totally in shock. I never expected any such thing. I couldn't believe that these people, who had recruited me to do a three year job, would fire me."

According to Hansen's testimony, Schultz was "extremely upset" and went into an adjacent kitchen. Hansen followed her. Schultz testified that Hansen told her "in a very stern tone of voice," that she had never heard him use, that it was very important that she "sign this letter now" and that if she decided to fight them she would "never win." She also testified that Hansen said that if she did not sign the letter, she would not receive the letter of recommendation. Schultz, in shock, agreed to sign the letter because she had recently recovered from major surgery and needed the six months of health insurance.

The next day, CAA counsel wrote to Schultz, ordering her to remove all personal effects and turn in her key. He told her, "Your presence at the office is not desired and will not be permitted as of August 25, 1989."

Schultz filed a claim for unemployment compensation. After a claims examiner ruled that she was ineligible for benefits because her resignation had been voluntary, she appealed. The ALJ reversed, concluding that "a careful review of the evidence and testimony at the appeals hearing fails to support the decision that Schultz voluntarily left her position. The evidence rather supports a finding that her leaving was involuntary." This appeal followed.

An employee who leaves work voluntarily without good cause connected with the work is disqualified from receiving unemployment benefits. The threshold issue in this case is whether the employer's actions were coercive to the point of compelling an involuntary resignation. Because we answer that question in the affirmative, we do not reach the question whether, if the employee resigned voluntarily, there was "good cause" for doing so. Whether the employee's action was compelled by the employer rather than based on the employee's volition must be determined by reference to all the circumstances surrounding the decision to leave.

Situations reflected in our termination cases involving voluntariness generally fall into: "shape up or ship out" (voluntary) and "quit or be fired" (involuntary). Schultz's comes closer to "quit or be fired" than "shape up or ship out."

The Columbia Chapter initiated Schultz's resignation and drafted the resignation letter without consulting her. The resignation letter mentioned a positive employment reference, and a letter of recommendation was attached to the resignation letter. Hansen, an Executive Committee member, suggested to Schultz that she would be best served by accepting the proposed resignation rather than remaining. There is no evidence that the employer offered Schultz any palatable option other than resignation. She was not told improvement would result in a work relationship satisfactory to her employer. Schultz, therefore, in effect was told to quit or be fired.

Based on these facts, the ALJ was justified in concluding as a matter of law that the employer's conduct caused an involuntary separation.

Affirmed.

4

Rodger Kaplan v. Columbia Department of Employment Services

Columbia Supreme Court (1982)

Rodger Kaplan challenges a ruling by the Department of Employment Services (DOES) that disqualified him from receiving unemployment benefits on the ground that he voluntarily left his previous employment without good cause connected with the work. We agree with Kaplan that the final decision is unsupported by substantial evidence of record.

On June 28, 1980, Kaplan, who had been employed for nearly two years at Club East II, resigned from his position there. An administrative law judge (ALJ) determined that the employment had been voluntarily terminated without good cause connected with the work.

Kaplan testified that the management of the club, a 24-hour facility, had repeatedly failed to keep its promises to him and also engaged in coercive employment practices. He was told that shift assignments would be made on the basis of seniority of the work staff, but the practice was never followed. With regard to salary, he was promised an increase from $4.00 to $4.50 an hour, but received a lesser amount. Whenever a shortage of monies was received during a particular work shift, the manager routinely required all employees on the shift to make up the deficiency. When an employee reported late for his shift, the manager required the employee on duty to continue until a replacement arrived. The manager then insisted that the employee who had worked extra hours collect his compensation for the work from the tardy co-worker. On several days, Kaplan was not paid for overtime work.

In ruling against Kaplan, the ALJ set forth the circumstances described but concluded that, in leaving his employment, Kaplan had not acted as a reasonable and prudent person in the labor market. He concluded that Kaplan had left because of "general dissatisfaction with his work" and not for good cause.

5

Since in this instance it is undisputed that Kaplan voluntarily left his employment, we need only review the question of whether Kaplan's decision to resign was without good cause.

Regulations promulgated by the Department of Employment Services provide examples of circumstances that do and do not constitute good cause. *Columbia Code of Regulations, sections 311.6, 311.7.* Circumstances that do <u>not</u> constitute good cause include "minor reduction in wages," "refusal to obey reasonable employer rules," and "general dissatisfaction with work." *Id, Section 311.6.* Circumstances that <u>do</u> constitute good cause include "failure to provide remuneration for employee services," "material change in terms of employment resulting in lower pay," and "racial or sexual discrimination or harassment." *Id, Section 311.7.*

These regulations offer non-exclusive illustrations of the respective factors to be used in determining good cause. The determination of good cause is factual in nature and should be judged by the standard of a reasonably prudent person under similar circumstances. The ALJ articulated this more general legal test. Thus our inquiry is whether there was sufficient evidence to support the decision. We conclude there was not.

In addition to the complaints regarding promised salary and work schedules, we think it significant that Kaplan was required to work overtime and referred to other employees to seek compensation for the work done. The failure to provide remuneration for employee services constitutes good cause. The employer also required that all employees on a shift were held collectively responsible, regardless of fault, for any deficiency in receipts. Taking these circumstances as a whole, without opposing evidence, we hold that there is insufficient evidence in the record to support the ALJ's decision that Kaplan did not act as a reasonable and prudent employee under the circumstances.

Accordingly, we reverse.

6

Jaime Delgado v. Columbia Department of Employment Services

Columbia Supreme Court (1993)

Petitioner Jaime Delgado asks us to review a decision by the Department of Employment Services (DOES) denying him unemployment benefits upon the ground that he voluntarily left his job without good cause connected with the work. We agree with Delgado that the administrative law judge (ALJ) failed to make sufficient findings to support her decision that Delgado's leaving was without good cause.

Delgado worked as a Spanish Coordinator for the United Programming Organization (UPO) from May 1990 to August 9, 1991 when he resigned.

Delgado immediately applied for unemployment benefits. On his claim form, he marked "Reason for Separation: Left Voluntarily," without providing any further explanation. Based on the application, the DOES claims examiner found Delgado ineligible for benefits because he had left for unspecified personal reasons. Delgado filed an administrative appeal.

At the hearing, Delgado explained that UPO had been experiencing severe financial difficulties, that employees had been furloughed, and that he believed, in light of the employer's economic crises, that his own continued employment was in jeopardy. Delgado further explained that he had encountered "a lot of resistance" from the Executive Director's support staff to carrying out his job, a situation that "made it very uncomfortable to stay." The employer did not contest any of these allegations.

The ALJ found that Delgado "left of his own volition" for a personal reason that was not "objectively job-related or directly connected with the work." The ALJ described these personal reasons as "general dissatisfaction with his work." *See, Columbia Code of Regulations, section 311.6.* The ALJ concluded that Delgado had not shown that his voluntary departure was for "good cause connected with the work." She ruled that Delgado was disqualified from receiving unemployment benefits.

7

We have consistently held that the Unemployment Compensation Act is remedial humanitarian legislation of vast import. Its benefits sections must be liberally and broadly construed for the benefit of unemployed workers. The Act has wiped out the acute and almost unbearable hardships that accompany unanticipated loss of employment. The purpose of Columbia's unemployment compensation statute is to protect employees against economic dependency caused by temporary unemployment and to reduce the need for other welfare programs. The remedial goals of the legislation apply in "voluntary quit" cases such as this.

Delgado alleges that UPO was in a financial crisis, that employees had been furloughed, that he believed that his position was at risk, and, implicitly, that he would soon be out of work if he did not secure another job. Second, he alleges that resistance from his superior's support staff made his job "very uncomfortable."

The ALJ only addressed Delgado's allegations of resistance from supervisors. The ALJ made no attempt at the hearing to elicit facts relevant to the situation at UPO – whether the employer was, in fact, in financial peril or if Delgado reasonably believed that it was. No inquiry was made as to the nature and extent of the alleged furloughs. The ALJ made no findings regarding the pressures that allegedly made it difficult for Delgado to stay on.

If Delgado had left UPO because he believed he could find better work elsewhere, recovery would be foreclosed under our decisions. But this case is unlike those where an employee resigned, intending to take a similar position with another company at a higher wage. Here, Delgado alleged that he voluntarily left UPO at least in part because UPO's financial instability seriously threatened his job security, and because other employees on the staff of his boss had made it difficult for him to stay on. These reasons merit scrutiny under the "reasonable and prudent person" test. Furthermore, the sufficiency of a claimant's asserted justifications must be considered in light of the remedial purposes of the statute.

8

We do not suggest that an employee's concerns about possible discharge on account of his employer's actual or perceived financial straits or the employee's own difficulties with supervisors would necessarily constitute good cause. In order to constitute good cause, the circumstances that compel the decision must be real, substantial, and reasonable; there must be some compulsion produced by extraneous and necessitous or compelling circumstances.

Having alleged financial crises and employee furloughs, as well as activities on the part of aides to his boss that made it difficult for him to stay, Delgado satisfied the threshold requirement that he articulate material issues of fact. He was entitled to have these issues adequately explored and then resolved by specific findings.

We reverse the agency's decision and remand for further proceedings consistent with this opinion.

Practice California Performance Test:
Step-by-Step Demonstration 1

Haynes v. National Bank of Columbia (2017)

[Roadmap modeled on scratch paper.]

Step 1.	**Scan the instructions, the file table of contents, and the library table of contents (1 minute)**

Instructions

You should have already thoroughly read the instruction page once. When you are completing a PT, look for three important details: the jurisdiction (usually in paragraph two), the contents of the packet (usually in paragraph three), and any specific weighting information, which, if supplied, would be noted at the bottom of the instructions. Take a second to skim the instructions to ensure no changes were made to the standard instructions.

Haynes Instructions

1. The problem is set in the State of Columbia.
2. The packet contains a file and library.
3. No special weighting information is included.

Client File Table of Contents

Look this over to get a general feel for what the case is about, how many pages of facts there are, and the type of documents you will be working with.

Haynes File Table of Contents

Since the case name is <u>Haynes v. National Bank of Columbia,</u> we know this is a civil case, rather than a criminal case. We will be working with approximately four pages of facts.

- The first file document is a memorandum from Susan Mont, so she must be our boss.
- The second document is an "Intake Interview of Conrad Haynes," so he is likely our client since an intake interview is the sort of thing a firm would do with a client.
- The third document is named "Determination by Claims Examiner," so this case has something to do with a bank, and we can theorize that it has something to do with some type of insurance claim.

Library Table of Contents

You are still trying to get a general feel for what the case is about and to quickly determine the type of law you will be working with. You want to make note if you have statutes and/or cases and how many of each. You also want to note the jurisdiction or court the cases come from to possibly start getting the picture of the type of task you have ahead as well as whether the cases are binding or merely persuasive authority.

Haynes Library Table of Contents

There are three cases in approximately eight pages, and all originate from the Columbia Supreme Court, which is our jurisdiction. All three cases have different plaintiffs, but they seem to be against the same defendant, the Columbia Department of Employment Services, so we can theorize that Haynes is involved in some sort of employment issue.

HAYNES v. NATIONAL BANK OF COLUMBIA

INSTRUCTIONS

1.   This performance test is designed to evaluate your ability to handle a select number of legal authorities in the context of a factual problem involving a client.

2.   The problem is set in the <u>fictional State of Columbia, one of the United States</u>.

3.   You will have two sets of materials with which to work: <u>a File and a Library</u>.

4.   The File contains factual materials about your case. The first document is a memorandum containing the instructions for the tasks you are to complete.

5.   The Library contains the legal authorities needed to complete the tasks. The case reports may be real, modified, or written solely for the purpose of this performance test. If the cases appear familiar to you, do not assume that they are precisely the same as you have read before. Read each thoroughly, as if it were new to you. You should assume that cases were decided in the jurisdictions and on the dates shown. In citing cases from the Library, you may use abbreviations and omit page citations.

6.   You should concentrate on the materials provided, but you should also bring to bear on the problem your general knowledge of the law. What you have learned in law school and elsewhere provides the general background for analyzing the problem; the File and Library provide the specific materials with which you must work.

7.   This performance test is designed to be completed in 90 minutes. Although there are no parameters on how to apportion that 90 minutes, you should allow yourself sufficient time to thoroughly review the materials and organize your planned response. Since the time allotted for this session of the examination includes two (2) essay questions in addition to this performance test, time management is essential.

8.   Your response will be graded on its compliance with instructions and on its content, thoroughness, and organization.

Civil Case

HAYNES v. NATIONAL BANK OF COLUMBIA

Possible insurance case.

1

HAYNES v. NATIONAL BANK OF COLUMBIA

LIBRARY

All cases are <u>Supreme Court level</u> and in our jurisdiction.

All cases concern Columbia Department of Employment Services, so our case likely involves employment.

1

| Step 2. | **Read the task memo (and format memo, if provided, and identify the macrostructure for your answer) (5–7 minutes)** |

Task Memo

This is the most important document in the packet, so slow down and read it very carefully. Follow all directions exactly. If the task memo refers to another document as a source of important information, read that document carefully, too.

Your goal is to identify three key pieces of information:

1. Information about your client: Who is your client? What is your client's legal issue? What is your client's goal?
2. Specific information about the task: What is the task? Who is the audience? Has more than one task been assigned? Are there directions about things to include and exclude?
3. The macro-structure of your answer: Can you start your roadmap?

Haynes Task Memo

- **Client info:** As we suspected, Conrad Haynes is our client. He worked as a bank teller for National Bank of Columbia (Bank). After leaving his job, he was denied unemployment compensation. Bank alleges he left the position voluntarily. We are representing Haynes in an administrative appeal. His goal is to receive unemployment compensation.
- **Task info:** We are preparing an argument to include in our appeal brief, so our tone will be persuasive. Our audience is an administrative law judge (ALJ), so our vocabulary will be more formal. We can only use facts already in the record, which is limited to an interview with Haynes and one with Sandra Bennett. There is only one task assigned. We have been instructed not to include a separate statement of facts, but to use the facts in the analysis.
- **Task structure:** Our brief will have two main sections:
  1. Haynes's resignation should be construed as involuntary; and
  2. If found voluntary, it was for good cause.
  Since we've seen a lot of performance tests, we already suspect the first point is not certain to go in our favor. We have been told to assert Haynes's arguments and rebut potential arguments, so within each section of the argument we may include two parts. We will note this on our roadmap so we don't forget. There is no format memo, so we will use common sense to craft headings. We have enough information to start our roadmap.

PAGER MONT AND WHITE

Attorneys at Law

3216 Morningside Drive

Roslyn, Columbia

www.PagerMont.com

TO: Applicant

FROM: Susan Mont, Senior Partner

DATE: July 28, 2015

SUBJECT: Conrad Haynes Case

Conrad Haynes was referred to our firm by the Columbia Bar Association Pro Bono Project and we have agreed to represent him in an administrative **appeal** of the **denial** of his claim for unemployment compensation.   His former employer, the National Bank of Columbia, opposes his claim, alleging that he voluntarily left his job as a bank teller and thus is ineligible for benefits.

Unemployment compensation appeals are decided by an administrative law judge (ALJ) in the Office of Administrative Appeals (OAA) on the record before the claims examiner -- in this case, the interviews of ① Mr. Haynes and that of ② Sandra Bennett, a bank employee.

Prepare an **argument** to include in our appeal brief.   Be sure to argue both that ① Haynes' resignation should be construed as involuntary **and** that ② if voluntary, it was for good cause.   We will need to convince the ALJ that the circumstances that led our client to resign do not disqualify him from receiving benefits.   We will have to marshal facts effectively to **persuade** the ALJ that Haynes should not be disqualified. Make sure to assert arguments in his favor **and** to rebut potential arguments against this conclusion.

Do not prepare a separate statement of facts.   Your draft should relate specific facts to the legal tests and conclude how your analysis would establish that the client should prevail.

| Step 3. | **Start roadmap (time included in steps 2–7)** |

Roadmap

Having a well-planned roadmap is the key to writing a passing performance test. We can start our roadmap using the macrostructure from the task memo and add to it as we gather more information. We recommend that you make a note at the top of the roadmap listing all essential information, including the client and opposing party, the client's goal, task specifics about included or excluded parts, the tone and vocabulary, any task weighting, and a time goal for when you want to start writing your answer. Your time goal will vary depending on which approach you employ to organize your performance test. If your written answer is already done because you input the headings and complete rules, etc., directly into your computer as you organized, you will need less time. If you need to write your answer in its entirety because you organized by creating a full shorthand roadmap on paper, you will need more time. Since the response will have two sections, it is recommended that you roadmap each on a separate piece of paper.

> *Important note:* When roadmapping for your own use on paper, the result is unlikely to be as thorough or neat as this example. Liberally use abbreviations and symbols to remind yourself where in the file you can find the information you need to use in each section. When roadmapping on the computer, type the rules you know you will use directly into the appropriate section after briefing, but still create a skeleton roadmap on paper setting out the macrostructure. Only write as much as you need to guide you in properly drafting your answer.

Haynes Roadmap

From the task memo we know all the key task information. We also know our argument will be broken up into two sections: (1) arguing the resignation was <u>involuntary</u>, and (2) that if the resignation is found to be voluntary, it was for <u>good cause.</u> From the task memo, we are unable to determine what, if any, subsections will be needed, although we know we will need to rebut any counterarguments. See the attached roadmap containing the important information we have available so far.

Haynes Roadmap

π Δ Haynes v. NBC Bank Client: Haynes Issue: Denial unemployment Goal: Collect unemployment	Start writing at _____ Task: Appeal argument Audience: Judge/formal/persuasive Include: Arguments and rebuttal Exclude: Statement of facts	

1. Haynes resignation should be construed as involuntary (assert/rebut)

2. If voluntary, Haynes' resignation was for good cause (assert/rebut)

Step 4.   **Skim the client file/facts (2 minutes)**

Skim the Client File/Facts

We don't yet know the applicable law, so we won't yet be able to identify the legally significant facts. Skimming the facts gives us enough of the big picture story to satisfy our curiosity and provides clues to what materials we have to work with once we do identify the applicable law from the library.

Haynes Client File Skim

Below is my quick takeaway from the skim of the facts:

- **From the Haynes intake interview:** Haynes quit his job at bank (NBC), Frog Hollow (FH) branch, six weeks ago. He worked for NBC for 3 years, but for only 6 months at FH branch. In Sept. 2014 he was temporarily assigned to FH. He did a good job and was invited to apply for CSR opening. He went through the interview process, was hired, and started at FH in Nov. 2014. Upon hire, Haynes learns CSR job is not authorized. Haynes is upset and frequently asks about CSR job. At review in Mar. 2015, Haynes is deemed "not a team player." Haynes feels misled and quits. Haynes applies for unemployment.
- **From the Determination by Claims Examiner:** The rule for unemployment eligibility is that one can't receive benefits if he voluntarily left a job without good cause, which you should notice mirrors the language from the second half of the assigned task. Haynes left because of general job dissatisfaction. Sandra Bennett was Haynes's boss (and she is mentioned in the task memo as the other source of information in the record upon which the appeal will be decided). The claims examiner determined Haynes voluntarily quit and was not forced.
- **Our assessment from the skim of the facts:** Most of Haynes's story is in the interview, and a few facts provided by Bennett appear in the second document. Haynes was upset about not getting the promised CSR job and felt misled, so he quit. The applicable rule is that he can't receive unemployment benefits if he voluntarily left without good cause. We need to know how "good cause" is interpreted.

DEPARTMENT OF EMPLOYMENT SERVICES

SUBJECT: Intake Interview of Conrad Haynes

FROM: Jane Epstein, Claims Examiner

DATE: May 11, 2015

Conrad Haynes is a 28-year-old father of two who quit his job at the National Bank of Columbia (NBC), Frog Hollow Branch, 6 weeks ago. He expected at the time that he resigned that, with his experience and abilities, he would be able to find a new job quickly. Because of the number of bank failures and mergers, he has not gotten an interview.

Haynes worked for NBC for a total of 3 years, but had been at the Frog Hollow Branch for the last 6 months of his employment. Before going to Frog Hollow, he worked as a "Roving Teller," substituting in branches all through the city and suburbs of San Carlos as needed in any particular week. While working as a Roving Teller for the region, Haynes took evening courses at Central Community College, taking advantage of NBC's tuition payment program; he ultimately got the degree of Associate in Business. His hope, he said, was to advance beyond the lowest level teller job and get into a management position at the bank.

In September 2014, Haynes was temporarily assigned to Frog Hollow to fill in for a teller who was on leave due to a medical issue. He got along well with Sandy Bennett, the branch manager there. She told him that she was impressed with the fact that he was able to perform many aspects of the teller job that were "above his pay grade." Because he had worked in so many branches, filling in for people in various jobs, he had learned to do the work at each of the three levels of teller as well as that of "Customer Service Representative." Bennett noticed that he was a hard worker, that he took initiative, and that he got along well with customers.

Even while serving as a fill-in, he was able to form relationships with customers that enabled him to sell other bank services. On at least three occasions that he could

4

remember, "his" customers opened brokerage accounts upon his suggestion and two took out loans to purchase new cars. These are examples of work normally done by a "Customer Service Representative." Haynes said that Bennett was very pleased with each of these occurrences and praised his ability to connect the customers with the bank's other products.

Bennett invited him to apply for an opening at her branch as a Customer Service Representative (CSR) and he gladly did so. He saw it as a stepping stone to management positions at the bank. He said that he very much liked the kind of customer contact that the job entailed and that he welcomed the opportunity for higher level training about the banking business. Getting the job would also result in an increase in pay of at least $5,000 per year because the pay grade for the job is higher than any teller position.

Haynes was interviewed by a committee of three people for the CSR job and one week later was told by Bennett that he had the job and that she would arrange a transfer from the city-wide Roving Teller position to the Frog Hollow Branch and that he would start one week later, on the first of November 2014.

When Haynes reported for work on what was to have been his first day in the new job, Bennett called him in and said that the CSR job "had not been authorized" by senior management and that she was sorry. She said that she did not know when the authorization might come through. Instead, she said, he could continue to work as a teller and "be patient" until something changed. Haynes said he was very disappointed by this news but felt he had no choice but to do his job well and strive to get ahead.

Haynes believed he had been offered and accepted a position as CSR at Frog Hollow. When he got his paycheck he found himself in the lowest level teller position, which paid the lowest salary. He explained that there are three levels of teller: Teller, Senior Teller, and Teller Manager. After he started at Frog Hollow, his supervisors often asked him to take on some of the tasks that Senior Tellers and Teller Managers were supposed to do. Bennett also asked him to train and mentor other tellers "because the other tellers didn't like doing it." He was not paid more for this extra

5

responsibility.

Haynes thought that it was unfair that he wasn't paid for it or given the formal recognition that he felt he deserved. About four months ago he asked Bennett for at least a promotion in the teller ranks, but she said that he needed more time on the job. When he said it wasn't fair to do the job of the more senior tellers without being paid for it, she told him that if he was dissatisfied with his work, he should quit.

After that, Haynes spoke with Bennett every two weeks to ask when the CSR job would be his. Each time, Bennett stalled him and advised patience.

Haynes said that on March 25, 2015 he received a written performance appraisal that was positive but that said that he "wasn't a team player." He suspected that this comment was the result of his complaints to Bennett about his promised job.

The next day, Haynes once more talked to Bennett about the CSR job and pointed out that in his performance appraisal the things that were listed as his strengths were all the things that would make him an excellent customer service representative. Bennett responded that, "It just isn't going to happen." She told Haynes that NBC had been bought by a large nationwide bank, that there was a new senior management team in place, that there was attrition going on in the total number of employees the bank would employ, and that no one's job was secure. She said, "My boss thinks you aren't ready for promotion. And you should know that you have no future at this bank."

Haynes said, "I felt completely defeated, misled about the job I had been promised, so I quit." The next day Haynes resigned and gave two weeks' notice. Bennett told him that the policy of the bank was that when someone quit, the employment ended immediately, and thus the last day of his employment was right then.

Haynes applied for unemployment benefits, stating that he left because "I had no choice when I learned that they lied to me about my position." I informed Haynes that I would interview a representative of the bank and that he would get my decision in the mail.

6

STATE OF COLUMBIA
DEPARTMENT OF EMPLOYMENT SERVICES

ADJUDICATION BRANCH

196 Magnolia Street
Celiana, Columbia

JUNE 22, 2015

CLAIMANT:

CONRAD HAYNES
17 BEMBE ROAD
ROSLYN, COLUMBIA

EMPLOYER:

NATIONAL BANK OF COLUMBIA
FROG HOLLOW BRANCH
2173 WILLOW STREET
ROSLYN, COLUMBIA

DETERMINATION BY CLAIMS EXAMINER

The Columbia Unemployment Compensation Act provides that an individual shall be disqualified from receiving benefits if it is found that he/she voluntarily left his/her most recent work without good cause connected with the work. (*Col. Unemployment Comp. Code, section 110.*) `Rule`

Per the statement you, Conrad Haynes, provided to the Department of Employment Services, you left your most recent employment on March 27, 2015 because of general dissatisfaction with your job. You said that you resigned from your position with the National Bank of Columbia immediately after you were told that you were not getting a promotion that you believed had been promised to you.

Sandra Bennett, the branch manager of the bank, was your supervisor. She

7

stated you were not yet ready for a promotion. She also said that you had often expressed dissatisfaction with your work, despite being given opportunities to work as a permanent teller. She said that you left your job of your own volition.

Accordingly, it is determined that you voluntarily left available employment and that your employer did not force you to leave. It is also determined that you did not have good cause connected with your work to quit your position and that you left because of general unhappiness with your job.

For these reasons, you are disqualified from receiving benefits.

_____*JANE EPSTEIN*_____

Jane Epstein
Claims Examiner

8

Step 5.   Actively read the library and synthesize rules (15–20 minutes)

Read the Library and Deconstruct and Synthesize Rules as Needed

We are looking for the rules we can use to solve the problem posed and any analysis we can borrow from the cases. Depending on the task, we may need to synthesize cases or identify which rule among competing rules should be adopted. To most efficiently assess the library, read the materials in the order presented, since most often the rules are provided in the same order that they can be used to solve the problem, given the task macrostructure. Book brief the cases and add information to your roadmap as you go. Annotate your cases with notes so you don't waste time rewriting sentences into your roadmap. Determine how to best use any statutes. Each case in the library was included because it is likely to be needed to solve the problem, so it is up to you to determine how each can best be used. We typically note at the top of each case where it will be used in our answer and whether it is favorable or not for our client by writing a plus or minus sign on the top. Continue to look for clues as to how you should structure your answer.

Haynes Cases

Three cases in eight pages makes the library a bit more law heavy than fact heavy. This is a persuasive task, so we are looking for law and analysis that will bolster our argument, but since we need to rebut counterarguments, we will keep an eye out for rules and analysis that bolsters our opponent's argument. After reading the cases, it isn't clear which cases our opponent will use, so we deduce that information will come from the facts. So add a reminder "Rebut?" at the bottom of each section so you don't forget to include appropriate rebuttal as instructed.

- **Case 1: <u>CAA.</u>** This case primarily belongs in section one on how to determine if a leave is voluntary or involuntary. It repeats the code section we saw in the facts, a "totality of circumstances" standard to apply, and we learn that an employer's action can be so coercive that quitting can be considered as an involuntary leave. <u>CAA</u> contains many facts that we may use to make a factual analogy to the Haynes matter, depending on what factual details we find in our case when we go through the facts more carefully. <u>CAA</u> also mentioned the standard applicable for the good cause determination, so we dropped that rule in the second section of our roadmap, although this case provides no analysis on this point.
- **Case 2: <u>Kaplan</u>.** This case expands on the law for section two, namely that good cause is determined using a reasonable person type standard. The statute also provides three examples of what would constitute good cause and what would not. The case offers some examples of the employer's "failure to pay" that establish good cause, which we may be able to analogize once we learn more about our facts. However, another section of code 311.7 may be on point as well, since one of the proffered examples of good cause is a "material change resulting in lower pay." This should catch your eye, since Haynes was hired for the CSR position and something went wrong. Add this example to your analysis section but be sure to note that no case facts are on point to analogize. We think we have two reasons for a good cause argument.
- **Case 3: <u>Delgado.</u>** This case also expands on section two regarding good cause. A paragraph at the top of the second page discusses the policy behind the Unemployment Compensation Act, broadly construed. This will help Haynes, and it will make a nice persuasive introduction to this section, so we plan to take it out of case order and insert it at the top of section two on our roadmap. This case was a little less straightforward in presentation, but it provides an additional "good cause" reason that was not included in the non-exclusive list of examples in code 311.7 cited in <u>Kaplan</u>. The case indicates an "employer's financial crisis" resulting in job insecurity may be sufficient to establish good cause, although the case was remanded for further proceedings to develop this evidence. We suspect this may potentially be a third reason for good cause, depending on our facts. Otherwise, all we can use this case for is the policy section and the "real, substantial, and reasonable . . . circumstances" language.

Point 1: Involuntary
Resignation

Columbia Association of Accountants v. Columbia Department of Employment Services

Columbia Supreme Court (1991)

In this claim for unemployment compensation benefits, an administrative law judge (ALJ) reversed the decision of a claims examiner of the Department of Employment Services (DOES) who had ruled that Lindsey Schultz was <u>ineligible</u> for unemployment compensation because she had <u>voluntarily left her employment</u>. The ALJ concluded that Schultz's resignation was <u>coerced and thus involuntary</u> and that she is entitled to unemployment benefits. The Columbia Association of Accountants (CAA) appealed.

Issue
Case History

An individual who <u>leaves</u> his or her most recent work <u>involuntarily or with good cause connected with the work</u> shall be <u>eligible for unemployment compensation</u> benefits. *Columbia Unemployment Compensation Code, section 110.* Whether an individual leaves <u>voluntarily or involuntarily</u> is determined in accordance with the <u>totality of the circumstances</u>. Whether an individual leaves <u>with or without good cause</u> is determined in accordance with the test: "<u>What would a reasonable and prudent person in the labor market do in the same circumstances?</u>"

General Rule

Voluntary/
Involuntary
Standard

Good Cause
Standard

Schultz was employed by the Cincinnati (Ohio) Chapter of the CAA until January 1989, when she joined the Columbia Chapter as Executive Vice President. After seven months, Arnold Prince, president of the Columbia Chapter, asked Schultz to stay after an Executive Committee meeting. Schultz testified that Prince gave no indication that anything was wrong or that she should be concerned. The day before the meeting, Schultz called the secretary of the chapter, William Hansen, to ask what he could tell her about the meeting. Schultz said Hansen told her that "there was some dissatisfaction and some anger" on both sides of the employment relationship and that "we need to talk some things over."

Case Facts

After the meeting, five of the Committee members met with Schultz. Prince told

2

her that "we have no choice but to ask for your resignation." Hansen then gave Schultz a draft letter of resignation to which a positive letter of recommendation was attached. The resignation letter provided for an additional six months of salary and health benefits upon termination of employment, as well as a "suitable positive employment reference." The letter also contained extensive waiver provisions absolving the CAA of liability attributable to Schultz's leaving her job.

Case Facts

Schultz testified before the ALJ that: "I was absolutely and totally in shock. I never expected any such thing. I couldn't believe that these people, who had recruited me to do a three year job, would fire me."

Haynes was also recruited to apply.

According to Hansen's testimony, Schultz was "extremely upset" and went into an adjacent kitchen. Hansen followed her. Schultz testified that Hansen told her "in a very stern tone of voice," that she had never heard him use, that it was very important that she "sign this letter now" and that if she decided to fight them she would "never win." She also testified that Hansen said that if she did not sign the letter, she would not receive the letter of recommendation. Schultz, in shock, agreed to sign the letter because she had recently recovered from major surgery and needed the six months of health insurance.

Case Facts

The next day, CAA counsel wrote to Schultz, ordering her to remove all personal effects and turn in her key. He told her, "Your presence at the office is not desired and will not be permitted as of August 25, 1989."

Schultz filed a claim for unemployment compensation. After a claims examiner ruled that she was ineligible for benefits because her resignation had been voluntary, she appealed. The ALJ reversed, concluding that "a careful review of the evidence and testimony at the appeals hearing fails to support the decision that Schultz voluntarily left her position. The evidence rather supports a finding that her leaving was involuntary." This appeal followed.

Claims Finding

ALJ Finding

3

An employee who leaves work voluntarily without good cause connected with the work is disqualified from receiving unemployment benefits.   The threshold issue in this <u>case is whether the employer's actions were coercive to the point of</u> <u>compelling an **involuntary resignation**</u>.   Because we answer that question in the affirmative, we do not reach the question whether, if the employee resigned voluntarily, there was "good cause" for doing so.   Whether the employee's action was compelled by the employer rather than based on the employee's volition must be determined by reference to <u>all the circumstances</u> surrounding the decision to leave.

Involuntary Resignation Rule

Case for Point 1 Only

Rule

Situations reflected in our termination cases involving voluntariness generally fall into: <u>"shape up or ship out"</u> (voluntary) and <u>"quit or be fired"</u> (involuntary).   <u>Schultz's</u> comes closer to <u>"quit or be fired"</u> than "shape up or ship out."

Voluntary/ Involuntary Rule

The Columbia Chapter <u>initiated Schultz's resignation and drafted</u> <u>the resignation letter without consulting her.</u>   The resignation letter mentioned a <u>positive employment reference</u>, and a letter of <u>recommendation was attached</u> <u>to the resignation letter</u>. Hansen, an Executive Committee member, suggested to Schultz that she would be best <u>served by accepting the proposed resignation</u> rather than remaining.   There is no evidence that the employer <u>offered Schultz</u> <u>any palatable</u> option <u>other than resignation.</u> She <u>was not told improvement would</u> <u>result in a work</u> <u>relationship</u> satisfactory to her employer.   Schultz, therefore, in effect was told to <u>quit or</u> <u>be fired</u>.

Analyze to our case facts.

Based on these facts, the ALJ was justified in concluding as a matter of law that the employer's conduct caused an involuntary separation.

Affirmed.

Employee Wins = Involuntary Resignation

4

$\oplus$

Rodger Kaplan v. Columbia Department of Employment Services

Columbia Supreme Court (1982)

Rodger <u>Kaplan challenges</u> a ruling by the Department of Employment Services (DOES) that disqualified him from receiving unemployment benefits on the ground that he <u>voluntarily left his previous employment</u> **without good cause** connected with the work.   We agree with Kaplan that the final decision is unsupported by substantial evidence of record.

Issue

On June 28, 1980, Kaplan, who had been employed for nearly <u>two years</u> at Club East II, <u>resigned</u> from his position there.   An administrative law judge (ALJ) determined that the employment had been <u>voluntarily</u> terminated <u>without good cause</u> connected with the work.

Case History

Kaplan testified that the <u>management</u> of the club, a 24-hour facility, had repeatedly <u>failed to keep its promises to him</u> and also engaged in <u>coercive employment</u> practices.   He was told that <u>shift assignments would be made on the basis of seniority</u> of the work staff, <u>but the practice was never followed.</u>   With regard to salary, he was <u>promised an increase from $4.00 to $4.50</u> an hour, but <u>received a lesser amount.</u> Whenever a shortage of monies was received during a particular work shift, the manager routinely <u>required all employees on the shift to make up the deficiency.</u>   When an <u>employee reported late</u> for his shift, the manager <u>required the employee on duty to continue until a replacement</u> arrived.   The manager then insisted that the employee who had worked extra hours <u>collect his compensation for the work from the tardy co-worker.</u> On several days, <u>Kaplan was not paid for overtime work.</u>

Case Facts

In ruling against Kaplan, the <u>ALJ</u> set forth the circumstances described but concluded that, in <u>leaving</u> his employment, Kaplan <u>had not acted as a reasonable and prudent person in the labor market.</u>   He concluded that Kaplan had left because of "general dissatisfaction with his work" and <u>not for good cause.</u>

ALJ Finding

5

Since in this instance it is undisputed that Kaplan <u>voluntarily left</u> his employment, we need only review the question of whether Kaplan's decision to resign <u>was without good cause.</u>

Regulations promulgated by the Department of Employment Services provide <u>examples</u> of circumstances that <u>do and do not</u> constitute good cause. *Columbia Code of Regulations, sections 311.6, 311.7.* Circumstances that **do not** constitute good cause include "<u>minor reduction in wages</u>," "<u>refusal to obey reasonable employer rules</u>," and "<u>general dissatisfaction with work</u>." *Id, Section 311.6.* Circumstances **that do** constitute good cause include "<u>failure to provide remuneration for employee services</u>," "<u>material change in terms</u> of employment resulting <u>in lower pay</u>," and "<u>racial or sexual discrimination</u> or harassment." *Id, Section 311.7.*

These regulations offer <u>non-exclusive</u> illustrations of the respective factors to be used in determining good cause. The determination of good cause is factual in nature and should be judged by the standard of a <u>reasonably prudent person under similar circumstances.</u> The ALJ articulated this more general legal test. Thus our inquiry is whether there was sufficient evidence to support the decision. We conclude there was not.

In addition to the complaints regarding promised <u>salary</u> and work <u>schedules</u>, we think it significant that Kaplan was required to <u>work overtime and referred to other employees</u> to <u>seek compensation</u> for the work done. The <u>failure to provide remuneration for employee services constitutes good cause.</u> The employer also required that all employees on a shift were held collectively responsible, regardless of fault, for any <u>deficiency in receipts.</u> Taking these circumstances as a whole, without opposing evidence, we hold that there is insufficient evidence in the record to support the ALJ's decision that Kaplan did not act as a reasonable and prudent employee under the circumstances.

Accordingly, <u>we **reverse.**</u>

6

Jaime Delgado v. Columbia Department of Employment Services

Columbia Supreme Court (1993)

Petitioner Jaime Delgado asks us to review a decision by the Department of Employment Services (DOES) denying him unemployment benefits upon the ground that he <u>voluntarily left his job</u> without good cause connected with the work. We agree with Delgado that the administrative law judge (ALJ) failed to make sufficient findings to support her decision that <u>Delgado's leaving was without good cause.</u>

Case History

Delgado worked as a <u>Spanish Coordinator</u> for the United Programming Organization (UPO) from May 1990 to August 9, 1991 when <u>he resigned.</u>

Case History

Delgado immediately applied for unemployment benefits. On his claim form, he marked "Reason for Separation: <u>Left **Voluntarily,**</u>" without providing any further explanation. Based on the application, the DOES claims examiner <u>found Delgado</u> ineligible for benefits because he had left for unspecified personal reasons. Delgado filed an <u>administrative appeal.</u>

At the hearing, Delgado explained that <u>UPO had been experiencing severe financial difficulties,</u> that <u>employees had been furloughed</u>, and that he believed, in light of the employer's economic crises, that his <u>own continued employment was in jeopardy.</u> Delgado further explained that he had encountered <u>"a lot of resistance"</u> from the Executive Director's support staff to carrying out his job, a situation that "made it very <u>uncomfortable to stay."</u> The employer <u>did not contest</u> any of these allegations.

Case Facts

The <u>ALJ</u> found that Delgado "left of his own volition" for a personal reason that was not "objectively job-related or directly connected with the work." The ALJ described these personal reasons as <u>"general dissatisfaction with his work."</u> *See, Columbia Code of Regulations, section 311.6.* The ALJ concluded that Delgado had not shown that his voluntary departure was for "good cause connected with the work." She ruled that Delgado was disqualified from receiving unemployment benefits.

ALJ Finding

We have consistently held that the Unemployment Compensation Act is remedial humanitarian legislation of vast import. Its <u>benefits sections must be liberally and broadly construed for the benefit of unemployed workers.</u> The Act has wiped out the acute and almost unbearable hardships that accompany unanticipated loss of employment. The <u>purpose of Columbia's unemployment compensation statute is to **protect employees against economic dependency caused by temporary unemployment**</u> and to reduce the need for other welfare programs. The remedial goals of the legislation apply in <u>"voluntary quit"</u> cases such as this.

Delgado alleges that UPO was in a <u>financial crisis,</u> that employees had been furloughed, that he believed that his position was at risk, and, implicitly, that he would soon be out of work if he did not secure another job. Second, he alleges that <u>resistance</u> from his superior's support staff made his job "very uncomfortable."

The ALJ <u>only addressed</u> Delgado's allegations of <u>resistance</u> from supervisors. The <u>ALJ made **no attempt**</u> at the hearing to elicit facts relevant to the situation at UPO – whether the employer was, in fact, in <u>financial peril</u> or if Delgado reasonably believed that it was. No inquiry was made as to the <u>nature and extent of the alleged furloughs.</u> The ALJ made <u>no findings</u> regarding the pressures that allegedly made it difficult for Delgado to stay on.

<u>If</u> Delgado had left UPO because he <u>believed he could find better work elsewhere, recovery would be foreclosed</u> under our decisions. But this case is unlike those where an employee resigned, intending to take a similar position with another company at a higher wage. Here, Delgado alleged that he voluntarily left UPO at least <u>in part</u> because UPO's <u>financial instability</u> seriously <u>threatened his **job security**</u>, and because <u>other employees on the staff of his boss had made it difficult for him to stay on.</u> These reasons merit scrutiny under the <u>"reasonable and prudent person"</u> test. Furthermore, the sufficiency of a claimant's asserted justifications must be considered in light of the remedial purposes of the statute.

| Rule |
| Act Policy |
| Case History |
| Case Facts/ History |
| Rule No Good Cause |
| Possible good cause; need more information. |

8

<u>We do not suggest</u> that an employee's concerns about possible discharge on account of his employer's actual or perceived financial straits or the employee's own difficulties with supervisors <u>would necessarily constitute good cause.</u>   In order to constitute good cause, the circumstances that compel the decision must be <u>real, substantial, and reasonable;</u> there must be <u>some compulsion produced by extraneous and necessitous or compelling circumstances.</u>

Rule

Having alleged <u>financial crises</u> and <u>employee furloughs</u>, as well as activities on the part of aides to his boss that made it difficult for him to stay, Delgado <u>satisfied the threshold</u> requirement that he articulate material issues of fact.   He was entitled to have these issues <u>adequately explored and then resolved by specific findings.</u>

We reverse the agency's decision and remand for **further proceedings** consistent with this opinion.

Employee gets further
hearing to explore
circumstances.

9

Haynes Roadmap

<table>
<tr><td>

π   Δ
<u>Haynes   v.   NBC Bank</u>

Client: Haynes
Issue: Denial unemployment
Goal: Collect unemployment

</td><td>

Start writing at _____

Task: Appeal argument
Audience: Judge/formal/ persuasive
Include: Arguments and rebuttal
Exclude: Statement of facts

</td></tr>
</table>

1. Haynes resignation should be construed as <u>involuntary</u> (assert/rebut)
   R: Leave involuntarily or with good cause connected to the work can get unemployment benefits. <u>Code, 110; CAA</u>
   R: Voluntarily/involuntarily standard = totality of circumstances. <u>CAA</u>
   R: Employer actions can be so coercive they compel an involuntary resignation. <u>CAA</u>
   R: Shape up or ship out = voluntary; Quit or be fired = involuntary. <u>CAA</u>

   RE: <u>CAA</u>
   • E/er initiated resignation
   • E/er drafted resignation letter without consulting e/ee
   • Resignation letter attached to positive recommendation
   • E/ee told best served by accepting proposed resignation
   • E/ee given no other option
   • No improvement possible

   C: Quit or be fired, which is involuntary

   Rebut?

2. If voluntary, Haynes's resignation was for <u>good cause</u> (assert/rebut)
   R: *Policy*. Act broadly and liberally construed to protect employees. <u>Delgado</u>
   R: Good cause standard = reasonable and prudent person in labor market, same circumstances. <u>CAA</u>
   R: (Nonexclusive) examples of good cause/not good cause in code. <u>Kaplan citing Columbia Code of Regulations, sec. 311.6, 311.7</u>
   R: Not good cause = minor reduction in wages; refusal to obey reasonable rules; general dissatisfaction with work. <u>311.6</u>
   R: Good cause = failure to pay remuneration for employee services; material change in terms of employment resulting in lower pay; and racial/sexual discrimination or harassment. <u>311.7</u>

   RE: <u>Kaplan</u>
   • Salary promises & schedule
   • Failure to pay: work OT & get pay from coworker, or unpaid
   • Material change resulting in lower pay (no case facts)

   C: Good cause found

   R: If employee leaves in belief he can find better work, no good cause. <u>Delgado</u>
   R: The circumstances compelling decision to leave must be real, substantial, and reasonable; a compulsion produced by extraneous, necessitous, or compelling circumstances. <u>Delgado</u>

RE: <u>Delgado</u>
- E/er financial crisis
- Threat to job security/furlough
- Difficult to stay on

C: Possible financial instability, threat to job security could be good cause, remanded for further proceedings

Rebut?

| Step 6. | **Actively read client file/facts (10–15 minutes)** |

Client File/Case Facts

Now that we know from the library the rules governing this situation, we must look for legally significant facts to apply to the rules to solve the problem. We want to look for helpful facts, harmful facts, and any missing facts, if pertinent to the task assigned. Add the legally significant facts into your roadmap as you go.

Haynes Facts

On the first and second pages of the intake interview (pages 4 and 5 of the file) you should note the language that can be used to argue Haynes was not paid proper remuneration for his services since it appears he was doing work above his pay grade, both before and after being hired at the FH branch. The second page (page 5 of the file) contains a paragraph with facts we can use to prove Haynes experienced a material change in position resulting in lower pay. The third page (page 6 of the file) contains two sections we can use in the voluntary/involuntary analysis and a paragraph that can be used to argue the bank was undergoing a financial crisis. There aren't many facts we can use from the Determination by Claims Examiner, but we can note that the issues pertaining to NBC's financial issues were not considered, similar to the <u>Delgado</u> case.

Since you have your roadmap, it's easy to go through and line the facts up with the rules where they can be used. You should also underline and annotate the facts at the side of the page so they are easy to find while you're writing your response. Also include in your roadmap facts to use for a rebuttal to the logical arguments NBC will make so you don't forget to include them in your response. Before you move on to write, make sure you've used all available facts to address all points raised by the facts in the underlying cases. It is during this double-check that you will add many of the facts you will use to argue that the resignation was involuntary since you didn't notice that no other option or improvement plan was given to Haynes during your first read-through of the facts. After pondering where the facts line up and looking at the totality of what we know, we want to revisit our organization, since breaking arguments up into smaller pieces where possible will make the final presentation easier to follow. You might decide that the second section can logically be broken up into three subsections, since there are three separate reasons that Haynes may have had good cause to quit:

1. Failure to pay remuneration for employee services;
2. Material change in terms of employment resulting in lower pay; and
3. Real, substantial, and reasonable circumstances, such as employer's financial crisis.

Make a note on the roadmap by bolding the key terms. We're almost ready to write.

DEPARTMENT OF EMPLOYMENT SERVICES

SUBJECT: Intake Interview of Conrad Haynes

FROM: Jane Epstein, Claims Examiner

DATE: May 11, 2015

Conrad Haynes is a 28-year-old father of two who <u>quit his job</u> at the National Bank of Columbia <u>(NBC)</u>, Frog Hollow Branch, 6 weeks ago. He expected at the time that he resigned that, with his experience and abilities, he would be able to find a new job quickly. Because of the number of bank failures and mergers, he has not gotten an interview.

Haynes worked for <u>NBC for a total of 3 years</u>, but had been at the Frog Hollow Branch for the last 6 months of his employment. Before going to Frog Hollow, he worked as a <u>"Roving Teller," substituting</u> in branches all through the city and suburbs of San Carlos as needed in any particular week. While working as a Roving Teller for the region, Haynes <u>took evening courses at Central Community College</u>, taking advantage of NBC's tuition payment program; he ultimately got the degree of Associate in Business. <u>His hope</u>, he said, <u>was to advance beyond</u> the lowest level teller job and get into a management position at the bank.

In September 2014, Haynes was <u>temporarily assigned to Frog Hollow to fill in for</u> a teller who was on leave due to a medical issue. He got along well with Sandy Bennett, the branch manager there. She told him that <u>she was impressed</u> with the fact that he was able to perform <u>many aspects of the teller job that were "above his pay grade."</u> Because he had worked in so many branches, filling in for people in various jobs, <u>he had learned to do the work at each of the three levels of teller</u> as well as that of <u>"Customer Service Representative."</u> Bennett noticed that he was a <u>hard worker</u>, that he <u>took initiative,</u> and that <u>he got along well with customers.</u>

> $
> Properly
> paid?

Even while serving as a fill-in, he was able to <u>form relationships with customers</u> that enabled him to <u>sell other bank services.</u> On at least three occasions that he could

> $
> Properly
> paid?

4

remember, "his" customers opened brokerage accounts upon his suggestion and two took out loans to purchase new cars. These are examples of work normally done by a "Customer Service Representative." Haynes said that Bennett was very pleased with each of these occurrences and praised his ability to connect the customers with the bank's other products.

***
Failure to pay properly

Bennett invited him to apply for an opening at her branch as a Customer Service Representative (CSR) and he gladly did so. He saw it as a stepping stone to management positions at the bank. He said that he very much liked the kind of customer contact that the job entailed and that he welcomed the opportunity for higher level training about the banking business. Getting the job would also result in an increase in pay of at least $5,000 per year because the pay grade for the job is higher than any teller position.

$5,000↑

Haynes was interviewed by a committee of three people for the CSR job and one week later was told by Bennett that he had the job and that she would arrange a transfer from the city-wide Roving Teller position to the Frog Hollow Branch and that he would start one week later, on the first of November 2014.

Hired CSR

When Haynes reported for work on what was to have been his first day in the new job, Bennett called him in and said that the CSR job "had not been authorized" by senior management and that she was sorry. She said that she did not know when the authorization might come through. Instead, she said, he could continue to work as a teller and "be patient" until something changed. Haynes said he was very disappointed by this news but felt he had no choice but to do his job well and strive to get ahead.

***
Material change: lower pay

Haynes believed he had been offered and accepted a position as CSR at Frog Hollow. When he got his paycheck he found himself in the lowest level teller position, which paid the lowest salary. He explained that there are three levels of teller: Teller, Senior Teller, and Teller Manager. After he started at Frog Hollow, his supervisors often asked him to take on some of the tasks that Senior Tellers and Teller Managers were supposed to do. Bennett also asked him to train and mentor other tellers "because the other tellers didn't like doing it." He was not paid more for this extra responsibility.

***
Failure to pay properly

5

Haynes thought that it was unfair that he wasn't paid for it or given the formal recognition that he felt he deserved. About four months ago he <u>asked Bennett</u> for at least a <u>promotion</u> in the teller ranks, but she said that he <u>needed more time</u> on the job. When he said it <u>wasn't fair</u> to do the job of the more senior tellers without being paid for it, she told him that if <u>he was dissatisfied with his work, he should quit.</u>

***
 Voluntary/
Involuntary

After that, Haynes spoke with Bennett <u>every two</u> weeks to <u>ask when the CSR job</u> would be his. Each time, <u>Bennett stalled</u> him and advised patience.

Haynes said that on March 25, 2015 he received a written performance appraisal that was positive but that said that he "wasn't a team player." He suspected that this comment was the result of his complaints to Bennett about his promised job.

The next day, Haynes once more talked to Bennett about the CSR job and pointed out that in his performance appraisal the things that were listed as his strengths were all the things that would make him an excellent customer service representative. Bennett responded that, <u>"It just isn't going to happen."</u> She told Haynes that NBC had been <u>bought by a large nationwide bank,</u> that there was a <u>new senior management</u> team in place, that there was <u>attrition</u> going on in the total number of employees the bank would employ, and that <u>no one's job was secure.</u> She said, "My boss thinks you aren't ready for promotion. And you should know that <u>you have no future at this bank."</u>

Bank
financial
crisis

Voluntary/
Involuntary

Haynes said, "I felt completely defeated, misled about the job I had been promised, <u>so I quit."</u> The next day Haynes resigned and gave two weeks' notice. Bennett told him that the policy of the bank was that when someone quit, the employment ended immediately, and thus the last day of his employment was right then.

<u>Haynes applied for unemployment benefits, stating that he left because "I had no choice</u> when I learned that they <u>lied to me about my position."</u> I informed Haynes that I would interview a representative of the bank and that he would get my decision in the mail.

6

STATE OF COLUMBIA
DEPARTMENT OF EMPLOYMENT SERVICES

ADJUDICATION BRANCH

196 Magnolia Street
Celiana, Columbia

JUNE 22, 2015

CLAIMANT:

CONRAD HAYNES
17 BEMBE ROAD
ROSLYN, COLUMBIA

EMPLOYER:

NATIONAL BANK OF COLUMBIA
FROG HOLLOW BRANCH
2173 WILLOW STREET
ROSLYN, COLUMBIA

DETERMINATION BY CLAIMS EXAMINER

The Columbia Unemployment Compensation Act provides that an individual shall [Rule] be disqualified from receiving benefits if it is found that he/she voluntarily left his/her most recent work without good cause connected with the work. (*Col. Unemployment Comp. Code, section 110.*)

Per the statement you, Conrad Haynes, provided to the Department of Employment Services, you left your most recent employment on March 27, 2015 because of general dissatisfaction with your job. You said that you resigned from your position with the National Bank of Columbia immediately after you were told that you were not getting a promotion that you believed had been promised to you.

Sandra Bennett, the branch manager of the bank, was your supervisor. She

7

stated you were <u>not yet ready for a promotion.</u>   She also said that you had often <u>expressed dissatisfaction with your work</u>, despite being given opportunities to work as a permanent teller.   She said that you left your job of your own volition.

Accordingly, it is determined that you voluntarily left available employment and that your employer did not force you to leave.   It is also determined that you did not have good cause connected with your work to quit your position and that you left because of general unhappiness with your job.

For these reasons, you are disqualified from receiving benefits.

> No mention of NBC financial crisis.

_____*JANE EPSTEIN*_____

Jane Epstein
Claims Examiner

8

Haynes Roadmap

	Start writing at _____
π Δ Haynes v. NBC Bank	
Client: Haynes Issue: Denial unemployment Goal: Collect unemployment	Task: Appeal argument Audience: Judge/formal/ persuasive Include: Arguments and rebuttal Exclude: Statement of facts

1. Haynes's resignation should be construed as <u>involuntary</u> (assert/rebut)

   R: Leave involuntarily or with good cause connected to the work can get unemployment benefits. <u>Code, 110; CAA</u>

   R: Voluntarily/involuntarily standard = totality of circumstances. <u>CAA</u>

   R: Employer actions can be so coercive they compel an involuntary resignation. <u>CAA</u>

   R: Shape up or ship out = voluntary; quit or be fired = involuntary. <u>CAA</u>

   RE: <u>CAA</u>
   - E/er initiated resignation
   - E/er drafted resignation letter without consulting e/ee
   - Resignation letter attached to positive recommendation
   - E/ee told best served by accepting proposed resignation
   - E/ee given no other option
   - No improvement possible

   A: <u>Haynes</u>
   - Hired CSR, but low teller $, no promotion, "isn't going to happen"
   - If dissatisfied, quit, no future at bank
   - No other option given
   - No improvement plan given

   C: Quit or be fired, which is involuntary

   Rebut?
   - No drafted letter
   - No threat w/ recommendation
   - Not initiated by bank

2. If voluntary, Haynes's resignation was for <u>good cause</u> (assert/rebut)

   R: *Policy.* Act broadly and liberally construed to protect employees. <u>Delgado</u>

   R: Good cause standard = reasonable and prudent person in labor market, same circumstances. <u>CAA</u>

   R: (Non-exclusive) examples of good cause/not good cause in code. <u>Kaplan citing Columbia Code of Regulations, sec. 311.6, 311.7</u>

   R: Not good cause = minor reduction in wages; refusal to obey reasonable rules; general dissatisfaction with work. <u>311.6</u>

   R: Good cause = (2a) failure to pay remuneration for employee services; (2b) material change in terms of employment resulting in lower pay; and racial/sexual discrimination or harassment. <u>311.7</u>

   RE: <u>Kaplan</u>
   - Salary promises & schedule
   - Failure to pay: work OT & get pay from coworker, or unpaid
   - Material change resulting in lower pay (no case facts)

A: <u>Haynes</u>
- 5k increase not paid
- Work above grade before; work above grade after w/ low salary
- Hired as CSR, but lowest teller pay

C: Good cause found

Rebut?
- 5K minor reduction
- Opportunity full-time teller

R: If employee leaves in belief he can find better work, no good cause. <u>Delgado</u>
R: The circumstances compelling decision to leave must be **(2c) real, substantial and reasonable**; a compulsion produced by extraneous, necessitous, or compelling **circumstances.** <u>Delgado</u>

RE: <u>Delgado</u>
- E/er **financial crisis**
- Threat to job security/furlough
- Difficult to stay on

A: <u>Haynes</u>
- CSR not authorized by agent
- NBC bought out, attrition, job
- Not secure, no future

C: Possible financial instability, threat to job security could be good cause, remanded for further proceedings

Rebut?
- Crisis overstated

> **Step 7.** **Reread the task memo and refine your roadmap to solve the problem posed (5 minutes)**

Reread the Task Memo, See the Big Picture, and Solve the Problem
Before you start writing, always take a moment to ensure you are solving the problem posed and haven't gotten off track while going through the documents. Reread the task memo to refocus on precisely what you've been asked to do. Make sure that you are clear on your client's goal, plan to use the appropriate tone and vocabulary in your response, and follow all directions in the task memo. Consider your presentation's organization to ensure your response is clear and easy to follow. Lastly, consider the complexity of the various sections and components of your answer to assess how you think the grader will allocate points and devise a plan to spend your time accordingly.

Haynes Big Picture
You are writing an argument, so you want to ensure that your tone, including your headings, will be persuasive. If you haven't already thought to provide subheadings for section two or determined how best to use the policy argument, you may see how to work those in now. Though the argument has two main sections, it is not likely they are of equal 50/50 weight, since section two contains three subsections. Thus, your response will essentially have four subsections (1, 2a, 2b, and 2c). They are not quite of equal weight, however, based on the laws and facts available to make our arguments. Our best guess is one-third on point one and two-thirds on all of point two combined; our plan will allot our time accordingly.

> **Step 8.** **Write an answer that solves the problem posed (about 45 minutes)**

SAMPLE ANSWER FOR HAYNES

MEMORANDUM

TO: Susan Mont, Senior Partner
FROM: Applicant
DATE: February 28, 2017
RE: Conrad Haynes: Appeal Brief Argument

Introduction

Pursuant to your request, below is the argument section of Haynes's unemployment compensation appeal brief, asserting (1) Haynes's resignation from NBC is involuntary, and (2) even if his resignation is found to be voluntary, it was for good cause. As such, Haynes is entitled to receive benefits.

ARGUMENT

I. HAYNES'S RESIGNATION WAS INVOLUNTARY, AND HE IS ENTITLED TO BENEFITS BECAUSE HE WAS INVITED TO QUIT AND TOLD HE HAD "NO FUTURE" OR OPTIONS FOR IMPROVEMENT.

An individual who leaves his or her most recent work involuntarily or with good cause connected with the work shall be eligible for unemployment compensation benefits. <u>Columbia Assoc. of Accountants (CAA)</u>; <u>Columbia Unemployment Compensation Code, Sec. 110</u>. Whether an individual leaves voluntarily or involuntarily is determined in accordance with the totality of circumstances. <u>CAA</u>. An employer's action can be so coercive that the employee is compelled to resign, which is considered an involuntary resignation and permits the employee to receive unemployment benefits. <u>CAA</u>. Termination cases involving whether an employee voluntarily left his employment generally fall into "shape up or ship out" (voluntary) or "quit or be fired" (involuntary). <u>CAA</u>.

In <u>CAA</u>, the employer surprised employee Schultz with a pre-drafted resignation letter, which he demanded she sign. Schultz was told she would be "best served by accepting the proposed resignation." No other palatable options or opportunities to improve her performance were offered. The court found Schultz's resignation was involuntary, since she was in effect told to quit or be fired. <u>CAA</u>.

Similarly, NBC essentially told Haynes to "quit or be fired," and Haynes did not leave his job voluntarily. NBC coerced Haynes to quit when they hired him for one position but then used a bait and switch to place him in a lesser paying job, telling him to quit if he was dissatisfied. After working three years for NBC as a roving fill-in teller, Haynes was recruited for and hired as a customer service representative (CSR) for the Frog Hollow branch. After starting, Haynes discovered there was no CSR position; instead he had the lowest-level teller position. His supervisor, branch manager Bennett, repeatedly lied and misled Haynes into thinking the CSR promotion would materialize. Eventually, Bennett told Haynes the promotion "just isn't going to happen" and that if he was dissatisfied, he should quit since he had "no future" at the bank. Similar to employee Schultz in <u>CAA</u>, Haynes was not provided with other options, or provided with an improvement plan to obtain the promised position, as he would have been if the message were "shape up or ship out."

Although NBC did not initiate Haynes's resignation by pre-drafting a letter and attaching a positive recommendation as an inducement, as in <u>CAA</u>, the message to Haynes was "quit or be fired" rather than "shape up or ship out" since Haynes, like Schultz in <u>CAA</u>, was not provided a palatable option to quitting.

In applying the totality of circumstances test, Haynes was coerced into quitting by NBC, making his resignation involuntary and entitling him to benefits.

Role-play for a professional presentation.

Include a brief introduction.

Persuasive headings explain why you win using "because" and key facts.

Organize rules from broad to narrow, and underline case names so it is easy for the grader to find.

To save time, only recite key facts that you will analogize.

We use a new paragraph to signal our analysis, leading with our conclusion and using pointed language like "bait and switch" to persuade.

Signal the rebuttal with a new paragraph using a word like "although," so it's easy to find.

It is good practice to end each section with a conclusion.

II. IF HAYNES'S RESIGNATION IS DEEMED VOLUNTARY, IT WAS FOR GOOD CAUSE, AND HE IS ENTITLED TO BENEFITS BECAUSE NBC DID NOT PAY HIM FOR WORK PERFORMED, THERE WAS A MATERIAL CHANGE IN THE TERMS OF EMPLOYMENT RESULTING IN LOWER PAY, AND THE EMPLOYER WAS HAVING A REAL FINANCIAL CRISIS CAUSING JOB INSECURITY.

The benefits sections of the Unemployment Compensation Act must be liberally and broadly construed for the benefit of unemployed workers. Delgado. The purpose of the statute is "to protect employees against economic dependency caused by temporary unemployment and to reduce the need for other welfare programs," and this applies to voluntary quit cases. Delgado. Haynes, a young father of two, seeks the Act's protection and benefits since he has been unable to find another job because of many bank failures and mergers and will be forced to depend on welfare.

An employee who has voluntarily left employment, but for good cause connected with the work, can still receive unemployment benefits. Kaplan, CAA, Col. Code sec. 110. The determination of good cause should be judged by what a reasonable and prudent person in the labor market would do in the same circumstances. Kaplan. Even if Haynes voluntarily left his employment, he did so for good cause and is entitled to benefits.

Columbia Code section 311.7 sets forth several nonexclusive examples that constitute good cause, such as "failure to provide remuneration for employee services," "material change in terms of employment resulting in lower pay," and "racial or sexual discrimination or harassment." Kaplan. Circumstances that do not constitute good cause include "minor reduction in wages" and "general dissatisfaction with work." Kaplan, Col. Code sec. 311.6. As outlined below, Haynes had several "good cause" reasons for quitting that render him eligible for benefits.

A. NBC Failed to Pay Remuneration to Haynes for His Services When Haynes Was Required to Perform Work Above His Pay Grade Without Compensation.

Good cause was found in the Kaplan case when salary and schedule promises did not materialize and the employee was required to work overtime and collect pay from his coworkers or not be paid at all. The court found Kaplan acted as a reasonable and prudent employee under the circumstances when he resigned and that he was entitled to benefits. Kaplan.

Similarly, here, NBC as part of an ongoing practice, failed to provide remuneration for Haynes's services when he was repeatedly forced to perform job duties above his pay grade without appropriate pay. He was promised a CSR position at a $5,000 increase, but he was given the lowest-level teller position while repeatedly being required to perform higher-level teller functions, such as training other tellers.

While Haynes was compensated, it was at a lower rate than the work dictated. NBC may argue the $5,000 increase Haynes was promised, but did not receive, is a "minor reduction in wages" and not good cause, but this argument will fail. In Kaplan, the court found a 50-cent salary reduction significant, when considered along with the other circumstances. Similarly, the $5,000 missing salary is much more substantial, but it is still only part of the circumstances showing good cause.

A reasonably prudent employee in the same circumstances would not want to continue completing higher-level tasks without being appropriately compensated, thus Haynes's resignation was with good cause.

B. NBC Materially Changed the Terms of Haynes's Employment Resulting in Lower Pay When He Was Given the Lowest Teller Position After Being Hired for a CSR Position.

A material change in the terms of employment resulting in lower pay constitutes good cause for voluntarily leaving a position. Kaplan, Col. Code sec. 311.7. Here, Haynes interviewed and was hired for a CSR position paying $5,000 more, but when he showed up for work

---

The policy argument was necessary, but it could effectively work in various places. It is also persuasive to use facts that show Haynes in a sympathetic light.

When possible, break an argument into subsections to guide the grader and provide clarity. This micro-organization came from the library.

In the interest of time, we opt to write a very brief rule explanation.

Since we can skip a rule explanation, we opt to merge our rule and analysis into one paragraph.

he was given the lowest-paying teller position. Upon inquiry, his boss told him repeatedly over months to "be patient" and promised the CSR position would materialize, but it never did. This type of material change in title and pay falls squarely within the examples of good cause found in Columbia Code section 311.7.

Although Haynes was provided the opportunity to be a full-time teller instead of a roving teller, that was not the position and pay level he agreed to when he accepted the job.

Thus, this material change in position resulting in lower pay provided good cause for Haynes to resign.

C. Haynes Resigned Because of a "Real, Substantial, and Reasonable" Fear of Job Insecurity Caused by NBC's Financial Crisis.

In order to constitute "good cause," the circumstances that compel the decision to leave employment must be "real, substantial, and reasonable . . . some compulsion produced by extraneous and necessitous or compelling circumstances." <u>Delgado</u>. In <u>Delgado</u>, the court determined an employer financial crisis and employee furloughs causing job insecurity may be sufficient to establish good cause and remanded the case for further proceedings.

> We can use this for the principle stated (finding an additional "good cause" reason), but since it was remanded, we won't analogize facts.

Here, very recently a large nationwide bank bought NBC, a new senior management team was put in place, and attrition was going on to reduce the number of bank employees. Further, Haynes's boss told him the CSR position was "not authorized by senior management," that "no one's job was secure," and that he had "no future at this bank." It is reasonable to assess that NBC is in a financial crisis given the buyout and subsequent belt tightening; Haynes thus has real, reasonable, and substantial reasons for job insecurity based on NBC's financial crisis.

NBC may claim they are not having a financial crisis and that this is overstated, but similar to <u>Delgado</u>, the ALJ here made no attempt to determine if NBC was in financial peril. Further, this was a reasonable interpretation by Haynes given the sequence of events, providing him with sufficient good cause.

Haynes resigned for good cause based on the real, substantial, and reasonable concern that NBC's financial crisis made his job insecure and not because he had general dissatisfaction with his work.

> Always conclude with what you want and why you should get it.

CONCLUSION

Haynes is entitled to receive unemployment compensation benefits because his resignation was involuntary because he was coerced into resigning by NBC. Further, even if the resignation was involuntary, it was for good cause. Since the unemployment statutes are broadly construed for the benefit of workers, Haynes should be awarded unemployment compensation.

Self-Assessment Grid: Haynes

Argument for Appeal Brief		

Overall organization and presentation

☐ Organized like a brief argument with intro, argument, and conclusion
☐ Persuasive tone and formal vocabulary
☐ Organized/presented in some logical way with at least two sections
☐ Appropriate use of persuasive headings to persuade and guide grader
☐ Cite to rules, codes, and cases in appropriate places
☐ Presented rule and rule explanation before analysis
☐ Used all cases appropriately
☐ Analogized cases where helpful, comparing case facts to ours
☐ Rebutted potential arguments where appropriate
☐ Used all pertinent facts well
☐ Followed all directions in task memo, including no statement of facts

Rules (from library)	Rule Explanation (library case facts)	Analysis (our case facts)
Introduction		
Briefly describe the task and identify the two arguments: (1) Haynes's resignation is involuntary, and (2) even if involuntary, it was for good cause.		
Argument		
I. Haynes' resignation was involuntary because of employer coercion		
☐ An individual who leaves his or her most recent work involuntarily or with good cause connected with the work shall be eligible for unemployment compensation benefits. <u>CAA, Code 110</u>. ☐ Whether the departure was voluntary or involuntary is determined by the totality of circumstances. <u>CAA</u>. ☐ An employer's action(s) can be so coercive that the employee is compelled to resign, which is considered an involuntary resignation and permits the employee to receive unemployment benefits. <u>CAA</u>. ☐ Termination cases involving whether an employee voluntarily left his employment generally fall into "shape up or ship out" (voluntary) or "quit or be fired" (involuntary). <u>CAA</u>.	☐ The **employer initiated** the severance by surprising employee Schultz and **demanding she sign a pre-drafted resignation letter.** ☐ Employee was induced to sign by attaching **positive recommendation.** ☐ Employee was told she should "sign the letter now," that if she decided to fight she would "never win," and she would be "best served by accepting the proposed resignation." ☐ **No other palatable options or opportunities to improve her performance were offered other than resignation.** ☐ **The court found the resignation was involuntary,** since Schultz was in effect told to "quit or be fired."	☐ After working three years for NBC as a roving fill-in teller, Haynes was recruited for and **hired as a customer service representative (CSR)** for the Frog Hollow branch. ☐ After starting, Haynes discovered there was no CSR position; he instead was given the **lowest-paid level of teller position.** ☐ His supervisor, branch manager Bennett, repeatedly lied and misled Haynes into thinking the CSR promotion would materialize. ☐ Eventually, Bennett told Haynes the promotion **"just isn't going to happen,"** that he was **"not ready for a promotion,"** and that **if dissatisfied, he should quit,** since he had **"no future"** at the bank. ☐ As in <u>CAA</u>, Haynes was **not provided with other options or provided with an improvement plan.** ☐ [Rebuttal needed] NBC did not initiate Haynes's resignation by pre-drafting a letter and attaching a positive recommendation, but Haynes was not provided a palatable option other than quitting. ☐ Haynes's resignation was involuntary.

Continued>

II. If resignation was voluntary, it was for good cause.		
☐ The benefits sections of the Unemployment Compensation Act must be liberally and broadly construed for the benefit of unemployed workers. <u>Delgado</u>. [Could include this in various places.] ☐ The purpose of the statute is "to protect employees against economic dependency caused by temporary unemployment and to reduce the need for other welfare programs," and this applies to voluntary quit cases. <u>Delgado</u>. ☐ An employee who has voluntarily left employment, but for good cause connected with the work, can still receive unemployment benefits. <u>Kaplan, CAA, Code 110</u>. ☐ The determination of good cause should be judged by what a reasonable and prudent person in the labor market would do in the same circumstances. <u>Kaplan</u>. ☐ Non-exclusive examples constituting good cause include "failure to provide remuneration for employee services," "material change in terms of employment resulting in lower pay," and "racial or sexual discrimination or harassment." <u>Kaplan, Code 311.7</u>. ☐ Circumstances that do not constitute good cause include "minor reduction in wages" and "general dissatisfaction with work." <u>Kaplan</u>, <u>Code 311.6</u>.		☐ Haynes, a young father of two, seeks the Act's protection and benefits since he has been unable to find another job because of many bank failures and mergers and because without it he would face unbearable hardships and be forced to depend on welfare programs. ☐ Haynes was not dissatisfied with his work, but rather wanted recognition for his good work and to be paid accordingly. ☐ Even if Haynes voluntarily left his employment, he did so for good cause and is entitled to benefits.
A. NBC failed to pay remuneration for services.		
[Note: The rules stated above in section II are used throughout sections II A, B, and C, but the rules could be placed in this section. Using three subheadings is best, but a well-organized argument without subheadings would work so long as the three points were clearly made.]	☐ Good cause was found when salary and schedule promises did not materialize and the employee was required to work overtime and collect pay from his coworkers or not be paid at all. <u>Kaplan</u>. ☐ The court found Kaplan acted as a reasonable and prudent employee under the circumstances when he resigned and that he was entitled to benefits. <u>Kaplan</u>.	☐ Haynes was promised a CSR position at a $5,000 increase, but he was given the lowest-paying level of teller position while being repeatedly required to perform higher-level teller (senior teller or teller manager) functions, such as training other tellers. ☐ [Rebuttal needed] NBC may argue the $5,000 increase is a "minor reduction in wages." ☐ But, in <u>Kaplan</u> the court found a 50-cent salary reduction significant, and $5,000 is much more substantial. ☐ Haynes had good cause because NBC failed to pay him the proper remuneration.

Continued>

B. NBC materially changed the terms of employment, resulting in lower pay.		
☐ A material change in the terms of employment resulting in lower pay constitutes good cause for voluntarily leaving a position. <u>Kaplan</u>, <u>Code 311.7</u>.	☐ Employees were asked to seek compensation from their coworkers, which could be a material change in the terms of employment. <u>Kaplan</u>.	☐ Haynes interviewed and was hired for a CSR position paying $5,000 more than his then current position, but he was instead given the lowest-paying teller position. ☐ Upon inquiry, his boss told him repeatedly over months to "be patient" and promised the CSR position would materialize, but it didn't. ☐ [Rebuttal] Although Haynes was provided the opportunity to be a full-time teller instead of a roving teller, that was not the position and pay level he agreed to when he accepted the job. ☐ Haynes had good cause because there was a material change in employment.
C. NBC's financial crisis caused real, substantial, and reasonable job insecurity.		
☐ To constitute "good cause," the circumstances that compel the decision to leave employment must be "real, substantial, and reasonable . . . some compulsion produced by extraneous and necessitous or compelling circumstances." <u>Delgado</u>.	☐ The court determined an employer's financial crisis and employee furloughs causing job insecurity may be sufficient to establish good cause, and it remanded the case for further proceedings. <u>Delgado</u>. ☐ The employer made it difficult to stay on. <u>Delgado</u>.	☐ A large nationwide bank bought NBC, a new senior management team was put in place, and attrition was going on to reduce the number of bank employees. ☐ Haynes's boss told him the CSR position was "not authorized by senior management," that "no one's job was secure," and that he had "no future at this bank." ☐ NBC is in a financial crisis, given the buyout and subsequent belt tightening, creating job insecurity for Haynes. ☐ Haynes's boss made it difficult to stay on when she urged him to "be patient" and told him he had "no future." ☐ [Rebuttal needed] NBC may claim a financial crisis is overstated, but similar to <u>Delgado</u>, the ALJ here made no attempt to determine if NBC was in financial peril. ☐ Haynes had good cause because of NBC's financial crisis.
Conclusion		
☐ Haynes is entitled to receive unemployment compensation benefits because his resignation was involuntary, and, even if voluntary, it was for good cause.		

DEMONSTRATION 2

UNITED STATES v. BLAKE C. DAVIS

July 2017

California
Bar
Examination

Performance Test

INSTRUCTIONS AND FILE

UNITED STATES v. BLAKE C. DAVIS

UNITED STATES v. BLAKE C. DAVIS

INSTRUCTIONS

1.   This performance test is designed to evaluate your ability to handle a select number of legal authorities in the context of a factual problem involving a client.

2.   The problem is set in the <u>fictional State of Columbia, one of the United States.</u>

3.   You will have two sets of materials with which to work: <u>a File and a Library.</u>

4.   The File contains factual materials about your case. The first document is a memorandum containing the instructions for the tasks you are to complete.

5.   The Library contains the legal authorities needed to complete the tasks. The case reports may be real, modified, or written solely for the purpose of this performance test. If the cases appear familiar to you, do not assume that they are precisely the same as you have read before. Read each thoroughly, as if it were new to you. You should assume that cases were decided in the jurisdictions and on the dates shown. In citing cases from the Library, you may use abbreviations and omit page citations.

6.   You should concentrate on the materials provided, but you should also bring to bear on the problem your general knowledge of the law. What you have learned in law school and elsewhere provides the general background for analyzing the problem; the File and Library provide the specific materials with which you must work.

7.   This performance test is designed to be completed in 90 minutes. Although there are no parameters on how to apportion that 90 minutes, you should allow yourself sufficient time to thoroughly review the materials and organize your planned response. Since the time allotted for this

session of the examination includes two (2) essay questions in addition to this performance test, time management is essential.

8.   Your response will be graded on its compliance with instructions and on its content, thoroughness, and organization.

Alfaro, Blevin & Cohn, LLP

MEMORANDUM

TO: Applicant

FROM: Timothy Alfaro

DATE: July 25, 2017

RE: United States v. Blake C. Davis

We represent Blake Davis who may be charged with: (1) the misdemeanor of resisting agents from the U.S. Customs and Border Protection Service ("CBP"), and (2) the felony of possession of cocaine. Mr. Davis views the incident, which took place aboard a cruise ship after it docked at Port Columbia, as an unfortunate incident prompted by a significant investigative error made by the Customs officers who made the arrest.

Maria Castile, the Assistant U.S. Attorney who is reviewing the case, seems inclined to seek an indictment against Mr. Davis. Ms. Castile, however, is willing to consider a plea bargain. Following a lengthy counseling session yesterday, Mr. Davis wants to try to get a plea agreement but does not want a felony conviction on his record.

What I want to do is convince Ms. Castile to accept a guilty plea to misdemeanor resisting.

To support this offer, please draft a letter to Ms. Castile that argues that: the search of Mr. Davis' cabin aboard the cruise ship was unreasonable under the Fourth Amendment to the United States Constitution and hence a possession charge should not be brought because the drugs were illegally seized and will be suppressed. Do not prepare a statement of facts, but use the facts in making your legal arguments.

INTERVIEW TRANSCRIPT

July 18, 2017

Blake Davis (BLAKE): Thanks for seeing us.

Tim Alfaro (TIM): I'm glad both of you could come in. It should simplify getting all the information we'll need.

Ann Davis (ANN): We are so upset about this situation. We really appreciate your help.

TIM: We'll do our best. Now, I know that you were arrested, Blake, for assaulting a U.S. Customs agent and for possession of cocaine as you were about to get off of a cruise ship.

BLAKE: That's right, but it was a huge mistake. We had no idea there were drugs hidden in the wall. The Customs folks got the wrong cabin, they busted in with a drug dog and tossed all of our belongings, and then tried to grab my briefcase from me.

TIM: Why don't you start at the beginning and tell me what happened?

BLAKE: Alright. Well, we had booked this cruise on the *Esprit* months ago to celebrate our 40th wedding anniversary. I didn't realize at the time that I would be buried in work that would force me to bring along stuff that had to get done by the time we returned to Columbia City. It only was because of the need to protect the work product that I got in any trouble.

TIM: Where do you work and what type of work product are you talking about?

BLAKE: I'm an engineer with Allied Industries and I've been working with corporate counsel and others to put together a patent application for breakthrough technology that will revolutionize our business. I had to submit the

final paper work right after we got off the ship. I was told by the lawyers, the chief engineer, and the CEO to make sure no one got a look at any of the papers.

TIM: How does this tie in with your encounter with the Customs agents?

ANN: It all happened the morning we were to disembark. We got up early to finish packing; we planned to wheel our luggage off the ship. I got room service, just a light continental breakfast. Blake went up to the buffet area because he wanted a full breakfast.

BLAKE: I took my briefcase with me because I wanted to recheck some final details.

ANN: Right. Well, I was on the balcony sipping coffee when I heard a knock on the door. I thought it was our cabin steward checking to see if we needed anything before disembarking. So I opened the door and there were a man and a woman. She had a dog on a leash – a black Labrador, I think.

TIM: Did they ask you your name?

ANN: Yes, the gentleman said, "Who are you?" and I said, "Ann Davis. What's all this about?" He told me he was from U.S. Customs and they were there to search our cabin for contraband.

TIM: Were they in uniform and did they state their names?

ANN: Sure. I told them we didn't know anything about contraband but he – Oliphant, now I remember – told me to step into the corridor and remain there while they conducted the search. I told him it was some kind of mistake but I did what he asked.

BLAKE: That's when I showed up. I told them who I was and asked them what they were doing. They asked me to step aside and I did. Then they went in.

TIM: From your position could you see what the two agents were doing?

ANN: They propped the door open so I was able to see most of the cabin, except the corner where it was blocked by the bathroom.

TIM: What did you see?

ANN: First, they poked into everything, looking under the bed, opening drawers. I couldn't figure out what they were after. Then they put our three pieces of luggage on the bed and pressed down on them; our bags are soft-sided. Then the dog was brought over to the luggage. It sniffed at each one and then the dog went over to the balcony door and just sat down. After that, the two agents opened each bag and dumped everything on the bed; after we had spent all that time packing them neatly! Then they pawed through every darn thing we owned, every piece of clothing, our toiletries, rifling through the pages of our books, probing into each suitcase – everything. They didn't find anything they were interested in, just like I had told them. When they finished with the luggage, leaving all of our stuff strewn across the bed in piles and some on the floor, they turned their attention to where the dog was sitting. I saw them squat down and poke around with something, maybe a pencil. The guy pulled a panel off the wall and took out a small plastic bag. I had no idea what they found.

TIM: Okay, what did the Customs agents say or do?

BLAKE: At some point, the lead guy, Oliphant, said that they had "reliable information" that we had illegal drugs. I told him that was nonsense, we knew nothing about drugs, and I was outraged they had ransacked our private stateroom. That's when he demanded that I turn over my briefcase.

TIM: What happened then?

BLAKE: I told him "no way," that the briefcase contained confidential business materials and no one could look through it. Period. He told me I was required to give it to him, that they already found narcotics, and he suspected there was more in my briefcase. I told him he was nuts and to go away. That's when he

tried to grab the case from me. I wouldn't let go. He and the woman officer threw me to the floor and put the cuffs on me. Then Oliphant took the key to the briefcase from my pocket and tossed everything in it on the bed with our other stuff. That's when he found my passport and, gosh, was he surprised! He and the woman agent conferred and then he asked me if I was Blake C. Davis. I said, "Of course; that's what I told you!" He said there had been a mistake. They were looking for *Blaine C. Daviss* with an extra "s" -- spelled D-A-V-I-S-S; some other guy. They had been informed that this other Daviss had a cabin on the same deck, but on the other side of the ship. They took the cuffs off of me and apologized, but said that I would have to accompany them and that I'd be charged with resisting a legal search and possession of cocaine.

TIM: Okay. Thanks so much. Let me get in touch with the U.S. Attorney's Office and see where this situation stands and what we have to do to try to quash it. That seems like the first thing we have to address.

ANN and BLAKE: Okay. Thanks.

DEPARTMENT OF HOMELAND SECURITY

U.S. CUSTOMS AND BORDER PROTECTION

INCIDENT – ARREST REPORT

1. PORT WHERE INCIDENT-ARREST OCCURRED: Port Columbia

2. CBP OFFICER IN CHARGE: Ralph Oliphant #06254

3. NAME OF VESSEL: Sun Cruise Line - *Esprit*

4. DATE: July 16, 2017

5. SUBJECT: Davis, Blake C.

6. SEX: Male

7. HEIGHT: 5' 7"

8. WEIGHT: 140 lbs.

9. AGE: 61

10. RACE/ETHNICITY: White

The undersigned CBP Officer, assisted by Canine Enforcement Officer Veronica Brown, conducted a scheduled vessel search of Sun Cruise Line's *Esprit* when it docked in Port Columbia, in Columbia, following a seven-day cruise that included day-long visits to Acapulco, Mexico and three other foreign ports. As standard

procedure before boarding the ship to conduct routine enforcement actions, I accessed the Treasury Enforcement Communications System's ("TECS") computerized database to determine if it contained any enforcement information about passengers or crew members traveling on the *Esprit*.

Included in the TECS report on the *Esprit* was a "lookout" for a white male, Blaine C. Daviss, 6' 4", 260 lbs., 21 years old. The information was filed by an undercover CBP officer stationed in Acapulco who had observed Daviss during the period when the ship was docked at that port. The TECS report revealed that Daviss had traveled to other drug source countries in the Caribbean and South America on other occasions, had a criminal record (two arrests, one conviction for heroin possession and sale), had purchased his ticket at the last minute and in cash, and was traveling alone. The TECS report also indicated Daviss was observed in Acapulco in the company of three suspected drug dealers for a period of about 30 minutes.

Based on all of the data available in the TECS system for the *Esprit*, I identified Daviss to investigate when our CBP team boarded the ship. I accessed the passenger/crew manifest from the TECS database, but in doing so I erroneously listed Daviss' stateroom as 8132 instead of 8086. Cabin 8132 was assigned to *Blake C. Davis*, the subject of this report, who was listed on the manifest on the line immediately above Daviss. Both had staterooms on Deck 8 but on opposite sides of the ship, Daviss on the port side and Davis on the starboard side.

After boarding the ship, Canine Enforcement Officer Brown, her drug-sniffing dog, and I approached cabin 8132, at which point the dog "alerted" in the hallway. The "alert" indicated that cocaine had been deposited at the site within a year. I knocked on the door of the cabin and it was opened by a middle-aged

white female. I identified myself as a CBP Officer and introduced Officer Brown. Upon my request, the woman told us she was Ann Davis(s). I instructed Ms. Davis(s) to step into the hallway while we conducted a search for narcotics. She complied. At that point, the subject arrived and identified himself. I instructed him to comply. He complied. When the dog entered the stateroom, he moved to the corner of the cabin by the glass door that opened onto the balcony and alerted by sitting down. I opened each piece of luggage, removed the contents and conducted a thorough search of the items and the bags. I found nothing suspicious. I then moved to the area where the dog alerted and, with the assistance of Officer Brown and the dog, pulled a panel off the wall and found a white substance in a large plastic bag that later tested positive for cocaine.

While I was conducting a search of the rest of the cabin, the subject started protesting loudly. I explained we had evidence he was in possession of drugs, that a suspicious substance had been found, and asked him to turn over his briefcase. He refused to do so, claiming it contained confidential business documents. Officer Brown and I wrestled Davis(s) to the floor and forcibly took possession of the briefcase and handcuffed him. A search of the briefcase revealed no contraband. However, when I examined the passport in the case, I learned that the subject's name was *Blake C. Davis*. It was only then I realized we had made an error. We took Davis into custody. Subsequently, we searched stateroom 8086, found a large quantity of cocaine, and arrested *Blaine C. Daviss* for felony possession of cocaine with intent to distribute.

SIGNATURE:

_____*Ralph Oliphant*_____

RALPH OLIPHANT #06254

July 2017

California
Bar
Examination

PERFORMANCE TEST
LIBRARY

UNITED STATES v. BLAKE C. DAVIS

LIBRARY

United States v. Clark
U.S. Court of Appeals, 15th Circuit (2014)...

United States v. Clark

U.S. Court of Appeals, 15th Circuit (2014)

Daniel Clark was convicted in the U.S. District Court for the Eastern District of Columbia of violating *21 U.S.C. § 846* (possession with intent to distribute a controlled substance) following the denial of a motion to suppress evidence. On appeal, Clark asserts the United States Custom Service failed to procure a warrant to search his cabin aboard the M/V *Enchanted Isle* where he was employed as a seaman. The judgment of the District Court is affirmed.

I. Facts

On September 7, 2010, the *Enchanted Isle* returned to her home port, Sealand, at approximately 4:30 a.m. after visiting Cozumel, Mexico, the Grand Cayman Islands and Jamaica. The ship was to depart again at about 4:00 p.m. U.S. Customs agents, with the cooperation of the vessel owner, routinely boarded and searched the ship upon reentry at Sealand.

Robert Sedge, a Customs Service agent, had received information from a reliable informant that two crew members, Alan Arch and Daniel Clark, would be transporting illegal narcotics. At approximately 2:30 p.m., Alan Arch, was seen by Sedge passing a package to Larry Bates. Although Clark was with Arch, there was no evidence Clark gave anything to Bates. Bates later was arrested by other Customs agents and a package containing shoes with cocaine hydrochloride innersoles was seized from him. This information was relayed to Sedge who, without a warrant, boarded the *Enchanted Isle* with a drug-trained dog.

Sedge went directly to the cabin assigned to Clark and, after knocking and being admitted by Clark's roommate, entered the cabin, whereupon the dog alerted to the presence of drugs. Sedge did not have Clark's permission to enter the room; the roommate admitted Sedge based solely on the latter's claimed authority to do so. Clark's roommate informed Sedge that his was the top bunk and pointed out his belongings, with the inference that the remainder belonged to Clark. Upon searching the cabin and Clark's belongings, Sedge found two pairs of shoes with innersoles made of cocaine hydrochloride, one on the lower bunk and another between the bulkhead and the bed. These were the materials that were the subject of Clark's motion to suppress and are the basis of his appeal.

II. **Discussion**

The *Fourth Amendment* protects "against unreasonable searches and seizures." Whether a search is reasonable will depend upon its nature and all of the circumstances surrounding it but, as a general matter, warrantless searches are unreasonable. Searches conducted at the nation's borders, however, represent a well-established exception to the warrant requirement. The exception applies not only at the physical boundaries of the United States, but also at "the functional equivalent" of a border, including the first port where a ship docks after arriving from a foreign country. The search here, conducted as the *Enchanted Isle* arrived in Sealand, was therefore a border search.

Provided a border search is routine, it may be conducted, not just without a warrant, but without probable cause, reasonable suspicion, or any suspicion of wrongdoing. The expectation of privacy is less at the border than in the interior and the *Fourth Amendment* balance between the interests of the Government and the privacy right of the individual is much more in favor of the Government. Even at the border, however, an individual is entitled to be free from an unreasonable search and privacy interests must be balanced against the sovereign's interests. Consequently, certain searches, classified as "non-routine," require reasonable suspicion of wrongdoing to pass constitutional muster.

The question here, therefore, is not whether the Customs officers were required to have a warrant or probable cause in order to search Clark's private cabin, but, rather, whether reasonable suspicion was necessary. The parties agree that no suspicion is required in order for a Customs officer to board and search a cruise ship as part of a routine border search. They disagree, however, as to whether any *Fourth Amendment* protection applies to a search of a private sleeping cabin aboard a cruise ship.

To answer this question, we must first decide whether the border search at issue was routine or non-routine and, so doing, set forth the correct standard required under the *Fourth Amendment*. We turn to a determination of whether this search was conducted in accordance with it.

To ascertain whether a border search can be classified as routine, we must examine the degree to which it intrudes on a person's privacy. Highly intrusive border searches that implicate the dignity and privacy interests of the person being searched require reasonable suspicion. In the present case, Clark argues that the search of a cruise ship cabin is not a routine border search because the *Fourth Amendment's* primary purpose is the protection of privacy in one's home and the search of a home, by its nature, is highly intrusive. He makes a compelling argument that an individual's expectation of privacy in a cabin of a ship is no different from any other temporary place of abode. Because the search of his living quarters aboard the cruise ship intruded upon that most private of places – his home – he says it should be considered non-routine. In response to Clark's arguments, the Government contends that the search of the cabin was a routine border search and should be analyzed in the same way as that of a vehicle.

It is an open question whether the search of a cabin of a cruise ship sufficiently intrudes upon an individual's privacy to render it non-routine, so that reasonable suspicion of criminal activity is required. Indeed, there is a surprising dearth of authority on the matter.

The authority the Government cites for the proposition that a search of a crew member's cabin amounts to a routine border search is readily distinguishable from the present case. In *United States v. Braun (S.D. Fla. 2004)*, the "routine" aspect of the search was the use of trained canines to detect narcotic odor from the hallways of newly-arrived cruise ships in Key West. The search of Braun's cabin occurred only after the drug-sniffing dog had alerted to the presence of drugs in the cabin while still in the hallway. While the court stated the search was a routine border search, clearly it was referring to the use of the dogs to "search" the ship's hallways, not the search of the cabin once there was reasonable suspicion based on the alert and all of the other circumstances. Here, by contrast, the dog did not alert until after the cabin was opened and the animal entered the room. The dog's alerting, therefore, cannot establish reasonable suspicion for the search. The routine search in *Braun*, done without reasonable suspicion, was of the ship's hallways -- public space; the search of Braun's cabin was done only after there was reasonable suspicion (or even probable cause) to search.

The relatively few decisions in this area counsel in favor of the approach urged by Clark. Other courts correctly recognize that the search of private living quarters aboard a ship at the functional equivalent of a border is a non-routine search and must be supported by reasonable suspicion of criminal conduct. The cruise ship cabin is both living quarters and located at the national border. As a result, one principle underlying the case law on border searches – namely, that a port of entry is not a traveler's home – runs headlong into the overriding respect for the sanctity of the home embedded in our traditions since the origins of the Republic, foremost in our nation's *Fourth Amendment* jurisprudence. We find that requiring reasonable suspicion strikes the proper balance between the interests of the government and the privacy rights of the individual. It also best comports with the case law, which treats border searches permissively but gives special protection to an individual's dwelling place, however temporary. We, therefore, join those courts that require reasonable suspicion to search a cabin of a passenger or crew member aboard a ship.

Here, the search was highly intrusive on Clark's privacy. Uninvited and in Clark's absence, the officers entered his *de facto* home, searched through his belongings, and subjected his private space to inspection by a drug-sniffing dog. Because of the high expectation of privacy and level of intrusiveness, the search cannot be considered "routine" and must therefore be supported by reasonable suspicion of illegal activity.

Under the reasonable suspicion standard, law enforcement officers, including Customs officers, must have reasonable suspicion, based on specific and articulable facts, that the suspect committed, is committing, or is about to commit, a crime in order to conduct a search. In our view, the information known to the agent, including the informant's tip, his own observations, and the arrest and seizure of cocaine from Bates justified reasonable suspicion that Clark (and Arch) had contraband aboard the *Enchanted Isle*.

Clark argues that any suspicion the agent might have had *about him* was unreasonable because it supposedly arose from various mistakes the agent had made about his relationship with Arch. To be sure, suspicion is unreasonable if it arises from mistakes that are themselves unreasonable. But quibbles aside, Clark points to no evidence revealing *any* mistake by the agent, lest still any *unreasonable* one.

III. Disposition

For the foregoing reasons, we AFFIRM the denial of the motion to suppress and uphold Clark's conviction.

Practice California Performance Test:
Step-by-Step Demonstration 2

United States v. Blake C. Davis (Cal. July 2017)

[Roadmap modeled on the computer.]

| Step 1. | **Scan the instructions, the file table of contents, and the library table of contents (1 minute)** |

Instructions

You should have already thoroughly read the instruction page once. When you are completing a PT, look for three important details: the jurisdiction (usually in paragraph two), the contents of the packet (usually in paragraph three), and any specific weighting information, which, if supplied, would be noted at the bottom of the instructions. Take a second to skim the rest of the instructions to ensure no changes were made in the standard instructions.

Davis Instructions

1. The problem is set in the State of Columbia.
2. The packet contains a file and a library.
3. No special weighting information is included.

Client File Table of Contents

Look this over to get a general feel for what the case is about, how many pages of facts there are, and the type of documents you will be working with.

Davis File Table of Contents

Since the case name is <u>United States v. Blake C. Davis,</u> the federal government is involved, but the names alone don't clarify whether it is a civil or a criminal case (since the federal government files suits in both civil and criminal matters). There are approximately nine pages of facts we will be working with.

- The first file document is a memorandum from Timothy Alfaro, who is likely the person who will direct us on what to do and whom we represent.
- The second file document is an "interview transcript" transcribing a conversation involving the defendant Davis, Timothy Alfaro, and a woman named Ann Davis (likely related to the defendant).
- The third file document is an arrest report from the Dept. of Homeland Security, which is likely related to the defendant Davis and which also implies that this is a criminal case as opposed to a civil case.

Library Table of Contents

You are still trying to get a general feel for what the case is about, and you need to quickly determine the type of law you will be working with. You want to make a note of what and how many statutes and/or cases are included. You also want to note the jurisdiction/court of each case; this will help you begin to form a picture of the task and will help you determine whether the cases are binding or merely persuasive authority.

Davis Library

Only one case is available to work with here. It is from the U.S. Court of Appeals in the 15th Circuit and dates from 2014 (three years prior to the time given in the task: 2017). It is not yet clear if the 15th Circuit is the federal circuit court that oversees the State of Columbia. Similar to our case, this case has the United States as the first party and "Clark," which appears to be an individual, also similar to our case, as the defendant.

UNITED STATES v. BLAKE C. DAVIS

INSTRUCTIONS

1. This performance test is designed to evaluate your ability to handle a select number of legal authorities in the context of a factual problem involving a client.

2. The problem is set in the <u>fictional State of Columbia, one of the United States.</u>

3. You will have two sets of materials with which to work: <u>a File and a Library</u>.

4. The File contains factual materials about your case. The first document is a memorandum containing the instructions for the tasks you are to complete.

5. The Library contains the legal authorities needed to complete the tasks. The case reports may be real, modified, or written solely for the purpose of this performance test. If the cases appear familiar to you, do not assume that they are precisely the same as you have read before. Read each thoroughly, as if it were new to you. You should assume that cases were decided in the jurisdictions and on the dates shown. In citing cases from the Library, you may use abbreviations and omit page citations.

6. You should concentrate on the materials provided, but you should also bring to bear on the problem your general knowledge of the law. What you have learned in law school and elsewhere provides the general background for analyzing the problem; the File and Library provide the specific materials with which you must work.

7. This performance test is designed to be completed in 90 minutes. Although there are no parameters on how to apportion that 90 minutes, you should allow yourself sufficient time to thoroughly review the materials and organize your planned response. Since the time allotted for this

session of the examination includes two (2) essay questions in addition to this performance test, time management is essential.

8.   Your response will be graded on its compliance with instructions and on its content, thoroughness, and organization.

Not clear if civil or criminal case.

UNITED STATES v. BLAKE C. DAVIS

Instructions ....

FILE

This is the task memo from our boss.

Memorandum to Applicant from Timothy Alfaro ....

Likely a transcript with our client.

Interview Transcript...

Department of Homeland Security Incident -- Arrest Report ....

Likely an incident involving our client, which may indicate it is a criminal case.

UNITED STATES v. BLAKE C. DAVIS

<u>LIBRARY</u>

United States v. Clark
U.S. Court of Appeals, 15th Circuit (2014)...

We only have one case, and it is not clear whether the 15th Circuit is the Circuit in the Columbia jurisdiction.

Step 2. Read the task memo (and format memo, if provided, and identify the macrostructure for your answer) (7–10 minutes)

Task Memo

This is the most important document in the packet, so slow down and read it very carefully. Follow all directions exactly. Your goal is to identify three key pieces of information:

1. Information about your client: Who is your client? What is your client's legal issue? What is your client's goal?
2. Specific information about the task: What is the task? Who is the audience? Has more than one task been assigned? Do the directions specify things to include and exclude?
3. The macrostructure of your answer: Can you start your roadmap?

Davis Task Memo

- **Client info:** As we suspected, Davis is a criminal defendant. We represent Mr. Davis, who is accused of resisting agents from the U.S. Customs and Border Patrol (misdemeanor) and possessing cocaine (felony). The incident giving rise to these accusations took place aboard a cruise ship docked at Port Columbia. Mr. Davis wants to try to get a plea agreement but does not want a felony conviction on his record.

- **Task info:** We are asked to draft a letter to Ms. Castile, the Asst. U.S. Attorney reviewing the case, who is inclined to seek an indictment against Mr. Davis. Our letter will try to convince Ms. Castile to accept a guilty plea to the misdemeanor resisting charge. The letter will be persuasive, as it should also convince Ms. Castile that the search giving rise to the felony cocaine charge was unreasonable and in violation of Mr. Davis's Fourth Amendment rights, because the drugs were illegally seized. The letter will not require a statement of facts.

- **Task structure:** Our letter will focus on the Fourth Amendment and why the search and seizure against Mr. Davis were unreasonable and should be suppressed. As with most performance tests in which the task focuses on a particular law or area of law, the structure for the Fourth Amendment discussion in the letter will likely be found in the case provided. Since there is no format memo, common sense dictates that our letter structure should organize the Fourth Amendment discussion in a way similar to the way it is organized in the case. Using this as a guideline, we can start our roadmap. We will also likely need to include some discussion (even if brief) about the defendant's ability to accept a plea and Ms. Castile's ability to offer him a plea.

Alfaro, Blevin & Cohn, LLP

MEMORANDUM

TO: Applicant

FROM: Timothy Alfaro

DATE: July 25, 2017

RE: United States v. Blake C. Davis

We represent Blake Davis who may be charged with: (1) the misdemeanor of resisting agents from the U.S. Customs and Border Protection Service ("CBP"), and (2) the felony of possession of cocaine. Mr. Davis views the incident, which took place aboard a cruise ship after it docked at Port Columbia, as an unfortunate incident prompted by a significant investigative error made by the Customs officers who made the arrest.

Maria Castile, the Assistant U.S. Attorney who is reviewing the case, seems inclined to seek an indictment against Mr. Davis. Ms. Castile, however, is willing to consider a plea bargain. Following a lengthy counseling session yesterday, Mr. Davis wants to try to get a plea agreement but does not want a felony conviction on his record.

What I want to do is convince Ms. Castile to accept a guilty plea to misdemeanor resisting.

To support this offer, please draft a letter to Ms. Castile that argues that: the search of Mr. Davis' cabin aboard the cruise ship was unreasonable under the Fourth Amendment to the United States Constitution and hence a possession charge should not be brought because the drugs were illegally seized and will be suppressed. Do not prepare a statement of facts, but use the facts in making your legal arguments.

Step 3. Start roadmap (time included in steps 2–7)

Roadmap

Having a well-planned roadmap is the key to writing a passing performance test. We can start our roadmap using the macrostructure from the task memo and add to it as we gather more information. We recommend that you make a note at the top of the roadmap listing all essential information, including the client and opposing party, the client's goal, task specifics concerning included or excluded parts, the tone and vocabulary, any task weighting, and a time goal for when you want to start writing your answer. Your time goal will vary depending on which approach your employ to organize your answer. If your written answer is already done because you input the headings and complete rules, etc., directly into your computer as you organized, you will need less time. If you need to write your answer in its entirety because you organized by creating a full shorthand roadmap on paper, you will need more time. Since we have two sections, it is recommended that you roadmap each on a separate piece of paper.

> *Important note:* When roadmapping for your own use on paper, the result is unlikely to be as thorough or neat as this example. Liberally use abbreviations and symbols to remind yourself where in the file you can find the information you need to use in each section. When roadmapping on the computer, type the rules you know you will use directly into the appropriate section after briefing, but still create a skeleton roadmap on paper setting out the macrostructure. Only write as much as you need to guide you in properly drafting your answer. **This performance test demonstration will show you how each part would look if you were typing it on the computer as you organize.**

Davis Roadmap

From the task memo, we know we will be writing an analysis in letter format of why Mr. Davis's Fourth Amendment rights prohibit Ms. Castile from using the seizure of the cocaine against Mr. Davis, thus convincing her to allow Mr. Davis to plea to a misdemeanor of resisting agents. The structure for the Fourth Amendment discussion will likely come from the case in the library. For now, we can set up a letter format addressing Ms. Castile, creating an introduction (or part of it for now) and filling in more detail after we read the case.

Mr. Alfaro,

Pursuant to your request, below is the letter we can send to Ms. Castile requesting that she accept a plea from Mr. Davis to the misdemeanor of resisting agents. The letter should convince her not to pursue the felony possession charge since the cocaine was obtained through an illegal search. Please let me know if you need any additional help with Mr. Davis's case.

Applicant

Alfaro, Blevin, & Cohn, LLP

July 25, 2017

U.S. Asst. Attorney's Office
Attention: Maria Castile

Re: U.S. v. Blake C. Davis

Dear Ms. Castile,

We represent Blake C. Davis and are writing this letter to encourage you to forgo seeking an indictment against Mr. Davis. Below we will discuss Mr. Davis's desire to seek a plea agreement for misdemeanor resisting. We will also discuss why the Fourth Amendment protects Mr. Davis from an unreasonable search by the government and how the drugs in this incident were illegally seized, and thus why the possession charge should be suppressed. Please review this letter and respond at your earliest convenience.

Fourth Amendment

(We will add in headings and more format/rules for our letter once we have gone through the entire case.)

Based on the above, we request that you allow Mr. Davis to accept a plea for misdemeanor resisting and that you do not seek any felony charges against Mr. Davis for possession.

If you have any questions or concerns, please do not hesitate to contact me.

Respectfully yours,

Applicant

Step 4. **Skim the client file/facts (2 minutes)**

Skim the Client File/Facts

We know that the Fourth Amendment is involved. While we don't yet have the exact structure the case will set out for the Fourth Amendment, our "general knowledge of the law," which we were instructed to use in the instructions, should give us an idea of what facts we might be looking for when we skim the file/facts. For example, we know that government action and some reasonable expectation of privacy are likely involved. We also know that the question of whether a search warrant was issued will likely matter; if one was not, we will need to consider any facts suggesting a warrantless search exception. Skimming the facts gives us enough of the big picture to satisfy our curiosity, and it provides clues for what materials we have to work with once we do identify the specific structure the library provides for the Fourth Amendment.

Davis File Skim

Below is my quick takeaway from the skim of the facts:

- **Interview transcript:** Davis and his wife Ann were taking a cruise for their 40th wedding anniversary. Incident occurred when they were about to disembark at port. They claim it was a mistake—something about <u>Daviss</u> with an extra <u>s</u> was the guy they were looking for. Agents searched their cabin but later apologized. Davis didn't want them to search his work briefcase—confidential info there.

- **Arrest report:** Location was Port Columbia. Agents were looking for a 21-year-old who was 260 lbs., white, 6'4", Blaine Daviss (two s's at end of name), and instead arrested Blake (not Blaine) Davis with one <u>s</u> at the end of his name, 61 years old, 140 lbs., and 5'7"—also mentions cabin numbers (will look at details of those later). Info about a sniffing dog too.

- **Assessment from the skim of the facts:** Most of the details are in the interview, but the arrest report seems like those facts about the mistaken arrest and search will be what we need to prove the search was unreasonable since it appears that the agents searched someone who didn't at all resemble the description of the suspect they were looking for. (Also note the arrest report details we focused on while skimming it—the last name with double -<u>s</u> at the end mentioned in the interview was made very noticeable because it was in all capitals. We paid special attention to that in the arrest report, and since the other details about the suspect were right next to the name it was easy to identify and include the information here now.) We need to see how this mistaken identity can help us convince Ms. Castile to drop her pursuit of the indictment for the felony possession charge.

INTERVIEW TRANSCRIPT

July 18, 2017

> Since we are just skimming the facts, the facts that are noteworthy from this first skim are underlined.

Blake Davis (BLAKE): Thanks for seeing us.

> Note the people involved in the interview and who they are.

Tim Alfaro (TIM): I'm glad both of you could come in. It should simplify getting all the information we'll need.

Ann Davis (ANN): We are so upset about this situation. We really appreciate your help.

TIM: We'll do our best. Now, I know that you were arrested, Blake, for assaulting a U.S. Customs agent and for possession of cocaine as you were about to get off of a cruise ship.

BLAKE: That's right, but it was a huge mistake. We had no idea there were drugs hidden in the wall. The Customs folks got the wrong cabin, they busted in with a drug dog and tossed all of our belongings, and then tried to grab my briefcase from me.

TIM: Why don't you start at the beginning and tell me what happened?

BLAKE: Alright. Well, we had booked this cruise on the *Esprit* months ago to celebrate our 40th wedding anniversary. I didn't realize at the time that I would be buried in work that would force me to bring along stuff that had to get done by the time we returned to Columbia City. It only was because of the need to protect the work product that I got in any trouble.

TIM: Where do you work and what type of work product are you talking about?

BLAKE: I'm an engineer with Allied Industries and I've been working with corporate counsel and others to put together a patent application for breakthrough technology that will revolutionize our business. I had to submit the

final paper work right after we got off the ship. I was told by the lawyers, the chief engineer, and the CEO to make sure no one got a look at any of the papers.

TIM: How does this tie in with your encounter with the Customs agents?

ANN: It all happened the morning we were to disembark. We got up early to finish packing; we planned to wheel our luggage off the ship. I got room service, just a light continental breakfast. Blake went up to the buffet area because he wanted a full breakfast.

BLAKE: I took my briefcase with me because I wanted to recheck some final details.

ANN: Right. Well, I was on the balcony sipping coffee when I heard a knock on the door. I thought it was our cabin steward checking to see if we needed anything before disembarking. So I opened the door and there were a man and a woman. She had a dog on a leash – a black Labrador, I think.

TIM: Did they ask you your name?

ANN: Yes, the gentleman said, "Who are you?" and I said, "Ann Davis. What's all this about?" He told me he was from U.S. Customs and they were there to search our cabin for contraband.

TIM: Were they in uniform and did they state their names?

ANN: Sure. I told them we didn't know anything about contraband but he – Oliphant, now I remember – told me to step into the corridor and remain there while they conducted the search. I told him it was some kind of mistake but I did what he asked.

BLAKE: That's when I showed up. I told them who I was and asked them what they were doing. They asked me to step aside and I did. Then they went in.

TIM: From your position could you see what the two agents were doing?

ANN: They propped the door open so I was able to see most of the cabin, except the corner where it was blocked by the bathroom.

TIM: What did you see?

ANN: First, they poked into everything, looking under the bed, opening drawers. I couldn't figure out what they were after. Then they put our three pieces of luggage on the bed and pressed down on them; our bags are soft-sided. Then the dog was brought over to the luggage. It sniffed at each one and then the dog went over to the balcony door and just sat down. After that, the two agents opened each bag and dumped everything on the bed; after we had spent all that time packing them neatly! Then they pawed through every darn thing we owned, every piece of clothing, our toiletries, rifling through the pages of our books, probing into each suitcase – everything. They didn't find anything they were interested in, just like I had told them. When they finished with the luggage, leaving all of our stuff strewn across the bed in piles and some on the floor, they turned their attention to where the dog was sitting. I saw them squat down and poke around with something, maybe a pencil. The guy pulled a panel off the wall and took out a small plastic bag. I had no idea what they found.

TIM: Okay, what did the Customs agents say or do?

BLAKE: At some point, the lead guy, Oliphant, said that they had "reliable information" that we had illegal drugs. I told him that was nonsense, we knew nothing about drugs, and I was outraged they had ransacked our private stateroom. That's when he demanded that I turn over my briefcase.

TIM: What happened then?

BLAKE: I told him "no way," that the briefcase contained confidential business materials and no one could look through it. Period. He told me I was required to give it to him, that they already found narcotics, and he suspected there was more in my briefcase. I told him he was nuts and to go away. That's when he

tried to grab the case from me. I wouldn't let go. He and the woman officer threw me to the floor and put the cuffs on me. Then Oliphant took the key to the briefcase from my pocket and tossed everything in it on the bed with our other stuff. That's when he found my passport and, gosh, was he surprised! He and the woman agent conferred and then he asked me if I was Blake C. Davis. I said, "Of course; that's what I told you!" He said there had been a mistake. They were looking for *Blaine C. Daviss* with an extra "s" -- spelled D-A-V-I-S-S; some other guy. They had been informed that this other Daviss had a cabin on the same deck, but on the other side of the ship. They took the cuffs off of me and apologized, but said that I would have to accompany them and that I'd be charged with resisting a legal search and possession of cocaine.

TIM: Okay. Thanks so much. Let me get in touch with the U.S. Attorney's Office and see where this situation stands and what we have to do to try to quash it. That seems like the first thing we have to address.

ANN and BLAKE: Okay. Thanks.

While you are skimming facts, certain facts such as the use of all caps in the names stand out, so be sure to read those sentences; same with dates and other stand-out facts in various case files.

DEPARTMENT OF HOMELAND SECURITY

U.S. CUSTOMS AND BORDER PROTECTION

INCIDENT – ARREST REPORT

1.   PORT WHERE INCIDENT-ARREST OCCURRED: Port Columbia

2.   CBP OFFICER IN CHARGE: Ralph Oliphant #06254

3.   NAME OF VESSEL: Sun Cruise Line - *Esprit*

4.   DATE: July 16, 2017

5.   SUBJECT: Davis, Blake C.

6.   SEX: Male

7.   HEIGHT: 5' 7"

8.   WEIGHT: 140 lbs.

9.   AGE: 61

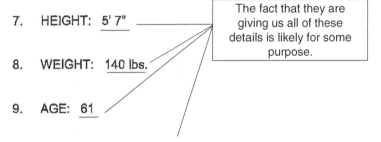

The fact that they are giving us all of these details is likely for some purpose.

10.   RACE/ETHNICITY: White

The undersigned CBP Officer, assisted by Canine Enforcement Officer Veronica Brown, conducted a scheduled vessel search of Sun Cruise Line's *Esprit* when it docked in Port Columbia, in Columbia, following a seven-day cruise that included day-long visits to Acapulco, Mexico and three other foreign ports. As standard

procedure before boarding the ship to conduct routine enforcement actions, I accessed the Treasury Enforcement Communications System's ("TECS") computerized database to determine if it contained any enforcement information about passengers or crew members traveling on the *Esprit*.

Included in the TECS report on the *Esprit* was a "lookout" for a white male, Blaine C. Daviss, 6' 4", 260 lbs., 21 years old. The information was filed by an undercover CBP officer stationed in Acapulco who had observed Daviss during the period when the ship was docked at that port. The TECS report revealed that Daviss had traveled to other drug source countries in the Caribbean and South America on other occasions, had a criminal record (two arrests, one conviction for heroin possession and sale), had purchased his ticket at the last minute and in cash, and was traveling alone. The TECS report also indicated Daviss was observed in Acapulco in the company of three suspected drug dealers for a period of about 30 minutes.

> Already we can see a discrepancy with whom they were looking for and whom they arrested.

Based on all of the data available in the TECS system for the *Esprit*, I identified Daviss to investigate when our CBP team boarded the ship. I accessed the passenger/crew manifest from the TECS database, but in doing so I erroneously listed Daviss' stateroom as 8132 instead of 8086. Cabin 8132 was assigned to *Blake C. Davis*, the subject of this report, who was listed on the manifest on the line immediately above Daviss. Both had staterooms on Deck 8 but on opposite sides of the ship, Daviss on the port side and Davis on the starboard side.

After boarding the ship, Canine Enforcement Officer Brown, her drug-sniffing dog, and I approached cabin 8132, at which point the dog "alerted" in the hallway. The "alert" indicated that cocaine had been deposited at the site within a year. I knocked on the door of the cabin and it was opened by a middle-aged

white female. I identified myself as a CBP Officer and introduced Officer Brown. Upon my request, the woman told us she was Ann Davis(s). I instructed Ms. Davis(s) to step into the hallway while we conducted a search for narcotics. She complied. At that point, the subject arrived and identified himself. I instructed him to comply. He complied. When the dog entered the stateroom, he moved to the corner of the cabin by the glass door that opened onto the balcony and alerted by sitting down. I opened each piece of luggage, removed the contents and conducted a thorough search of the items and the bags. I found nothing suspicious. I then moved to the area where the dog alerted and, with the assistance of Officer Brown and the dog, pulled a panel off the wall and found a white substance in a large plastic bag that later tested positive for cocaine.

While I was conducting a search of the rest of the cabin, the subject started protesting loudly. I explained we had evidence he was in possession of drugs, that a suspicious substance had been found, and asked him to turn over his briefcase. He refused to do so, claiming it contained confidential business documents. Officer Brown and I wrestled Davis(s) to the floor and forcibly took possession of the briefcase and handcuffed him. A search of the briefcase revealed no contraband. However, when I examined the passport in the case, I learned that the subject's name was *Blake C. Davis*. It was only then I realized we had made an error. We took Davis into custody. Subsequently, we searched stateroom 8086, found a large quantity of cocaine, and arrested *Blaine C. Daviss* for felony possession of cocaine with intent to distribute.

SIGNATURE:

_____*Ralph Oliphant*_____

RALPH OLIPHANT #06254

This is how your answer should look at this point if you are adding details as you organize your answer:

Mr. Alfaro,

Pursuant to your request, below is the letter we can send to Ms. Castile requesting that she accept a plea from Mr. Davis to the misdemeanor of resisting agents. The letter should convince her not to pursue the felony possession charge since the cocaine was obtained through an illegal search. Please let me know if you need any additional help with Mr. Davis's case.

Applicant

Alfaro, Blevin, & Cohn, LLP

July 25, 2017

U.S. Asst. Attorney's Office
Attention: Maria Castile

Re: U.S. v. Blake C. Davis

Dear Ms. Castile,

We represent Blake C. Davis and are writing this letter to encourage you to forgo seeking an indictment against Mr. Davis. Below we will discuss Mr. Davis's desire to seek a plea agreement for misdemeanor resisting. We will also discuss why the Fourth Amendment protects Mr. Davis from an unreasonable search by the government and how the drugs in this incident were illegally seized, and thus why the possession charge should be suppressed. Please review this letter and respond at your earliest convenience.

Fourth Amendment

(We will add in headings and more format/rules for our letter once we have gone through the entire case.)

When reading case — look at mistaken identity facts (if any).

At the time of the incident, U.S. Customs agents were looking for a 21-year-old male who was 260 lbs. and 6'4" with the name Blaine Daviss (with two s's at end of the name). Instead they searched and arrested Blake (not Blaine) Davis, whose name has one -s̲ at the end of his name. Further Mr. Davis was a 61-year-old, 140 lb., 5'7" male, which is drastically different from the description of the person they were looking for.

Based on the above, we request that you allow Mr. Davis to accept a plea for misdemeanor resisting and that you do not seek any felony charges against Mr. Davis for possession.

If you have any questions or concerns, please do not hesitate to contact me.

Respectfully yours,

Applicant

Step 5.	**Actively read the library and synthesize rules (20–30 minutes)**

[Since we are using the computer to input headings, rules, case reasoning, etc., directly into our answer as we go through each step, we need more time here than if our roadmap were being done on scratch paper.]

Read the Library and Deconstruct and Synthesize Rules as Needed

Look for the rules you can use to solve the problem posed and any analysis that can be borrowed from the cases. Depending on the task, we may need to synthesize cases or identify which rule among competing rules should be adopted. To most efficiently assess the library, read the materials in the order presented, since most often the rules are provided in the same order that they will be used to solve the problem, given the task macrostructure. Book brief the cases and add information to the roadmap as you go. Annotate your cases with notes so you don't waste time rewriting sentences into your roadmap. Determine how best to use any statutes. Each case in the library was included because it is likely needed to solve the problem, so it is up to you to determine how each can best be used. We typically note at the top of each case where it will be used in our answer and whether it is favorable or not for our client by writing a plus or minus sign at the top. Continue to look for clues as to how you should structure your answer.

Davis Case

The library contains only one case, but, at six pages long, it is longer than most cases provided in PTs with multiple cases. We know we need to find the structure for our organization for the Fourth Amendment in this case since it is the only case available. Further, this is a persuasive task, so we are looking for reasoning that will bolster our argument to Ms. Castile in favor of Mr. Davis. We also need to be prepared to address any possible counterarguments Ms. Castile might have in regard to our arguments, so we will also look for reasoning we might need to distinguish the cases.

- **U.S. v. Clark:** This case also involves a search aboard a cruise ship, but it involves a search of a ship in port between cruises, prior to departure, and the search is of a crewman's room. We can distinguish our facts, since Mr. Davis wasn't a crewman, and the search did not take place between cruises. The facts in Clark involve cocaine being delivered — we need to read our facts carefully to see if we can distinguish the identity and reasonable suspicion facts better than Clark did. Clark distinguishes between routine and non-routine searches at borders (which includes where a ship docks after arriving from a foreign country). The court distinguished Clark from Braun and found that Clark's search was non-routine, unlike Braun's, in which the dogs sniffed the halls regularly. The court looks at the degree to which the search intrudes on a person's privacy. If the place searched is private living quarters, then the agents need reasonable suspicion of criminal conduct to search. In Clark the court found such reasonable suspicion. To obtain a different result, since the court in Clark held for the government, we need to compare our facts to show how, with Davis, agents did not have such reasonable suspicion. Several rules were mentioned that we now can input into our roadmap/answer. (Here we will input the entire rules into the answer as if you would if you were writing it as you followed each step.)

When you are done reading the case come back and write a plus or negative sign to remind you of whether the case is or isn't favorable for us.

— for us

United States v. Clark

U.S. Court of Appeals, 15th Circuit (2014)

Issue and case history

Daniel Clark was convicted in the U.S. District Court for the Eastern District of Columbia of violating *21 U.S.C. § 846* (possession with intent to distribute a controlled substance) following the denial of a motion to suppress evidence. On appeal, Clark asserts the United States Custom Service failed to procure a warrant to search his cabin aboard the M/V *Enchanted Isle* where he was employed as a seaman. The judgment of the District Court is affirmed.

Since D lost below and that is aff'd, that is not good for us; we will need to distinguish this case.

Cases don't always label the facts section for you like this.

I. Facts

On September 7, 2010, the *Enchanted Isle* returned to her home port, Sealand, at approximately 4:30 a.m. after visiting Cozumel, Mexico, the Grand Cayman Islands and Jamaica. The ship was to depart again at about 4:00 p.m. U.S. Customs agents, with the cooperation of the vessel owner, routinely boarded and searched the ship upon reentry at Sealand.

Key facts underlined here would be highlighted in yellow on my paper. Have a system of highlighting for "book" briefing, such as facts in yellow, rules in blue, and reasoning in pink: this makes it easier to find things later.

Robert Sedge, a Customs Service agent, had received information from a reliable informant that two crew members, Alan Arch and Daniel Clark, would be transporting illegal narcotics. At approximately 2:30 p.m., Alan Arch, was seen by Sedge passing a package to Larry Bates. Although Clark was with Arch, there was no evidence Clark gave anything to Bates. Bates later was arrested by other Customs agents and a package containing shoes with cocaine hydrochloride innersoles was seized from him. This information was relayed to Sedge who, without a warrant, boarded the *Enchanted Isle* with a drug-trained dog.

Sedge went directly to the cabin assigned to Clark and, after knocking and being admitted by Clark's roommate, entered the cabin, whereupon the dog alerted to the presence of drugs. Sedge did not have Clark's permission to enter the room; the roommate admitted Sedge based solely on the latter's claimed authority to do so. Clark's roommate informed Sedge that his was the top bunk and pointed out his belongings, with the inference that the remainder belonged to Clark. Upon searching the cabin and Clark's belongings, Sedge found two pairs of shoes with innersoles made of cocaine hydrochloride, one on the lower bunk and another between the bulkhead and the bed. These were the materials that were the subject of Clark's motion to suppress and are the basis of his appeal.

> Again, not all cases signal when the discussion begins.

II. **Discussion**

> These boxed rules would all be highlighted in blue on my paper book brief.

The *Fourth Amendment* protects "against unreasonable searches and seizures." Whether a search is reasonable will depend upon its nature and all of the circumstances surrounding it but, as a general matter, warrantless searches are unreasonable. Searches conducted at the nation's borders, however, represent a well-established exception to the warrant requirement. The exception applies not only at the physical boundaries of the United States, but also at "the functional equivalent" of a border, including the first port where a ship docks after arriving from a foreign country. The search here, conducted as the *Enchanted Isle* arrived in Sealand, was therefore a border search.

> Facts in this case = border search

> This whole paragraph is rules and would be highlighted blue. But you should still underline key elements or buzz words for the rule.

Provided a border search is routine, it may be conducted, not just without a warrant, but without probable cause, reasonable suspicion, or any suspicion of wrongdoing. The expectation of privacy is less at the border than in the interior and the *Fourth Amendment* balance between the interests of the Government and the privacy right of the individual is much more in favor of the Government. Even at the border, however, an individual is entitled to be free from an unreasonable search and privacy interests must be balanced against the sovereign's interests. Consequently, certain searches, classified as "non-routine," require reasonable suspicion of wrongdoing to pass constitutional muster.

Broader issue

The question here, therefore, is not whether the Customs officers were required to have a warrant or probable cause in order to search Clark's private cabin, but, rather, whether reasonable suspicion was necessary. The parties agree that no suspicion is required in order for a Customs officer to board and search a cruise ship as part of a routine border search. They disagree, however, as to whether any *Fourth Amendment* protection applies to a search of a private sleeping cabin aboard a cruise ship.

This will be an area we need to look at in our facts.

Narrower issue

To answer this question, we must first decide whether the border search at issue was routine or non-routine and, so doing, set forth the correct standard required under the *Fourth Amendment*. We turn to a determination of whether this search was conducted in accordance with it.

We are paying attention to how the court organizes their 4th Am. approach, as this will likely be the frame for our roadmap.

This is another rule that would be highlighted in blue.

To ascertain whether a border search can be classified as routine, we must examine the degree to which it intrudes on a person's privacy. Highly intrusive border searches that implicate the dignity and privacy interests of the person being searched require reasonable suspicion. In the present case, Clark argues that the search of a cruise ship cabin is not a routine border search because the *Fourth Amendment's* primary purpose is the protection of privacy in one's home and the search of a home, by its nature, is highly intrusive. He makes a compelling argument that an individual's expectation of privacy in a cabin of a ship is no different from any other temporary place of abode. Because the search of his living quarters aboard the cruise ship intruded upon that most private of places -- his home -- he says it should be considered non-routine. In response to Clark's arguments, the Government contends that the search of the cabin was a routine border search and should be analyzed in the same way as that of a vehicle.

Underline how each side argues for future reference, since the court usually agrees with one of them.

It is an open question whether the search of a cabin of a cruise ship sufficiently intrudes upon an individual's privacy to render it non-routine, so that reasonable suspicion of criminal activity is required. Indeed, there is a <u>surprising dearth of</u> <u>authority on the matter.</u>

> This might help us since we will need to distinguish this case.

> Pay attention to cases cited within cases and the jx.

The authority the <u>Government cites</u> for the proposition that a search of a crew member's cabin amounts to a <u>routine border search</u> is readily distinguishable from the present case. In <u>*United States v. Braun (S.D. Fla. 2004)*</u>, the "<u>routine</u>" aspect of the search was the <u>use of trained canines to detect narcotic odor from</u> <u>the hallways of newly-arrived cruise ships</u> in Key West. The <u>search of Braun's</u> <u>cabin occurred only after the drug-sniffing dog had alerted to the presence of</u> <u>drugs in the cabin while still in the hallway.</u> While the court stated the search was a <u>routine border search,</u> clearly it was referring to the use of the dogs to "search" the ship's hallways, not the search of the cabin once there was reasonable suspicion based on the alert and all of the other circumstances. <u>Here, by contrast, the dog did not alert until after the cabin was opened and the</u> <u>animal entered the room.</u> The dog's alerting, therefore, cannot establish reasonable suspicion for the search. The routine search in *Braun*, done without reasonable suspicion, was of the ship's hallways -- public space; the search of Braun's cabin was done only after there was reasonable suspicion (or even probable cause) to search.

> The court distinguishes the case the gov. cites.

> New rule added

> Sounds good for D, but we know that the court ultimately finds against him.

<u>The relatively few decisions in this area counsel in favor of the approach urged</u> <u>by Clark.</u> Other courts correctly recognize that <u>the search of private living</u> <u>quarters aboard a ship at the functional equivalent of a border is a non-routine</u> <u>search and must be supported by reasonable suspicion of criminal conduct.</u> The cruise ship cabin is both living quarters and located at the national border. As a result, one principle underlying the case law on border searches – namely, that a port of entry is not a traveler's home – runs headlong into the overriding respect for the sanctity of the home embedded in our traditions since the origins of the Republic, foremost in our nation's *Fourth Amendment* jurisprudence. <u>We find</u> <u>that requiring reasonable suspicion strikes the proper balance between the</u>

> Another rule to note

> Court's reasoning

interests of the government and the privacy rights of the individual. It also best comports with the case law, which treats border searches permissively but gives special protection to an individual's dwelling place, however temporary. We, therefore, join those courts that require reasonable suspicion to search a cabin of a passenger or crew member aboard a ship.

> Holding, but also shows a split in authority.

Here, the search was highly intrusive on Clark's privacy. Uninvited and in Clark's absence, the officers entered his *de facto* home, searched through his belongings, and subjected his private space to inspection by a drug-sniffing dog. Because of the high expectation of privacy and level of intrusiveness, the search cannot be considered "routine" and must therefore be supported by reasonable suspicion of illegal activity.

> This is the next step the court (and our approach) will need to go through.

> This rule (in blue on our paper) goes to the reas. suspicion std. after analyzing the type of search.

Under the reasonable suspicion standard, law enforcement officers, including Customs officers, must have reasonable suspicion, based on specific and articulable facts, that the suspect committed, is committing, or is about to commit, a crime in order to conduct a search. In our view, the information known to the agent, including the informant's tip, his own observations, and the arrest and seizure of cocaine from Bates justified reasonable suspicion that Clark (and Arch) had contraband aboard the *Enchanted Isle*.

> Court's reasoning against D

Clark argues that any suspicion the agent might have had *about him* was unreasonable because it supposedly arose from various mistakes the agent had made about his relationship with Arch. To be sure, suspicion is unreasonable if it arises from mistakes that are themselves unreasonable. But quibbles aside, Clark points to no evidence revealing *any* mistake by the agent, lest still any *unreasonable* one.

> More court reasoning against D

III. Disposition

For the foregoing reasons, we AFFIRM the denial of the motion to suppress and uphold Clark's conviction.

> Gov. wins. Try to find distinguishable facts when you read the library.

Now that you have briefed the case, if you are inputting your rules as you go through the steps, you can update your letter by adding in headings showing how you are organizing the issues and by adding in all rules and policies. Essentially, using this approach, you will be writing your performance test response as you go through each step.

Mr. Alfaro,

Pursuant to your request, below is the letter we can send to Ms. Castile requesting that she accept a plea from Mr. Davis to the misdemeanor of resisting agents. The letter should convince her not to pursue the felony possession charge since the cocaine was obtained through an illegal search. Please let me know if you need any additional help with Mr. Davis's case.

Applicant

Alfaro, Blevin, & Cohn, LLP

July 25, 2017

U.S. Asst. Attorney's Office
Attention: Maria Castile

Re: U.S. v. Blake C. Davis

Dear Ms. Castile,

We represent Blake C. Davis and are writing this letter to encourage you to forgo seeking an indictment against Mr. Davis. Below we will discuss Mr. Davis's desire to seek a plea agreement for misdemeanor resisting. We will also discuss why the Fourth Amendment protects Mr. Davis from an unreasonable search by the government and how the drugs in this incident were illegally seized, and thus why the possession charge should be suppressed. Please review this letter and respond at your earliest convenience.

Fourth Amendment Protections

As you already know, Ms. Castile, the Fourth Amendment protects against unreasonable searches and seizures. As the court in Clark observed, whether a search is reasonable will depend upon its nature and all of the circumstances surrounding it. Specific to our case, the courts have further found that searches conducted at the first port where a ship docks after arriving from a foreign country constitute the equivalent to a border search and thus a warrant is not required. Clark.

In Clark, the court was analyzing a situation in which a cruise ship was between cruises; the cruise ship had just returned from various countries and it was set to depart that same day. The defendant Clark was a crewman aboard the ship. Clark.

Routine v. Non-routine Border Searches

The Clark court noted that border searches that are routine may be conducted without a warrant and without probable cause, reasonable suspicion, or any suspicion of wrongdoing. However, an individual's privacy interests must be balanced against the sovereign's interests, and as a result, non-routine searches do require reasonable suspicion of wrongdoing to pass constitutional muster. Clark.

While the search in Braun (cited by Clark) was a routine search that the agents often did after returning from foreign countries, by having dogs sniff the hallways and alert them to any drugs, here, as in Clark . . . (Need to look at facts in detail to add more here but the court in Clark found that Clark's was a non-routine search as the dogs didn't alert the agents to search his room but rather they sought him out.)

Reasonable Suspicion Standard

Under the reasonable suspicion standard, in order to conduct a search law enforcement officers, including Customs officers, must have reasonable suspicion, based on specific and articulable facts, that the suspect committed, is committing, or is about to commit a crime. The suspicion is unreasonable if it arises from mistakes that themselves are unreasonable. Clark.

In Clark, the court found that even though Clark did have a right to privacy in his room, the agents had reasonable suspicion to enter his room because a reliable informant told agents that Clark and another were transporting illegal narcotics. This information was then substantiated when one of the crewmen was seen passing a package that was seized and found to contain cocaine. Clark.

Mr. Davis's incident is substantially distinguishable from Clark. At the time of Mr. Davis's incident, U.S. Customs agents were looking for a 21-year-old male who was 260 lbs. and 6'4" with the name Blaine Daviss (with two s's at end of the name). Instead they searched and arrested Blake (not Blaine) Davis, who has one -s at the end of his name. Further Mr. Davis was 61 years old, 140 lbs., and 5'7", a description drastically different from the description of the person they were looking for.

Based on the above, we request that you allow Mr. Davis to accept a plea for misdemeanor resisting and that you do not seek any felony charges against Mr. Davis for possession.

If you have any questions or concerns, please do not hesitate to contact me.

Respectfully yours,

Applicant

Step 6.	**Actively read the client file/facts (15–20 minutes)**

[Since we are inputting facts and analysis directly into our answer as we go through each step, we need more time here than we would if our roadmap were being written on scratch paper.]

Client File/Case Facts

Now that we know from the library the rules governing this situation, we must look for legally significant facts to apply to the rules to solve the problem. We want to look for helpful facts, harmful facts, and any missing facts, if pertinent to the task assigned. Add the legally significant facts into your roadmap as you go or input them into your answer in complete sentences if you are organizing your performance test in that manner.

Davis Facts Interview

From the interview we see that both Davis and his wife are witnesses (unlike Clark, who was alone).

- Cruise for 40th wedding anniversary; last morning before disembarking was when the incident occurred.
- Mr. Davis was buried in work so he had to bring work stuff with him, including confidential information about a patent application he was working on with legal counsel; he is an engineer.
- Mr. Davis was advised by legal counsel, the chief engineer, and the CEO that nobody could see any of the papers. He took his briefcase with him to breakfast to recheck the final papers, as he had to file the paperwork right after disembarking.
- Mrs. Davis had custom agents with a dog knock on their door and ask her to step into the corridor and remain there while they searched the cabin. Mr. Davis was still at breakfast. She told them it was a mistake.
- Agents searched all of their luggage and found nothing; dog was sitting by the balcony door; finally after taking out all of their belongings they went to where the dog was and poked around and found a small plastic bag.
- When Mr. Davis returned, agents demanded to see his briefcase because they thought more narcotics would be there; he refused, so they threw him on the floor and handcuffed him.
- While going through the briefcase, they found his passport and discovered it did not have the name of the man they were looking for. They said they had made a mistake, but that Mr. Davis would be charged with resisting a legal search and possession of cocaine.

Davis Facts Arrest Report

Include under the arrest report details about the suspect and Mr. Davis noted in roadmap earlier:

- The suspect was traveling alone and had purchased his ticket at the last minute.
- Officer erroneously listed Daviss's (suspect) stateroom as 8132 instead of 8086. Mr. and Mrs. Davis were in 8132. Both were on Deck 8 but on opposite sides of the ship.
- Dog alerted them in the hallway of 8132.
- Officers subsequently searched 8086 and found large amounts of cocaine.

Our Assessment of the Detailed Facts

Now that you have the rules and organization input into your answer, you can line up facts with each part of the argument/rule in the letter. You should annotate and highlight the pertinent facts listed above as you read them. Pay attention to the facts that are similar in both cases, which you will need to rebut, as well as to facts that distinguish the Davis incident from Clark. Once you input these facts into your answer your answer should be nearly complete, since you have been writing it as you go through each step.

INTERVIEW TRANSCRIPT

July 18, 2017

Since we already skimmed the facts, now we are simply adding to them and marking them up more, looking for key distinguishing facts from the <u>Clark</u> case.

Note the people involved in the interview and who they are.

Blake Davis (BLAKE): Thanks for seeing us.

Tim Alfaro (TIM): I'm glad both of you could come in. It should simplify getting all the information we'll need.

Ann Davis (ANN): We are so upset about this situation. We really appreciate your help.

TIM: We'll do our best. Now, I know that you were arrested, Blake, for assaulting a U.S. Customs agent and for possession of cocaine as you were about to get off of a cruise ship.

BLAKE: That's right, but it was a huge mistake. We had no idea there were drugs hidden in the wall. The Customs folks got the wrong cabin, they busted in with a drug dog and tossed all of our belongings, and then tried to grab my briefcase from me.

Sounds different from Clark case.

TIM: Why don't you start at the beginning and tell me what happened?

BLAKE: Alright. Well, we had booked this cruise on the *Esprit* months ago to celebrate our 40th wedding anniversary. I didn't realize at the time that I would be buried in work that would force me to bring along stuff that had to get done by the time we returned to Columbia City. It only was because of the need to protect the work product that I got in any trouble.

TIM: Where do you work and what type of work product are you talking about?

BLAKE: I'm an engineer with Allied Industries and I've been working with corporate counsel and others to put together a patent application for breakthrough technology that will revolutionize our business. I had to submit the

final paper work right after we got off the ship. I was told by the lawyers, the chief engineer, and the CEO to make sure no one got a look at any of the papers.

TIM: How does this tie in with your encounter with the Customs agents?

ANN: It all happened the morning we were to disembark. We got up early to finish packing; we planned to wheel our luggage off the ship. I got room service, just a light continental breakfast. Blake went up to the buffet area because he wanted a full breakfast.

BLAKE: I took my briefcase with me because I wanted to recheck some final details.

ANN: Right. Well, I was on the balcony sipping coffee when I heard a knock on the door. I thought it was our cabin steward checking to see if we needed anything before disembarking. So I opened the door and there were a man and a woman. She had a dog on a leash – a black Labrador, I think.

TIM: Did they ask you your name?

ANN: Yes, the gentleman said, "Who are you?" and I said, "Ann Davis. What's all this about?" He told me he was from U.S. Customs and they were there to search our cabin for contraband.

TIM: Were they in uniform and did they state their names?

ANN: Sure. I told them we didn't know anything about contraband but he – Oliphant, now I remember – told me to step into the corridor and remain there while they conducted the search. I told him it was some kind of mistake but I did what he asked.

> No permission to enter?

BLAKE: That's when I showed up. I told them who I was and asked them what they were doing. They asked me to step aside and I did. Then they went in.

TIM: From your position could you see what the two agents were doing?

ANN: They propped the door open so I was able to see most of the cabin, except the corner where it was blocked by the bathroom.

TIM: What did you see?

ANN: First, they poked into everything, looking under the bed, opening drawers. I couldn't figure out what they were after. Then they put our three pieces of luggage on the bed and pressed down on them; our bags are soft-sided. Then the dog was brought over to the luggage. It sniffed at each one and then the dog went over to the balcony door and just sat down. After that, the two agents opened each bag and dumped everything on the bed; after we had spent all that time packing them neatly! Then they pawed through every darn thing we owned, every piece of clothing, our toiletries, rifling through the pages of our books, probing into each suitcase – everything. They didn't find anything they were interested in, just like I had told them. When they finished with the luggage, leaving all of our stuff strewn across the bed in piles and some on the floor, they turned their attention to where the dog was sitting. I saw them squat down and poke around with something, maybe a pencil. The guy pulled a panel off the wall and took out a small plastic bag. I had no idea what they found.

> Different from case where dog alerted from hallway.

> W/o dog alerting them?

TIM: Okay, what did the Customs agents say or do?

BLAKE: At some point, the lead guy, Oliphant, said that they had "reliable information" that we had illegal drugs. I told him that was nonsense, we knew nothing about drugs, and I was outraged they had ransacked our private stateroom. That's when he demanded that I turn over my briefcase.

TIM: What happened then?

BLAKE: I told him "no way," that the briefcase contained confidential business materials and no one could look through it. Period. He told me I was required to give it to him, that they already found narcotics, and he suspected there was more in my briefcase. I told him he was nuts and to go away. That's when he

> Resisting facts

tried to grab the case from me. I wouldn't let go. He and the woman officer threw me to the floor and put the cuffs on me. Then Oliphant took the key to the briefcase from my pocket and tossed everything in it on the bed with our other stuff. That's when he found my passport and, gosh, was he surprised! He and the woman agent conferred and then he asked me if I was Blake C. Davis. I said, "Of course; that's what I told you!" He said there had been a mistake. They were looking for *Blaine C. Daviss* with an extra "s" -- spelled D-A-V-I-S-S; some other guy. They had been informed that this other Daviss had a cabin on the same deck, but on the other side of the ship. They took the cuffs off of me and apologized, but said that I would have to accompany them and that I'd be charged with resisting a legal search and possession of cocaine.

TIM: Okay. Thanks so much. Let me get in touch with the U.S. Attorney's Office and see where this situation stands and what we have to do to try to quash it. That seems like the first thing we have to address.

ANN and BLAKE: Okay. Thanks.

While you are skimming facts, certain facts such as the use of all caps in the names stand out, so be sure to read those sentences; same with dates and other stand-out facts in various case files.

DEPARTMENT OF HOMELAND SECURITY

U.S. CUSTOMS AND BORDER PROTECTION

INCIDENT – ARREST REPORT

1.   PORT WHERE INCIDENT-ARREST OCCURRED: Port Columbia

2.   CBP OFFICER IN CHARGE: Ralph Oliphant #06254

3.   NAME OF VESSEL: Sun Cruise Line - *Esprit*

4.   DATE: July 16, 2017

5.   SUBJECT: Davis, Blake C.

6.   SEX: Male

7.   HEIGHT: 5' 7"

> The fact that they are giving us all of these details is likely for some purpose.

8.   WEIGHT: 140 lbs.

9.   AGE: 61

10.   RACE/ETHNICITY: White

> Facts go to routine or non-routine border search rules.

The undersigned CBP Officer, assisted by Canine Enforcement Officer Veronica Brown, conducted a scheduled vessel search of Sun Cruise Line's *Esprit* when it docked in Port Columbia, in Columbia, following a seven-day cruise that included day-long visits to Acapulco, Mexico and three other foreign ports. As standard

procedure before boarding the ship to conduct routine enforcement actions, I accessed the Treasury Enforcement Communications System's ("TECS") computerized database to determine if it contained any enforcement information about passengers or crew members traveling on the *Esprit*.

As to discrepancy with whom they were looking for and whom they arrested, this can help us distinguish Clark; here arguably info not reliable to warrant reas. suspicion like in Clark.

Included in the TECS report on the *Esprit* was a "lookout" for a white male, Blaine C. Daviss, 6' 4", 260 lbs., 21 years old. The information was filed by an undercover CBP officer stationed in Acapulco who had observed Daviss during the period when the ship was docked at that port. The TECS report revealed that Daviss had traveled to other drug source countries in the Caribbean and South America on other occasions, had a criminal record (two arrests, one conviction for heroin possession and sale), had purchased his ticket at the last minute and in cash, and was traveling alone. The TECS report also indicated Daviss was observed in Acapulco in the company of three suspected drug dealers for a period of about 30 minutes.

Lots of mistakes with Davis—ticket purchased early for anniversary and not alone—and officers knew that when they knocked and wife answered door.

Based on all of the data available in the TECS system for the *Esprit*, I identified Daviss to investigate when our CBP team boarded the ship. I accessed the passenger/crew manifest from the TECS database, but in doing so I erroneously listed Daviss' stateroom as 8132 instead of 8086. Cabin 8132 was assigned to *Blake C. Davis*, the subject of this report, who was listed on the manifest on the line immediately above Daviss. Both had staterooms on Deck 8 but on opposite sides of the ship, Daviss on the port side and Davis on the starboard side.

More mistakes

After boarding the ship, Canine Enforcement Officer Brown, her drug-sniffing dog, and I approached cabin 8132, at which point the dog "alerted" in the hallway. The "alert" indicated that cocaine had been deposited at the site within a year. I knocked on the door of the cabin and it was opened by a middle-aged

So could be anyone's in past year?

white female. I identified myself as a CBP Officer and introduced Officer Brown. Upon my request, the woman told us she was Ann Davis(s). I instructed Ms. Davis(s) to step into the hallway while we conducted a search for narcotics. She complied. At that point, the subject arrived and identified himself. I instructed him to comply. He complied. When the dog entered the stateroom, he moved to the corner of the cabin by the glass door that opened onto the balcony and alerted by sitting down. I opened each piece of luggage, removed the contents and conducted a thorough search of the items and the bags. I found nothing suspicious. I then moved to the area where the dog alerted and, with the assistance of Officer Brown and the dog, pulled a panel off the wall and found a white substance in a large plastic bag that later tested positive for cocaine.

> So opened luggage when dog not alerting there?

While I was conducting a search of the rest of the cabin, the subject started protesting loudly. I explained we had evidence he was in possession of drugs, that a suspicious substance had been found, and asked him to turn over his briefcase. He refused to do so, claiming it contained confidential business documents. Officer Brown and I wrestled Davis(s) to the floor and forcibly took possession of the briefcase and handcuffed him. A search of the briefcase revealed no contraband. However, when I examined the passport in the case, I learned that the subject's name was *Blake C. Davis*. It was only then I realized we had made an error. We took Davis into custody. Subsequently, we searched stateroom 8086, found a large quantity of cocaine, and arrested *Blaine C. Daviss* for felony possession of cocaine with intent to distribute.

> Missed all other clues?

SIGNATURE:

_____*Ralph Oliphant*_____

RALPH OLIPHANT #06254

Mr. Alfaro,

Pursuant to your request, below is the letter we can send to Ms. Castile requesting that she accept a plea from Mr. Davis to the misdemeanor of resisting agents. The letter should convince her not to pursue the felony possession charge since the cocaine was obtained through an illegal search. Please let me know if you need any additional help with Mr. Davis's case.

Applicant

Alfaro, Blevin, & Cohn, LLP

July 25, 2017

U.S. Asst. Attorney's Office
Attention: Maria Castile

Re: U.S. v. Blake C. Davis

Dear Ms. Castile,

We represent Blake C. Davis and are writing this letter to encourage you to forgo seeking an indictment against Mr. Davis. Below we will discuss Mr. Davis's desire to seek a plea agreement for misdemeanor resisting. We will also discuss why the Fourth Amendment protects Mr. Davis from an unreasonable search by the government and how the drugs in this incident were illegally seized, and thus why the possession charge should be suppressed. Please review this letter and respond at your earliest convenience.

Fourth Amendment Protections

As you already know, Ms. Castile, the Fourth Amendment protects against unreasonable searches and seizures. As the court in Clark observed, whether a search is reasonable will depend upon its nature and all of the circumstances surrounding it. Specific to our case, the courts have further found that searches conducted at the first port where a ship docks after arriving from a foreign country constitute the equivalent to a border search and thus a warrant is not required. Clark.

In Clark, the court was analyzing a situation in which a cruise ship was between cruises, the cruise ship had just returned from various countries, and it was set to depart that same day. The defendant Clark was a crewman aboard the ship. Clark.

Here, unlike Clark, Mr. Davis, was a passenger simply trying to celebrate his 40th wedding anniversary with his wife. Further, it was the last day of their cruise, when they were getting ready to disembark, so arguably they were not at the "first port where a ship docks after arriving from a foreign country." They were at the port of Columbia, not a foreign country or, arguably, a border. However, it is possible since the cruise visited other foreign countries and ports that their prior port was overseas. Even if the court finds that this port was equivalent to a border search, this was a non-routine search with no reasonable suspicion, which would require the courts to suppress the evidence found as the result of a search in violation of Mr. Davis's Fourth Amendment rights.

Routine v. Non-routine Border Searches

The Clark court noted that border searches that are routine may be conducted without a warrant and without probable cause, reasonable suspicion, or any suspicion of wrongdoing. An individual's privacy interests must be balanced against the sovereign's interests, however, and as a result, non-routine searches do require reasonable suspicion of wrongdoing to pass constitutional muster. Clark.

While the search in Braun (cited by Clark) was a routine search often performed by agents after ships returned from foreign countries by having dogs sniff the hallways and alert them to any drugs, here, as in Clark, Mr. Davis's room was searched alone as an isolated and non-routine search. Thus, the government would need to show reasonable suspicion to search the Davis cabin.

Reasonable Suspicion Standard

Under the reasonable suspicion standard, in order to conduct a search law enforcement officers, including Customs officers, must have reasonable suspicion, based on specific and articulable facts, that the suspect committed, is committing, or is about to commit a crime. The suspicion is unreasonable if it arises from mistakes that themselves are unreasonable. <u>Clark</u>.

In <u>Clark</u>, the court found that even though Clark did have a right to privacy in his room, the agents had reasonable suspicion to enter his room because a reliable informant had told agents that Clark and another were transporting illegal narcotics. This information was then substantiated when one of the crewmen was seen passing a package that was seized and found to contain cocaine. <u>Clark</u>.

Mr. Davis's incident is substantially distinguishable from <u>Clark</u>. At the time of Mr. Davis's incident, U.S. Customs agents were looking for a 21-year-old male who was 260 lbs. and 6'4" with the name Blaine Daviss (with two s's at the end of his name). Instead they searched and arrested Blake (not Blaine) Davis, whose name has one -<u>s</u> at the end. Further, Mr. Davis was a 61-year-old, 140 lb., 5'7" male, which drastically differs from the description of the person agents were seeking. Further, the suspect was traveling alone and had purchased a last-minute ticket, whereas Mr. and Mrs. Davis were traveling together for their anniversary for a long-planned trip. Moreover, here the agents, using a drug-sniffing dog, proceeded to search the Davises' entire room and all of their luggage, dumping everything into piles, when the dog didn't even alert them to the luggage but rather went to the balcony door and sat down there instead.

In addition, after the agents found a small bag in the wall, which could have been placed there by any person, even prior to this cruise, they demanded that Mr. Davis give them his briefcase. Since the dog never alerted the agents to the briefcase, and since all of their bags and luggage were clean, there was no reasonable suspicion to believe that his work briefcase contained any cocaine. In fact, Mr. Davis explained to them that he had protected work product information in the briefcase, which is why he didn't want to show them the contents. And, in fact, when they did open it anyway after throwing him on the ground and cuffing him, they found no cocaine but rather realized they had been searching the wrong person and the wrong room, based on his passport name and the room number. Not only did the agents search a man who did not fit the description of the suspect, but they also searched the wrong room due to their own error, which was not reasonable since the room they were supposed to search was room 8086 and the Davises were in room 8132, which was on the opposite side of the ship. Thus, their mistake was not reasonable as these agents should be able to read and input numbers correctly and know roughly where in the ship the room to be searched is located. Further, there could have been no reasonable mistake as to the description since it was completely different from the suspect's description such that no reasonable person could have mistaken these two men.

Based on the above, we request that you allow Mr. Davis to accept a plea for misdemeanor resisting and that you do not seek any felony charges against Mr. Davis for possession.

If you have any questions or concerns, please do not hesitate to contact me.

Respectfully yours,

Applicant

| Step 7. | **Reread the task memo and refine your roadmap to solve the problem posed (5 minutes)** |

Reread the Task Memo, See the Big Picture, and Solve the Problem

Before you start writing, always take a moment to ensure you are solving the problem posed and haven't gotten off track while going through the documents. Reread the task memo to refocus on precisely what you've been asked to do. Make sure that you are clear on your client's goal, plan to use the appropriate tone and vocabulary in your response and follow all directions in the task memo. Consider your presentation's organization to ensure your response is clear and easy to follow. Lastly, consider the complexity of the various sections and components of your answer to assess how you think the grader will allocate points and devise a plan to spend your time accordingly.

Davis Big Picture

After rereading the task memo, be sure that you are writing a letter. While traditional letters might not have headings, on performance tests, letters should have headers, just not the formal header you would use in a memorandum. The header will make it easier for you to organize your answer and easier for the grader to follow it. Further, since you are trying to convince Ms. Castile to allow Mr. Davis to accept a plea bargain, your letter needs to be persuasive. So double check that your tone is appropriately convincing. You might not have noticed on the first read, but the task memo specifically asks you to argue that the search was "unreasonable." You should have seen that word used in the case law, but make sure as you go back through your answer that your letter makes this argument as it relates to the case law. Finally, you were told not to write a statement of facts, so make sure you followed the directions and didn't waste your time writing one.

| Step 8. | **Write an answer that solves the problem posed (about 45 minutes)** |

Since you have been writing your answer the entire time as you went through each step, it should be mostly, if not completely, finished. Spend your remaining time rereading your answer and making sure that everything is cohesive, written in complete sentences, and flows as it should. You can also use any additional time to bolster your introduction, making sure you address the person who initially requested the information, if you didn't already do so. Add in a conclusion, if you haven't already done so, and add any facts you may have only summarized earlier to save time.

Make sure you address the requestor prior to doing what you were asked to do.

Make the heading look like a letter to the extent you can and NEVER use your real name.

Always do an introduction of what you are going to write about. It provides the grader with a roadmap to your letter.

Even though you are writing a letter still use headings to organize your letter. Make them persuasive and brief.

If time permits, use the facts in prior cases to analogize or distinguish yours before moving on to your analysis.

It is common to find yourself "fixing up" your facts and adding in more detail or rewording things as you complete your last step and finalize your writing.

SAMPLE ANSWER FOR DAVIS

Mr. Alfaro,

Pursuant to your request, below is the letter we can send to Ms. Castile requesting that she accept a plea from Mr. Davis to the misdemeanor of resisting agents. The letter should convince her not to pursue the felony possession charge since the cocaine was obtained through an illegal search. Please let me know if you need any additional help with Mr. Davis's case.

Applicant

_____

Alfaro, Blevin, & Cohn, LLP

July 25, 2017

U.S. Asst. Attorney's Office
Attention: Maria Castile

Re: U.S. v. Blake C. Davis

Dear Ms. Castile,

We represent Blake C. Davis in regard to his potential indictment and charges for the misdemeanor of resisting agents and felony possession of cocaine. We are writing this letter to encourage you to forgo seeking an indictment and filing charges against Mr. Davis. Below we will discuss why the Fourth Amendment protects Mr. Davis from an unreasonable search by the government and how the drugs found in the wall to his cruise cabin were illegally seized, and thus why the possession charge should be suppressed. Despite his innocence, Mr. Davis is still willing to accept a plea to the misdemeanor of resisting agents. Please review this letter and respond at your earliest convenience.

The Search of Mr. Davis's Cabin Violated Fourth Amendment Protections

The Fourth Amendment protects people against unreasonable searches and seizures. As the court in Clark observed, whether a search is reasonable will depend upon its nature and all of the circumstances surrounding it. Generally, warrantless searches are considered unreasonable. Specific to our case, the courts have further found that searches conducted at the first port where a ship docks after arriving from a foreign country constitute the equivalent to a border search and thus a warrant is not required. Clark.

In Clark, the court was analyzing a situation in which a cruise ship was between cruises, the cruise ship had just returned from various countries, and it was set to depart that same day. The defendant Clark was a crewman aboard the ship. Clark.

Here, unlike Clark, Mr. Davis, was a passenger simply trying to celebrate his 40th wedding anniversary with his wife. Further, it was the last day of their cruise, when they were getting ready to disembark, so arguably they were not at the "first port where a ship docks after arriving from a foreign country." They were at the port of Columbia, not a foreign country or, arguably, a border. However, it is possible since the cruise visited other foreign countries and ports that their prior port was overseas. Even if the court finds that this port was equivalent to a border search, this was a non-routine search with no reasonable suspicion, which would require the courts to suppress the evidence found as the result of a search in violation of Mr. Davis's Fourth Amendment rights.

The Search of Mr. Davis's Cabin was a Non-routine Border Search and Officers Needed Reasonable Suspicion to Search His Cabin

The Clark court noted that border searches that are routine may be conducted without a warrant and without probable cause, reasonable suspicion, or any suspicion of wrongdoing.

However, an individual's privacy interests must be balanced against the sovereign's interests, and, as a result, non-routine searches do require reasonable suspicion of wrongdoing to pass constitutional muster. <u>Clark</u>.

While the search in <u>Braun</u> (cited by <u>Clark</u>) was a routine search that agents often did after returning from foreign countries by having dogs sniff the hallways and alert them to any drugs, here, as in <u>Clark</u>, Mr. Davis's room was searched alone as an isolated and non-routine search. Thus, the government would need to show reasonable suspicion to search the Davises' cabin.

Further, the court must balance Mr. Davis's privacy rights against the sovereign's interest. Here, since Mr. Davis was using the cabin as his room and home, he would have a right to privacy in such room, just as the court in <u>Clark</u> found that Clark had a right to privacy in his room where he was living as a crewman. Since Mr. Davis did have an expectation of privacy to his room and this was a non-routine search similar to that in <u>Clark</u>, the agents must have had reasonable suspicion to enter Mr. Davis's room and conduct a warrantless search, even if it was at a border equivalent where the government has an interest in keeping people and the premises safe from prior foreign paraphernalia.

Officers Did Not Have a Reasonable Suspicion to Search Mr. Davis's Cabin, and Reasonable Suspicion Cannot be Based on the Officer's Unreasonable Mistakes

Under the reasonable suspicion standard, in order to conduct a search law enforcement officers, including Customs officers, must have reasonable suspicion, based on specific and articulable facts, that the suspect committed, is committing, or is about to commit a crime. The "suspicion is unreasonable if it arises from mistakes that themselves are unreasonable." <u>Clark.</u>

In <u>Clark</u>, the court found that even though Clark did have a right to privacy in his room, the agents had reasonable suspicion to enter his room because a reliable informant told agents that Clark and another were transporting illegal narcotics. This information was then substantiated when one of the crewmen was seen passing a package that was seized and found to contain cocaine. <u>Clark</u>.

Mr. Davis's incident is substantially distinguishable from <u>Clark</u> since here the agent made numerous unreasonable mistakes. At the time of Mr. Davis's incident, U.S. Customs agents were looking for a 21-year-old male who was 260 lbs. and 6'4" with the name Blaine, not Blake, Daviss (with two s's at end of the name). Instead, they searched and arrested Blake (not Blaine) Davis, whose last name has one -<u>s</u> at the end, not two. Further, Mr. Davis was a 61-year-old, 140 lb., 5'7" male, which is drastically different from the description of the person the agents were seeking. No reasonable person could mistake a person who was more than 100 pounds heavier, 40 years younger, and several inches shorter, and a jury would likely agree with this interpretation. Further, the suspect was traveling alone and had purchased a last-minute ticket, whereas Mr. and Mrs. Davis were traveling together for their anniversary, a long-planned trip. When the agents first knocked prior to any search, seeing Mrs. Davis answer the door should have alerted them that they had the wrong suspect, as this would show that Mr. Davis was not traveling alone. Moreover, here the agents using a drug sniffing dog proceeded to search the Davises' entire room and all of their luggage, dumping everything into piles, when the dog didn't even alert them to the luggage but rather went to the balcony door and sat down there instead.

In addition, after the agents found a small bag in the wall, which could have been placed there by any person prior to this cruise, as even the arrest report acknowledges that it could have been placed there any time in the past year, they demanded that Mr. Davis give them his briefcase. Since the dog never alerted the agents to the briefcase and since all of the Davises' bags and luggage were clean, there was no reasonable suspicion to believe that Mr. Davis's work briefcase contained any cocaine. In fact, he explained to them that he had protected work product information in the briefcase, which is why he didn't want to show them the contents. And in fact when they did open it anyway after throwing him on the ground and handcuffing him, they found no cocaine but rather realized they had been searching the wrong person and the wrong room based on his passport name and the room number.

When a case cites another case that provides important information, be sure to name and use it so the grader easily sees you know how important it is.

Most of your time should be on this section since the task memo told us that reasonableness would be our argument. So allocate your time properly so you can be sure to place most of your analysis in this section.

Use as many facts as you can to bolster your argument. If you didn't have time at first, add in more details later if time permits.

Mention of the drug-sniffing dog could have been used anywhere here. Most likely it was best in your reasonable suspicion section, but you also could have used it in the routine v. non-routine discussion, as the case discussed dogs there too. The key was using these facts somewhere.

Use of certain words can make your analysis more persuasive (such as "did not even slightly"). Always keep your tone in mind as you write.

As you conclude, always ask the recipient to do what you want them to do, just as you did in the beginning.

Not only did the agents search a man who did not even slightly resemble the description of the suspect, but they also searched the wrong room due to their own error, which was not reasonable since the room they were supposed to search was room 8086 and the Davises were in room 8132, which was on the opposite side of the ship. As agents who are responsible for checking the cruise ship, they should know which rooms are on which side of the ship. Thus, their mistake was not reasonable as these agents should be able to read and input numbers correctly and know roughly where in the ship the room to be searched is located.

Conclusion

Overall, the court will review all of the evidence considering the totality of the circumstances. Here, there is not simply one mistake but numerous mistakes by experienced agents. The totality of these unreasonable mistakes would lead a jury or a court to find that the search was not protected under the Fourth Amendment.

Based on the above, we request that you allow Mr. Davis to accept a plea for misdemeanor resisting arrest charge and that you do not seek any felony charges against Mr. Davis for possession.

If you have any questions or concerns, please do not hesitate to contact me.

Respectfully yours,

Applicant

Self-Assessment Grid: Davis

Persuasive Letter

Overall organization and presentation

- ☐ An introduction to the requester stating that you have written the letter below as requested
- ☐ Organized like a letter, with salutation, signature line, introductory paragraph, and conclusion
- ☐ Persuasive tone and formal vocabulary, since writing to another attorney
- ☐ Organized/presented in some logical way (various options available, but the reasonable suspicion argument should be separated within the letter)
- ☐ Appropriate use of headings to persuade and guide the grader, even though it is a letter (formal headers as in a memo are unnecessary)
- ☐ Properly cite to rules in the only case, as well as the case cited within the only case
- ☐ Presented rule and rule explanation before analysis
- ☐ Analogized/distinguished cases where helpful and appropriate
- ☐ Used all pertinent facts well
- ☐ Followed all directions in task memo, including no statement of facts

Rules (from library)	Rule Explanation (library case facts)	Analysis (our case facts)
Introduction		

Briefly describe to the requestor the task you have been asked to complete. Then, set up the letter format and include a brief introduction that identifies that Davis has the potential to be indicted and charged with a misdemeanor for resisting agents and a felony for possession of cocaine. Make it known to Ms. Castile that Davis will plead guilty to the misdemeanor but that she should not pursue the felony indictment/charge as the search of Davis's cabin was unreasonable under the Fourth Amendment because the agents did not have reasonable suspicion to conduct the search and thus a court would suppress the evidence.

Letter Body		
Fourth Amendment Protections Were Violated		
☐ The Fourth Amendment protects people against unreasonable searches and seizures. <u>Clark</u> ☐ Whether a search is reasonable will depend upon its nature and all of the circumstances surrounding it. <u>Clark</u> ☐ Generally, warrantless searches are considered unreasonable. <u>Clark</u> ☐ Searches conducted at the first port where a ship docks after arriving from a foreign country constitute the equivalent to a border search, and a warrant is not required to search. <u>Clark</u>	☐ A cruise ship was between cruises, the cruise ship had just returned from various countries, and it was set to depart that same day. ☐ Defendant Clark was a crewman aboard the ship.	☐ Mr. Davis was a passenger simply trying to celebrate his 40th wedding anniversary with his wife. ☐ It was the last day of their cruise when they were getting ready to disembark. ☐ They were at the port of Columbia.
Search of Cabin was Non-Routine Border Search		
☐ Border searches that are routine may be conducted without a warrant and without probable cause, reasonable suspicion, or any suspicion of wrongdoing. <u>Clark</u> ☐ An individual's privacy interests must be balanced against the sovereign's interests and as a result, non-routine searches do require reasonable suspicion of wrongdoing to pass constitutional muster. <u>Clark</u>	☐ The search in <u>Braun</u> (cited by <u>Clark</u>) was a routine search that agents often did when a ship returned from foreign countries by having dogs sniff the hallways and alert them to any drugs. ☐ Clark's search was found to be a non-routine search since the agents sought out his room rather than agents responding to dogs alerting them. Also it was Clark's private cabin.	☐ Mr. Davis's room alone was searched as an isolated and non-routine search, and no dogs alerted agents to his room location. ☐ While on board the cruise Mr. Davis was using the cabin as his room and temporary home where he kept all of his personal belongings.

Reasonable Suspicion Can't Be Met by Unreasonable Mistakes

☐ In order to conduct a search, law enforcement officers, including Customs officers, must have reasonable suspicion, based on specific and articulable facts, that the suspect committed, is committing, or is about to commit a crime. <u>Clark</u>

☐ The suspicion is unreasonable if it arises from mistakes that themselves are unreasonable. <u>Clark</u>

☐ Clark did have a right to privacy in his room.

☐ The agents had reasonable suspicion to enter his room because a reliable informant told agents that Clark and another were transporting illegal narcotics.

☐ This information was then substantiated when one of the crewmen was seen passing a package that was seized and found to contain cocaine.

☐ At the time of Mr. Davis's incident, U.S. Customs agents were **looking for a 21-year-old male who was 260 lbs. and 6'4". with the name Blaine Daviss.**

☐ Agents searched and arrested **Blake (not Blaine) Davis**, whose last name has one -<u>s</u> at the end as opposed to two.

☐ **Mr. Davis was a 61-year-old, 140 lb., 5'7" male.** Drastic differences show an unreasonable mistake.

☐ The suspect was **traveling alone and had purchased a last-minute ticket.**

☐ Mr. and Mrs. Davis were **traveling together** for their anniversary, a **planned trip.**

☐ When the agents first knocked, Mrs. Davis answered the door, alerting the agents that the room they entered did not house a single traveler, which should have alerted them to their mistake prior to the search.

☐ The agents, using a drug-sniffing dog, searched their entire room and all of their luggage, dumping everything into piles, when the **dog never alerted them to the contents of the luggage**—another unreasonable mistake.

☐ The drug-sniffing dog didn't alert agents to the luggage, but rather went to the balcony door and sat down there instead, while the agents continued to search the luggage.

☐ Agents found a small bag in the wall, which could have been placed there by any person prior to this cruise, as even the arrest report acknowledges that it could have been placed there any time in the past year.

☐ The agents demanded that Mr. Davis give them his briefcase.

☐ Mr. Davis explained to them that he had protected work product information in the briefcase.

☐ When the agents opened the briefcase after throwing Mr. Davis on the ground and handcuffing him, they found no cocaine but rather realized they had been searching the wrong person and the wrong room based on his passport name.

☐ The agents were supposed to search **room 8086 and the Davises were in room 8132, which was on the opposite side of the ship.**

Conclusion

☐ The court will review all evidence based on the totality of the circumstances, and the numerous errors and unreasonable mistakes will result in the court finding the search was unreasonable under the circumstances.

☐ Be sure to request that Ms. Castile allow **Mr. Davis to accept a plea for misdemeanor resisting agents** and that she **not seek any felony charges against Mr. Davis for possession.**

PT: SELECTED ANSWER 1

Dear Ms. Castille,

Our firm, Alfaro, Blevin & Cohn, represents Blake C. Davis in the matter of the United States v. Davis. As you may recall, Mr. Davis has been charged with 1) the misdemeanor of resisting agents from the U.S. Customs and Border Protection Service ("CBP"), and 2) the felony of possession of cocaine. We are writing to you today to inform you that it is our contention that the search of Mr. Davis' cabin aboard the cruise ship was unreasonable under the Fourth Amendment to the United States Constitution because the CBP officers did not have the requisite reasonable suspicion necessary to conduct the search of Mr. Davis' cabin. As a result, the possession charge should not be brought against Mr. Davis because the drugs were illegally seized, and will be suppressed in a trial against Mr. Davis. However, Mr. Davis will agree to accept a guilty plea to misdemeanor arresting if the felony charge is dropped.

A. *The Fourth Amendment Required the CBP Officers to Have Reasonable Suspicion Prior to Searching Mr. Davis' Cabin*

The Fourth Amendment of the US Constitution protects people against unreasonable searches and seizures. Generally, the court will find that warrantless searches are unreasonable, however the court will look to the nature and all of the surrounding circumstances before making that determination. One exception to this rule is when those searched are made at the nation's borders, which includes the functional equivalent of a border such as the first port where a ship docks after arriving from a foreign country. Generally, a search at a border or functional equivalent of a border may be conducted without a warrant, probable cause, reasonable suspicion, or in fact any suspicion of a wrong doing. United States v. Clark. This is due to the fact that the expectation of privacy is less at a border crossing, and the interest of the government is much greater. However, this does not mean that the government's right to search is absolute at the border. Any search that is non-routine still requires that the government has reasonable suspicion of wrongdoing prior to the conducting of such a search.

1. *The Search of Mr. Davis' Room was a Non-Routine Search and Reasonable Suspicion Was Required*

A person has the right to be free from unreasonable searches and seizures in their home because any search of the home is considered to be highly intrusive. Under 15th Circuit law, any border search that implicates the dignity and privacy interests of a person requires reasonable suspicion. Id. This includes the cabin of a passenger on a cruise ship because the cabin is merely a temporary abode for the passenger, and therefore should be afforded similar protections as the person's home. In Clark, the court there found that the search of the defendant's room was a non-routine search because it was his temporary home while on the ship. Entering the cabin, searching an individual's private belongings, and subjecting their private space to a search by a drug-sniffing dog was beyond the level of routine. Id. Contrast this with United States v. Braun, where the court there found that a routine search occurred. However, the search was routine because the officers used trained canines to detect narcotic odors in the hallway. After the dog alerted the police to the presence of drugs, the officers then searched the room. However, the court there found that the search in the hallway by the dogs was routine, and not the search of the cabin.

Furthermore, when a search of a cruise ship cabin is conducted at the border, the officers must have reasonable suspicion to search the cabin. Id. Reasonable suspicion is required to provide some protection to an individual on a cruise ship because it best strikes the proper balance between the government interests and the privacy rights of an individual. Id.

Here, Mr. and Mrs. Davis were traveling aboard the ship as passengers, and the cruise ship had just returned from Mexico, making their first stop back in the

United State. Accordingly, this was a border search and Mr. Davis does not deny that there is a lower expectation of privacy. However, the cabin still constituted the Davis' temporary abode, any completely warrantless and suspicionless search of the cabin violated their Fourth Amendment rights. The cabin was their de facto home, it held all their belongings while they were on this trip, and therefore, the search by the CBP officers was a non-routine search. Additionally, the officers brought in a drug-sniffing dog, searched all of the Davis' belongings, and entered their de facto home, just as the officers did in Clark. This also corresponds with the holding in Braun, as the search of the room would still be non-routine. As such, the officers were required to have reasonable suspicion before entering the room and searching the Davis' belonging.

2. *The CBP Officers Did Not Have Reasonable Suspicion to Enter the Davis' Cabin*

As the room constituted the Davis' temporary abode, the officers needed reasonable suspicion to enter into the cabin. Reasonable suspicion requires that the officers have specific, articulable facts that the suspect committed, is committing, or is about to commit a crime before conducting a search. Id. In Clark, the officers were found to have had reasonable suspicion based upon the information known to the officers, including a tip from a reliable informant, as well as the officer's own observations, and the arrest and seizure of drugs from an acquaintance of the defendant. In Braun, the officers failed to have reasonable suspicion prior to entering the room because the dog did not alert them to the presence of drugs there, it was only after the dog entered the room did the dog alert. Furthermore, the court in Clark stated in dicta that suspicion based upon an unreasonable mistake would not be a reasonable suspicion supporting a non-routine search.

Here, for the following reasons, the CBP officers did not have the reasonable suspicion required. First, the officers made an unreasonable mistake in coming to the Davis' room in the first place. The officers were acting based upon information obtained from an informant who was an undercover officer. However, the information that the officers obtained was to be on a lookout for a white male named Blaine C. Daviss. Mr. Daviss was in room 8086, on the same floor but the opposite side of the ship from the Mr. and Mrs. Davis. Certainly officers who conducted routine searches of ships for drugs would know how to find the correct room. Officer Oliphant acknowledged his mistake in his report, but blamed it on a harmless error due to the names being next to each other on the manifest. We acknowledge that this alone might be a reasonable mistake, however when looked at in the totality of the circumstances here, the officers failed to have reasonable suspicion.

Second, Officer Oliphant then states in his report that upon arriving at the incorrect state room, the dog alerted in the hallway as to the presence of cocaine. However, Office Oliphant acknowledges there that cocaine could have been deposited at that site at any time in the past year. This is not enough to establish reasonable suspicion as there was no indication there was presently cocaine, or that the cocaine was in the room, but only that at some point cocaine had been there. The court in Braun did find that an alert to the presence of drugs while in the hallway could be enough to establish reasonable suspicion because the search of the hallway was a routine search. However, in that situation, the officers were conducting a routine search of the hallways that they always conducted for ships arriving at Key West. In our present situation, the officers were only on the ship and in that hallway because they were planning to go to Mr. Davis' room, which as established above, was a mistake. However, even the situation at this point could still be a reasonable mistake as there had been some alert, but the court will most likely find that the facts here were different because it was not a routine search, and reasonable suspicion was still required, which when looked at in the totality of the circumstances, the officers failed to meet.

Third, when the officers knocked on the door, Mrs. Davis opened the door, who as Officer Oliphant stated, was a middle aged white female. They had been told that Mr. Daviss was 21 years old and traveling by himself. This fact should have indicated to them that they had the wrong room. Instead, the officers told her they were looking for contraband and she had to step into the hallway. They did not ask, and so never obtained her consent to enter.

Fourth, Mr. Davis showed up at this point and the officers began to talk to him. He signaled to them that he was in fact the Mr. Davis. The officers had been told by their informant that the Mr. Daviss they were looking for was 6'4, 260 pounds, and 21 years old. Mr. Davis is also a white male, but the similarities stop there. Mr. Davis is 5'7, 140 pounds, and 61 years old. When he told them he was Mr. Davis, neither officer realized at that point their mistake and instead informed Mr. Davis he had to stay out of the room. This was an unreasonable mistake at that point. They knew what their suspect looked like, and knew Mr. Davis could not be him. Yet they proceeded to enter the room, all because of the fact that cocaine might have been at that location within the past year. This one fact is not enough to rise to the level of reasonable suspicion, yet still the officers proceeded.

Fifth, when entering the room, the canine ignored all the belongings and most of the room, and went over and sat by the window. However, the officers now ignored this and began pressing on the luggage, and then had the dog specifically sniff the luggage, but the dog again ignored the luggage. The officers ignored this lack of an alert, and proceeded to search through every piece of luggage, invading Mr. and Mrs. Davis' privacy. They had no reasonable suspicion at that time to search the luggage, or to even be in the room.

Sixth, they finally paid attention to the "alert" and went over to where the dog was sitting and looked in the surrounding area, and it was only then they found the cocaine. The dog was enough to provide reasonable suspicion due to the alert. However, as the court in Clark said when interpreting Braun, the alert of the canine inside of the room was not enough to establish reasonable suspicion to be within that room. Accordingly, the invasion of the Davis' privacy was not justified at this point by the alert because the officers were not allowed to be in their cabin. It was then that the officers forcibly removed the briefcase from Mr. Davis, which he prevented them from doing so because of the confidential information contained within. The officers then looked at Mr. Davis' passport, and stated that it was only then they realized their mistake and that they had searched the wrong room. However, they should have realized that mistake when Mr. Davis returned to the room and identified himself. Accordingly, the officers here made a very unreasonable mistake, and did not have reasonable suspicion to search the room. Therefore, the search will be found to be unreasonable, and the seized cocaine will be suppressed at the trial.

B. *Conclusion*

As stated above, it is our proposal that the government drops their felony charge against Mr. Davis because it has no chance of success due to the fact that the seized cocaine will be suppressed and without it, the government has no case against Mr. Davis. The officers did not have the required level of reasonable suspicion prior to conducting the non-routine search of Mr. Davis' cruise cabin, and therefore the search violated his Fourth Amendment rights against unreasonable searches and seizures. Mr. Davis will in turn plead guilty to his misdemeanor offense for resisting arrest.

Sincerely,

Applicant

PT: SELECTED ANSWER 2

FROM: Applicant

TO: Ms. Maria Castile

DATE: July 25, 2017

RE: United States v. Blake C. Davis

Dear Ms. Castile,

I, along with Timothy Alfaro, represent Mr. Blake C. Davis in his charges of (1) misdemeanor of resisting agents from the U.S. Customs and Border Protection Service (CBP) and (2) felony possession of cocaine. After a discussion with Mr. Davis regarding the charges, we are amendable to a plea bargain regarding the charges as well. Mr. Davis is willing to plead guilty to a misdemeanor of resisting CBP agents. Mr. Davis does not want to have a felony conviction on his record, but is willing to plead guilty to a misdemeanor for an efficient resolution of this matter.

The charges against Mr. Davis regarding felony possession of cocaine should be dropped because the search of Mr. Davis' cabin abroad the cruise ship was unreasonable under the 4th Amendment to the United States Constitution and hence a possession charge should not be brought because the drugs were illegally seized and will be suppressed.

First, the border search at issue was non-routine, and thus CBP agents needed reasonable suspicion to conduct search. Second, the CBP agents did not have reasonable suspicion to search the cabin and made unreasonable mistakes that did not justify their suspicion.

Therefore, our offer of Mr. Davis' pleading guilty to the misdemeanor charge should be accepted because the felony charge of possession of cocaine would be suppressed at trial because of the illegal search.

The Search of Mr. Davis' Cabin is Non-Routine and Requires Reasonable Suspicion for CBP Agents to Search and Enter the Cabin

"The 4th Amendment protects against unreasonable searches and seizures. Whether a search is reasonable will depend upon its nature and all of the circumstances surrounding it but, as a general matter, warrantless searches are unreasonable. Searches conducted at the nation's borders, however, represent a well-established exception to the warrant requirement. The exception applies not only at the physical boundaries of the United States, but also at the "functional equivalent" of a border, including the first port where a ship docks after arriving from a foreign country." *United States v. Clark,* U.S. Court of Appeals, 15th Circuit (2014).

The court in *Clark* states that as long as the border search is routine, it may be conducted without a warrant, probable cause, reasonable exception, or any suspicion of wrongdoing. No suspicion is required in order for a Customs officer to board and search a cruise ship as part of a routine border search. However, even at the border, an individual is entitled to reasonable searches only and their privacy interests must be balanced against the government's interests. Therefore, searches that are classified as "non-routine" require reasonable suspicion of wrongdoing to pass constitutional muster.

To determine whether the border search is routine, the degree to which it intrudes on a person's privacy must be determined. Any search that implicates the dignity and privacy interest of the person being searched is highly intrusive and requires reasonable suspicion.

The court in *Clark* concluded that a search of private living quarters abroad a ship at the functional equivalent of a border is a non-routine search and must be supported by reasonable suspicion of criminal conduct. The court held in *United States v. Braun*, that the routine aspect of a search is the use of trained drug-dogs in a "search" of the public hallways of the cruise ship. A search of the public areas of cruise ship is routine and does not require any reasonable suspicion, however, a search of the cruise ship cabin is non-routine and requires reasonable suspicion.

In Mr. Davis' case, the CBP agents actually searched the Davis' cabin with their drug dog. According to the court in *Clark*, a search of private living quarters aboard a ship at the functional equivalent of a border is a non-routine search and must be supported by reasonable suspicion of criminal conduct. While the CBP agents may have been following procedures and conducting routine enforcement actions by searching the cruise ship when it entered port, their search of Mr. Davis' cabin is not routine.

The CBP agent's search of the Mr. Davis' property was highly intrusive, the agents not only searched throughout the entire cabin but also opened and probed every item that the Davis' owned. Such an intrusive and detailed searched is not routine and the invasion into the sanctity of privacy must be supported with reasonable suspicion to be valid under the 4th Amendment.

Thus, the search conducted by the CBP was non-routine and must be supported with reasonable suspicion.

<u>The Search of Mr. Davis' Cabin is Unreasonable and any Evidence should be Suppressed because the Search was not Supported with Reasonable Suspicion and the Agents made Unreasonable Mistakes to lead to the Search</u>

Under the reasonable suspicion standard, law enforcement officers, including

Customs officers, must have reasonable suspicion, based on specific and articulable facts, that the suspect committed, is committing, or is about to commit, a crime in order to conduct a search. *Clark*. The court held that the search of the defendant's cabin was reasonable because the agents had reasonable suspicion of a crime and the defendant was unable to point to any evidence of unreasonable mistakes by the agents.

However, in Mr. Davis' case, the CBP made several unreasonable mistakes that led to a search of Mr. Davis' cabin and the agents did not have any actual information that Davis is guilty of a crime.

First, Agent Oliphant made an unreasonable mistake when he took down the wrong cabin number in the TECS database due to his inability to notice a difference between the two last names. The mistake is clearly unreasonable because the names, although similar, are not identical and an agent conducting a warrantless search of a living quarter should have been more careful. The difference between Blaine versus Blake and Daviss versus Davis is clear, and it is unreasonable for the agent to make such a mistake.

Agent Oliphant may argue that the dog "alerted" in the hallway next to Mr. Davis' cabin and that is enough reasonable suspicion to enter the cabin to conduct a search. In *United States v. Braun*, a dog's alert to drugs outside the hallway of the cabin during a routine search is enough to create reasonable suspicion for a non-routine search of the defendant's cabin. However, if not for the unreasonable mistake by Agent Oliphant when taking down the room number, the CBP agents would not have been conducting a search on that side of the cruise ship. If the Agent had taken down the correct number and did not make an unreasonable mistake, the CBP agents and the drug dog would be searching the opposite side of the ship because Daviss resides on the port side and David on the state side. Thus, the drug dog's alert only arose because of Agent Oliphant's unreasonable mistake in taking down the room number.

Second, the CBP agents may also argue that the drug dog's action once inside the room also gave rise to reasonable suspicion because the dog alerted to the existence of drugs near the outer wall. However, the court in *Clark* also held that a drug dog's alert to drugs after entering the cabin is not reasonable suspicion, and the search is unreasonable. The dog's alert that arose after the agents made an unreasonable search does not establish reasonable suspicion for the search.

Lastly, Agent Oliphant also made an unreasonable mistake regarding the identity of Mr. Davis. The TECS report clearly indicated that Daviss was a white male that was 6'4", 260 lbs and aged 21 years. Mr. Davis by comparison is aged 61 years, weighing 140 lbs and only 5'7". Once Mr. Davis entered into the cabin, the CBP agents should have realized that they have the wrong cabin and the wrong suspect.

Even if the CBP's mistake regarding the cabin number and the identity of Mr. Davis is reasonable, their inability to recognize that they have the wrong suspect the moment that Mr. Davis entered into the cabin is clearly unreasonable. The CBP agents should have stopped the search of the cabin the moment they recognized that Mr. Davis is not the suspect that they are looking for. However, the CBP continued their illegal search of the cabin and managed to find a bag of cocaine that the Davis' had no knowledge of.

The CBP agents did not have reasonable suspicion to search Mr. Davis' cabin because their conduct was not based on specific and articulable facts that the Mr. Davis is committing a crime. With the known information by the agents and in light of the unreasonable mistakes the agents made throughout their conduct, the search and seizure of the cocaine from Mr. Davis' cabin is clearly not justified by reasonable suspicion.

Conclusion

The search of Mr. Davis' cabin by the CBP agents was highly invasive and non-routine, and under the 4th Amendment it must be supported with reasonable suspicion for it not to be illegal. However, the CBP agents did not have reasonable suspicion to search the cabin and made unreasonable mistakes in their process of looking up information and conducting the search. Thus, the felony possession of cocaine should be dropped because the search of Mr. Davis' cabin abroad the cruise ship was unreasonable under the 4th Amendment and any possession charge should not be brought because the drugs were illegally seized and will be suppressed.

We hope you consider our offer of Mr. Davis' accepting a guilty plea for the misdemeanor of resisting arrest and drop the charges against Mr. Davis for felony possession.

Thank you,

Applicant

DEMONSTRATION 3

MEANEY v. TRUSTEES OF THE UNIVERSITY OF COLUMBIA

February 2018

California
Bar
Examination

Performance Test
INSTRUCTIONS AND FILE

MEANEY v. TRUSTEES OF THE UNIVERSITY OF COLUMBIA

MEANEY v. TRUSTEES OF THE UNIVERSITY OF COLUMBIA

INSTRUCTIONS

1. This performance test is designed to evaluate your ability to handle a select number of legal authorities in the context of a factual problem involving a client.

2. The problem is set in the fictional State of Columbia, one of the United States.

3. You will have two sets of materials with which to work: a File and a Library.

4. The File contains factual materials about your case. The first document is a memorandum containing the instructions for the tasks you are to complete.

5. The Library contains the legal authorities needed to complete the tasks. The case reports may be real, modified, or written solely for the purpose of this performance test. If the cases appear familiar to you, do not assume that they are precisely the same as you have read before. Read each thoroughly, as if it were new to you. You should assume that cases were decided in the jurisdictions and on the dates shown. In citing cases from the Library, you may use abbreviations and omit page citations.

6. You should concentrate on the materials provided, but you should also bring to bear on the problem your general knowledge of the law. What you have learned in law school and elsewhere provides the general background for analyzing the problem; the File and Library provide the specific materials with which you must work.

7. This performance test is designed to be completed in 90 minutes. Although there are no parameters on how to apportion that 90 minutes, you should allow yourself sufficient time to thoroughly review the materials and organize your planned response. Since the time allotted for this session of the examination includes two (2) essay questions in addition to this performance test, time management is essential.

8. Your response will be graded on its compliance with instructions and on its content, thoroughness, and organization.

FOGEL & DAVIS, LLP

One Walton Avenue

Belleville, Columbia

MEMORANDUM

TO: Applicant

FROM: Melissa Saphir

DATE: February 27, 2018

RE: Meaney v. Trustees of the University of Columbia

We have been retained by the Trustees of the University of Columbia to defend them in a breach of contract action.

The late Edward Kemper (Edward) was a wealthy businessman and a generous donor to the University. Pursuant to an agreement, Edward transferred a garden to the Trustees, which the Trustees agreed to retain in perpetuity as the "Kemper Scottish Garden." Sometime later, Edward married Sarah Meaney (Sarah). Before her death two years ago, Sarah had grown quite fond of the Kemper Scottish Garden -- so much so that it came to be known as "Sarah's Scottish Garden." Notwithstanding the agreement, the Trustees recently made the difficult decision to sell the garden so as to use the proceeds for pressing educational purposes.

The plaintiff in the breach of contract action I referred to is Brendan Meaney. Meaney is the only child of Sarah by a prior marriage. By his action, Meaney is seeking to prevent the Trustees from selling the garden.

I believe that we may be able to persuade the court to dismiss Meaney's breach of contract action on the ground that Meaney lacks standing. To confirm my belief, I need to determine whether Edward transferred the garden to the Trustees by way of contract or gift and, if by way of gift, by way of what kind of gift.

To that end, please prepare an objective memorandum assessing whether Edward did indeed transfer the garden to the Trustees by way of contract or gift and, if by way of gift, by way of what kind of gift. Do not include a statement of facts, but use the facts in your analysis.

AGREEMENT

The Trustees of the University of Columbia (hereinafter "the Trustees") desire to obtain a garden parcel of real property now owned and occupied by Emily Gordon, located in Belleville, Columbia, commonly known as 625 Sierra Way.

Edward Kemper (hereinafter "Kemper") desires to facilitate such acquisition by acquiring the garden parcel and by transferring it to the Trustees, subject to certain restrictions as provided for herein.

Therefore, in consideration of the foregoing, the Trustees and Kemper do hereby agree as follows:

1. Kemper will acquire the garden parcel and transfer it to the Trustees.
2. The Trustees will cause the garden parcel to bear the name "Kemper Scottish Garden," use it for educational purposes, and retain it in perpetuity.

Kemper retains the right to modify the terms of this Agreement as necessary and appropriate to its purpose.

Dated: December 18, 1964.

_____*Edward Kemper*_____

Edward Kemper

___ *Harold Williamson*_____

Harold Williamson

Chairman of the Board of Trustees

February 2018

California
Bar
Examination

Performance Test

LIBRARY

MEANEY v. TRUSTEES OF THE UNIVERSITY OF COLUMBIA

LIBRARY

Behrens Research Foundation v. Fairview Memorial Hospital
Columbia Court of Appeals (2008)...

Collins v. Lincoln
Columbia Court of Appeals (2009) ....

Holt v. Jones
Columbia Supreme Court (1994) ....

BEHRENS RESEARCH FOUNDATION v.
FAIRVIEW MEMORIAL HOSPITAL
Columbia Court of Appeals (2008)

Behrens Research Foundation (Behrens), a non-profit public benefit corporation, gave Fairview Memorial Hospital (Fairview), a healthcare institution, a gift of $1 million. Fairview had a well-recognized Department of Cardiothoracic Surgery. Behrens had had a longstanding interest in advancing cardiothoracic surgery. Not long thereafter, as a result of various unforeseen changes, including departures of key staff, Fairview closed the department.

Behrens brought the underlying action in the District Court seeking an injunction directing Fairview either to reopen its Department of Cardiothoracic Surgery or to return Behrens' $1 million gift. Fairview moved to dismiss the action under Columbia Rule of Civil Procedure 12(b)(6), claiming that Behrens did not have standing to sue. The District Court granted the motion and entered a judgment of dismissal.

On appeal, Behrens contends that it did indeed have standing to sue.

We disagree.

It is well settled in Columbia that a donor is the master of his or her gift.

Because that is so, a donor can make a gift that is *absolute.* The donor can give property *unconditionally*, without (1) restricting use or disposition of the property, (2) retaining power to modify the gift, or (3) reserving a right to sue to enforce a restriction or to undo the gift in case of a restriction's breach by causing the property to revert to the donor him- or herself or to a third person. When a gift is absolute, the donor has relinquished, and the donee has assumed, full dominion over the property -- i.e., the ability to use or dispose of the property at any time, in any manner, and for any purpose.

But a donor can also make a gift that is *not absolute.* The donor can give property *conditionally*, (1) restricting use or disposition, (2) retaining power of modification, and/or (3) reserving a right of enforcement or reversion. When a gift is not absolute, the donor has not relinquished, and the donee has not assumed, full dominion over the property; rather, both donor and donee share power over the property's use or disposition.

Although a donor is indeed master of his or her gift, the law presumes that a gift is *absolute* unless it clearly appears otherwise. In line with this presumption, the law further presumes that a donor has *not* restricted use or disposition, has *not* retained power of modification, and has *not* reserved a right of enforcement or reversion, unless it clearly appears otherwise.

These presumptions prove fatal to Behrens' position. The record on appeal contains the instrument by which Behrens made its $1 million gift to Fairview. In pertinent part, the instrument recites only that Behrens "hereby delivers" and Fairview "hereby accepts" the gift. Neither expressly, nor by implication, does the instrument evidence any reservation on Behrens' part of a right of enforcement. Behrens did not reserve any such right for itself. We cannot make up for its omission.

Affirmed.

COLLINS v. LINCOLN

Columbia Court of Appeals (2009)

Anita Collins brought an action for declaratory relief in the District Court against Stephen Lincoln, her adult son. In order to resolve various tax questions now pending before the State of Columbia Tax Board, Collins seeks a determination that the instrument by which she transferred certain property to Lincoln reflected a gift rather than a transfer by contract. Following a bench trial, the District Court entered judgment in Collins' favor, issuing the determination that she had sought. Lincoln appeals. We affirm.

The facts are undisputed: By deed dated June 26, 2002, Collins transferred to Lincoln a 260-acre vineyard in Parker County including a 20,000-square-foot Victorian main residence, guest house, pool, tennis courts, sports field, exercise studio, lake, olive orchard, and a stone winery with a tasting room and a permit to produce 5,500 cases of wine a year. The deed recited that Collins transferred the property to Lincoln "in consideration for his promise to use his best efforts to maintain the property in an ecologically sustainable manner." As of the date in question, the assessed value of the property was more than $35 million. Collins was then 65 years old, a widow, and the Chair of the Board of Directors of the Parker County Rural Conservancy, a locally-prominent environmental organization; Lincoln was 30 years old, unmarried, and the Rural Conservancy's Volunteer Coordinator; each was the other's sole living relative.

Property may be passed by gift. The elements of a gift consist of: (1) intent on the part of the donor to make a gift; (2) delivery, either actual or constructive, of property by the donor; (3) acceptance of the property by the donee; and (4) lack of consideration for the gift.

Property may also be passed by transfer by contract. The elements of a transfer by contract consist of: (1) an offer to buy or sell; (2) acceptance of the offer; and (3) consideration passing between the buyer and seller.

Gifts and transfers by contracts have two similar elements. First, a gift requires delivery by the donor and a transfer by contract requires offer by the buyer or seller. Second, a gift requires acceptance by the donee and a transfer by contract requires acceptance by the seller or buyer.

But one element is different. While a transfer by contract requires the *presence* of consideration, a gift requires the *absence* of consideration. In other words, without consideration, the passing of property is by gift, whereas with consideration, it is by transfer by contract.

Consideration has two requirements. The promisee must bargain with the promisor and must confer, or agree to confer, a benefit or must suffer, or agree to suffer, a burden.

The absence of consideration is clear when a gift is absolute. *See, Behrens Research Foundation v. Fairview Memorial Hospital* (Colum. Ct. App. 2008). In that instance, the donee does not bargain with the donor or confer, or agree to confer, any benefit. Neither does the donee bargain with the donor or suffer, or agree to suffer, any burden. Instead, the donor simply delivers the property and the donee simply accepts it.

But the absence of consideration is not clear when a gift is not absolute. *See, Behrens Research Foundation.* In that instance, the donee could be said to bargain with the donor, and could be said to confer, or agree to confer, a "benefit" on the donor or to suffer, or agree to suffer, a "burden." Consider the situation in which a university agrees to name a campus building in a donor's honor or to use the building for a specified purpose. The university could be said to "bargain" with the donor -- negotiating the terms for the naming of the building or its use for the specified purpose -- and to confer, or agree to confer, a benefit or to suffer, or agree to suffer, a burden -- the naming of the building or its use for the specified purpose. Such a "bargain" and "benefit" and "burden" do not preclude a gift.

The presence or absence of consideration does not turn on the presence or absence of the term "consideration" in the instrument. For example, in *Salmon v. Wilson* (Colum. Supreme Ct. 1971), the Supreme Court held that a deed by which a father transferred 10 acres of land valued at $500,000 to his adult daughter effected a gift, even though the deed recited that he transferred the property to her "in consideration for $500." The Supreme Court reasoned that, in light of all of the circumstances, the $500 paid by the daughter to her father was "nominal and immaterial," and it was "clearly" the father's intent to "donate the land to his daughter and not to sell it to her."

Ultimately, what controls are the motives manifested by the parties. If the parties are motivated by a desire to buy and sell the property through a commercial transaction, there is a transfer by contract. But if the parties are motivated by a desire to deliver and accept the property through a non-commercial transaction, there is a gift.

Attacking the District Court's determination that the deed by which Collins transferred the property in question reflected a gift rather than a transfer by contract, Lincoln claims that the deed impliedly recited Collins' "offer" to transfer the property and his "acceptance" of the offer, and expressly recited the "consideration" -- his "promise to use his best efforts to maintain the property in an ecologically sustainable manner." The "burden" of a promise to "use best efforts" is hard to quantify. But we have little doubt that it is adequate. Because that is so, such a promise could surely support a transfer by contract. But the fundamental question is whether there was in fact a transfer by contract rather than a gift. The answer is no. From all that appears, Collins and Lincoln were not motivated by a desire to buy and sell the property through a commercial transaction, but instead by a desire to deliver and accept the property through a non-commercial transaction. Collins was Lincoln's mother, and he was her son. Each was the other's only living relative, and each was an environmentalist. As the Supreme Court concluded in *Salmon*, so do we conclude here: In light of all of the circumstances, Lincoln's "promise" to Collins "to use his best efforts to maintain the property in an ecologically sustainable manner" was nominal and immaterial, and it was clearly Collins' intent to donate the property to him and not to sell it.

Affirmed.

HOLT v. JONES

Columbia Supreme Court (1994)

Almost one hundred years ago, Ralph Polk created the Polk Trust by giving the Trustees of the University of Columbia a parcel of 10 acres in Silveyville, as a campus for the then newly-founded College of Physicians and Surgeons, and a sum of $5 million for the upkeep of the grounds. The Trustees of the University of Columbia are ex officio trustees of the Polk Trust.

Plaintiffs are three trustees of the University of Columbia and the Polk Trust. Defendants are the seven remaining trustees and the Attorney General of the State of Columbia.

Plaintiffs filed a complaint in the District Court. They alleged that defendant trustees had wrongfully diverted assets of the Polk Trust and sought an injunction to prohibit further wrongful diversion.

The Attorney General filed an answer to the complaint, denying plaintiffs' allegation for want of information and belief. In her answer, the Attorney General stated: "The Attorney General has reviewed the management of the Polk Trust and has determined that suit is not warranted."

Defendant trustees moved to dismiss the action on the ground that plaintiffs did not have standing to sue. The District Court granted the motion and entered judgment accordingly. The Court of Appeals affirmed. We granted certiorari.

The sole issue -- which is a question of first impression in Columbia -- is whether plaintiffs, as minority trustees of the Polk Trust, have standing to sue.

In accordance with the common law, all jurisdictions recognize that the Attorney General has standing to sue to enforce provisions of non-private trusts. At the same time, a substantial majority of jurisdictions have adopted the position that the Attorney General's standing is not exclusive. These jurisdictions accord standing to any person with a special interest.

The common law recognizes the problem of providing adequate enforcement of provisions of non-private trusts.

The primary type of non-private trust is the so-called charitable trust. A charitable trust is created, as a matter of fact, whenever a settlor manifests an intent to give property, in trust, for a charitable purpose and actually gives the property, in trust, for such purpose. A charitable trust is also created, as a matter of law, whenever a person gives property to an educational, philanthropic, healthcare, or similar institution for an education, philanthropy, healthcare, or similar purpose.

Since there is usually no one who is willing to assume the burdens of suing to enforce the provisions of a non-private trust, the Attorney General has been accorded standing. But, in light of limited resources, the Attorney General cannot reasonably assume the burdens of suing to enforce the provisions of all non-private trusts.

The present case is representative. In her answer, the Attorney General stated that she had determined that suit was not warranted. But she also admitted that she had no information or belief as to plaintiffs' allegation that defendant trustees had wrongfully diverted property of the Polk Trust.

Although the Attorney General has primary responsibility for the enforcement of provisions of non-private trusts, the need for adequate enforcement is not wholly fulfilled by the authority given to him or her. There is no rule or policy against supplementing the Attorney General's standing by allowing standing to persons with a special interest, i.e., persons who are trustees or beneficiaries or would otherwise have an ownership interest in the property.

For this reason, we join the substantial majority of jurisdictions that have adopted the position that the Attorney General's standing is not exclusive. We hold that any person with a special interest has standing to sue to enforce provisions of the trust.

The trustees of a non-private trust, as trustees, have a special interest in the trust. The trustees are also in the best position to learn about breaches of trust and to bring the relevant facts to a court's attention.

Therefore, we conclude that plaintiffs, as trustees of the Polk Trust, have standing to sue to enforce its provisions.

Reversed and remanded.

Practice California Performance Test:
Step-by-Step Demonstration 3

Meaney v. Trustees of the University of Columbia (Feb. 2018)

[Roadmap modeled on scratch paper.]

Step 1.	Scan the instructions, the file table of contents, and the library table of contents (1 minute)

Instructions

You should have already thoroughly read the instruction page once. When completing a practice PT, or on exam day, examine the instructions for three important details: the jurisdiction (usually in paragraph two), the contents of the packet (usually in paragraph three), and any specific weighting information, which, if supplied, would be noted at the bottom of the document. Take a second to skim the rest of the document to ensure no changes were made to the standard instructions.

Meaney Instructions

1. The problem is set in the State of Columbia.
2. The packet contains a file and library.
3. No special weighting information is supplied. The instructions look like the standard instructions.

Client File Table of Contents

Try to get a general feel for what the case is about, how many pages of facts are included, and the type of documents you will be working with.

Meaney File Table of Contents

Since the case name is <u>Meaney v. Trustees of the University of Columbia</u>, we know this is a civil case, rather than a criminal case. The case file contains only two documents.

*   The first file document is a memorandum from Melissa Saphir, so she must be our boss.
*   The second document is an "Agreement," so a good guess it that the case involves a dispute about this agreement.

Library Table of Contents

When looking at the library table of contents, try to expand your general feel for what the case is about and to determine the type of law involved. Make note of whether you have statutes and/or cases and how many of each. You will also want to note the court the cases come from, to begin forming a picture of the type of task you face as well as whether the cases are binding or merely persuasive authority.

Meaney Library Table of Contents

The library table of contents lists three cases, including one from the Columbia Supreme Court, our jurisdiction. The other two are from the Columbia Court of Appeals.

MEANEY v. TRUSTEES OF THE UNIVERSITY OF COLUMBIA

INSTRUCTIONS

1.   This performance test is designed to evaluate your ability to handle a select number of legal authorities in the context of a factual problem involving a client.

2.   The problem is set in the <u>fictional State of Columbia</u>, one of the United States.

3.   You will have two sets of materials with which to work: <u>a File and a Library</u>.

4.   The File contains factual materials about your case. The first document is a memorandum containing the instructions for the tasks you are to complete.

5.   The Library contains the legal authorities needed to complete the tasks. The case reports may be real, modified, or written solely for the purpose of this performance test. If the cases appear familiar to you, do not assume that they are precisely the same as you have read before. Read each thoroughly, as if it were new to you. You should assume that cases were decided in the jurisdictions and on the dates shown. In citing cases from the Library, you may use abbreviations and omit page citations.

6.   You should concentrate on the materials provided, but you should also bring to bear on the problem your general knowledge of the law. What you have learned in law school and elsewhere provides the general background for analyzing the problem; the File and Library provide the specific materials with which you must work.

7.   This performance test is designed to be completed in 90 minutes. Although there are no parameters on how to apportion that 90 minutes, you should allow yourself sufficient time to thoroughly review the materials and organize your planned response. Since the time allotted for this session of the examination includes two (2) essay questions in addition to this performance test, time management is essential.

8.   Your response will be graded on its compliance with instructions and on its content, thoroughness, and organization.

MEANEY v. TRUSTEES OF THE UNIVERSITY OF COLUMBIA

Instructions ....

FILE

This is the task memo from our boss.

Memorandum to Applicant from Melissa Saphir...

Agreement ....

MEANEY v. TRUSTEES OF THE UNIVERSITY OF COLUMBIA

LIBRARY

Behrens Research Foundation v. Fairview Memorial Hospital
Columbia Court of Appeals (2008)..

Collins v. Lincoln
Columbia Court of Appeals (2009) ....

Holt v. Jones
Columbia Supreme Court (1994) ....

All cases are in our jurisdiction.

Step 2. **Read the task memo (and format memo, if provided, and identify the macrostructure for your answer) (5–7 minutes)**

Task Memo

This is the most important document in the packet so slow down and read it very carefully. Follow all directions exactly. If the task memo refers to another document as a source of important information, read that document carefully, too. Your goal is to identify three key pieces of information:

1. Information about your client: Who is your client? What is your client's legal issue? What is your client's goal?
2. Specific information about the task: What is the task? Who is the audience? Has more than one task been assigned? Are there directions about things to include and exclude?
3. The macrostructure of your answer: Can you start your roadmap?

Meaney Task Memo

- **Client info:** The Trustees of the University of Columbia are our clients. We've been hired to defend them in a breach of contract action brought by Meaney, stepson of the late Edward Kemper, who once had transferred a garden to the Trustees. Their goal is to sell the garden without interference from Meaney.
- **Task info:** We are preparing an objective memorandum assessing whether Edward transferred the garden to the Trustees by contract or gift, and, if by gift, the type of gift. Our tone will be objective and lean toward formal, since our audience is our boss, a lawyer. Note that two paragraphs in the task memo provide facts about the case. Only one task is assigned. We have been instructed that our boss is handling the standing issue and not to include a separate statement of facts, but to use the facts in the analysis.
- **Task structure:** Our brief will have two main sections. These will address the following questions:

  1. Did Edward transfer the garden by way of contract or gift?
  2. If by way of gift, what kind of gift was it?

  No format memo is provided, so we will use common sense to craft headings. This material provides enough information to start our roadmap.

FOGEL & DAVIS, LLP

One Walton Avenue

Belleville, Columbia

MEMORANDUM

TO: Applicant

FROM: Melissa Saphir

DATE: February 27, 2018 — Our client

RE: Meaney v. Trustees of the University of Columbia
              π   Δ

We have been retained by the Trustees of the University of Columbia to **defend** them in a breach of contract action.

The late Edward Kemper (Edward) was a wealthy businessman and a generous donor to the University. Pursuant to an agreement, Edward transferred a garden to the Trustees, which the Trustees agreed to retain in perpetuity as the "Kemper Scottish Garden." Sometime later, Edward married Sarah Meaney (Sarah). Before her death two years ago, Sarah had grown quite fond of the Kemper Scottish Garden -- so much so that it came to be known as "Sarah's Scottish Garden." Notwithstanding the agreement, the Trustees recently made the difficult decision to sell the garden so as to use the proceeds for pressing educational purposes. | Case Facts

The plaintiff in the breach of contract action I referred to is Brendan Meaney. Meaney is the only child of Sarah by a prior marriage. By his action, Meaney is seeking to prevent the Trustees from selling the garden. | Case Facts

I believe that we may be able to persuade the court to dismiss Meaney's breach of contract action on the ground that Meaney lacks standing. To confirm my belief, I need to determine whether Edward transferred the garden to the Trustees by way of contract or gift and, **if** by way of gift, by way of what kind of gift.

To that end, please prepare an **<u>objective memorandum</u>** assessing whether Edward did indeed transfer the garden to the Trustees by way <u>of contract or gift</u>①and, if by way of ②<u>gift, by way of what kind of gift</u>. <u>Do not include a statement of facts, but use the facts in your analysis.</u>

| Step 3. | **Start roadmap (time included in steps 2–7)** |

Roadmap

Having a well-planned roadmap is the key to writing a passing performance test. We can start our roadmap using the macrostructure from the task memo, adding to it as we gather more information. We recommend that you make a note at the top of the roadmap listing all essential information, including the client and opposing party, the client's goal, task specifics concerning included or excluded parts, the tone and vocabulary, any task weighting, and a time goal for when you want to start writing your answer. Since we have two sections, it is recommended that you roadmap each on a separate piece of paper.

> ***Important note:*** When roadmapping for your own use on paper, the result is unlikely to be as thorough or neat as this example. Liberally use abbreviations and symbols to remind yourself where in the file you can find the information you need to use in each section. When roadmapping on the computer, type the rules you know you will use directly into the appropriate section after briefing, but still create a skeleton roadmap on paper setting out the macrostructure. Only write as much as you need to guide you in properly drafting your answer.

Meaney Roadmap

From the task memo we know all the key task information. We also know our argument will be broken up into two sections addressing these questions:

1. Was the garden transferred by *contract or gift*?
2. If by way of gift, *what kind of gift*?

From the task memo, we are unable to determine what, if any, subsections will be appropriate. In the fourth paragraph, our boss mentions that she wants to persuade the court to dismiss Meaney's case for lack of standing. Further, she wants the information from this memorandum to confirm her belief that Meaney lacks standing. Despite this extra information, we want to clearly focus on the task assigned, which concerns the merits of the underlying case (contract or type of gift); the standing issue was not assigned. See the attached roadmap containing the important information we have available so far.

Meaney Roadmap

π Δ Meaney v. Trustees	Start writing at _____
Client: Trustees Issue: Garden by contract or gift Goal: Sell garden w/out interference	Task: Memorandum Audience: Lawyer-boss/objective Exclude: Statement of facts

1. Garden transferred by contract or gift?

2. If by gift, what kind of gift?

Step 4.	**Skim the client file/facts (2 minutes)**

Skim the Client File/Facts

We don't yet know the applicable law, so we won't yet be able to identify the legally significant facts. Skimming the facts gives us enough of the big picture story to satisfy our curiosity and provides clues about the materials we have to work with once we do identify the applicable law from the library.

Meaney Client File Skim
Below is our quick takeaway from a skim of the facts:

- **From the task memo:** We have already read the two paragraphs of case facts that were included in the task memo. That information indicates that Edward was a generous donor. He gave the garden, which was to remain in perpetuity as the "Kemper Scottish Garden." Edward's wife liked the garden so much that it became known as "Sarah's Scottish Garden." The trustees want to sell it for pressing educational purposes. Sarah's son, Edward's stepson, seeks to prevent the Trustees from selling the garden.
- **From the Agreement:** Some of the language, such as using the word "consideration," gives the appearance of a contract. Kemper promised to acquire and transfer the parcel, and the Trustees promised to name the garden the "Kemper Scottish Garden," to use it for educational purposes, and to retain it in perpetuity. Further, Kemper retained the right to modify the terms of the Agreement.
- **Our assessment from the skim of the facts:** Since so few facts are available, we read, rather than skim them. Most performance tests provide more facts to work with.

FOGEL & DAVIS, LLP

One Walton Avenue

Belleville, Columbia

MEMORANDUM

TO: Applicant

FROM: Melissa Saphir

DATE: February 27, 2018   ┌─────────────┐
                                                                             │ Our client │
                                                                             └─────────────┘
RE: Meaney v. Trustees of the University of Columbia
                    π   Δ

We have been retained by the <u>Trustees</u> of the University of Columbia to **defend** them in a <u>breach of contract</u> action.

The late Edward Kemper (Edward) was a <u>wealthy businessman</u> and a <u>generous donor</u> to the University.   Pursuant to an <u>agreement</u>, Edward transferred a garden to the Trustees, which the Trustees <u>agreed to retain in perpetuity</u> as the "<u>Kemper Scottish Garden</u>."   Sometime later, Edward married <u>Sarah Meaney</u> (Sarah). Before her death two years ago, Sarah had grown quite fond of the Kemper Scottish Garden -- so much so that it came to be known as "<u>Sarah's Scottish Garden</u>."   Notwithstanding the agreement, the Trustees recently made the difficult decision to <u>sell the garden</u> so as to use the <u>proceeds for pressing educational purposes.</u>   ┌────────────┐ │ Case Facts │ └────────────┘

The plaintiff in the breach of contract action I referred to is Brendan Meaney. Meaney is the <u>only child</u> of Sarah by a prior marriage. By his action, Meaney is seeking to <u>prevent the Trustees from selling</u> the garden.   ┌────────────┐ │ Case Facts │ └────────────┘

I believe that we may be able to <u>persuade</u> the court to <u>dismiss</u> Meaney's breach of contract action on the ground that Meaney lacks <u>standing</u>. To confirm my belief, I need to determine whether Edward transferred the garden to the Trustees by way of <u>contract or gift</u> and, **if** by way of <u>gift</u>, by way of <u>what kind</u> of gift.

To that end, please prepare an **objective memorandum** assessing whether Edward did indeed transfer the garden to the Trustees by way of contract or gift ① and, if by way of gift, by way of what kind of gift. ② Do not include a statement of facts, but use the facts in your analysis.

AGREEMENT

The Trustees of the University of Columbia (hereinafter "the Trustees") desire to <u>obtain a garden parcel</u> of real property now owned and occupied by Emily Gordon, located in Belleville, Columbia, commonly known as 625 Sierra Way.

Edward <u>Kemper</u> (hereinafter "Kemper") desires to facilitate such acquisition by <u>acquiring the garden parcel</u> and by <u>transferring it to the Trustees</u>, subject to <u>certain restrictions</u> as provided for herein.

Therefore, **in consideration** of the foregoing, the Trustees and Kemper do hereby agree as follows:

1.   Kemper will <u>acquire the garden parcel and transfer</u> it to the Trustees.

2.   The Trustees will cause the garden parcel to bear the name <u>"Kemper Scottish Garden,"</u> use it for <u>educational purposes</u>, and retain it in perpetuity.

Kemper <u>retains the right to modify</u> the terms of this Agreement as necessary and appropriate to its purpose.

Dated: December 18, 1964.

_____*Edward Kemper*_____
Edward Kemper

___   *Harold Williamson*_____
Harold Williamson

Chairman of the Board of Trustees

| Step 5. | **Actively read the library and synthesize rules (15–20 minutes)** |

Read the Library and Deconstruct and Synthesize Rules as Needed

We are looking for the rules we can use to solve the problem posed, and any analysis we can borrow from the cases. Depending on the task, we may need to synthesize cases or identify which rule among competing rules should be adopted. To most efficiently assess the library, read the materials in the order presented, since most often the rules are provided in the same order that they can be used to solve the problem, given the task macrostructure. Book brief the cases and add information to the roadmap as you go. Annotate your cases with notes so you don't waste time rewriting sentences into your roadmap. Determine how to best use any statutes. Each case in the library was included because it is likely to be needed to solve the problem, so it is up to you to determine how each can best be used. We typically note at the top of each case where it will be used in our answer and whether it is favorable or not for our client by writing a plus or minus sign on the top. Continue to look for clues as to how you should structure your answer.

Meaney Cases
The three cases occupy eight pages, and, given the lack of facts, this PT will be law heavy. This is an objective task, so we are looking for the controlling law and analysis to assess how this case would turn out. As well as looking for the law and analysis that bolsters our client's side, we are looking for law and analysis that bolsters our opponents' argument.

- **Case 1: Behrens.** This case provides rules about types of gifts, which can be absolute or conditional. This case may hurt our case since it makes it clear that, while a gift is presumed absolute, if it appears otherwise and the donor has retained the power to modify or enforce, it will be a conditional gift, as is likely the case for Trustees. The court holds that donors of absolute gifts do not have standing to sue since they did not reserve a right of enforcement. This case goes in section two.
- **Case 2: Collins:** This case explains the difference between a contract and a gift and goes in section one. We will want to use the two cases within the case to make factual analogies. Citing Behrens, the court explains that naming rights or promises to use a building for a certain purpose, while giving the appearance of bargaining and conferring a benefit and burden, does not preclude the finding of a gift. This may help us. Citing Salmon, the court found that citing the word "consideration" was not determinative. Rather, the court looks to the donor/seller's intent. This finding also helps us, since our agreement cited the word "consideration." In Collins, the court found a mom gifted a vineyard to her son when in consideration for the transfer he promised to use his "best efforts" to ecologically sustain the property.
- **Case 3: Holt.** The issue in this case is who has standing to sue on behalf of a trust, and it finds that those with a "special interest," such as trustees or beneficiaries (who would otherwise have an interest in the property), may sue. This is interesting, since standing was mentioned in the task memo as an issue reserved for our boss, and we haven't been assigned the standing issue. The case also defines a charitable trust, which we can use in our second section when we determine the type of gift.

BEHRENS RESEARCH FOUNDATION v.

FAIRVIEW MEMORIAL HOSPITAL

Columbia Court of Appeals (2008)

> Point 2:
> Type of gift

Behrens Research Foundation (Behrens), a non-profit public benefit corporation, gave Fairview Memorial Hospital (Fairview), a healthcare institution, a gift of $1 million. Fairview had a well-recognized Department of Cardiothoracic Surgery. Behrens had had a longstanding interest in advancing cardiothoracic surgery. Not long thereafter, as a result of various unforeseen changes, including departures of key staff, Fairview closed the department.

> Case Facts

Behrens brought the underlying action in the District Court seeking an injunction directing Fairview either to reopen its Department of Cardiothoracic Surgery or to return Behrens' $1 million gift. Fairview moved to dismiss the action under Columbia Rule of Civil Procedure 12(b)(6), claiming that Behrens did not have standing to sue. The District Court granted the motion and entered a judgment of dismissal.

> Case Facts

On appeal, Behrens contends that it did indeed have standing to sue.

We disagree.

It is well settled in Columbia that a donor is the master of his or her gift.

> Rule

Because that is so, a donor can make a gift that is *absolute*. The donor can give property *unconditionally*, without (1) restricting use or disposition of the property, (2) retaining power to modify the gift, or (3) reserving a right to sue to enforce a restriction or to undo the gift in case of a restriction's breach by causing the property to revert to the donor him- or herself or to a third person. When a gift is absolute, the donor has relinquished, and the donee has assumed, full dominion

> Gift

> Rule:
> Absolute gift

> Rule

over the property -- i.e., the ability to use or dispose of the property at any time, in any manner, and for any purpose.

But a donor can also make a gift that is *not absolute.* The donor can give property *conditionally*, (1) restricting use or disposition, (2) retaining power of modification, and/or (3) reserving a right of enforcement or reversion. When a gift is not absolute, the donor has not relinquished, and the donee has not assumed, full dominion over the property; rather, both donor and donee share power over the property's use or disposition.

Conditional gift

Although a donor is indeed master of his or her gift, the law presumes that a gift is *absolute* unless it clearly appears otherwise. In line with this presumption, the law further presumes that a donor has *not* restricted use or disposition, has *not* retained power of modification, and has *not* reserved a right of enforcement or reversion, unless it clearly appears otherwise.

Rule

Rule

These presumptions prove fatal to Behrens' position. The record on appeal contains the instrument by which Behrens made its $1 million gift to Fairview. In pertinent part, the instrument recites only that Behrens "hereby delivers" and Fairview "hereby accepts" the gift. Neither expressly, nor by implication, does the instrument evidence any reservation on Behrens' part of a right of enforcement. Behrens did not reserve any such right for itself. We cannot make up for its omission.

Holding

Absolute gift, so, no standing to sue hospital.

Affirmed.

Must distinguish: Edward reserved rights, so conditional gift.

Mom	Son

COLLINS v. LINCOLN

Columbia Court of Appeals (2009)

Point 1:
Difference between
contract and gift

Anita Collins brought an action for declaratory relief in the District Court against Stephen Lincoln, her adult son. In order to resolve various tax questions now pending before the State of Columbia Tax Board, Collins seeks a determination that the <u>instrument</u> by which she <u>transferred certain property to Lincoln</u> reflected a <u>gift</u> rather than a transfer by contract. Following a bench trial, the District Court entered judgment in <u>Collins' favor</u>, issuing the determination that she had sought. Lincoln appeals. We affirm.

The facts are undisputed: By deed <u>dated</u> June 26, 2002, Collins transferred to Lincoln a <u>260-acre vineyard</u> in Parker County including a 20,000-square-foot Victorian main residence, guest house, pool, tennis courts, sports field, exercise studio, lake, olive orchard, and a stone winery with a tasting room and a permit to produce 5,500 cases of wine a year. The deed recited that Collins transferred the property to Lincoln <u>"in consideration</u> for his <u>promise to use his best efforts to maintain the property</u> in an <u>ecologically sustainable manner</u>." As of the date in question, the assessed value of the property was more than $35 million. Collins was then 65 years old, a widow, and the Chair of the Board of Directors of the Parker County Rural Conservancy, a locally-prominent environmental organization; Lincoln was 30 years old, unmarried, and the Rural Conservancy's Volunteer Coordinator; each was the other's sole living relative.

Case Facts

Property may be passed <u>by gift</u>. The elements of a gift consist of: (1) <u>intent</u> on the part of the donor to make a gift; (2) <u>delivery</u>, either actual or constructive, <u>of property</u> by the donor; (3) <u>acceptance</u> of the property by the donee; and (4) <u>lack of consideration</u> for the gift.

Rule:
Gift Definiton

Property may also be passed by transfer by <u>contract</u>. The elements of a transfer by contract consist of: (1) <u>an offer to buy or sell</u>; (2) <u>acceptance</u> of the offer; and (3) <u>consideration</u> passing between the buyer and seller.

Rule: Contract

Gifts and transfers by contracts have two similar elements. First, a gift requires <u>delivery</u> by the donor and a transfer by contract requires <u>offer</u> by the buyer or seller. Second, a gift requires <u>acceptance</u> by the donee and a transfer by contract requires <u>acceptance</u> by the seller or buyer.

How similar

But <u>one element</u> is different. While a transfer by contract requires the *presence* of consideration, <u>a gift requires the *absence* of consideration</u>. In other words, without consideration, the passing of property is by gift, whereas with consideration, it is by transfer by contract.

Difference between gift and contract

Consideration has two requirements. The promisee must <u>bargain with the promisor</u> and must confer, or agree to confer, a <u>benefit</u> or must suffer, or <u>agree to suffer, a burden</u>.

Rule: Consideration

The <u>absence of consideration is clear when a gift is absolute</u>. *See, Behrens* Research Foundation v. Fairview Memorial Hospital (Colum. Ct. App. 2008). In that instance, the donee does not bargain with the donor or confer, or agree to confer, any benefit. Neither does the donee bargain with the donor or suffer, or agree to suffer, any burden. Instead, the donor simply delivers the property and the donee simply accepts it.

Rule: Apply Behrens

But the <u>absence of consideration is not clear when a gift is not absolute</u>. *See, Behrens Research Foundation.* In that instance, the donee could be said to bargain with the donor, and could be said to confer, or agree to confer, a "benefit" on the donor or to suffer, or agree to suffer, a "burden." Consider the situation in which a university <u>agrees</u> to name a campus building in a donor's honor or to use the building for a specified purpose. The university could be said to "bargain" with the donor -- <u>negotiating</u> the <u>terms for the naming</u> of the building or its use for the specified purpose -- and <u>to confer</u>, or agree to confer, a benefit or to suffer, or agree to suffer, a burden -- the naming of the building or its use for the specified purpose. Such a "bargain" and "benefit" and "burden" do not preclude a gift.

Factual example: Can be gift even with bargain benefit

The presence or absence of consideration does not turn on the presence or absence of the term <u>"consideration"</u> in the instrument. For example, in *Salmon v. Wilson* (Colum. Supreme Ct. 1971), the Supreme Court held that a <u>deed</u> by which a father transferred 10 acres of land valued at $500,000 to his adult daughter effected a gift, even though the deed recited that he transferred the property to her "in <u>consideration for $500</u>." The Supreme Court reasoned that, in light of all of the circumstances, the $500 paid by the daughter to her father was "<u>nominal and immaterial,</u>" and it was "clearly" the father's intent to "donate the land to his daughter and not to sell it to her."

Factual example: Even with $500 consideration

Ultimately, what controls are the <u>motives manifested</u> by the parties. <u>If the parties are motivated</u> by a <u>desire to buy and sell the property through</u> a commercial transaction, there is a transfer by contract. But if the parties are <u>motivated by a desire to deliver</u> and accept the property through a non-commercial transaction, <u>there is a gift.</u>

Rule

Attacking the District Court's determination that the deed by which Collins transferred the property in question reflected a gift rather than a transfer by contract, Lincoln claims that the deed impliedly recited Collins' "offer" to transfer the property and his "acceptance" of the offer, and expressly recited the "consideration" -- his "promise to use his best efforts to maintain the property in an ecologically sustainable manner." <u>The "burden" of a promise to "use best efforts" is hard to quantify.</u> But we <u>have little doubt that it is adequate.</u> Because that is so, <u>such a promise could surely support a transfer</u> by contract. But the fundamental question is whether there was in fact a transfer by contract rather than a gift. The answer is no. From all that appears, Collins and Lincoln were

Vague OK

not motivated by a desire to buy and sell the property through a commercial transaction, but instead by a desire to deliver and accept the property through a non-commercial transaction. Collins was Lincoln's mother, and he was her son. Each was the other's only living relative, and each was an environmentalist. As the Supreme Court concluded in *Salmon*, so do we conclude here: In light of all of the circumstances, Lincoln's "promise" to Collins "to use his best efforts to maintain the property in an ecologically sustainable manner" was nominal and immaterial, and it was clearly Collins' intent to donate the property to him and not to sell it.

Affirmed.

Case holding

Case facts

HOLT v. JONES

Columbia Supreme Court (1994)

Almost one hundred years ago, Ralph Polk created the Polk Trust by giving the Trustees of the University of Columbia a parcel of 10 acres in Silveyville, as a campus for the then newly-founded College of Physicians and Surgeons, and a sum of $5 million for the upkeep of the grounds. The Trustees of the University of Columbia are ex officio trustees of the Polk Trust.

Plaintiffs are three trustees of the University of Columbia and the Polk Trust. Defendants are the seven remaining trustees and the Attorney General of the State of Columbia.

Plaintiffs filed a complaint in the District Court.   They alleged that defendant trustees had wrongfully diverted assets of the Polk Trust and sought an injunction to prohibit further wrongful diversion.

The Attorney General filed an answer to the complaint, denying plaintiffs' allegation for want of information and belief. In her answer, the Attorney General stated: "The Attorney General has reviewed the management of the Polk Trust and has determined that suit is not warranted."

Defendant trustees moved to dismiss the action on the ground that plaintiffs did not have standing to sue. The District Court granted the motion and entered judgment accordingly. The Court of Appeals affirmed. We granted certiorari.

The sole issue -- which is a question of first impression in Columbia -- is whether plaintiffs, as minority trustees of the Polk Trust, have standing to sue.

In accordance with the common law, all jurisdictions recognize that the Attorney General has standing to sue to enforce provisions of non-private trusts.

At the same time, a substantial majority of jurisdictions have adopted the position that the Attorney General's standing is not exclusive. These jurisdictions <u>accord standing to any person with a special interest.</u>

The common law recognizes the problem of providing adequate enforcement of provisions of non-private trusts.

The <u>primary type of non-private trust is the so-called charitable trust.</u> <u>A charitable trust is created, as a matter of fact</u>, whenever a settlor <u>manifests an intent to give property</u>, in trust, for a charitable purpose and actually gives the property, in trust, for such purpose. <u>A charitable trust is also created, as a matter of law,</u> whenever a person gives property to an <u>educational</u>, philanthropic, healthcare, or similar institution for an education, philanthropy, healthcare, or similar purpose.

Since there is <u>usually no one who</u> is willing to assume the burdens of suing to enforce the provisions of a non-private trust, the <u>Attorney General has been</u> accorded standing. But, in light of limited resources, the Attorney General cannot reasonably assume the burdens of suing to enforce the provisions of all non-private trusts.

The present case is representative. In her answer, the Attorney General stated that she had determined that <u>suit was not warranted</u>. But she also admitted that she had <u>no information</u> or belief as to plaintiffs' allegation that defendant trustees had wrongfully diverted property of the Polk Trust.

Although the Attorney General has <u>primary responsibility</u> for the enforcement of provisions of non-private trusts, the need for adequate enforcement is not wholly fulfilled by the authority given to him or her. There is no <u>rule or policy</u> against supplementing the Attorney General's standing by allowing standing to persons <u>with a special interest</u>, i.e., persons <u>who are trustees or beneficiaries or would otherwise</u> have an ownership interest in the property.

For this reason, we join the substantial majority of jurisdictions that have adopted the position that the <u>Attorney General's standing is not exclusive</u>. We hold that <u>any person</u> with a <u>special interest has standing to sue to enforce provisions of</u> the trust.

Holding

Rule

The trustees of a non-private trust, as trustees, have a special interest in the trust. The <u>trustees are also in the best position to learn about breaches of trust</u> and to bring the relevant facts to a court's attention.

Therefore, we conclude that plaintiffs, as trustees of the Polk Trust, have <u>standing</u> to sue to enforce its provisions.

Reversed and remanded.

Meaney Roadmap

π Δ Meaney v. Trustees	Start writing at _____
Client: Trustees Issue: Garden by contract or gift Goal: Sell garden w/out interference	Task: Memorandum Audience: Lawyer-boss/objective Exclude: Statement of facts

1. Garden transferred by *contract or gift*?

   R: Gift = (1) intent of donor to gift, (2) delivery of property, (3) acceptance by donee, (4) no consideration. Collins

   R: Contract = (1) offer to buy or sell, (2) acceptance of offer, (3) consideration. Collins

   R: Difference = consideration. Collins

   R: Consideration requires (1) promisee must bargain w/ promisor, and (2) must confer a benefit or suffer a burden. Collins

   RE: Collins, citing Behrens
   - Donor delivers & donee accepts

   C: No consideration, absolute gift

   RE: Collins, citing example
   - Ex: Named building or specified purpose
   - Bargaining included
   - Confer benefit or suffer burden

   C: Conditional gift is still gift, not contract

   RE: Collins, citing Salmon
   - Father transfered land for $500
   - $500 nominal, immaterial
   - Word "consideration" not dispositive

   C: Intent to give, not sell

   R: Party motives control. Commercial transaction motivation = contract; Noncommercial transaction motivation = gift. Collins

   RE: Collins
   - "Best efforts" consideration?
   - But, mom > son; only relative
   - Both environmentalists

   C: Intent to donate, so gift

2. If by gift, *what kind of gift*?

   R: Donor of absolute gift did not have standing. Behrens

   R: Donor is the master of gift. Behrens

   R: Absolute gift, w/out (1) restricting use, (2) retain power to modify, or (3) reserve right to sue. Absolute = unconditional = donee gets full dominion. Behrens

   R: Non-absolute gift = conditional, (1) restricting use/disposition, (2) retain power to modify, (3) reserving right to enforce/reversion. Donee does not have full dominion. Behrens

   R: Gift presumed absolute, unless clearly appears otherwise. Behrens

RE: <u>Behrens</u>
- "deliver," "accepts"
- Instrument clear no reservation

C: Absolute gift

R: Person w/ special interest has standing to enforce charitable trust. <u>Holt</u>

R: Charitable trust created as matter of law when intent to give property in trust for educational, philanthropic, healthcare, etc. purpose. <u>Holt.</u>

| Step 6. | **Actively read the client file facts (10–15 minutes)** |

Client File/Case Facts

Now that we know from the library the rules governing this situation, we must look for legally significant facts to apply to the rules to solve the problem. We want to look for helpful facts, harmful facts, and any missing facts, if pertinent to the task assigned. Add the legally significant facts into your roadmap as you go.

Meaney Case Facts

We have already read the facts, since there were so few. Now, we will go back through them and strategically line them up with the legal arguments on our roadmap. Although it won't take long to reread our facts, we should spend some time thinking about them and not rush through them, possibly missing key arguments. When there are few facts to work with, it is important not to miss anything, since it will be a glaring omission. Remember, every fact may be here to be used, so we are actively looking for what we can do with the facts presented. We recall our task memo recited an atypical number of facts, so we start there. We remind ourselves this is an objective memorandum, so we are careful to look for arguments for both sides. After lining up the facts, we make some changes in the second part. We decide to reorder some of the law so that the presentation will flow better, and we break the second section into two logical subsections: (1) Absolute or conditional gift; and (2) Charitable trust. We add the subheadings to our roadmap.

We're almost ready to write, but we need to decide what, if anything, to do with the standing issue. We should be careful not to get too distracted by it, since it was not specifically assigned as an issue for us to resolve and thus is unlikely to be worth many points. In addition, we likely don't have enough facts or law to make a determination. We think about what would be the best way to handle this issue if this were a real-world assignment. Since the cases discussing standing come up in the second part of the memo, we decide to discuss it briefly in the concluding section. [Note: Both released passing answers handled this differently. Answer one stated in the introduction that it would not address the merits of the standing issue; answer two addressed it briefly in section two, right before the conclusion.]

FOGEL & DAVIS, LLP

One Walton Avenue

Belleville, Columbia

MEMORANDUM

TO: Applicant

FROM: Melissa Saphir

DATE: February 27, 2018

RE: Meaney v. Trustees of the University of Columbia

            π   Δ

> Our client

We have been retained by the <u>Trustees</u> of the University of Columbia to **defend** them in a <u>breach of contract</u> action.

> Case Facts

The late Edward Kemper (Edward) was a <u>wealthy businessman</u> and a <u>generous donor</u> to the University. Pursuant to an <u>agreement</u>, Edward transferred a garden to the Trustees, which the Trustees <u>agreed to retain in perpetuity</u> as the "<u>Kemper Scottish Garden.</u>" Sometime later, Edward married <u>Sarah Meaney</u> (Sarah). Before her death two years ago, Sarah had grown quite fond of the Kemper Scottish Garden -- so much so that it came to be known as "<u>Sarah's Scottish Garden.</u>" Notwithstanding the agreement, the Trustees recently made the difficult decision to <u>sell the garden</u> so as to use the <u>proceeds for pressing educational purposes.</u>

> Case Facts

The plaintiff in the breach of contract action I referred to is Brendan Meaney. Meaney is the <u>only child</u> of Sarah by a prior marriage. By his action, Meaney is seeking to <u>prevent the Trustees from selling</u> the garden.

I believe that we may be able to <u>persuade</u> the court to <u>dismiss</u> Meaney's breach of contract action on the ground that Meaney lacks <u>standing</u>. To confirm my belief, I need to determine whether Edward transferred the garden to the Trustees by way of <u>contract or gift</u> and, **if** by way of <u>gift</u>, by way of <u>what kind</u> of gift.

To that end, please prepare an **<u>objective memorandum</u>** assessing whether Edward did indeed transfer the garden to the Trustees by way <u>of contract or gift</u>①and, if by way of <u>gift, by way of what kind of gift</u>.② <u>Do not include a statement of facts, but use the facts in your analysis.</u>

AGREEMENT

The Trustees of the University of Columbia (hereinafter "the Trustees") desire to <u>obtain a garden parcel</u> of real property now owned and occupied by Emily Gordon, located in Belleville, Columbia, commonly known as 625 Sierra Way.

Edward <u>Kemper</u> (hereinafter "Kemper") desires to facilitate such acquisition by <u>acquiring the garden parcel</u> and by <u>transferring it to the Trustees</u>, subject to <u>certain restrictions</u> as provided for herein.

Therefore, **in consideration** of the foregoing, the Trustees and Kemper do hereby agree as follows:

1. Kemper will <u>acquire the garden parcel and transfer</u> it to the Trustees.
2. The Trustees will cause the garden parcel to bear the name <u>"Kemper Scottish Garden,"</u> use it for <u>educational purposes</u>, and retain it in perpetuity.

Kemper <u>retains the right to modify</u> the terms of this Agreement as necessary and appropriate to its purpose.

Dated: December 18, 1964.

_____*Edward Kemper*_____
Edward Kemper

___   *Harold Williamson*_____
Harold Williamson

Chairman of the Board of Trustees

Meaney Roadmap

<table>
<tr>
<td>

π   Δ
<u>Meaney v. Trustees</u>

Client: Trustees
Issue: Garden by contract or gift
Goal: Sell garden w/out interference

</td>
<td>

Start writing at _____

Task: Memorandum
Audience: Lawyer-boss/objective
Include: ?? Standing argument
Exclude: Statement of facts

</td>
</tr>
</table>

1. Garden transferred by *contract or gift*?

   R: Gift = (1) intent of donor to gift, (2) delivery of property, (3) acceptance by donee, (4) no consideration. <u>Collins</u>

   R: Contract = (1) offer to buy or sell, (2) acceptance of offer, (3) consideration. <u>Collins</u>

   R: Difference = consideration. <u>Collins</u>

   R: Consideration requires (1) promisee must bargain w/ promisor, and (2) must confer a benefit or suffer a burden. <u>Collins</u>

   RE: <u>Collins, citing Behrens</u>
   - Donor delivers & donee accepts
   C: No consideration, absolute gift
   A: <u>Meaney</u>
   - Not as clear here
   C: Not absolute gift

   RE: <u>Collins, citing example</u>
   - Ex: Named building or specified purpose
   - Bargaining included
   - Confer benefit or suffer burden
   C: Conditional gift is gift, not contract
   A: <u>Meaney</u>
   - "Kemper Scottish Garden"
   - Transfer subject to restrictions
   - Benefit = name, burden educational purpose
   C: Likely conditional gift

   RE: <u>Collins, citing Salmon</u>
   - Father transfer land for $500
   - $500 nominal, immaterial
   - Word "consideration" not dispositive
   C: Intent to give, not sell
   A: <u>Meaney</u>
   - No $, name right, educ. purpose
   - Name nominal since change to "Sarah's Scottish Garden"
   - "In consideration" not contract
   C: Intent to give, not sell

R: Party motives control. Commercial transaction motivation = contract; Noncommercial transaction motivation = gift. Collins

RE: Collins
- "Best efforts" consideration?
- But, mom > son; only relative
- Both environmentalists

C: Intent to donate, so gift

A: Meaney
- Name, "educational purposes"
- But, wealthy, generous donor

C: Motivation noncommercial

2. If by gift, *what kind of gift?*

   R: Donor is the master of gift. Behrens

   A. Conditional gift

   R: Absolute gift, w/out (1) restricting use, (2) retain power to modify, or (3) reserve right to sue. Absolute = unconditional = donee gets full dominion. Behrens

   RE: Behrens
   - "deliver," "accepts"
   - Instrument clear no reservation

   C: Absolute gift

   A: Meaney
   - Did restrict use
   - Retained power to modify

   C: Not absolute

   R: Non-absolute gift = conditional,
   - Restricting use/disposition,
   - Retain power to modify,
   - Reserving right to enforce/reversion.

   A: Meaney
   - Restrict to garden, educational
   - Retained power to modify
   - "Subject to" restrictions

   C: Likely conditional gift

   R: Donee does not have full dominion. Behrens
   R: Gift presumed absolute, unless clearly appears otherwise. Behrens

   B. Charitable trust

R: Charitable trust created as matter of law when intent to give property in trust for educational, philanthropic, healthcare, etc. purpose. <u>Holt.</u>

A: <u>Meaney</u>
  • Educational purpose

C: Possible charitable trust

Conclusion

<u>Standing</u>

R: Donor of absolute gift did not have standing. <u>Behrens</u>

R: Person w/ special interest has standing to enforce charitable trust. <u>Holt</u>

Step 7.   **Reread the task memo and refine your roadmap to solve the problem posed (5 minutes)**

Re-Read the Task Memo, See the Big Picture, and Solve the Problem

Before you start writing, always take a moment to ensure you are solving the problem posed and haven't gotten off track while going through the documents. Re-read the task memo to refocus on precisely what you've been asked to do. Make sure that you are clear on your client's goal, plan to use the appropriate tone and vocabulary in your response, and follow all directions in the task memo. Consider your presentation's organization to ensure your response is clear and easy to follow. Lastly, consider the complexity of the various sections and components of your answer to assess how you think the grader will allocate points and devise a plan to spend your time accordingly.

Meaney Big Picture

If we hadn't already decided what to do with the standing issue, we would figure that out now. If we hadn't already decided to break section two into two sections, this might be when we decide to do so. We consider breaking section one into subsections, but decide against it, since it doesn't contain a logical break and the concepts twirl together, although we may choose differently as we craft the answer. We also reread the task memo and take another look at the facts to make sure we didn't miss any key arguments. The memorandum is objective, so we will create objective headings to guide the reader. The memorandum has two main sections, and the first section seems likely to require more time, even though the second section will have two subsections.

Step 8.   **Write an answer that solves the problem posed (about 45 minutes)**

SAMPLE ANSWER FOR MEANEY

FOGEL & DAVIS, LLP
One Walton Avenue
Belleville, Columbia

MEMORANDUM

TO: Melissa Saphir
FROM: Applicant
DATE: February 27, 2018
RE: Meaney v. Trustees of the University of Columbia

I. INTRODUCTION

Pursuant to your request in the case referenced above, I have prepared an objective memorandum assessing whether Edward Kemper transferred the garden to the Trustees by way of contract or gift, and if by way of a gift, what kind of gift.

In sum, the transfer was most likely by gift instead of by contract, and the gift was likely not an absolute gift, but was rather a conditional gift or charitable trust.

II. ANALYSIS

A. The garden transfer was likely a gift rather than by contract because the parties were motivated to effectuate a noncommercial transaction.

Property may be passed by gift, or by transfer by contract. The elements of a gift consist of: (1) intent on the part of the donor to make a gift; (2) delivery, either actual or constructive, of property by the donor; (3) acceptance of the property by the donee; and (4) lack of consideration for the gift. Collins v. Lincoln. The elements of a transfer by contract consist of: (1) an offer to buy or sell; (2) acceptance of the offer; and (3) consideration passing between the buyer and seller. Collins. The difference between the two is consideration. While a transfer by contract requires the *presence* of consideration, a gift requires the *absence* of consideration. Collins. Consideration has two elements. The promisee must bargain with the promisor, and must confer, or agree to confer, a benefit or must suffer, or agree to suffer, a burden. Collins.

The absence of consideration is clear when a gift is absolute. Where a donor simply delivers property, and the donee simply accepts the property, there is no bargaining or benefit or burden and the gift is absolute. Collins, citing Behrens. The absence of consideration is not clear when a gift is not absolute. The Collins court cited an example where a university might agree to name a campus building in the donor's honor or use the building for a specified purpose. While it appears the university "bargained" with the donor for the naming rights and specified purpose, and conferred a "benefit" or "burden," this type of bargain, benefit and burden do not preclude finding the transfer was a gift. Collins.

Similarly, while the Kemper agreement has the appearance of a contract and specifies some restrictions, it will not preclude a finding that the transfer was a gift. The agreement specifies the garden will be called the "Kemper Scottish Garden" and indicates the garden will be used for educational purposes and be retained in perpetuity. Meaney can argue the naming rights were bargained for, and that the Trustees agreeing to the educational use imposes a burden. However, as explained in Collins, these are not the types of benefits or burdens that preclude the finding of a gift.

Further, the presence or absence of consideration does not turn on the presence or absence of the word "consideration" in the instrument. <u>Collins</u>. For example, the Supreme Court held a deed by which a father transferred 10 acres of land valued at $500,000 to his daughter was a gift, even though the deed recited the transfer was "in consideration for $500." <u>Collins, citing Salmon</u>. Under the circumstances, despite the language of contract used, the court found the $500 paid was "nominal and immaterial," and that it was clearly the father's intent to donate, rather than sell the land to his daughter. <u>Collins, citing Salmon.</u>

Here, the instrument used to transfer the garden also recites classic words of contract, such as "consideration," but that is similarly not dispositive. In our case, no money was exchanged. Rather, the instrument recites naming rights, and that the garden be used for educational purposes, in perpetuity. However, similar to the "consideration" in <u>Salmon</u>, the naming rights here were probably "nominal and immaterial" to the agreement, as evidenced that for several years the garden name came to be known as "Sarah's Scottish Garden" and there were no complaints. Had the name been material, it is likely Kemper, or Sarah, or Meaney would have sued earlier.

Ultimately, the parties' motives control. If the parties are motivated by a desire to buy and sell property through a commercial transaction, there is a transfer by contract. But if the parties are motivated by a desire to deliver and accept transfer through a noncommercial transaction, there is a gift. <u>Collins</u>. In <u>Collins</u>, the court found that while a promise to "use best efforts to maintain property in an ecologically sustainable manner" could theoretically be sufficient consideration to support a transfer by contract, it did not reach such a result in that case where the transfer was otherwise from a mother to her son of a property valued at $35 million. The court found the mother's intent was to donate the land, rather than sell it, despite the recitation of consideration regarding maintaining the property ecologically.

It is likely the court would come to a similar conclusion in our case. Kemper was a generous and wealthy donor to the university. Nothing suggests there was a commercial motive for this transfer. While the instrument specifies the "consideration" of the garden name and its educational use, Kemper's intent appears to be to gift the garden, rather than sell it to the university for the named "consideration."

Ultimately, the determination turns on Kemper's motives. This agreement does not appear to represent a commercially motivated transaction. Consequently, it is most likely the transfer was a gift.

B. There are several categories of gifts.

A donor is the master of his or her gift. <u>Behrens v. Fairview.</u> A gift can be absolute, conditional, or take the form of a charitable trust.

1. The garden transfer was likely a conditional gift, rather than absolute gift, because Kemper restricted use and retained power to modify the agreement.

A donor can make an absolute gift, where the property is given "*unconditionally*, without (1) restricting use or disposition of the property, (2) retaining power to modify the gift, or (3) reserving a right to sue to enforce a restriction or to undo the gift in case of a restriction's breach by causing property to revert to the donor. . . ." <u>Behrens</u>. Where a donor simply delivers property, and the donee simply accepts the property, there is no bargaining or benefit or burden and the gift is absolute. <u>Collins, citing Behrens</u>. In our case, the transfer was not as simple, since Kemper placed conditions on the garden gift regarding its name and use, so the garden will not be deemed an absolute gift.

But, a donor can make a gift that is not absolute and give the property *conditionally*, (1) restricting use or disposition, (2) retaining power of modification, or, (3) reserving a right of enforcement or reversion. <u>Behrens</u>. The law presumes a gift is absolute, unless it clearly states otherwise. <u>Behrens</u>. However, here in the instrument itself Kemper explicitly

> With so few facts, this was an important argument.

> We opted to address case facts very briefly to save time.

> Use the facts available to demonstrate a noncommercial motivation.

> We originally wrote some of this in section A, but realized it worked better here and moved it.

restricted the use of the garden to use for an educational purpose, and specifically retained "the right to modify the terms of this Agreement as necessary to its purpose." This clearly demonstrates that the gift here was conditional, and thus it is unlikely a court would find it absolute.

2. The garden transfer may have created a charitable trust.

Another type of gift is a charitable trust. A charitable trust is created, as a matter of fact, whenever a settlor manifests an intent to give property, in trust, for a charitable purpose and actually gives the property, in trust, for such purpose. Holt v. Jones. Kemper had such a charitable intent and gave the garden for such a purpose, which appears to create a charitable trust as a matter of fact. A charitable trust is also created, as a matter of law, whenever a person gives a property to an educational, philanthropic, healthcare, or similar institution for an educational, philanthropy, healthcare or similar purpose. Holt. Here, Kemper acquired and transferred the garden to the university explicitly for an educational purpose, so it would fall squarely under the definition of a charitable trust created as a matter of law. While the instrument did not create a charitable trust on its face, the gift may satisfy the requirements for a charitable trust, as outlined above.

> We weren't certain this would be a charitable trust, so we hedged.

III. CONCLUSION

Kemper likely transferred the garden to the university by means of a gift, rather than by contract, since his motivation appeared to be noncommercial. Since Kemper restricted property use, and retained modification rights, the gift will likely be deemed a conditional gift, rather than an absolute gift. It is also possible the gift will be found to have created a charitable trust, which has implications for the standing argument. While the standing issue was not assigned in the memo, it is worth noting that should the gift be considered a charitable trust, and only persons with a "special interest" have standing to sue. Holt. Further, donors of absolute gifts do not have standing to sue. Behrens. A determination of standing requirements for conditional gifts was beyond the scope of this memo.

> We weren't comfortable not addressing standing, so we folded it into the conclusion in a commonsense and logical way.

Self-Assessment Grid: Meaney

Objective Memorandum

Overall Organization and Presentation

- ☐ Organized like a memorandum with intro, analysis section, and conclusion
- ☐ Objective tone and formal vocabulary
- ☐ Organized/presented in some logical way, with at least two sections
- ☐ Appropriate use of headings to summarize and guide the grader
- ☐ Cite to rules and cases in appropriate places
- ☐ Presented rule and rule explanation before analysis
- ☐ Used all cases appropriately, including citing to cases within a case
- ☐ Analogized cases where helpful, comparing case facts to ours
- ☐ Used all pertinent facts well
- ☐ Followed all directions in task memo, including no statement of facts

Rules (from library)	Rule Explanation (library case facts)	Analysis (our case facts)
Introduction		
☐ Briefly describe task and identify the two sections: (1) Was the garden transferred by contract or gift? (2) If by gift, what type of gift? ☐ Briefly summarize your findings.		
Analysis		
A. Garden transferred by contract or gift?		
☐ The elements of a gift: (1) intent on the part of the donor to make a gift; (2) delivery, either actual or constructive, of property by the donor; (3) acceptance of the property by the donee; and (4) lack of consideration for the gift. <u>Collins</u> ☐ The elements of a contract: (1) an offer to buy or sell; (2) acceptance of the offer; and (3) consideration passing between the buyer and seller. <u>Collins</u>. ☐ While a transfer by contract requires the *presence* of consideration, a gift requires the *absence* of consideration. <u>Collins</u>. ☐ Consideration has two elements. The promisee must bargain with the promisor, and must confer, or agree to confer, a benefit or must suffer, or agree to suffer, a burden. <u>Collins</u>. ☐ If the parties are motivated by a desire to buy and sell property through a commercial transaction, there is a transfer by contract. But **if the parties are motivated by a desire to deliver and accept transfer through a noncommercial transaction, there is a gift.** <u>Collins</u>.	☐ A university might agree to name a campus building in the donor's honor or use the building for a specified purpose. While it appears the university "bargained" with donor for the naming rights and specified purpose, and conferred a "benefit" or "burden," **this type of bargain, benefit, and burden do not preclude finding the transfer was a gift.** <u>Collins</u>. ☐ The presence or absence of consideration does not turn on the presence or absence of the word "consideration" in the instrument. <u>Collins</u>. ☐ A deed by which a father transferred 10 acres of land valued at $500,000 to his daughter was a gift, even though the deed recited the transfer was "in consideration for $500." <u>Collins, citing Salmon</u>. ☐ $500 was "nominal and immaterial," and it was clearly the father's intent to donate, rather than sell the land to his daughter. <u>Collins, citing Salmon.</u> ☐ A promise to "use best efforts to maintain property in an ecologically sustainable manner" could support a transfer by contract, but it did not where the transfer was from a **mother to her son** of a property valued at $35 million. The court found the mother's intent was to donate the land, rather than sell it. <u>Collins.</u>	☐ Kemper agreement has the appearance of a contract and specifies restrictions, but this will not preclude a finding that the transfer was a gift. ☐ **The agreement specifies the garden will be called the "Kemper Scottish Garden" and indicates the garden will be used for educational purposes and be retained in perpetuity.** ☐ **The instrument** used to transfer the garden also **recites** classic words of contract, such as "consideration." ☐ The instrument recites naming rights, and that the garden be used for educational purposes, in perpetuity. ☐ **Naming rights** here were probably "nominal and immaterial" to the agreement, as evidenced that for several years the garden name **came to be known as "Sarah's Scottish Garden."** ☐ Kemper was a generous and wealthy donor to the university, supporting the idea of a gift.

B. There are several types of gifts		
1. Conditional gift, rather than absolute gift		
☐ A donor can make an absolute gift, where the property is given "*unconditionally*, without (1) restricting use or disposition of the property, (2) retaining power to modify the gift, or (3) reserving a right to sue to enforce a restriction or to undo the gift in case of a restriction's breach by causing property to revert to the donor. . . ." Behrens ☐ Where a donor simply delivers property, and the donee simply accepts the property, there is no bargaining or benefit or burden and the gift is absolute. Collins, citing Behrens. ☐ A donor can make a gift that is not absolute and give the property *conditionally*, (1) restricting use or disposition, (2) retaining power of modification, or, (3) reserving a right of enforcement or reversion. Behrens. ☐ The law presumes a gift is absolute, unless it clearly states otherwise. Behrens.		☐ Kemper placed conditions on the garden gift regarding its name and use, so the garden will not be deemed an absolute gift. ☐ The instrument itself named the garden after Kemper, **restricted the use of the garden to use for an educational purpose**, and specifically retained "the **right to modify the terms** of this Agreement as necessary to its purpose."
2. Charitable trust		
☐ A charitable trust is created, as a matter of fact, whenever a settlor manifests an intent to give property, in trust, for a charitable purpose and actually gives the property, in trust, for such purpose. Holt ☐ A charitable trust is created, as a matter of law, whenever a person gives a property to an educational, philanthropic, healthcare, or similar institution for an educational, philanthropy, healthcare, or similar purpose. Holt.		☐ Kemper gave the garden for a charitable purpose. ☐ Kemper transferred the garden to the university for an educational purpose.
Standing (issue could have been included in various places or omitted entirely)		
☐ Only persons with a "special interest" have standing to sue. Holt. ☐ Donors of absolute gifts do not have standing to sue. Behrens.		Note: No analysis on this point was required to pass.
Conclusion		
☐ The garden was likely a **conditional gift** or charitable trust.		

PT: SELECTED ANSWER 1

PRIVILEGED & CONFIDENTIAL

CONTAINS ATTORNEY WORK PRODUCT

FOGEL & DAVIS LLP

One Walton Avenue

Belleville, Columbia

MEMORANDUM

TO: Melissa Saphir

FROM: Applicant

DATE: February 27, 2018

RE: Meaney v. Trustees of the University of Columbia

-- -----------------------------------

I. Questions Presented

This memorandum addresses two questions: (1) whether Edward Kemper ("Edward") transferred what is now known as the Kemper Scottish Garden or, to some, Sarah's Scottish Garden ("Garden") to the Trustees of the University of Columbia ("Trustees") by way of contract or gift; and, (2) if by way of gift, by way of what kind of gift. This memorandum does not intend to address the merits question of whether Plaintiff Brandon Meaney ("Meaney") has standing to sue the Trustees.

This memorandum concludes that: (1) Edward transferred the Garden to the Trustees by way of gift, not contract, even though the transfer contains the indicia of a contract; and that (2) Edward's transfer by gift likely constituted a conditional gift rather than an unconditional gift because of the express limitations placed on the Trustees, but that further research is required to determine whether Edward's conditional gift may also constitute a charitable trust.

II. Analysis

A. Whether Edward Transferred the Garden by Contract or Gift

Edward likely transferred the Garden by way of gift, even though many of the traditional hallmarks of transfer by contract are present in the 1964 Agreement signed by Edward and Harold Williamson ("Agreement"). Columbia law recognizes both gifts and contracts as legitimate mechanisms for the transfer of property. A property passes by gift when there exists: "(1) intent on the part of the donor to make a gift; (2) delivery, either actual or constructive, of property by the donor; (3) acceptance of the property by the donee; and (4) lack of consideration for the gift." *Collins v. Lincoln*, Library at 5 (Colum. Ct. App. 2009). Property passes by contract where there exists: "(1) an offer to buy or sell; (2) acceptance of the offer; and (3) consideration passing between the buyer and seller." *Id.* at 6.

1. Consideration Is Key, But Intent Is Often Dispositive

The key factor in determining whether a property passed by contract or gift, since both contracts and gifts share many elements, is the presence or absence of consideration. *See Collins*, Library at 6 ("While a transfer by contract requires the *presence* of consideration, a gift requires the *absence* of consideration. In other words, without consideration, the passing of property is by gift, whereas with consideration, it is by transfer of contract." (emphasis in original)). Consideration requires both a bargain between the promisee and the promisor and that the promisor confers, or agrees to confer, a benefit or suffers, or agrees to suffer, a burden. *Collins*, Library at 6.

The presence of buzzwords that signal consideration, including the word "consideration," do not suffice to render a transfer a contract. The Columbia Supreme Court has held that a $500 payment for land referred to as "consideration" in a contract did not convert a gift into a contract because, "in light of all the circumstances," the donor intended to "donate the land . . . and not sell it." *Salmon v. Wilson* (Colum. Supreme Ct. 1971), *quoted in Collins*, Library at 7. And in *Collins*, the Columbia Appeals Court held that a gift occurred, even though the transferring document contained the terms "offer," "acceptance," and "consideration," because the mother donor and son donee did not behave commensurate with a commercial transaction and the promise to use "best efforts" to maintain the property a certain way were "nominal and immaterial." Library at 7-8.

Even where indicia of a contract are present, whether a property transfer is a contract or gift ultimately depends on the "motives manifested by the parties." *Id.* at 7. For example, the parties' intent to transfer property by commercial transaction suggests a contract, while the parties' intent to transfer by a non-commercial transaction suggests a gift. *See id.*

   2.   The Agreement Contains Indicia of a Contract, But the Parties' Intent Suggests a Gift

The Agreement contains the markings and elements of a contract, but a court would likely find that the circumstances and parties' intent render it a gift. The Agreement contains the phrase "in consideration of the foregoing" and specifies that Edward incurred the burden of acquiring the Garden and transferring it to Trustees, while Trustees acquired the benefit of the Garden and the burdens of naming it "Kemper Scottish Garden," using it for educational purposes, and retaining it in perpetuity. *See* Agreement at 1. Because Edward appears to have acquired the Garden as part of the Agreement in an arm's length transaction with another, and because the Trustees agreed to name the Garden, use it for a particular purpose, and never sell it, there are certainly indicia of a bargain between Edward and the Trustees that created both burdens and benefits, as one would find in a contract. *See Collins*, Library at 6 (defining consideration as requiring a bargain and that the promisor confer a benefit or suffer a burden). And, unlike the transactions in *Salmon* and *Collins*, Edward and the Trustees have no familial relationship *id.* at 7. On the other hand, the Trustees did not make even a nominal payment for the land of the kind present in *Salmon*. *See id.* at 7 (quoting *Salmon*). And *Collins* reasoned that even, as here, a university "bargains" to grant naming rights to a donor and use property for a specific purpose, such a bargain does not "preclude a gift." *Id.* at 6-7 (citing *Behrens Research Foundation v. Fairview Memorial Hospital* (Colum. Ct. App. 2008)).

The Agreement here contains additional restrictions or "bargains" not contemplated by the *Collins*, *Behrens*, or *Salmon* courts: namely, the restriction that the Trustees agreement to "retain [the Garden] in perpetuity" and Edward's reserved right "to modify the terms of this Agreement as necessary and appropriate to its purpose." Agreement at 1. More research is required to determine whether Columbia courts have held these restrictions to suggest the presence of a contract or gift, but the totality of the circumstances appears to suggest that Edward gifted the Garden to the University. Edward paid what appears to be fair monetary consideration to another for the Garden and granted it immediately to the University for no monetary consideration in return. Edward specified in the Agreement use of the Garden for an educational purpose, which suggests the lack of a commercial transaction. And Edward's condition that the Trustees retain the Garden in perpetuity (note that this memorandum does not assess the legal propriety of a perpetual restriction on transfer by the Trustees) suggests that no further monetary value would be realized for the Garden.

Even though the Agreement contains many of the markings of a contract and contains arguably more "consideration" than was present in *Collins*, *Behrens*, or *Salmon*, the overall intent of the Agreement suggests that Edward gifted the Garden to the Trustees.

B. Whether Edward Conferred the Garden as an Absolute Gift or a

Conditional Gift

Edward likely gifted the Garden as a conditional gift, and possibly also as a charitable trust. "It is well settled in Columbia that a donor is the master of his or her gift." *Behrens*, Library at 2 (Colum. Ct. App. 2008). Gifts can be "absolute" or "conditional." A donor can give property unconditionally without restricting its use or disposition, retaining power to modify the gift, or reserving a right to sue to enforce a restriction or cause reversion of the property. *See id.* "When a gift is absolute, the donor has relinquished, and the donee has assumed, full dominion over the property -- i.e., the ability to use or dispose of the property at any time, in any manner, and for any purpose." *Id.* at 2-3. A donor can also give property conditionally by "(1) restricting use or disposition, (2) retaining power of modification, and/or (3) reserving a right of enforcement or reversion." *Behrens*, Library at 3. In the case of conditional gifts, donor and donee "share power over the property's use or disposition." *Id.*

1.   Edward Likely Conferred a Conditional, Not an Absolute, Gift

Columbia law "presumes that a gift is *absolute* unless it clearly appears otherwise" and that "a donor has *not* restricted use or disposition, has *not* retained power of modification, and has *not* reserved a right of enforcement or reversion, unless it clearly appears otherwise." *Behrens*, Library at 3 (emphasis in original). In *Behrens*, the court found that a gift of $1 million without restrictive terms, which only said that donor "hereby delivers" and donee "hereby accepts" the gift, gave an unconditional gift and relinquished control over the donee's use of the gift. *See Behrens*, Library at 3. And an absolute gift evinces clear absence of consideration, such as where "the donor simply delivers the property and the donee simply accepts it." *Collins*, Library at 6 (citing *Behrens*).

The Agreement contains conditions that would prevent it from being adjudged an absolute gift. The gift at issue in *Behrens* contained no restrictions at all, and simply transferred money with the terms "hereby delivers" and "hereby receives." *Behrens*, Library at 3. The Agreement, by contrast, contains explicit restrictions on the Trustees' use of the Garden: it must be named "Kemper Scottish Garden," it must be used for educational purposes, and the Trustees may never dispose of it. *See* Agreement at 1. In the Agreement, Edward further reserves a right to modify the Agreement "as necessary and appropriate to its purpose." The Agreement thus presents all of the factors for a conditional gift envisioned by the *Behrens* court but not presented in the facts of that case: restricted use, restricted disposition, and reserved rights. *Compare id.* at 1, *with Behrens*, Library at 3. Nor is this a case where "the donor simply delivers the property and the donee simply accepts it." *Collins*, Library at 6 (internal citation omitted).

A court would almost certainly find that Edward did not confer the Garden as an unconditional gift, without regard to the enforceability of the Agreement's conditions. Edward's retention of rights to modify the Agreement and restrictions on the Garden's use and disposition suggest a conditional gift.

2. Edward May Have Created a Charitable Trust

Edward's gift may also constitute a charitable trust, although more research than this memorandum provides is necessary to determine the interplay between charitable trusts and conditional gifts. The Columbia Supreme Court has held that a gift can also take the form of a charitable trust in certain circumstances. *See generally Holt v. Jones*, Library at 10 (Colum. Supreme Ct. 1994). Even where a property grant is not placed in trust by the donor, a charitable trust can be created by operation of law "whenever a person gives property to an educational, philanthropic, healthcare, or similar institution for an education, philanthropy, healthcare, or similar purpose." *Id.*

The Agreement, to be sure, does not create a trust of any kind. But a court may find under *Holt* that Edward's restriction on use of the Garden "for educational purposes" and gift of the Garden to the University of Columbia, an educational institution, may satisfy the criteria for the creation of a charitable trust by operation of law. More research is required to determine whether other aspects of Columbia law, or decisions of Columbia courts, would suggest the lack of a charitable trust. And more research is needed to determine what effect, if any, the legal creation of a charitable trust would have on Edward's rights, the Trustees' rights, Plaintiff's rights in the instant lawsuit, or other claims that may arise.

IV. Conclusion

Edward more likely than not transferred the Garden to the Trustees by gift, rather than by contract, because the totality of the Agreement and the accompanying intent of the parties suggests a non-commercial transaction lacking proper consideration. If Edward's transfer of the Garden constitutes a gift, it is much more likely than not to be deemed a conditional gift than an absolute gift due to the Agreement's restrictions on use and disposition and Edward's retention of modification rights. Edward's transfer of the Garden may also constitute a charitable trust because the Agreement conveys property to an educational institution for an educational purpose, but more research is required to assess this possibility and its effects on the other issues discussed herein.

Please feel free to contact me with any questions regarding this memorandum, or if you would like additional research and analysis performed.

PRIVILEGED & CONFIDENTIAL

CONTAINS ATTORNEY WORK PRODUCT

PT: SELECTED ANSWER 2

FOGEL & DAVIS, LLP

One Walton Avenue

Belleville, Columbia

TO: Melissa Saphir, Managing Attorney

FROM: Applicant

DATE: February 27, 2018

RE: Meaney v. Trustees of the University of Columbia

I. Introduction

In order to persuade the court to dismiss Brendan Meaney's breach of contract action on the ground that he lacks standing, you have asked me prepare an objective memo first analyzing whether the Edward Kemper transferred the garden to the Trustees by way of contract or gift, and if the garden was transferred by gift, what kind of gift.

In short, a court will likely find that the transfer was by a not absolute gift in the form of a charitable trust.

II. Legal Analysis

Property may be passed by gift or by transfer by contract. *Collins v. Lincoln*, Columbia Court of Appeals (2009). The elements of a gift consist of: (1) intent on the part of the donor to make a gift; (2) actual or constructive delivery of property by the donor; (3) acceptance of the property by the donee; and (4) lack of consideration for the gift. *Id*. Alternatively, the elements of a transfer by contract consist of: (1) an offer to buy or sell; (2) acceptance of the offer; and (3) consideration passing between the buyer and seller. *Id.* Accordingly, gifts and transfers by contract have two similar elements. A gift requires delivery by the donor and a transfer by contract requires offer by the buyer or seller. Additionally, a gift requires acceptance by the donee and a transfer by contract requires acceptance by the seller or buyer. But one element is different. While a contract requires the presence of consideration, a gift requires the absence of consideration. *Id.* In other words, without consideration, the passing of property is by gift, whereas with consideration, it is by transfer by contract.

A.   The relationship between Edward Kemper and the Trustees of University of Columbia manifested an intent that the transfer be by gift rather than by contract because the parties were motivated by a non-commercial transaction.

The element of consideration has two requirements: the promisee must bargain with the promisor and must confer, or agree to confer, a benefit or must suffer, or agree to suffer, a burden. *Id.* The absence of consideration is clear when a gift is absolute. See, *Behrens Research Foundation v. Fairview Memorial Hospital*, Columbia Court of Appeal (2008). This is plain when the donor simply delivers the property and the donee simply accepts it. But where the facts suggest a bargained for exchange, where the donee confers or agrees to confer a benefit to the donor, or where the donee suffers, or agrees to suffer, a burden, the type of transfer is not as plain.

In the situation where a university agrees to name a campus building in a donor's honor or to use a building for a specified purpose, the university can be said to have "bargained" with the donor. This is because there was a negotiation for the terms for the naming of the building or its use for the specified purpose, and to confer, or agree to confer, a benefit or to suffer, or agree to suffer, a burden. Here, it is arguable that the Trustees of the University of Columbia have "bargained" with Edward Kemper. Meaney will argue that because the garden parcel was to bear the name "Kemper Scottish Garden" and to be used for educational purposes in perpetuity in exchange for the parcel of property, that the exchange was bargained for. Additionally Meaney will argue that the Trustees of the University of Columbia negotiated the terms for the naming of the garden and agreed to suffer a burden, that is using the garden for educational purposes and retaining it in perpetuity. While this is likely, such a bargain and benefit and burden do not preclude a gift. *Id*.

The presence or absence of consideration does not turn on the presence or absence of the term "consideration" in the instrument. *Id.* For example, the Supreme Court held that a deed by which a father transferred 10 acres of land valued at $500,000 to his adult daughter effected a gift, even though the deed recited that he transferred the property to her in consideration for $500. *Salmon v. Wilson*, Supreme Court (1971). Rather than look at the terms of the deed objectively, the Supreme Court reasoned that, in light of the circumstances, the $500 paid by the daughter to her father was "nominal and immaterial," and it was "clearly" the father's intent to donate the land to his daughter and not to sell it to her. Here, we can show that Edward Kemper was a wealthy businessman and a generous donor to the University. To that end, he agreed to transfer a garden to the Trustees to use for educational purposes. Like in Salmon, we can argue that the naming of the garden was nominal and immaterial because the true purpose of the transfer was for educational purposes, not for the name of the garden to live on. To further show that the naming of the garden was a nominal and immaterial consideration, we can show that recently the garden came to be known as Sarah's Scottish Garden. Additionally, if naming of the garden was material, then Edward Kemper, having retained the right to modify the terms of the Agreement as necessary and appropriate to its purpose, would have taken actions to ensure that the name was not changed from Kemper Scottish Garden to Sarah's Scottish Garden. Additionally, in line with this argument, if the naming of the garden was material consideration for the transfer, Meaney would have brought suit earlier to enjoin the use of the name to require that the old name be used.

Ultimately, what controls are the motives manifested by the parties. *Collins*. If the parties are motivated by a desire to buy and sell property through a commercial transaction, there is a transfer by contract. *Id.* But if the parties are motivated by a desire to deliver and accept the property through a non-commercial transaction, there is a gift. *Id.* Here, we can argue that the transaction was a manifestation of the parties desire to deliver the property through a non-commercial transaction. To support our position, we will show that Edward Kemper was a wealthy businessman and a generous donor. He had no intent in benefiting financially from the transaction and he didn't need to. If he had intended to benefit from the transaction, then he would have sold the property rather than donate it, like he had often donated in the past.

To counter our position that the parties were not motivated by a commercial transaction, Meaney will likely argue that the agreement impliedly recited that the transfer was subject to the Trustee's acceptance of the terms and restrictions. He will argue that by signing the agreement, the Trustees are burdened with the promise to maintain the garden with the name Kemper Scottish Garden" for educational purposes in perpetuity. The Court in Collins stated, that the burden of a promise, although hard to quantify, is adequate, and could support a transfer by contract.

But the fundamental question is whether there was in fact a transfer by contract rather than a gift. The primary element in resolving this issue is determining whether the parties are motivated by a desire to buy and sell the property through a commercial transaction. Here, they most likely are not. The relationship of Edward Kemper to the University of Columbia is similar to the relationship of Collins to Lincoln. It was only natural, based on the parties' relationship and past donations, that Edward Kemper and the Trustees would intend for the transaction to be noncommercial in nature. Under the totality of the circumstances, it is most likely that the transfer was by gift rather than by contract.

B.   What Kind of Gift

A gift can be absolute, not absolute, or by charitable trust.

i. Gift Absolute versus Gift Not Absolute

It is well settled in Columbia that a donor is the master of his or her gift. The donor can give property by a gift that is absolute or that is not absolute. A gift that is absolute is without (1) restricting use or disposition of the property; (2) retaining power to modify the gift; or (3) reserving a right to sue to enforce a restriction or to undo the gift in case of a restriction's breach by causing the property to revert to the donor him-or herself or to a third person. *Behrens Research Foundation v. Fairview Memorial Hospital*, Columbia Court of Appeals (2008). When a gift is absolute, the donor has relinquished, and the donee has assumed, full dominion over the property--the ability to use or dispose of the property at any time, in any manner, for any purpose. Alternatively, a donor can make a gift that is not absolute. The donor can give property conditionally, (1) restricting use or disposition; (2) retaining power of modification; and/or (3) reserving a right of enforcement or reversion. *Id.* When a gift is not absolute, the donor has not relinquished, and the donee has not assumed, full dominion over the property; rather, both donor and donee share power over the property. *Id.*

The law presumes that a gift is absolute unless it clearly appears otherwise. *Id.* Additionally, the law presumes that donor has not restricted use or disposition, has not retained power of modification, and has not reserved a right of enforcement or reversion, unless it clearly appears otherwise. Here, in the Agreement between Edward Kemper and the Trustees of the University, Kemper explicitly retained the right to modify the terms of the Agreement as necessary and appropriate to its purpose. Unlike in Behrens, Edward Kemper reserved a right of enforcement or reversion, and retained power of modification. Under this analysis, it is likely that a court will find the gift to be not absolute.

ii. Charitable Trust

We can argue, though, that the gift was a non-private charitable trust. The primary type of non-private trust is the charitable trust. A charitable trust is created, as a matter of fact, whenever a settlor manifests an intent to give property, in trust for a charitable purpose and actually gives the property, in trust, for such purpose. Holt v. Jones, Columbia Supreme Court (1994). A charitable trust is also created, as a matter of law, whenever a settlor manifests an intent to give property to an educational, philanthropic, healthcare, or similar institution for an education, philanthropy, healthcare, or similar purpose. *Id*. Here, it is plain from the agreement that the property was transferred to the Trustees of University of Columbia to use it for educational purposes. Therefore, we can argue that it is both a charitable trust as a matter of law and as a matter of fact. It is a charitable trust as a matter of fact because Edward Kemper intended to give it in trust for a charitable purpose and actually gave the property in trust for such purpose. Additionally, we can argue that it is a charitable trust as a matter of law because the property was given to an educational institution for education. We can show that it was "given" to the educational institution because the terms of the agreement state that it is "transferred" to the Trustees and that it was to be acquired for the purpose of transferring it to Trustees.

If the gift, although likely not absolute, is found to be a non-private charitable trust, in accord with the majority of jurisdictions, only the attorney general and some persons with a special interest will have standing to sue. Persons with a special interest include those who are trustees or beneficiaries, or would otherwise have an ownership interest in the property. Here, it is unlikely that Meaney will be found to be a trustee or beneficiary, or to otherwise have an ownership interest in the property, and will likely not have standing to sue.

III. Conclusion

Because we will likely be able to show that the gift, although not absolute, is a non-private charitable trust, the Court will likely dismiss Meaney's suit for lack of standing.

This has been a challenging and interesting project. Please let me know if I can provide any additional research on this issue.

Signed,

Applicant

_____

Fogel & Davis, LLP

One Walton Avenue

Belleville, Columbia

DEMONSTRATION 4

IN THE MATTER OF ABIGAIL WATKINS

July 2018

California
Bar
Examination

Performance Test
INSTRUCTIONS AND FILE

IN THE MATTER OF ABIGAIL WATKINS

IN THE MATTER OF ABIGAIL WATKINS

<u>INSTRUCTIONS</u>

1. This performance test is designed to evaluate your ability to handle a select number of legal authorities in the context of a factual problem involving a client.

2. The problem is set in the fictional State of Columbia, one of the United States.

3. You will have two sets of materials with which to work: a File and a Library.

4. The File contains factual materials about your case. The first document is a memorandum containing the instructions for the tasks you are to complete.

5. The Library contains the legal authorities needed to complete the tasks. The case reports may be real, modified, or written solely for the purpose of this performance test. If the cases appear familiar to you, do not assume that they are precisely the same as you have read before. Read each thoroughly, as if it were new to you. You should assume that cases were decided in the jurisdictions and on the dates shown. In citing cases from the Library, you may use abbreviations and omit page citations.

6. You should concentrate on the materials provided, but you should also bring to bear on the problem your general knowledge of the law. What you have learned in law school and elsewhere provides the general background for analyzing the problem; the File and Library provide the specific materials with which you must work.

7. This performance test is designed to be completed in 90 minutes. Although there are no parameters on how to apportion that 90 minutes, you should allow yourself sufficient time to thoroughly review the materials and organize your planned response. Since the time allotted for this session of the examination includes two (2) essay questions in addition to this performance test, time management is essential.

8. Your response will be graded on its compliance with instructions and on its content, thoroughness, and organization.

LAW OFFICES OF TIA LUCCI

MEMORANDUM

TO: Applicant

FROM: Tia Lucci

SUBJECT: In the Matter of Abigail Watkins

DATE: July 24, 2018

This case involves a Columbia State Bar disciplinary action against our client, Abigail Watkins. On June 8, 2018, Watkins pled guilty to a single felony count of insider trading that occurred more than two years ago. The State Bar then initiated disciplinary proceedings against Watkins, seeking disbarment. Watkins hired us to prevent that.

We have just completed testimony in a hearing on the threshold issue of whether the facts and circumstances surrounding the insider trading by Watkins involved moral turpitude. The judge has requested simultaneous briefs on this issue. Please draft an argument for me to use in a brief asserting that:

1)   The conduct underlying the plea does not justify a finding of moral turpitude.

2)   Watkins' testimony at the hearing does not justify a finding of moral turpitude.

At this point, we seek to avoid a finding of moral turpitude. Do not argue about appropriate discipline.

Do not write a separate statement of facts. Instead, incorporate the facts into your persuasive argument, making sure to address both favorable and unfavorable facts.

UNITED STATES DISTRICT COURT

FOR THE NORTHERN DISTRICT OF COLUMBIA

UNITED STATES OF AMERICA, v. ABIGAIL WATKINS, Defendant.	Criminal Case No. 2018-999-111 VIOLATION: 15 U.S.C. 78j (Insider Trading)

PLEA AGREEMENT

      Pursuant to Rule 11 of the Federal Rules of Criminal Procedure, the United States of America and the defendant, Abigail Watkins, agree as follows:

1. The defendant is entering into this agreement and is pleading guilty freely and voluntarily without promise or benefit of any kind (other than contained herein), and without threats, force, intimidation, or coercion of any kind.

2. The indictment relates to a single sale of stock by the defendant. The defendant pleads guilty.

3. The defendant knowingly, voluntarily and truthfully admits the facts contained in the attached Factual Basis for Plea.

FOR THE DEFENDANT

Dated: ___June 8, 2018___

_____*Abigail Watkins*_____   _____*Tia Lucci*_____

Abigail Watkins   Tia Lucci

Defendant   Counsel for Defendant

FOR THE UNITED STATES

Dated: ___June 8, 2018___

____*Mary Butler*_____   _____*Stephanie Evans*___

Mary Butler   Stephanie Evans
Criminal Division   Securities Criminal Enforcement
   U.S. Department of Justice   U.S. Department of Justice

ATTACHMENT A

FACTUAL BASIS FOR THE PLEA OF ABIGAIL WATKINS

This agreement is submitted to provide a factual basis for Defendant's plea of guilty.

1. As a patent-trademark partner with Wakefield and Lester (Wakefield), Defendant represented Fort Software, Inc. (Fort) in patent and other matters since 2011.

2. On August 13, 2015, Samantha Darmond, Fort's general counsel, left a voice mail message on Defendant's phone to call her about "an urgent patent matter." On the morning of August 16, Defendant returned the call, and she and Darmond spoke. Darmond told Defendant that Silicon Microsystems (Silicon), a large publicly traded company, was planning to acquire Fort and that Darmond was coordinating Silicon's requests in its due diligence efforts as to Fort's patents. Darmond wanted Defendant to share patent files in the Wakefield office with Silicon's counsel so that Silicon could complete its due diligence review of Fort.

3. About midday on August 16, Defendant placed a brokerage "market order" to buy 1,000 shares of Fort. She paid $13.50 per share. This is the basis for the indictment.

4. The merger of Fort into Silicon was publicly announced before the market's opening on August 23. When the merger was consummated, shares of Fort stock were exchanged at a certain ratio for shares in Silicon. In October 2015, Defendant sold her Silicon shares for a $14,000 profit.

5. In May 2016, Defendant received a call from an agent at the Securities and Exchange Commission (SEC), who was looking into the trading of shares of Fort in the period before the merger. Defendant readily admitted to purchasing Fort in her own name on August 16. Defendant told the SEC that at the time of the August 16 purchase she was not aware of the planned merger.

Dated:

___June 8, 2018___   _____*Abigail Watkins*_____

                                      Abigail Watkins, Defendant

HEARING DEPARTMENT OF THE STATE BAR COURT
HEARING IN THE MATTER OF ABIGAIL WATKINS

July 20, 2018

Case No. 18-SF-1023

State Bar Court Judge Margaret Kenler

BY THE COURT: Mr. Simonds, you may proceed.

ASSISTANT CHIEF TRIAL COUNSEL MATT SIMONDS: Your honor, this morning the State Bar relies on the Factual Basis for the Plea Agreement. We're standing on the admissions that the Respondent made in her plea agreement and in that Factual Basis. Specifically, we rely on her statements that she made a purchase of stock in Fort Software with knowledge of an impending purchase of Fort by Silicon Microsystems, knowledge that she gained through conversations with lawyers representing Silicon Microsystems. I understand that the Respondent will also testify. We rest.

BY THE COURT: Ms. Lucci, you may proceed.

BY TIA LUCCI: Thank you, your honor. We call the Respondent, Abigail Watkins.

ABIGAIL WATKINS

EXAMINATION BY MS. LUCCI: Ms. Watkins, could you please briefly describe your professional education and preparation.

WATKINS: I have a J.D. and a degree in chemical engineering from Worcester Polytechnic Institute. I practiced intellectual property law for many years before joining Wakefield and Lester in 2006. I chair its intellectual property group.

LUCCI: You have been a member of the bar in Columbia since 1991, and before that in Virginia and the District of Columbia. Have you ever been disciplined or even cited or received notice of any charges involving any discipline?

WATKINS: Never, until now.

LUCCI: You represent Fort Software?

WATKINS: Yes, in 2011 I personally advised and represented Fort during its start-up phase and when it went public a few years later. I have followed Fort since then and intended to make a purchase of its stock. Everything I read online about Fort, the stock recommendations from rating agencies, were very positive on Fort. At that point the patents were public information. But I never did so.

LUCCI: Did you reconsider that decision?

WATKINS: Yes. In June 2015, Fort was trading at $10 a share, and by August it was at $13. Two major brokerage companies had upgraded Fort stock from a "buy" to a "strong buy." The technology message boards were talking up Fort as a likely merger target for its software. I know that I was planning to make a purchase. I wasn't going to lose out again.

LUCCI: In July 2015, you underwent surgery for a tear to your rotator cuff.

WATKINS: Yes, July 14th.

LUCCI: Your doctor gave and you filled prescriptions both for Percocet and Ambien?

WATKINS: Yes, Percocet for pain and the Ambien to help me sleep. Percocet is something with oxycodone and the doctor said it's a potent pain reliever, for severe pain, but that I could take one or two tablets every 4 hours. I took it a lot, although I now know that it had some side effects. I was told not to take it before driving, and no alcohol.

LUCCI: How much and how long did you take Percocet?

WATKINS: I don't know. The prescription was for 50 tablets. I took it on and off until it ran out.

LUCCI: Were you still taking Percocet at the time of the Fort-Silicon merger?

WATKINS: I don't know. My memory from the surgery in July until September is very poor. I was very distracted by the pain and the medications, and trying to maintain a normal full-time work schedule.

LUCCI: You returned to work five days after surgery?

WATKINS: Yes, although I had considerable pain and limited mobility.

LUCCI: Turning to the Fort merger, when did you hear from Fort?

WATKINS: In 2015, I was not actively representing Fort. My best recollection is that on August 16, 2015 I received a call from Fort's general counsel, Samantha Darmond, with whom I had not previously worked, or from an attorney at Jordan & Haines. I really can't remember which. Anyway, I was asked to send our patent files over to J & H.

LUCCI: In the conversation, do you remember anything being said about a pending merger, or due diligence, or the need for confidentiality?

WATKINS: No. I thought that Fort was going to be represented by J & H. It's a top intellectual property firm, and I considered it a positive development for Fort. I had the files assembled, but did nothing more. I didn't think it was urgent. I think it was the next day that I received another call from the attorney at J & H about the files.

LUCCI: On August 16, did you place an order to purchase 1,000 shares of Fort?

WATKINS: Yes.

LUCCI: Was it because you knew about the merger?

WATKINS: It is my best recollection of that purchase, that on that day I was acting on my general opinion and my previous interest in Fort, observations from the message boards and buy recommendations. And as I said, I thought J & H's involvement was also good news. Looking back now, I know that I made a mistake.

LUCCI: Nothing further.

CROSS-EXAMINATION BY ASSISTANT CHIEF TRIAL COUNSEL SIMONDS:

SIMONDS: Do you claim that the Percocet or Ambien made you commit insider stock trading?

WATKINS: No, of course not.

SIMONDS: Did you have symptoms of delirium, or inability to reason, or impaired ability to understand your moral or ethical duties?

WATKINS: No, of course not. But I didn't appreciate the effect that had on me, as I can now.

SIMONDS: Neither drug left you mentally impaired or diminished your mental capacity?

WATKINS: As to actual effects of those drugs, you are asking the wrong person. It is not for me to say.

SIMONDS: Since you only had 50 Percocets, if you had taken just three a day, less than your doctor said you could, it would have run out in 17 days, or a week or more before the call about the merger. Correct?

WATKINS: I don't know. I took it infrequently, in reaction to pain. Then I would take it for a day or two and then stop.

SIMONDS: You saw your doctor several times between the surgery and mid-August. Did you complain about the effects of Percocet, tell him that you were mentally impaired?

WATKINS: No. The doctor said that continued pain in that period was normal.

SIMONDS: You would agree that it would be hard for any alleged Percocet intoxication to have caused you to commit an insider stock purchase?

WATKINS: That's not what I am saying. The Percocet and the pain, however, may have distracted my thinking, left me insufficiently attentive to what Ms. Darmond was telling me, why I could have failed to register what was so important, and especially why I don't have a very clear memory of what she told me in conversations or voice messages. My partner and associates were telling me that I was unfocused during that time.

SIMONDS TO COURT: Objection and move to strike. Hearsay and unresponsive.

COURT: The statements of others as to her mental state are stricken.

SIMONDS: As to your testimony that your stock purchase on August 16th was not based on anything about a pending merger told to you by Ms. Darmond, but on message boards and the like -- Those boards and buy recommendations were because of expectations of a Fort merger. Correct?

WATKINS: Yes.

SIMONDS: It is true, isn't it, that you were told on August 16th to gather the Fort patent files and you in fact did that?

WATKINS: Yes, my billing record on that date is 0.7 hour to review the Fort files and prepare a transmittal letter to J & H.

SIMONDS: Ms. Watkins, you agreed in the plea agreement that Ms. Darmond told you of the merger and that it was confidential information, before you made the purchase of Fort stock on August 16th.

WATKINS: That is what I agreed to.

SIMONDS: But now in your direct testimony today you claim that what you agreed to in a guilty plea is not true?

WATKINS: No, only that I don't remember it that clearly, that I don't remember that she told me she was talking about an imminent merger. I grasped the task, to assemble our patent files to send to other counsel, but little more. I had someone put together the documents she wanted, but I did not consider the matter sufficiently urgent to do more, and instead waited to hear from someone from J & H.

SIMONDS: I don't understand. Do you deny what you agreed was true in the plea agreement?

WATKINS: I am trying to say that the statement in the plea agreement is contrary to my memory of the event. But I agreed to it because my attorneys explained that it was a good deal. I received probation instead of jail time. I knew that the version in the plea agreement was Ms. Darmond's recollection and what she'd say if she testified. I simply have no recollection of it. And so I can't deny that the August 16th conversation with Ms. Darmond took place, nor can I agree that it happened and led me to the stock order.

SIMONDS: But long before today, didn't you refute her version?

WATKINS: What do you mean?

SIMONDS: Eight months after the merger, the SEC called you. Correct?

WATKINS: Yes, totally out of the blue.

SIMONDS: Right. You had no warning and were taken by surprise by the call.

WATKINS: I was shaken, and as I was trying to collect my thoughts to answer the questions, I saw my life passing before my eyes.

SIMONDS: You had enough control to repeat your story that you didn't know about the merger when you made the August 16 purchase?

WATKINS: Yes, Mr. Simonds. I told that to the SEC and I am telling it today because it is my best recollection.

SIMONDS: Nothing further, your honor.

BY THE COURT: As we agreed, then, simultaneous briefs due in one week. We are adjourned.

July 2018

California
Bar
Examination

Performance Test

LIBRARY

IN THE MATTER OF ABIGAIL WATKINS

LIBRARY

CHADWICK v. STATE BAR

Columbia Supreme Court (1989)

We review the recommendation of the Review Department of the State Bar Court that petitioner, William Chadwick, be suspended from the practice of law following his misdemeanor conviction for violating federal statutes prohibiting insider trading and for related misconduct. The Review Department recommended that Chadwick be suspended from the practice of law for a period of five years; that execution of the suspension be stayed, subject to two years actual suspension. On appeal, we review the facts underlying Chadwick's conviction to determine whether they constitute moral turpitude.

Chadwick was admitted to the practice of law in Columbia in December 1973. Formerly, he was a partner in a large firm. Chadwick is currently a sole practitioner, primarily rendering legal advice about alternative investment structures. He has no prior record of discipline.

Chadwick's misconduct began in December 1981 when he acquired material, nonpublic information regarding a tender offer involving the Brunswick Corporation from a Martin Cooper, who was a bank officer and banker for the Whittaker Corporation. The Whittaker Corporation was the company attempting to take over the Brunswick Corporation. Chadwick purchased stock options of the Brunswick Corporation for himself. Later, the takeover of Brunswick by the Whittaker Corporation was publicly announced.

Chadwick was later contacted by the SEC. After consulting with counsel, Chadwick informed the SEC that he had relied upon material, nonpublic information concerning the Brunswick tender offer.

On July 1982, Chadwick was charged in U.S. District Court with one misdemeanor count of having violated 15 United States Code section 78(j). Chadwick pled guilty to the count as charged and was fined $10,000 and ordered to disgorge profits. The plea agreement establishes the facts relevant to the question of moral turpitude and facts that may be used to impeach Chadwick.

Thereafter, the State Bar issued an order to show cause charging Chadwick with willfully committing acts involving moral turpitude within the meaning of Business and Professions Code section 6101. These charges were based on Chadwick's illegal purchase of stock options, the acts that underlay his misdemeanor conviction.

As we have noted on numerous occasions, the concept of moral turpitude escapes precise definition. For purposes of the Rules of Professional Responsibility, moral turpitude has been described as an act of baseness, vileness or depravity in the private and social duties that a man owes to his fellowmen, or to society in general, contrary to the accepted and customary rule of right and duty between man and man. To summarize, it has been described as any crime or misconduct without excuse. The meaning and test is the same whether the dishonest or immoral act is a felony, misdemeanor, or no crime at all.

Chadwick argues that his willingness to comply with the SEC's investigation excuses his earlier conduct. However, the concept of excuse relates to Chadwick's conduct at the time of the violations to which he pled guilty. Here, Chadwick's guilty plea rests on facts that indicate no such excuse at the time he purchased the stock.

Chadwick also argues that, by entering into a plea agreement, he did not concede that the factual basis for the criminal plea would justify ethical discipline based on those facts. However, even if true, this proposition does not prevent this court from reviewing the factual basis of the plea to determine whether the conduct it describes justifies a finding of moral turpitude.

In this case, we agree with the Review Department's conclusion that the facts and circumstances of the particular offense and Chadwick's related conduct establish that Chadwick's acts involved moral turpitude. We adopt the Review Department's recommended discipline.

In the Matter of HAROLD SALAS, a Member of the State Bar

Review Department of the State Bar Court (2001)

In 1999, Harold Salas entered a plea to conspiracy to obstruct justice. After his conviction, the State Bar Court held a hearing to recommend appropriate discipline pursuant to Section 6102(a) of the Business and Professions Code. After the hearing, the State Bar Court recommended disbarment rather than discipline because it concluded that Salas had lied at the hearing.

In 1995, Respondent entered into a business relationship with Anna Bash, the owner/operator of Chekov Legal Services in the Little Russia neighborhood. Respondent paid Bash $5,000 per month to market his practice to the Russian community in the City of Angels and to provide him with a secretary and a translator. Respondent would assist Bash in providing legal services, many on a pro bono basis, and Bash would refer personal injury, criminal, and other fee cases to Respondent. Respondent admitted he agreed to split fees with Bash, a non-attorney, and that this was illegal.

The District Attorney's Office filed a criminal complaint against Respondent and Bash as co-defendants in a "capping" conspiracy, alleging that Respondent paid Bash for referring clients to him. There were several charges of referral and fee-splitting, including one that alleged that Respondent issued a check for $10,000 to Bash from the proceeds of a settlement of a personal injury case. The District Attorney claimed that the $10,000 payment was an illegal payment in exchange for Bash's referring the case to Respondent.

Respondent and Bash were each charged with three felony counts: (1) conspiracy to commit a crime; (2) capping; and (3) conspiracy to commit an act injurious to the public. Respondent pled no contest to count three as a misdemeanor; and the District Attorney dismissed counts one and two.

In the hearing below, Respondent testified that he owed Bash $10,000 for two months of services, and that he properly withdrew that amount from the settlement because it was a part of his contingency fee in the case. Respondent denied that the payment to Bash was for referral of the personal injury case to him.

After her own plea agreement, Bash testified against Respondent. Her testimony directly contradicted Respondent's. She did, however, confirm that she operated an office, which included substantial secretarial and translation services, and that Respondent was paying her $5,000 a month and that $10,000 was due when she was paid. She was adamant that the $10,000 was for the referral.

The State Bar Court did not accept Respondent's testimony about the payment, and questioned why he would advance it before the court. The State Bar Court concluded that his lack of candor in the proceedings itself warranted a finding of moral turpitude.

Based on our review of the record, we find that the State Bar Court's finding of moral turpitude was not supported by clear and convincing evidence that Respondent had testified falsely and hence was guilty of moral turpitude. The State Bar bears the burden to prove moral turpitude by clear and convincing evidence. We conclude that the State Bar did not carry its burden here.

Normally, we would defer to a finding of fact from the State Bar Court. But in this case, Respondent contends that the hearing officer did not apply the burden of proof correctly. Respondent argues that there is no reasonable and logical explanation for why he would insist on his version of this one payment, other than the fact that he believes it to be true. It would have been easier, he says, to admit responsibility for this referral as well. Respondent contends that directly contradicting the plea agreement would raise severe doubts as to his candor. However, he asserts that his repeated statement of the innocent purpose of this single payment does not contradict the plea agreement, which is silent on this point.

Any determination of moral turpitude must be found by clear and convincing evidence. This includes a determination that a witness's testimony lacks candor (i.e., the witness is lying). An honest if mistaken belief in his innocence does not signal a lack of candor. A lack of candor should not be founded merely on Respondent's different memory of events.

Applying the standard of proof by clear and convincing evidence means that reasonable doubts must be resolved in favor of the accused attorney. If equally reasonable inferences may be drawn from a proven fact, the inference to innocence must be chosen. If, as is the case here, it is equally likely that Respondent is telling the truth about controverted facts, the State Bar has not met its burden of establishing clear and convincing evidence of culpability.

Reversed and remanded.

Practice California Performance Test:
Step-by-Step Demonstration 4

In the Matter of Abigail Watkins (Cal. July 2018)

[Roadmap modeled on computer.]

| Step 1. | Scan the instructions, the file table of contents, and the library table of contents (1 minute) |

Instructions
You should have already thoroughly read the instruction page once. When you are completing a PT, look for three important details: the jurisdiction (usually in paragraph two), the contents of the packet (usually in paragraph three), and any specific weighting information, which, if supplied, would be noted at the bottom of the instructions. Take a second to skim the instructions to ensure no changes were made to the standard instructions.

Three important details for Watkins

1. The problem is set in the State of Columbia.
2. The packet contains a file and a library.
3. There is no special weighting information.

Client File Table of Contents
Look this over to get a general feel for what the case is about, how many pages of facts there are, and the type of documents you will be working with.

Watkins Observations

Since the case name is <u>In the Matter of Abigail Watkins</u>, you know you are not dealing with two adverse parties. The types of cases often labeled like this usually involve probate, bankruptcy, juvenile proceedings, disciplinary proceedings, or other proceedings in which one party applies to the court for something. This case contains approximately nine pages of facts to work with.

- The first file document is a memorandum from Tia Lucci, who is likely the person who will direct us on what she wants us to do and who we represent.
- The second file document is a plea agreement, <u>U.S. v. Abigail Watkins</u>, which alerts us to a prior case with adverse parties: the government is one of them and Watkins, the current named party, is the other. It is fair to assume that whatever we are being asked to do here relates to the prior case involving Ms. Watkins.
- The third file document is an attachment containing the factual basis for the plea of Abigail Watkins. This document will likely shed some light on the prior underlying case.
- The fourth and final file document is a transcript from the Hearing Dept. of the State Bar Court, which is likely to be the agency we will deal with in whatever task we have been asked to complete. This document also suggests that Ms. Watkins has a legal license, since the State Bar Court is mentioned, along with the effect of her underlying case on her licensing: that might be the issue we are being asked to work on. Note: Whenever an attorney is involved, be mindful of PR issues.

Library Table of Contents
You are still trying to get a general feel for what the case is about and quickly determine the type of law you will be working with. You want to make note if you have statutes and/or cases and how many of each. You also want to note the jurisdiction or court the cases come from to possibly start getting the picture of the type of task you have ahead as well as whether the cases are binding or merely persuasive authority.

Watkins Library

The file contains only one court case. It is from the Columbia Supreme Court. Although the case is dated 1989, it will be binding since the Columbia Supreme Court is the highest court in our jurisdiction. We also have been given a review of another case involving a member of the State Bar. This likely relates to the case at hand with Ms. Watkins.

IN THE MATTER OF ABIGAIL WATKINS

INSTRUCTIONS

1. This performance test is designed to evaluate your ability to handle a select number of legal authorities in the context of a factual problem involving a client.

2. The problem is set in the <u>fictional State of Columbia, one of the United States.</u>

3. You will have two sets of materials with which to work: <u>a File and a Library</u>.

4. The File contains factual materials about your case. The first document is a memorandum containing the instructions for the tasks you are to complete.

5. The Library contains the legal authorities needed to complete the tasks. The case reports may be real, modified, or written solely for the purpose of this performance test. If the cases appear familiar to you, do not assume that they are precisely the same as you have read before. Read each thoroughly, as if it were new to you. You should assume that cases were decided in the jurisdictions and on the dates shown. In citing cases from the Library, you may use abbreviations and omit page citations.

6. You should concentrate on the materials provided, but you should also bring to bear on the problem your general knowledge of the law. What you have learned in law school and elsewhere provides the general background for analyzing the problem; the File and Library provide the specific materials with which you must work.

7. This performance test is designed to be completed in 90 minutes. Although there are no parameters on how to apportion that 90 minutes, you should allow yourself sufficient time to thoroughly review the materials and organize your planned response. Since the time allotted for this session of the examination includes two (2) essay questions in addition to this performance test, time management is essential.

8. Your response will be graded on its compliance with instructions and on its content, thoroughness, and organization.

This is not a typical two-party case name, and it is not a criminal case. Likely an administrative issue, e.g., probate, bankruptcy, etc.

IN THE MATTER OF ABIGAIL WATKINS

Instructions ....

FILE

Task memo likely from our boss.

Memorandum to Applicant from Tia Lucci...

Likely an underlying criminal case related to our client.

Plea Agreement, U.S. v. Abigail Watkins ....

Details about the underlying case.

Attachment A: Factual Basis for the Plea of Abigail Watkins ....

Transcript from Hearing Department of the State Bar Court.............................…..

Hint that our current issue involves State Bar issues. Likely ethical attorney issues, and the above file documents are likely the facts underlying this current issue with the State Bar.

IN THE MATTER OF ABIGAIL WATKINS

LIBRARY

A case in our jx and involving the State Bar so likely similar to ours.

Chadwick v. State Bar
Columbia Supreme Court (1989) ....

In the Matter of Harold Salas, a Member of the State Bar
Review Department of the State Bar Court (2001)......................................

Unlike a case, this appears to be State Bar review/ decision likely similar to what we will be working on.

Read the task memo (and format memo, if provided, and identify the macrostructure for your answer) (7–10 minutes)

Task Memo

This is the most important document in the packet, so slow down and read it very carefully. Follow all directions exactly. Your goal is to identify three key pieces of information:

1. Information about your client: Who is your client? What is your client's legal issue? What is your client's goal?
2. Specific information about the task: What is the task? Who is the audience? Is there more than one task assigned? Are there directions about things to include and exclude?
3. The macrostructure of your answer: Can you start your roadmap?

Watkins Task Information

- **Client info:** As we suspected, Watkins is an attorney. We represent Ms. Watkins, who pled guilty to felony insider trading that occurred more than two years ago. The Columbia State Bar is now seeking disbarment. Watkins has hired us to prevent that.
- **Task info:** We are asked to draft a persuasive argument to be used in a brief by, presumably, another attorney, Tia Lucci. The judge requested the brief after a hearing providing testimony about whether the facts and circumstances surrounding the insider trading involved moral turpitude. The argument for the brief must assert that (1) the conduct underlying the plea does not justify a finding of moral turpitude, and (2) Watkins's testimony at the hearing does not justify a finding of moral turpitude. The audience for our brief will be the judge presiding over the case. We are told not to argue about appropriate discipline. We are also told not to write a separate statement of facts, but rather to use both favorable and unfavorable facts in our persuasive argument.
- **Task structure:** Our argument section for the brief will start with the two main issues that must be asserted, as mentioned above. No format memo is provided, so common sense will dictate an argument organized using the two questions asked in the task. Based on this, we can start our roadmap. We might need to break down each issue into subissues, depending on the case law and on any subarguments in the other disciplinary matter review in the library.

LAW OFFICES OF TIA LUCCI

MEMORANDUM

TO: Applicant

FROM: Tia Lucci

SUBJECT: In the Matter of Abigail Watkins

DATE: July 24, 2018

This case involves a Columbia State Bar disciplinary action against our client, Abigail Watkins. On June 8, 2018, Watkins pled guilty to a single felony count of insider trading that occurred more than two years ago. The State Bar then initiated disciplinary proceedings against Watkins, seeking disbarment. Watkins hired us to prevent that.

We have just completed testimony in a hearing on the threshold issue of whether the facts and circumstances surrounding the insider trading by Watkins involved moral turpitude. The judge has requested simultaneous briefs on this issue. Please draft an argument for me to use in a brief asserting that:

> Brief argument to a judge; persuasive.

> These are our two issues and the beginning of our roadmap structure.

> Both involve moral turpitude.

1)   The conduct underlying the plea does not justify a finding of moral turpitude.

2)   Watkins' testimony at the hearing does not justify a finding of moral turpitude.

> Focus on these two words here when reading file/library.

At this point, we seek to avoid a finding of moral turpitude. Do not argue about appropriate discipline.

> Make a note of what you are NOT supposed to do.

Do not write a separate statement of facts. Instead, incorporate the facts into your persuasive argument, making sure to address both favorable and unfavorable facts.

Step 3.   **Start roadmap (time included in steps 2–7)**

Roadmap

Having a well-planned roadmap is the key to writing a passing performance test. We can start our roadmap using the macrostructure from the task memo, adding to it as we gather more information. We recommend that you make a note at the top of the roadmap listing all essential information, including the client and opposing party, the client's goal, task specifics about included or excluded parts, the tone and vocabulary, any task weighting, and a time goal for when you want to start writing your answer, which will vary based on whether you input the organization and complete rules, etc., as you organize the performance test or you shorthand your roadmap the entire way and then type it all up later in complete sentences.

> *Important note:* When roadmapping for your own use on paper, the result is unlikely to be as thorough or neat as this example. Liberally use abbreviations and symbols to remind yourself where in the file you can find the information you need to use in each section. When roadmapping on the computer, type the rules you know you will use directly into the appropriate section after briefing, but still create a skeleton roadmap on paper setting out the macrostructure. Only write as much as you need to guide you in properly drafting your answer. **This performance test demonstration will show you how each part would look if you were typing it in on the computer as you organized it.**

Watkins Roadmap

From the task memo, we know we will be analyzing an argument to be inserted into a persuasive brief for the judge. The macrostructure will consist of the two issues in the task memo: (1) determining if Watkins's conduct justifies a finding of moral turpitude, and (2) determining if her testimony justifies a finding of moral turpitude. For now, we can set up an argument with an introduction (or at least part of one, for now), the two issues to be addressed, and the conclusion heading; we will fill in more later after we read the library.

To: Tia Lucci
From: Applicant
Re: In the Matter of Abigail Watkins
Date: July 24, 2018

Ms. Lucci,

Pursuant to your request, below is the argument section we can include in our persuasive brief to the judge. The argument should convince the judge that (1) Ms. Watkins's conduct underlying the plea does not justify a finding of moral turpitude, and (2) Ms. Watkins's testimony at the hearing does not justify a finding of moral turpitude. Thus, the judge should find there was no moral turpitude involved here. Please let me know if you need any additional help with Ms. Watkins's case.

Applicant

BRIEF ON BEHALF OF ABIGAIL WATKINS

<u>ARGUMENT</u>

MS. WATKINS'S CONDUCT UNDERLYING THE PLEA DOES NOT JUSTIFY A FINDING OF MORAL TURPITUDE BECAUSE . . . (need to fill in later).

MS. WATKINS'S TESTIMONY AT THE HEARING DOES NOT JUSTIFY A FINDING OF MORAL TURPITUDE BECAUSE . . . (need to fill in later).

For the foregoing reasons, neither Ms. Watkins's conduct nor her testimony at the hearing justify a finding of moral turpitude.

| Step 4. | Skim the client file/facts (2 minutes) |

Skim the Client File/Facts

We know that insider trading is involved in an underlying issue to which our client plead guilty to one count of felony insider trading. We also know that this incident occurred more than two years ago and that the Columbia State Bar is now seeking disbarment, which involves whether Ms. Watkins's actions involved a crime of moral turpitude. We will need to address two issues to the judge concerning whether to find moral turpitude.

Watkins File Skim

Below is our quick takeaway from the skim of the facts:

- **Plea Agreement**: Defendant Watkins pled guilty voluntarily to a single sale of stock for insider trading.
- **Factual Basis for the Plea:** Watkins is a patent-trademark partner with Wakefield and represented Fort in patent matters. Watkins spoke with Fort's GC about the Fort acquisition. Watkins bought shares of Fort after that discussion and then sold her shares for a profit.
- **Transcript from Hearing Dept. of State Bar Court**: Talks about buying shares of Fort, taking some medicine following a surgery, questions about billing hours for Fort talk, and discussion about Watkins's plea agreement and what she remembers from that.
- **Our assessment from the skim of the facts:** We will definitely need to review the facts in more detail later, especially the hearing transcript. We can see that Watkins did agree to a plea agreement, but there seems to be a question as to what exactly she agreed to in that plea. Also, we will need to look at in more detail her representation of Fort and her phone call to learn the extent to which she knew about the stock/merger/price increase when she bought and sold the shares. Since we don't have much here, you can just input a few of the facts you do know into your overall answer and note what you still need to look at in more detail when you return to the facts for a thorough read.

Since we are just skimming the facts, the facts that are noteworthy from this first skim are underlined.

UNITED STATES DISTRICT COURT

FOR THE NORTHERN DISTRICT OF COLUMBIA

UNITED STATES OF AMERICA, v. ABIGAIL WATKINS, Defendant.	Criminal Case No. 2018-999-111 VIOLATION: 15 U.S.C. 78j (Insider Trading)

Underlying criminal issue

PLEA AGREEMENT

Pursuant to Rule 11 of the Federal Rules of Criminal Procedure, the United States of America and the defendant, Abigail Watkins, agree as follows:

1. The defendant is entering into this agreement and is <u>pleading guilty freely and voluntarily without promise or benefit of any kind</u> (other than contained herein), and <u>without threats, force, intimidation, or coercion of any kind.</u>

2. The indictment relates to a <u>single sale of stock by the defendant.</u> The defendant pleads guilty.

3. The defendant <u>knowingly, voluntarily and truthfully admits the facts contained in the attached Factual Basis for Plea.</u>

FOR THE DEFENDANT

Dated: ___June 8, 2018___

____*Abigail Watkins*_____   ____*Tia Lucci*_____

Abigail Watkins   Tia Lucci

Defendant   Counsel for Defendant

FOR THE UNITED STATES

Dated: ___June 8, 2018___

____*Mary Butler*_____   _____*Stephanie Evans*___

Mary Butler   Stephanie Evans
Criminal Division   Securities Criminal Enforcement
   U.S. Department of Justice   U.S. Department of Justice

ATTACHMENT A

FACTUAL BASIS FOR THE PLEA OF ABIGAIL WATKINS

This agreement is submitted to provide a factual basis for Defendant's plea of guilty.

1. As a patent-trademark partner with Wakefield and Lester (Wakefield), Defendant represented Fort Software, Inc. (Fort) in patent and other matters since 2011.

2. On August 13, 2015, Samantha Darmond, Fort's general counsel, left a voice mail message on Defendant's phone to call her about "an urgent patent matter." On the morning of August 16, Defendant returned the call, and she and Darmond spoke. Darmond told Defendant that Silicon Microsystems (Silicon), a large publicly traded company, was planning to acquire Fort and that Darmond was coordinating Silicon's requests in its due diligence efforts as to Fort's patents. Darmond wanted Defendant to share patent files in the Wakefield office with Silicon's counsel so that Silicon could complete its due diligence review of Fort.

3. About midday on August 16, Defendant placed a brokerage "market order" to buy 1,000 shares of Fort. She paid $13.50 per share. This is the basis for the indictment.

4. The merger of Fort into Silicon was publicly announced before the market's opening on August 23. When the merger was consummated, shares of Fort stock were exchanged at a certain ratio for shares in Silicon. In October 2015, Defendant sold her Silicon shares for a $14,000 profit.

5. In May 2016, Defendant received a call from an agent at the Securities and Exchange Commission (SEC), who was looking into the trading of shares of Fort in the period before the merger. Defendant readily admitted to purchasing Fort in her own name on August 16. Defendant told the SEC that at the time of the August 16 purchase she was not aware of the planned merger.

Dated:

___June 8, 2018___   _____*Abigail Watkins*_____

                                                                 Abigail Watkins, Defendant

---

[margin note:] We will read the details again later after reading the library to see what facts matter.

HEARING DEPARTMENT OF THE STATE BAR COURT
HEARING IN THE MATTER OF ABIGAIL WATKINS

July 20, 2018

Case No. 18-SF-1023

State Bar Court Judge Margaret Kenler

BY THE COURT: Mr. Simonds, you may proceed.

ASSISTANT CHIEF TRIAL COUNSEL MATT SIMONDS: Your honor, this morning the State Bar relies on the Factual Basis for the Plea Agreement. We're standing on the admissions that the Respondent made in her plea agreement and in that Factual Basis. Specifically, we rely on her statements that she made a purchase of stock in Fort Software with knowledge of an impending purchase of Fort by Silicon Microsystems, knowledge that she gained through conversations with lawyers representing Silicon Microsystems. I understand that the Respondent will also testify. We rest.

BY THE COURT: Ms. Lucci, you may proceed.

BY TIA LUCCI: Thank you, your honor. We call the Respondent, Abigail Watkins.

ABIGAIL WATKINS

EXAMINATION BY MS. LUCCI: Ms. Watkins, could you please briefly describe your professional education and preparation.

WATKINS: I have a J.D. and a degree in chemical engineering from Worcester Polytechnic Institute. I practiced intellectual property law for many years before joining Wakefield and Lester in 2006. I chair its intellectual property group.

LUCCI: You have been a member of the bar in Columbia since 1991, and before that in Virginia and the District of Columbia. Have you ever been disciplined or even cited or received notice of any charges involving any discipline?

WATKINS: Never, until now.

LUCCI: You represent Fort Software?

Note the people involved.

Her knowledge will likely go to moral turpitude later, so we will pay close attention to this later on during our detailed read.

WATKINS: Yes, in 2011 I personally advised and represented Fort during its start-up phase and when it went public a few years later. I have followed Fort since then and intended to make a purchase of its stock. Everything I read online about Fort, the stock recommendations from rating agencies, were very positive on Fort. At that point the patents were public information. But I never did so.

LUCCI: Did you reconsider that decision?

WATKINS: Yes. In June 2015, Fort was trading at $10 a share, and by August it was at $13. Two major brokerage companies had upgraded Fort stock from a "buy" to a "strong buy." The technology message boards were talking up Fort as a likely merger target for its software. I know that I was planning to make a purchase. I wasn't going to lose out again.

LUCCI: In July 2015, you underwent surgery for a tear to your rotator cuff.

WATKINS: Yes, July 14th.

LUCCI: Your doctor gave and you filled prescriptions both for Percocet and Ambien?

WATKINS: Yes, Percocet for pain and the Ambien to help me sleep. Percocet is something with oxycodone and the doctor said it's a potent pain reliever, for severe pain, but that I could take one or two tablets every 4 hours. I took it a lot, although I now know that it had some side effects. I was told not to take it before driving, and no alcohol.

LUCCI: How much and how long did you take Percocet?

WATKINS: I don't know. The prescription was for 50 tablets. I took it on and off until it ran out.

LUCCI: Were you still taking Percocet at the time of the Fort-Silicon merger?

WATKINS: I don't know. My memory from the surgery in July until September is very poor. I was very distracted by the pain and the medications, and trying to maintain a normal full-time work schedule.

LUCCI: You returned to work five days after surgery?

WATKINS: Yes, although I had considerable pain and limited mobility.

LUCCI: Turning to the Fort merger, when did you hear from Fort?

WATKINS: In 2015, I was not actively representing Fort. My best recollection is that on August 16, 2015 I received a call from Fort's general counsel, Samantha Darmond, with whom I had not previously worked, or from an attorney at Jordan & Haines. I really can't remember which. Anyway, I was asked to send our patent files over to J & H.

LUCCI: In the conversation, do you remember anything being said about a pending merger, or due diligence, or the need for confidentiality?

WATKINS: No. I thought that Fort was going to be represented by J & H. It's a top intellectual property firm, and I considered it a positive development for Fort. I had the files assembled, but did nothing more. I didn't think it was urgent. I think it was the next day that I received another call from the attorney at J & H about the files.

LUCCI: On August 16, did you place an order to purchase 1,000 shares of Fort?

WATKINS: Yes.

LUCCI: Was it because you knew about the merger?

WATKINS: It is my best recollection of that purchase, that on that day I was acting on my general opinion and my previous interest in Fort, observations from the message boards and buy recommendations. And as I said, I thought J & H's involvement was also good news. Looking back now, I know that I made a mistake.

LUCCI: Nothing further.

CROSS-EXAMINATION BY ASSISTANT CHIEF TRIAL COUNSEL SIMONDS:

SIMONDS: Do you claim that the Percocet or Ambien made you commit insider stock trading?

WATKINS: No, of course not.

SIMONDS: Did you have symptoms of delirium, or inability to reason, or impaired ability to understand your moral or ethical duties?

WATKINS: No, of course not. But I didn't appreciate the effect that had on me, as I can now.

> *Again, knowledge will likely be an issue later.*

> *Note we are now on cross.*

> *A new party is involved now.*

SIMONDS: Neither drug left you mentally impaired or diminished your mental capacity?

WATKINS: As to actual effects of those drugs, you are asking the wrong person. It is not for me to say.

SIMONDS: Since you only had 50 Percocets, if you had taken just three a day, less than your doctor said you could, it would have run out in 17 days, or a week or more before the call about the merger. Correct?

WATKINS: I don't know. I took it infrequently, in reaction to pain. Then I would take it for a day or two and then stop.

SIMONDS: You saw your doctor several times between the surgery and mid-August. Did you complain about the effects of Percocet, tell him that you were mentally impaired?

WATKINS: No. The doctor said that continued pain in that period was normal.

SIMONDS: You would agree that it would be hard for any alleged Percocet intoxication to have caused you to commit an insider stock purchase?

WATKINS: That's not what I am saying. The Percocet and the pain, however, may have distracted my thinking, left me insufficiently attentive to what Ms. Darmond was telling me, why I could have failed to register what was so important, and especially why I don't have a very clear memory of what she told me in conversations or voice messages. My partner and associates were telling me that I was unfocused during that time.

SIMONDS TO COURT: Objection and move to strike. Hearsay and unresponsive.

COURT: The statements of others as to her mental state are stricken.

SIMONDS: As to your testimony that your stock purchase on August 16th was not based on anything about a pending merger told to you by Ms. Darmond, but on message boards and the like -- Those boards and buy recommendations were because of expectations of a Fort merger. Correct?

WATKINS: Yes.

SIMONDS: It is true, isn't it, that you were told on August 16th to gather the Fort patent files and you in fact did that?

WATKINS: Yes, my billing record on that date is 0.7 hour to review the Fort files and prepare a transmittal letter to J & H.

SIMONDS: Ms. Watkins, you agreed in the plea agreement that Ms. Darmond told you of the merger and that it was confidential information, before you made the purchase of Fort stock on August 16th.

WATKINS: That is what I agreed to.

SIMONDS: But now in your direct testimony today you claim that what you agreed to in a guilty plea is not true?

WATKINS: No, only that I don't remember it that clearly, that I don't remember that she told me she was talking about an imminent merger. I grasped the task, to assemble our patent files to send to other counsel, but little more. I had someone put together the documents she wanted, but I did not consider the matter sufficiently urgent to do more, and instead waited to hear from someone from J & H.

SIMONDS: I don't understand. Do you deny what you agreed was true in the plea agreement?

WATKINS: I am trying to say that the statement in the plea agreement is contrary to my memory of the event. But I agreed to it because my attorneys explained that it was a good deal. I received probation instead of jail time. I knew that the version in the plea agreement was Ms. Darmond's recollection and what she'd say if she testified. I simply have no recollection of it. And so I can't deny that the August 16th conversation with Ms. Darmond took place, nor can I agree that it happened and led me to the stock order.

SIMONDS: But long before today, didn't you refute her version?

WATKINS: What do you mean?

SIMONDS: Eight months after the merger, the SEC called you. Correct?

WATKINS: Yes, totally out of the blue.

SIMONDS: Right. You had no warning and were taken by surprise by the call.

WATKINS: I was shaken, and as I was trying to collect my thoughts to answer the questions, I saw my life passing before my eyes.

> Again, goes to knowledge; will matter later.

SIMONDS: You had enough control to repeat your story that you didn't know about the merger when you made the August 16 purchase?

WATKINS: Yes, Mr. Simonds. I told that to the SEC and I am telling it today because it is my best recollection.

SIMONDS: Nothing further, your honor.

BY THE COURT: As we agreed, then, simultaneous briefs due in one week. We are adjourned.

This is how your answer should look at this point if you are adding details as you organize your answer:

To: Tia Lucci
From: Applicant
Re: In the Matter of Abigail Watkins
Date: July 24, 2018

Ms. Lucci,

Pursuant to your request, below is the argument section we can include in our persuasive brief to the judge. The argument should convince the judge that (1) Ms. Watkins's conduct underlying the plea does not justify a finding of moral turpitude, and (2) Ms. Watkins's testimony at the hearing does not justify a finding of moral turpitude. Thus, the judge should find there was no moral turpitude involved here. Please let me know if you need any additional help with Ms. Watkins's case.

Applicant

ARGUMENT

MS. WATKINS'S CONDUCT UNDERLYING THE PLEA DOES NOT JUSTIFY A FINDING OF MORAL TURPITUDE BECAUSE . . . (need to fill in later).

Look more closely into plea agreement facts (note Watkins did voluntarily agree to plead guilty to insider trading). Consider Watkins's actual actions when she purchased and sold her shares — but first look at library and see what rules are applicable before going over factual details.

MS. WATKINS'S TESTIMONY AT THE HEARING DOES NOT JUSTIFY A FINDING OF MORAL TURPITUDE BECAUSE . . . (need to fill in later).

Look more closely into plea agreement facts and at the hearing transcript to learn more about Watkins's knowledge of Fort at the time she purchased and sold her shares — but first look at the library and see what rules are applicable before going over factual details.

For the foregoing reasons, neither Ms. Watkins's conduct nor her testimony at the hearing justify a finding of moral turpitude.

| Step 5. | **Actively read the library and synthesize rules (20–30 minutes)** |

Read the Library and Deconstruct and Synthesize Rules as Needed

We are looking for the rules we can use to solve the problem posed and any analysis we can borrow from the cases. Depending on the task, we may need to synthesize cases or identify which rule among competing rules should be adopted. To most efficiently assess the library, read the materials in the order presented, since most often the rules are provided in the same order that they can be used to solve the problem, given the task macrostructure. Book brief the cases and add information to the roadmap as you go. Annotate your cases with notes so you don't waste time rewriting sentences into your roadmap. Determine how to best use any statutes. Each case in the library was included because it is likely to be needed to solve the problem, so it is up to you to determine how each can best be used. We typically note at the top of each case where it will be used in our answer and whether it is favorable or not for our client by writing a plus or minus sign on the top. Continue to look for clues as to how you should structure your answer.

Watkins's Cases

The library contains only one court case; at two pages in length, it is shorter than most cases. The library also contains a three-page write-up from a review of another attorney's matter (likely similarly situated to our client), however. We know we need to find a structure for organizing our presentation encompassing (1) "conduct" that involves a finding of moral turpitude, and (2) "testimony" that could find the same. Further, because this is a persuasive task, we are looking for reasoning that bolsters our argument to the State Bar that our client should not be disbarred based on a lack of moral turpitude.

- <u>Chadwick v. State Bar:</u> This case is binding, as it is in the Columbia Supreme Court (our jurisdiction). This case involved an attorney who pled guilty to misdemeanor insider trading. The attorney was informed about a possible tender offer and purchased stock options from the company that was to be taken over. He later sold that stock for a profit. The court defined moral turpitude. (Add this definition into your roadmap/answer now if you are writing it as you brief the cases.) The court agreed with the review board and found against the attorney. This case will be used in our first section on attorney conduct.

- <u>Matter of Harold Salas:</u> This review dept. matter involves attorney misconduct (which is different from our insider trading case). It focuses on the standard the State Bar bears: clear and convincing evidence to prove moral turpitude. Here, since the attorney's testimony contradicted another witness's, the story of either one could have been believed, and any reasonable doubts must be resolved in favor of the accused attorney. This case will be used in our second section on testimony.

At this time enter all rules into the appropriate part of your roadmap/answer.

Note this case goes to the first issue of CONDUCT from the task memo (1); note how the task memo note told you to focus on two key words, CONDUCT being one of them.

Mark outcome up here for easy reference later.

— for attorney

CHADWICK v. STATE BAR

Columbia Supreme Court (1989)

Binding in our jx

Similar underlying crime to our client.

We review the recommendation of the Review Department of the State Bar Court that petitioner, William Chadwick, be suspended from the practice of law following his misdemeanor conviction for violating federal statutes prohibiting insider trading and for related misconduct. The Review Department recommended that Chadwick be suspended from the practice of law for a period of five years; that execution of the suspension be stayed, subject to two years actual suspension. On appeal, we review the facts underlying Chadwick's conviction to determine whether they constitute moral turpitude.

Issue and case history

Relevant facts underlined; would be highlighted in yellow on real paper "book brief" style.

Chadwick was admitted to the practice of law in Columbia in December 1973. Formerly, he was a partner in a large firm. Chadwick is currently a sole practitioner, primarily rendering legal advice about alternative investment structures. He has no prior record of discipline.

Chadwick's misconduct began in December 1981 when he acquired material, nonpublic information regarding a tender offer involving the Brunswick Corporation from a Martin Cooper, who was a bank officer and banker for the Whittaker Corporation. The Whittaker Corporation was the company attempting to take over the Brunswick Corporation. Chadwick purchased stock options of the Brunswick Corporation for himself. Later, the takeover of Brunswick by the Whittaker Corporation was publicly announced.

Need to see if our client did the same.

Chadwick was later contacted by the SEC. After consulting with counsel, Chadwick informed the SEC that he had relied upon material, nonpublic information concerning the Brunswick tender offer.

Similar to our client at first glance.

On July 1982, Chadwick was charged in U.S. District Court with one misdemeanor count of having violated 15 United States Code section 78(j). Chadwick pled guilty to the count as charged and was fined $10,000 and ordered

[Facts the court looks at for moral turpitude issue.]

to disgorge profits. The plea agreement establishes the facts relevant to the question of moral turpitude and facts that may be used to impeach Chadwick.

Thereafter, the State Bar issued an order to show cause charging Chadwick with willfully committing acts involving moral turpitude within the meaning of Business and Professions Code section 6101. These charges were based on Chadwick's illegal purchase of stock options, the acts that underlay his misdemeanor conviction.

[All rules underlined here would be highlighted in blue on our paper for easy future reference; seems like these rules defining moral turpitude would go in section (1) of our brief.]

As we have noted on numerous occasions, the concept of moral turpitude escapes precise definition. For purposes of the Rules of Professional Responsibility, moral turpitude has been described as an act of baseness, vileness or depravity in the private and social duties that a man owes to his fellowmen, or to society in general, contrary to the accepted and customary rule of right and duty between man and man. To summarize, it has been described as any crime or misconduct without excuse. The meaning and test is the same whether the dishonest or immoral act is a felony, misdemeanor, or no crime at all.

[Attorney argues.]

[Rule/Court reasoning against attorney; highlight reasoning in pink on paper.]

Chadwick argues that his willingness to comply with the SEC's investigation excuses his earlier conduct. However, the concept of excuse relates to Chadwick's conduct at the time of the violations to which he pled guilty. Here, Chadwick's guilty plea rests on facts that indicate no such excuse at the time he purchased the stock.

Chadwick also argues that, by entering into a plea agreement, he did not concede that the factual basis for the criminal plea would justify ethical discipline based on those facts. However, even if true, this proposition does not prevent this court from reviewing the factual basis of the plea to determine whether the conduct it describes justifies a finding of moral turpitude.

[Holding against attorney.]

In this case, we agree with the Review Department's conclusion that the facts and circumstances of the particular offense and Chadwick's related conduct establish that Chadwick's acts involved moral turpitude. We adopt the Review Department's recommended discipline.

Note this case goes to the second issue of TESTIMONY from the task memo (2). Note how the task memo note told you to focus on two key words, TESTIMONY being one of them.

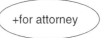

+for attorney

In the Matter of HAROLD SALAS, a Member of the State Bar

Review Department of the State Bar Court (2001)

In 1999, Harold Salas entered a plea to conspiracy to obstruct justice. After his conviction, the State Bar Court held a hearing to recommend appropriate discipline pursuant to Section 6102(a) of the Business and Professions Code.   After the hearing, the State Bar Court recommended disbarment rather than discipline because it concluded that Salas had lied at the hearing.

Different underlying action, so likely about the plea itself.

In 1995, Respondent entered into a business relationship with Anna Bash, the owner/operator of Chekov Legal Services in the Little Russia neighborhood. Respondent paid Bash $5,000 per month to market his practice to the Russian community in the City of Angels and to provide him with a secretary and a translator. Respondent would assist Bash in providing legal services, many on a pro bono basis, and Bash would refer personal injury, criminal, and other fee cases to Respondent. Respondent admitted he agreed to split fees with Bash, a non-attorney, and that this was illegal.

Facts in underlying case.

The District Attorney's Office filed a criminal complaint against Respondent and Bash as co-defendants in a "capping" conspiracy, alleging that Respondent paid Bash for referring clients to him. There were several charges of referral and fee-splitting, including one that alleged that Respondent issued a check for $10,000 to Bash from the proceeds of a settlement of a personal injury case. The District Attorney claimed that the $10,000 payment was an illegal payment in exchange for Bash's referring the case to Respondent.

Attorney agreed to only one count of conspiracy.

Respondent and Bash were each charged with three felony counts: (1) conspiracy to commit a crime; (2) capping; and (3) conspiracy to commit an act injurious to the public.   Respondent pled no contest to count three as a misdemeanor; and the District Attorney dismissed counts one and two.

In the hearing below, Respondent testified that he owed Bash $10,000 for two months of services, and that he properly withdrew that amount from the settlement because it was a part of his contingency fee in the case. Respondent denied that the payment to Bash was for referral of the personal injury case to him.

Discrepancy as to reason for payment.

After her own plea agreement, Bash testified against Respondent. Her testimony directly contradicted Respondent's. She did, however, confirm that she operated an office, which included substantial secretarial and translation services, and that Respondent was paying her $5,000 a month and that $10,000 was due when she was paid. She was adamant that the $10,000 was for the referral.

State Bar court reasoning against attorney.

The State Bar Court did not accept Respondent's testimony about the payment, and questioned why he would advance it before the court. The State Bar Court concluded that his lack of candor in the proceedings itself warranted a finding of moral turpitude.

This court's reasoning for attorney.

Rule: Highlight in blue.

Based on our review of the record, we find that the State Bar Court's finding of moral turpitude was not supported by clear and convincing evidence that Respondent had testified falsely and hence was guilty of moral turpitude. The State Bar bears the burden to prove moral turpitude by clear and convincing evidence. We conclude that the State Bar did not carry its burden here.

Attorney argues.

Normally, we would defer to a finding of fact from the State Bar Court. But in this case, Respondent contends that the hearing officer did not apply the burden of proof correctly. Respondent argues that there is no reasonable and logical explanation for why he would insist on his version of this one payment, other than the fact that he believes it to be true. It would have been easier, he says, to admit responsibility for this referral as well. Respondent contends that directly contradicting the plea agreement would raise severe doubts as to his candor. However, he asserts that his repeated statement of the innocent purpose of this single payment does not contradict the plea agreement, which is silent on this point.

All rules highlighted in blue on our paper go to testimony, so goes in section (2) of our roadmap.

> Any determination of moral turpitude must be found by clear and convincing evidence. This includes a determination that a witness's testimony lacks candor (i.e., the witness is lying). An honest if mistaken belief in his innocence does not signal a lack of candor. A lack of candor should not be founded merely on Respondent's different memory of events.

Another rule.

Court's reasoning for attorney.

Applying the standard of proof by clear and convincing evidence means that reasonable doubts must be resolved in favor of the accused attorney. If equally reasonable inferences may be drawn from a proven fact, the inference to innocence must be chosen. If, as is the case here, it is equally likely that Respondent is telling the truth about controverted facts, the State Bar has not met its burden of establishing clear and convincing evidence of culpability.

Reversed and remanded.

You have now briefed the case and review department record, so if you are inputting your rules as you go through the steps, you can update your brief as shown below by adding headings to organize the issues and adding all rules and policies. If you follow this approach, you are essentially writing out the performance test as you go through each step.

To: Tia Lucci
From: Applicant
Re: In the Matter of Abigail Watkins
Date: July 24, 2018

Ms. Lucci,

Pursuant to your request, below is the argument section we can include in our persuasive brief to the judge. The argument should convince the judge that (1) Ms. Watkins's conduct underlying the plea does not justify a finding of moral turpitude, and (2) Ms. Watkins's testimony at the hearing does not justify a finding of moral turpitude. Thus, the judge should find there was no moral turpitude involved here. Please let me know if you need any additional help with Ms. Watkins's case.

Applicant

BRIEF ON BEHALF OF ABIGAIL WATKINS

ARGUMENT

MS. WATKINS'S CONDUCT UNDERLYING THE PLEA DOES NOT JUSTIFY A FINDING OF MORAL TURPITUDE BECAUSE . . . (need to fill in later).

Moral turpitude has been described as an act of baseness, vileness, or depravity in the private and social duties that a man owes to his fellowmen, or to society in general, contrary to the accepted and customary rule of right and duty between man and man. Chadwick. Basically, moral turpitude is a crime or misconduct without any excuse. Chadwick. And the test is the same whether the dishonest or immoral act is a felony, misdemeanor, or no crime at all. Chadwick.

In Chadwick, the court found that Mr. Chadwick's conduct involving insider trading did constitute moral turpitude when he purchased stock after being told by a bank officer about a takeover. He later informed the SEC that he had relied upon material, nonpublic information concerning the tender offer. As a result, he pled guilty to a misdemeanor of insider trading. The court indicated that his willingness to comply with the SEC's investigation did not excuse his earlier conduct at the time of the violations to which he pled guilty.

Look into the facts more closely as to the plea agreement facts (note Watkins did voluntarily agree to plead guilty to insider trading) to see more about the actual actions Watkins took when she purchased and sold her shares.

MS. WATKINS'S TESTIMONY AT THE HEARING DOES NOT JUSTIFY A FINDING OF MORAL TURPITUDE BECAUSE . . . (need to fill in later).

The State Bar bears the burden to prove moral turpitude by clear and convincing evidence. Harold Salas. This includes a determination that a witness's testimony lacks candor. Harold Salas. An honest if mistaken belief in one's innocence does not signal a lack of candor. Harold Salas. A lack of candor should not be founded merely on a witness's different memory of events. Harold Salas. Any reasonable doubts must be resolved in favor of the accused attorney. Harold Salas.

In Harold Salas, the Review Department found that even though Salas had a different version than that of another witness as to whether he paid a non-attorney $10,000 for money due or as a referral fee, the court found that the plea agreement was silent as to why he paid the non-attorney $10,000 and, as such, it could not be assumed that he was the one lying. As such, the Bar did not prove by clear and convincing evidence that Salas was lying, and a determination of moral turpitude could not be found.

Look into the plea agreement facts more and at the hearing transcript to learn more about Watkins's knowledge of Fort when she purchased and sold her shares.

For the foregoing reasons, neither Ms. Watkins's conduct nor her testimony at the hearing justify a finding of moral turpitude.

| **Step 6.** | **Actively read the client file/facts (15–20 minutes)** |

Client File/Case Facts

Now that we know from the library the rules governing this situation, we must look for legally significant facts to apply to the rules to solve the problem. We want to look for helpful facts, harmful facts, and any missing facts, if pertinent to the task assigned. Add the legally significant facts into your roadmap as you go or input them into your answer in complete sentences if you are organizing your performance test in that manner.

Watkins's Client File/Case Facts

Plea Agreement Facts

If you are writing out your answer as you review the facts, you could enter these sentences into your answer as you read the facts, or you could wait to enter them until you have read all factual documents and have decided which items you need to include. (The latter is likely the best approach to ensure you don't go over on time.) It is still a good idea to use shorthand on paper first before entering the sentences you think would be useful, rather than writing down everything you see; time is limited, and you only want to include relevant, legally significant facts.

- Watkins pled guilty to violating 15 U.S.C. 78j for insider trading as it pertains to a single sale of stock.
- Watkins entered into the agreement freely and voluntarily without promise or benefit of any kind and without threats, force, intimidation, or coercion.
- Watkins also knowingly, voluntarily, and truthfully admits the facts contained in the factual basis.
- The agreement was dated June 8th.

Attachment A: Factual Basis for Plea

- Watkins was a patent-trademark partner with Wakefield and represented Fort in patent matters since 2011.
- On August 13, 2015, Fort's GC, Samantha Darmond, called Watkins for an urgent patent matter, to which Watkins responded the next day.
- Darmond told Watkins that Silicon, a large publicly traded company, was planning to acquire Fort, and she was calling in regard to Fort's patents at Silicon's request.
- Darmond wanted Watkins to share patent files in the Wakefield office with Silicon's GC so it could complete its due diligence.
- The day of the call, Watkins purchased 1,000 shares of Fort, the merger went through, and the stock prices went up; in October 2015 (two months after Watkins's purchase), Watkins sold her shares for a $14,000 profit.
- In a call with the SEC, Watkins told the SEC that at the time of the purchase she was not aware of the planned merger.

Hearing Transcript for State Bar Hearing

- State bar Chief Counsel is relying on Watkins's statements from the factual plea that she made a purchase of stock in Fort with knowledge of an impending purchase of Fort.
- Watkins has worked with Wakefield in its intellectual property group since 2006.
- In 2011, she personally advised and represented Fort during its start-up phase and when it went public a few years later.
- Watkins intended to purchase Fort stock back then but didn't.
- In June 2015, two major brokerage companies recommended purchasing Fort stock as a "strong buy," up from a "buy," and message boards were talking about Fort being a likely merger target.
- Watkins had surgery in July 2015 and was on pain and sleep medications for a while; she had poor memory from July until September.
- Watkins returned to work five days after the surgery.
- Watkins could not recall who called her on August 15 — the Fort GC or another attorney from J & H — nor could she remember that it was urgent, as she had received another call the following day about the patent files.

- When she placed an order to buy the stock, she was acting on her own opinion, the message boards, and her previous interest.
- Watkins had 50 pills of Percocet for pain. She didn't take them every day but rather intermittently when she had pain, and the medications may have distracted her thinking and made her insufficiently attentive.
- Co-workers told her she was unfocused during that time (HS, so stricken).
- Billing record from the phone call says to get the Fort files and a transmittal letter to J & H.
- In the plea agreement, Watkins agreed that Ms. Darmond told her of the merger and that it was confidential information, but Watkins states that this statement is contrary to what she remembers. Watkins states she agreed to it because her attorneys said she would receive probation instead of jail time, which was a good deal.
- Watkins said the plea agreement was based on Ms. Darmond's recollections and that she herself had no recollection.
- Watkins also told the SEC eight months later that she had no recollection.

Our Assessment of the Detailed Facts

Now that you have the rules and organization input into your answer, you can line up facts with each part of the argument/rule in the letter. You should annotate and highlight the pertinent facts listed above as you read them. Pay attention to similar facts that you will need to rebut as well as to facts that you can distinguish from those in <u>Chadwick</u>. Once you input these facts into your answer, your answer should be close to done, since you have been writing it as you go through each step.

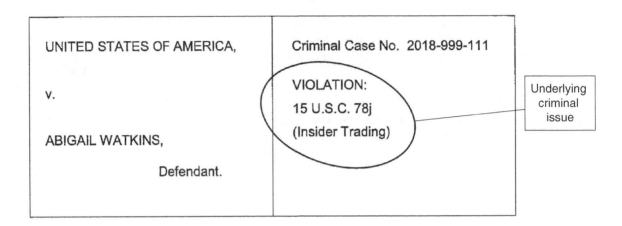

UNITED STATES DISTRICT COURT

FOR THE NORTHERN DISTRICT OF COLUMBIA

UNITED STATES OF AMERICA, v. ABIGAIL WATKINS, Defendant.	Criminal Case No. 2018-999-111 VIOLATION: 15 U.S.C. 78j (Insider Trading)

Underlying criminal issue

PLEA AGREEMENT

> Need to look at facts of plea carefully since Watkins is saying she voluntarily agreed to the plea agreement and the facts in the factual basis for the plea. Goes to moral turpitude for conduct in section (1) of our argument.

Pursuant to Rule 11 of the Federal Rules of Criminal Procedure, the United States of America and the defendant, Abigail Watkins, agree as follows:

1. The defendant is entering into this agreement and is <u>pleading guilty freely and voluntarily without promise or benefit of any kind</u> (other than contained herein), and <u>without threats, force, intimidation, or coercion of any kind.</u>

2. The indictment relates to a <u>single sale of stock by the defendant</u>. The <u>defendant pleads guilty.</u>

3. The defendant <u>knowingly, voluntarily and truthfully admits the facts contained in the attached Factual Basis for Plea.</u>

FOR THE DEFENDANT

Dated: ___June 8, 2018___

____Abigail Watkins_____
Abigail Watkins
Defendant

____Tia Lucci_____
Tia Lucci
Counsel for Defendant

FOR THE UNITED STATES

Dated: ___June 8, 2018___

____*Mary Butler*_____   _____*Stephanie Evans*___

Mary Butler   Stephanie Evans
Criminal Division   Securities Criminal Enforcement
   U.S. Department of Justice   U.S. Department of Justice

ATTACHMENT A

FACTUAL BASIS FOR THE PLEA OF ABIGAIL WATKINS

This agreement is submitted to provide a factual basis for Defendant's plea of guilty.

1. As a patent-trademark partner with Wakefield and Lester (Wakefield), Defendant represented Fort Software, Inc. (Fort) in patent and other matters since 2011.

2. On August 13, 2015, Samantha Darmond, Fort's general counsel, left a voice mail message on Defendant's phone to call her about "an urgent patent matter." On the morning of August 16, Defendant returned the call, and she and Darmond spoke. Darmond told Defendant that Silicon Microsystems (Silicon), a large publicly traded company, was planning to acquire Fort and that Darmond was coordinating Silicon's requests in its due diligence efforts as to Fort's patents. Darmond wanted Defendant to share patent files in the Wakefield office with Silicon's counsel so that Silicon could complete its due diligence review of Fort.

> Facts about the timing of the buy/sell and profits made.

3. About midday on August 16, Defendant placed a brokerage "market order" to buy 1,000 shares of Fort. She paid $13.50 per share. This is the basis for the indictment.

4. The merger of Fort into Silicon was publicly announced before the market's opening on August 23. When the merger was consummated, shares of Fort stock were exchanged at a certain ratio for shares in Silicon. In October 2015, Defendant sold her Silicon shares for a $14,000 profit.

> Goes to knowledge about the merger and her moral turpitude as to her conduct.

5. In May 2016, Defendant received a call from an agent at the Securities and Exchange Commission (SEC), who was looking into the trading of shares of Fort in the period before the merger. Defendant readily admitted to purchasing Fort in her own name on August 16. Defendant told the SEC that at the time of the August 16 purchase she was not aware of the planned merger.

Dated:

___June 8, 2018___   _____*Abigail Watkins*_____

                                       Abigail Watkins, Defendant

HEARING DEPARTMENT OF THE STATE BAR COURT
HEARING IN THE MATTER OF ABIGAIL WATKINS

July 20, 2018

Case No. 18-SF-1023

State Bar Court Judge Margaret Kenler

BY THE COURT: Mr. Simonds, you may proceed.

ASSISTANT CHIEF TRIAL COUNSEL MATT SIMONDS: Your honor, this morning the State Bar relies on the Factual Basis for the Plea Agreement. We're standing on the admissions that the Respondent made in her plea agreement and in that Factual Basis. Specifically, we rely on her statements that she made a purchase of stock in Fort Software with knowledge of an impending purchase of Fort by Silicon Microsystems, knowledge that she gained through conversations with lawyers representing Silicon Microsystems. I understand that the Respondent will also testify. We rest.

BY THE COURT: Ms. Lucci, you may proceed.

BY TIA LUCCI: Thank you, your honor. We call the Respondent, Abigail Watkins.

> Note the people involved.

> As we suspected, the State Bar is relying on her statements, so we need to show that her statements do not show moral turpitude.

ABIGAIL WATKINS

EXAMINATION BY MS. LUCCI: Ms. Watkins, could you please briefly describe your professional education and preparation.

WATKINS: I have a J.D. and a degree in chemical engineering from Worcester Polytechnic Institute. I practiced intellectual property law for many years before joining Wakefield and Lester in 2006. I chair its intellectual property group.

LUCCI: You have been a member of the bar in Columbia since 1991, and before that in Virginia and the District of Columbia. Have you ever been disciplined or even cited or received notice of any charges involving any discipline?

WATKINS: Never, until now.

LUCCI: You represent Fort Software?

> Shows she has had intent to purchase Fort stock for a while and not just now with an upcoming merger.

WATKINS: Yes, in 2011 I personally advised and represented Fort during its start-up phase and when it went public a few years later. I have followed Fort since then and intended to make a purchase of its stock. Everything I read online about Fort, the stock recommendations from rating agencies, were very positive on Fort. At that point the patents were public information. But I never did so.

LUCCI: Did you reconsider that decision?

> More evidence that shows she was planning on buying stock based on personal knowledge, not through inside information. Shows no moral turpitude in conduct, unlike <u>Chadwick</u> case.

WATKINS: Yes. In June 2015, Fort was trading at $10 a share, and by August it was at $13. Two major brokerage companies had upgraded Fort stock from a "buy" to a "strong buy." The technology message boards were talking up Fort as a likely merger target for its software. I know that I was planning to make a purchase. I wasn't going to lose out again.

LUCCI: In July 2015, you underwent surgery for a tear to your rotator cuff.

WATKINS: Yes, July 14th.

LUCCI: Your doctor gave and you filled prescriptions both for Percocet and Ambien?

WATKINS: Yes, Percocet for pain and the Ambien to help me sleep. Percocet is something with oxycodone and the doctor said it's a potent pain reliever, for severe pain, but that I could take one or two tablets every 4 hours. I took it a lot, although I now know that it had some side effects. I was told not to take it before driving, and no alcohol.

LUCCI: How much and how long did you take Percocet?

WATKINS: I don't know. The prescription was for 50 tablets. I took it on and off until it ran out.

LUCCI: Were you still taking Percocet at the time of the Fort-Silicon merger?

> We can use these memory issues to show a lack of knowledge = no moral turpitude.

WATKINS: I don't know. My memory from the surgery in July until September is very poor. I was very distracted by the pain and the medications, and trying to maintain a normal full-time work schedule.

LUCCI: You returned to work five days after surgery?

WATKINS: Yes, although I had considerable pain and limited mobility.

LUCCI: Turning to the Fort merger, when did you hear from Fort?

Can't even remember who she spoke with. Good to show lack of memory for content of conversation.

WATKINS: In 2015, I was not actively representing Fort. My best recollection is that on August 16, 2015 I received a call from Fort's general counsel, Samantha Darmond, with whom I had not previously worked, or from an attorney at Jordan & Haines. I really can't remember which. Anyway, I was asked to send our patent files over to J & H.

Not clear if sending over files shows merger known.

LUCCI: In the conversation, do you remember anything being said about a pending merger, or due diligence, or the need for confidentiality?

Facts that show lack of knowledge = no moral turpitude issue.

WATKINS: No. I thought that Fort was going to be represented by J & H. It's a top intellectual property firm, and I considered it a positive development for Fort. I had the files assembled, but did nothing more. I didn't think it was urgent. I think it was the next day that I received another call from the attorney at J & H about the files.

LUCCI: On August 16, did you place an order to purchase 1,000 shares of Fort?

WATKINS: Yes.

LUCCI: Was it because you knew about the merger?

Rational explanation for reason she purchased stock similar to Salas review = no moral turpitude if can go either way; State bar needs to prove by C & C evidence.

WATKINS: It is my best recollection of that purchase, that on that day I was acting on my general opinion and my previous interest in Fort, observations from the message boards and buy recommendations. And as I said, I thought J & H's involvement was also good news. Looking back now, I know that I made a mistake.

LUCCI: Nothing further.

Note we are now on cross.

CROSS-EXAMINATION BY ASSISTANT CHIEF TRIAL COUNSEL SIMONDS:

SIMONDS: Do you claim that the Percocet or Ambien made you commit insider stock trading?

WATKINS: No, of course not.

A new party is involved now.

SIMONDS: Did you have symptoms of delirium, or inability to reason, or impaired ability to understand your moral or ethical duties?

WATKINS: No, of course not. But I didn't appreciate the effect that had on me, as I can now.

SIMONDS: Neither drug left you mentally impaired or diminished your mental capacity?

WATKINS: As to actual effects of those drugs, you are asking the wrong person. It is not for me to say.

SIMONDS: Since you only had 50 Percocets, if you had taken just three a day, less than your doctor said you could, it would have run out in 17 days, or a week or more before the call about the merger. Correct?

WATKINS: I don't know. I took it infrequently, in reaction to pain. Then I would take it for a day or two and then stop.

SIMONDS: You saw your doctor several times between the surgery and mid-August. Did you complain about the effects of Percocet, tell him that you were mentally impaired?

WATKINS: No. The doctor said that continued pain in that period was normal.

SIMONDS: You would agree that it would be hard for any alleged Percocet intoxication to have caused you to commit an insider stock purchase?

WATKINS: That's not what I am saying. The Percocet and the pain, however, may have distracted my thinking, left me insufficiently attentive to what Ms. Darmond was telling me, why I could have failed to register what was so important, and especially why I don't have a very clear memory of what she told me in conversations or voice messages. My partner and associates were telling me that I was unfocused during that time.

SIMONDS TO COURT: Objection and move to strike. Hearsay and unresponsive.

COURT: The statements of others as to her mental state are stricken.

SIMONDS: As to your testimony that your stock purchase on August 16th was not based on anything about a pending merger told to you by Ms. Darmond, but on message boards and the like -- Those boards and buy recommendations were because of expectations of a Fort merger. Correct?

WATKINS: Yes.

SIMONDS: It is true, isn't it, that you were told on August 16th to gather the Fort patent files and you in fact did that?

> Simonds is trying to negate her loss of memory but it isn't working.

> Even though HS and can't come in, might still argue in brief that even others noticed her lack of focus.

> Even if based on a possible merger, doesn't negate that she could have bought stock based on this outside information, like Salas review.

> **Billing doesn't even mention merger.**

WATKINS: Yes, my billing record on that date is 0.7 hour to review the Fort files and prepare a transmittal letter to J & H.

SIMONDS: Ms. Watkins, you agreed in the plea agreement that Ms. Darmond told you of the merger and that it was confidential information, before you made the purchase of Fort stock on August 16th.

> **Goes to knowledge— moral turpitude of conduct and testimony—use in both sections to show her action was excused (unlike Chadwick) b/c of memory and testimony; honest since simply can't remember.**

WATKINS: That is what I agreed to.

SIMONDS: But now in your direct testimony today you claim that what you agreed to in a guilty plea is not true?

WATKINS: No, only that I don't remember it that clearly, that I don't remember that she told me she was talking about an imminent merger. I grasped the task, to assemble our patent files to send to other counsel, but little more. I had someone put together the documents she wanted, but I did not consider the matter sufficiently urgent to do more, and instead waited to hear from someone from J & H.

SIMONDS: I don't understand. Do you deny what you agreed was true in the plea agreement?

> **Two explanations, like in Salas.**

WATKINS: I am trying to say that the statement in the plea agreement is contrary to my memory of the event. But I agreed to it because my attorneys explained that it was a good deal. I received probation instead of jail time. I knew that the version in the plea agreement was Ms. Darmond's recollection and what she'd say if she testified. I simply have no recollection of it. And so I can't deny that the August 16th conversation with Ms. Darmond took place, nor can I agree that it happened and led me to the stock order.

SIMONDS: But long before today, didn't you refute her version?

WATKINS: What do you mean?

SIMONDS: Eight months after the merger, the SEC called you. Correct?

WATKINS: Yes, totally out of the blue.

SIMONDS: Right. You had no warning and were taken by surprise by the call.

WATKINS: I was shaken, and as I was trying to collect my thoughts to answer the questions, I saw my life passing before my eyes.

SIMONDS: You had <u>enough control to repeat your story that you didn't know</u> <u>about the merger when you made the August 16 purchase?</u>

WATKINS: Yes, Mr. Simonds. <u>I told that to the SEC and I am telling it today</u> <u>because it is my best recollection.</u>

SIMONDS: Nothing further, your honor.

BY THE COURT: As we agreed, then, simultaneous briefs due in one week. We are adjourned.

> Story consistent, which shows not lying = no moral turpitude issue.

To: Tia Lucci
From: Applicant
Re: In the Matter of Abigail Watkins
Date: July 24, 2018

Ms. Lucci,

Pursuant to your request, below is the argument section we can include in our persuasive brief to the judge. The argument should convince the judge that (1) Ms. Watkins's conduct underlying the plea does not justify a finding of moral turpitude, and (2) Ms. Watkins's testimony at the hearing does not justify a finding of moral turpitude. Thus, the judge should find there was no moral turpitude involved here. Please let me know if you need any additional help with Ms. Watkins's case.

Applicant

BRIEF ON BEHALF OF ABIGAIL WATKINS

<u>ARGUMENT</u>

MS. WATKINS'S CONDUCT UNDERLYING THE PLEA DOES NOT JUSTIFY A FINDING OF MORAL TURPITUDE BECAUSE AT THE TIME SHE PURCHASED FORT STOCK SHE DID NOT ACT UPON INSIDE CONFIDENTIAL INFORMATION AS SHE HAD NO RECOLLECTION OF THE CONVERSATION ABOUT THE POSSIBLE MERGER AND THUS SHE ACTED WITH AN EXCUSE.

Moral turpitude has been described as an act of baseness, vileness, or depravity in the private and social duties that a man owes to his fellowmen, or to society in general, contrary to the accepted and customary rule of right and duty between man and man. <u>Chadwick</u>. Basically, moral turpitude is a crime or misconduct without any excuse. <u>Chadwick</u>. And the test is the same whether the dishonest or immoral act is a felony, misdemeanor, or no crime at all. <u>Chadwick</u>.

In <u>Chadwick</u>, the court found that Mr. Chadwick's conduct involving insider trading did constitute moral turpitude when he purchased stock after being told by a bank officer about a takeover. He later informed the SEC that he had relied upon material, nonpublic information concerning the tender offer. As a result, he pled guilty to a misdemeanor of insider trading. The court indicated that his willingness to comply with the SEC's investigation did not excuse his earlier conduct at the time of the violations to which he pled guilty.

Similar to <u>Chadwick</u>, Ms. Watkins pled guilty to violating 15 U.S.C. 78j for insider trading as it pertains to a single sale of stock. Ms. Watkins agreed that she entered into the agreement freely and voluntarily without promise or benefit of any kind and without threats, force, intimidation, or coercion. Further she pled that she knowingly, voluntarily, and truthfully admitted the facts contained in the factual basis.

Also similar to <u>Chadwick</u>, Ms. Watkins was an attorney involved with the company purchased. She was a patent-trademark partner with Wakefield and represented Fort in patent matters since 2011. On August 13, 2015, Fort's General Counsel (GC), Samantha Darmond, called Ms. Watkins for an urgent patent matter to which Ms. Watkins responded the next day. Ms. Darmond told Ms. Watkins that Silicon, a large publicly traded company, was planning to acquire Fort, and she was calling in regard to Fort's patents at Silicon's request. Ms. Darmond wanted Ms. Watkins to share patent files in the Wakefield office with Silicon's GC so it could complete its due diligence. The day of the call, Ms. Watkins purchased 1,000 shares of Fort, the merger went through, and the stock prices went up; in October 2015 (two months after Watkins's purchase), Ms. Watkins sold her shares for a $14,000 profit.

While the actions of buying and selling stock are similar to <u>Chadwick</u>, the details surrounding the purchase are very different. Contrary to <u>Chadwick</u>, Ms. Watkins had recently had surgery and was taking medications for pain and sleep, which impacted her memory during the time of the stock purchase. Further, she stated in her plea agreement and again in a call with the SEC, that at the time of the purchase she was not aware of the planned merger, which is unlike <u>Chadwick</u>, who readily admitted he knew about the merger and acted upon that knowledge without any excuse. Ms. Watkins did have an excuse due to her memory issues from her medications. Further, when she placed an order to buy the Fort stock she was acting on her own opinion and the message boards that indicated the purchase of Fort stock was upgraded, from "buy" to "strong buy," due to a likely merger. Ms. Watkins also had a prior interest in purchasing Fort stock, but she never did so until this time. Thus, her actions were not "an act of baseness, vileness, or depravity in the private and social duties that a man owes to his fellowmen," but rather she was acting upon reasonable public information, and she acted with a poor memory due to medications and not with an intent to be immoral or without excuse as Chadwick had acted.

Unlike <u>Chadwick</u>, Ms. Watkins inadvertently committed insider trading with a rational excuse, which is not conduct that justifies a finding of moral turpitude.

MS. WATKINS'S TESTIMONY AT THE HEARING DOES NOT JUSTIFY A FINDING OF MORAL TURPITUDE BECAUSE THERE IS NO CLEAR AND CONVINCING EVIDENCE THAT HER TESTIMONY WAS DISHONEST OR INVOLVED A LACK OF CANDOR.

The State Bar bears the burden to prove moral turpitude by clear and convincing evidence. <u>Harold Salas</u>. This includes a determination that a witness's testimony lacks candor. <u>Harold Salas</u>. An honest if mistaken belief in one's innocence does not signal a lack of candor. <u>Harold Salas</u>. A lack of candor should not be founded merely on a witness's different memory of events. <u>Harold Salas</u>. Any reasonable doubts must be resolved in favor of the accused attorney. <u>Harold Salas</u>.

In <u>Harold Salas</u>, the Review Department found that even though Salas had a different version than that of another witness as to whether he paid a non-attorney $10,000 for money due or as a referral fee, the court found that the plea agreement was silent as to why he paid the non-attorney $10,000, and as such, it could not be assumed that he was the one lying. As such, the Bar did not prove by clear and convincing evidence that Salas was lying, and a determination of moral turpitude could not be found.

Similar to <u>Salas</u>, here the State Bar Chief Counsel is relying on Ms. Watkins's statements from the factual plea agreement that she made a purchase of stock in Fort with knowledge of an impending purchase of Fort. Ms. Watkins had worked with Wakefield in its intellectual property group since 2006, and in 2011, she personally advised and represented Fort during its start-up phase and again when it went public a few years later. Ever since then, Ms. Watkins had intended to purchase Fort stock but didn't up until this transaction.

While the factual basis for the plea agreement stated that Ms. Watkins agreed that Ms. Darmond told her of the merger and that it was confidential information, Ms. Watkins testified that this statement is contrary to what she remembers; she agreed to it because her attorneys said it was a good deal to receive probation instead of jail time. In fact, Ms. Watkins testified that in June 2015 two major brokerage companies recommended purchasing Fort stock as a "strong buy," up from a "buy," and that message boards were talking about Fort being a likely merger target. Based on her prior desire to purchase Fort stock as well as this new public information, Ms. Watkins decided to purchase the stock. She did not purchase the stock because she remembered any information relayed to her by Ms. Darmond.

Further, unlike <u>Salas</u>, here Ms. Watkins even has evidence as to why she would have been acting on her own knowledge and not Ms. Darmond's. Ms. Watkins had surgery in July 2015, was on pain and sleep medications for a while, and had poor memory from July until September. Further, while not admissible in the testimony hearing, colleagues at Ms. Watkins's office also indicated that she was unfocused during this time. She had returned to work five days after her surgery while being medicated with two different medicines for pain and sleep.

To further show why Ms. Watkins was not acting with a lack of candor, Ms. Watkins also testified that she could not even recall who called her on August 15th, the Fort General Counsel or another attorney from J & H, nor could she remember that it was urgent, as she had received another call the following day about the patent files, which she did not send right away. Ms. Watkins also indicated that her medications, which she took when she had pain, may have distracted her thinking and made her insufficiently attentive. Moreover, her billing record did not mention anything about a merger; rather, it just notes getting the Fort files and a transmittal letter to J & H.

All of Ms. Watkins's comments in her testimony are consistent with what she relayed to the SEC when they contacted her eight months after her transaction. While the plea agreement factual basis is based on Ms. Darmond's recollection, and Ms. Watkins agreed to Ms. Darmond's recollection for purposes of taking the plea to avoid jail time, Ms. Watkins has always maintained that she does not recall the discussion of the merger with Ms. Darmond, and, as such, that she did not lie to the SEC or in her testimony. Thus, Ms. Watkins did not act with a lack of candor. Since evidence supports Ms. Watkins's reasons for having no recollection, and since no evidence rebuts her contentions, the State Bar has failed to meet their burden to show clear and convincing evidence that Ms. Watkins's testimony amounts to a finding of moral turpitude. Further, since there are contradicting statements without evidence to the contrary, all reasonable doubts must be resolved in the favor of Ms. Watkins.

For the foregoing reasons, neither Ms. Watkins's conduct nor her testimony at the hearing justify a finding of moral turpitude.

| Step 7. | Reread the task memo and refine your roadmap to solve the problem posed (5 minutes) |

Reread the Task Memo, See the Big Picture, and Solve the Problem
Before you start writing, always take a moment to ensure you are solving the problem posed and haven't gotten off track while going through the documents. Reread the task memo to refocus on precisely what you've been asked to do. Make sure you are clear on your client's goal, plan to use the appropriate tone and vocabulary in your response, and follow all directions in the task memo. Consider your presentation's organization to ensure your response is clear and easy to follow. Lastly, consider the complexity of the various sections and components of your answer to assess how you think the grader will allocate points and devise a plan to spend your time accordingly.

Watkins: Refining the Roadmap
After rereading the task memo, be sure that you are writing an argument section for the brief. While full briefs have questions presented, facts, etc., here you are told specifically not to include a statement of facts. You are also only told to prepare the argument section for the brief for the two issues presented. It is a good idea to have headers, like a brief would have, and to make them stand out by putting them in bold or all caps or underlining them so they stand out for the grader to easily follow your answer. Further, your brief argument must be persuasive, so double-check that your tone is appropriately convincing.

| Step 8. | Write an answer that solves the problem posed (about 45 minutes) |

Since you have been writing your answer the entire time as you went through each step, it should be mostly, if not completely, finished. Now spend your remaining time rereading your answer to make sure everything is cohesive and flows well. You can also use any additional time to bolster your intro, making sure you address the person who initially requested the information, if you didn't already do so. Other possible last-minute steps include completing your headings, making them typographically distinctive; adding a conclusion if one isn't included as yet; and adding details on any facts you may have only summarized earlier to save time.

It is a good idea to have a quick intro addressed to the person who requested you to complete the task.

Remember, you are only asked to do the argument section, so stick to just that.

Start with headings that stand out for each of the two main questions; fill them in at the end when you are done with library/file.

Fill in facts from the library cases after reading those at the same time you input the rules. If you planned to come back later and add in more facts (time permitting), now is the time to do so.

If you don't have time to input a lot of facts just insert here the main facts you think must be included; if there is time at the end, you can add more details and bolster your factual analysis.

SAMPLE ANSWER FOR WATKINS

To: Tia Lucci
From: Applicant
Re: In the Matter of Abigail Watkins
Date: July 24, 2018

Ms. Lucci,

Pursuant to your request, below is the argument section we can include in our persuasive brief to the judge. The argument should convince the judge that (1) Ms. Watkins's conduct underlying the plea does not justify a finding of moral turpitude, and (2) Ms. Watkins's testimony at the hearing does not justify a finding of moral turpitude. Thus, the judge should find there was no moral turpitude involved here. Please let me know if you need any additional help with Ms. Watkins's case.

Applicant

BRIEF ON BEHALF OF ABIGAIL WATKINS

ARGUMENT

MS. WATKINS'S CONDUCT UNDERLYING THE PLEA DOES NOT JUSTIFY A FINDING OF MORAL TURPITUDE BECAUSE AT THE TIME SHE PURCHASED FORT STOCK SHE DID NOT ACT UPON INSIDE CONFIDENTIAL INFORMATION AS SHE HAD NO RECOLLECTION OF THE CONVERSATION ABOUT THE POSSIBLE MERGER AND THUS SHE ACTED WITH AN EXCUSE.

Moral turpitude has been described as an act of baseness, vileness, or depravity in the private and social duties that a man owes to his fellowmen, or to society in general, contrary to the accepted and customary rule of right and duty between man and man. Chadwick. Basically, moral turpitude is a crime or misconduct without any excuse. Chadwick. And the test is the same whether the dishonest or immoral act is a felony, misdemeanor, or no crime at all. Chadwick.

In Chadwick, the court found that Mr. Chadwick's conduct involving insider trading did constitute moral turpitude when he purchased stock after being told by a bank officer about a takeover. He later informed the SEC that he had relied upon material, nonpublic information concerning the tender offer. As a result, he pled guilty to a misdemeanor of insider trading. The court indicated that his willingness to comply with the SEC's investigation did not excuse his earlier conduct at the time of the violations to which he pled guilty.

Similar to Chadwick, Ms. Watkins pled guilty to violating 15 U.S.C. 78j for insider trading as it pertains to a single sale of stock. Ms. Watkins agreed that she entered into the plea agreement freely and voluntarily without promise or benefit of any kind and without threats, force, intimidation, or coercion. Further she pled that she knowingly, voluntarily, and truthfully admitted the facts contained in the factual basis.

Also similar to Chadwick, Ms. Watkins was an attorney involved with the company purchased. She was a patent-trademark partner with Wakefield and represented Fort in patent matters since 2011. On August 13, 2015, Fort's General Counsel (GC), Samantha Darmond, called Ms. Watkins for an urgent patent matter, to which Watkins responded the next day. Ms. Darmond told Ms. Watkins that Silicon, a large publicly traded company, was planning to acquire Fort, and she was calling in regard to Fort's patents at Silicon's request. Ms. Darmond wanted Ms. Watkins to share patent files in the Wakefield office with Silicon's GC so it could complete its due diligence. The day of the call, Ms. Watkins purchased

1,000 shares of Fort, the merger went through, and the stock prices went up; in October 2015 (two months after her purchase), Ms. Watkins sold her shares for a $14,000 profit.

While the actions of buying and selling stock are similar to <u>Chadwick</u>, the details surrounding the purchase are very different. Contrary to <u>Chadwick</u>, Ms. Watkins had recently had surgery and was taking medications for pain and sleep, which impacted her memory during the time of the stock purchase. Further, she stated in her plea agreement and again in a call with the SEC, that at the time of the purchase she was not aware of the planned merger, which is unlike <u>Chadwick</u>, who readily admitted he knew about the merger and acted upon that knowledge without any excuse. Ms. Watkins did have an excuse, due to her memory issues from her medications. Further, when she placed an order to buy the Fort stock she was acting on her own opinion and the message boards that indicated the purchase of Fort stock was upgraded from "buy" to "strong buy," due to a likely merger. She also had prior interest in purchasing Fort stock but never did so until this time. Thus, her actions were not "an act of baseness, vileness, or depravity in the private and social duties that a man owes to his fellowmen," but rather she was acting upon reasonable public information and she acted with a poor memory due to medications and not with an intent to be immoral or without excuse as Chadwick had acted.

Unlike <u>Chadwick</u>, Ms. Watkins inadvertently committed insider trading with a rational excuse, which is not conduct that justifies a finding of moral turpitude.

MS. WATKINS'S TESTIMONY AT THE HEARING DOES NOT JUSTIFY A FINDING OF MORAL TURPITUDE BECAUSE THERE IS NO CLEAR AND CONVINCING EVIDENCE THAT HER TESTIMONY WAS DISHONEST OR INVOLVED A LACK OF CANDOR.

The State Bar bears the burden to prove moral turpitude by clear and convincing evidence. <u>Harold Salas</u>. This includes a determination that a witness's testimony lacks candor. <u>Harold Salas</u>. An honest if mistaken belief in one's innocence does not signal a lack of candor. <u>Harold Salas</u>. A lack of candor should not be founded merely on a witness's different memory of events. <u>Harold Salas</u>. Any reasonable doubts must be resolved in favor of the accused attorney. <u>Harold Salas</u>.

In <u>Harold Salas</u>, the Review Department found that even though Salas had a different version of events than that of another witness as to whether he paid a non-attorney $10,000 for money due or as a referral fee, the court found that the plea agreement was silent as to why he paid the non-attorney $10,000, and as such, it could not be assumed that he was the one lying. As such, the Bar did not prove by clear and convincing evidence that Salas was lying, and a determination of moral turpitude could not be found.

Similar to <u>Salas</u>, here the State Bar Chief Counsel is relying on Ms. Watkins's statements from the factual plea that she made a purchase of stock in Fort with knowledge of an impending purchase of Fort. Ms. Watkins had worked with Wakefield in its intellectual property group since 2006 and in 2011, she personally advised and represented Fort during its start-up phase and when it went public a few years later. Ever since then, Ms. Watkins had intended to purchase Fort stock but didn't up until this transaction.

While the factual basis for the plea agreement stated that Ms. Watkins agreed that Ms. Darmond told her of the merger and that it was confidential information, Ms. Watkins testified that this statement is contrary to what she remembers, but she agreed because her attorneys said it was a good deal to receive probation instead of jail time. In fact, she testified that in June 2015, two major brokerage companies recommended purchasing Fort stock as a "strong buy," up from a "buy," and message boards were talking about Fort being a likely merger target. Based on her prior desire to purchase Fort stock, as well as this new public information, Ms. Watkins decided to purchase the stock. She did not purchase the stock because she remembered any information relayed to her by Ms. Darmond.

Further, unlike <u>Salas</u>, here Ms. Watkins even has evidence as to why she would have been acting on her own knowledge and not Ms. Darmond's. Ms. Watkins had surgery in July

---

Tie in the rule language with your analysis and facts.

Be sure to analogize and distinguish the facts in the library from your facts.

Conclude as to the first issue before moving on to the second issue.

You might find that some facts go to both arguments, so don't be afraid to use the same facts in more than one place in your brief.

2015, was on pain and sleep medications for a while, and had poor memory from July until September. Further, while not admissible in the testimony hearing, colleagues at Ms. Watkins's office also indicated that she was unfocused during this time. She returned to work five days after her surgery while being medicated on two different medicines for pain and sleep.

To further show why Ms. Watkins was not acting with a lack of candor, she also testified that she could not even recall who called her on August 15th, the Fort General Counsel or another attorney from J & H, nor could she remember that it was urgent, as she had received another call the following day about the patent files, which she did not send right away. She also indicated that her medications, which she took when she had pain, may have distracted her thinking and made her insufficiently attentive. Moreover, her billing record did not mention anything about a merger; rather, it just notes getting the Fort files and a transmittal letter to J & H.

> Again, be sure to tie back the rules to the analysis and the burden of proof.

All of Ms. Watkins's comments in her testimony are consistent with what she relayed to the SEC when they contacted her eight months after her transaction. While the plea agreement factual basis is based on Ms. Darmond's recollection, and Ms. Watkins agreed to Ms. Darmond's recollection for purposes of taking the plea to avoid jail time, Ms. Watkins has always maintained that she does not recall the discussion of the merger with Ms. Darmond and, as such, that she did not lie to the SEC or in her testimony. Thus, she did not act with a lack of candor. Further, since there are contradicting statements without evidence to the contrary, all reasonable doubts must be resolved in the favor of Ms. Watkins. Since evidence supports Ms. Watkins's reasons for having no recollection and since no evidence rebuts her contentions, the State Bar has failed to meet its burden to show clear and convincing evidence that Ms. Watkins's testimony amounts to a finding of moral turpitude.

CONCLUSION

> Add an overall conclusion for both issues at the end.

For the foregoing reasons, neither Ms. Watkins's conduct nor her testimony at the hearing justify a finding of moral turpitude.

Self-Assessment Grid: Watkins

Persuasive Brief Argument		

Overall organization and presentation

- ☐ An introduction to the requester stating that you have written the argument section for the brief, as requested
- ☐ Organization for a persuasive brief, with headings and a conclusion
- ☐ Persuasive tone and formal vocabulary, since writing to the court
- ☐ Organization/presentation in the format requested, with two issues addressed separately
- ☐ Appropriately used headings to persuade and guide grader (brief persuasive style headings recommended)
- ☐ Properly cited rules in the case/board review
- ☐ Presentation placed rule and rule explanation before analysis
- ☐ Cases analogized/distinguished, where helpful and appropriate
- ☐ All pertinent facts used effectively
- ☐ All directions in task memo followed, including no statement of facts

Rules (from library)	Rule Explanation (library case facts)	Analysis (our case facts)
Introduction		
Addressing the requestor, briefly describe the task you have been asked to complete. Then set up the brief argument format based on the two issues you need to address.		
Argument		
Watkins's conduct does not justify a finding of moral turpitude.		
☐ Moral turpitude has been described as an act of baseness, vileness, or depravity in the private and social duties that a man owes to his fellowmen, or to society in general, contrary to the accepted and customary rule of right and duty between man and man. <u>Chadwick</u> ☐ Moral turpitude is a crime or misconduct without any excuse. <u>Chadwick</u> ☐ The test is the same whether the dishonest or immoral act is a felony, misdemeanor, or no crime at all. <u>Chadwick</u>	☐ The court found that Mr. Chadwick's conduct involving insider trading did constitute moral turpitude when he purchased stock after being told by a bank officer about a takeover. ☐ He later informed the SEC that he had relied upon material, nonpublic information concerning the tender offer. As a result, he pled guilty to a misdemeanor of insider trading. ☐ The court indicated that his willingness to comply with the SEC's investigation did not excuse his earlier conduct at the time of the violations to which he pled guilty.	☐ Ms. Watkins pled guilty to violating 15 U.S.C. 78j for insider trading as it pertains to a single sale of stock. ☐ Ms. Watkins agreed that she entered into the agreement freely and voluntarily without promise or benefit of any kind and without threats, force, intimidation, or coercion. ☐ She pled that she knowingly, voluntarily, and truthfully admitted the facts contained in the factual basis. ☐ She was a patent-trademark partner with Wakefield and represented Fort in patent matters since 2011. ☐ On 8/13/15 Fort's GC, Samantha Darmond, called Ms. Watkins for an urgent patent matter to which Watkins responded the next day. ☐ Ms. Darmond told Ms. Watkins that Silicon, a large publicly traded company, was planning to acquire Fort, and she was calling in regard to Fort's patents at Silicon's request. ☐ Ms. Darmond wanted Ms. Watkins to share patent files in the Wakefield office with Silicon's GC so it could complete its due diligence. ☐ The day of the call, Ms. Watkins purchased 1,000 shares of Fort, the merger went through, and the stock prices went up; in Oct. 2015, Ms. Watkins sold her shares for a $14,000 profit. ☐ Ms. Watkins had recently had surgery and was taking medications for pain and sleep, which impacted her memory during the time of the stock purchase.

Continued>

Argument		
		☐ Ms. Watkins stated in her plea, and again in a call with the SEC, that at the time of the purchase she was not aware of the planned merger, which is unlike <u>Chadwick</u>, who readily admitted he knew about the merger and acted upon that knowledge without any excuse. ☐ Further, when Ms. Watkins placed an order to buy the Fort stock she was acting on her own opinion and on the message boards that indicated the purchase of Fort stock was upgraded from "buy" to "strong buy" due to a likely merger. ☐ Ms. Watkins's actions were not an act of baseness, vileness, or depravity in the private and social duties that a man owes to his fellowmen but rather she was acting upon reasonable public information and she acted with a poor memory due to medications and not with an intent to be immoral or without excuse, as Chadwick had acted.

Watkins's testimony does not justify a finding of moral turpitude.

☐ The State Bar bears the burden to prove moral turpitude by clear and convincing evidence. This includes a determination that a witness's testimony lacks candor. <u>Salas</u> ☐ An honest if mistaken belief in one's innocence does not signal a lack of candor. <u>Salas</u> ☐ A lack of candor should not be founded merely on a witness's different memory of events. <u>Salas</u> ☐ Any reasonable doubts must be resolved in favor of the accused attorney. <u>Salas</u>	☐ The Review Department found that Salas had a different version than that of another witness as to whether he paid a non-attorney $10,000 for money due or as a referral fee. ☐ The court found that the plea agreement was silent as to why he paid the non-attorney $10,000 and, as such, that it could not be assumed that Salas was the one lying. ☐ The Bar did not prove by clear and convincing evidence that Salas was lying, and a determination of moral turpitude could not be found.	☐ The State Bar Chief Counsel is relying on Ms. Watkins's statements from the factual plea that she made a purchase of stock in Fort with knowledge of an impending purchase of Fort. ☐ Ms. Watkins had worked with Wakefield in its intellectual property group since 2006, and in 2011 she personally advised and represented Fort during its start-up phase and when it went public a few years later. ☐ Ever since then, Ms. Watkins had intended to purchase Fort stock but didn't up until this transaction. ☐ While the factual basis for the plea agreement stated that Ms. Watkins agreed that Ms. Darmond told her of the merger and that it was confidential information, Ms. Watkins testified that this statement is contrary to what she remembers but that she agreed because her attorneys said it was a good deal to receive probation instead of jail time. ☐ She testified that in June 2015 two major brokerage companies recommended purchasing Fort stock as a "strong buy," up from a "buy," and message boards were talking about Fort being a likely merger target.

Continued>

Watkins's testimony does not justify a finding of moral turpitude.		
		☐ Ms. Watkins had surgery in July 2015 and was on pain and sleep medications for a while and had poor memory from July until September.
		☐ Colleagues at Ms. Watkins's office also indicated that she was unfocused during this time.
		☐ She returned to work five days after her surgery, while being medicated on two different medicines for pain and sleep.
		☐ Ms. Watkins also testified that she could not even recall who called her on August 15th, the Fort General Counsel or another attorney from J & H, nor could she remember that it was urgent, as she had received another call the following day about the patent files, which she did not send right away.
		☐ She also indicated that her medications, which she took when she had pain, may have distracted her thinking and made her insufficiently attentive.
		☐ Her billing record did not mention anything about a merger, but rather just noted getting the Fort files and a transmittal letter to J & H.
		☐ All of her comments in her testimony are consistent with what she relayed to the SEC when they contacted her eight months after her transaction.
		☐ Since there are contradicting statements without evidence to the contrary, all reasonable doubts must be resolved in the favor of Ms. Watkins.
		☐ Since evidence supports Ms. Watkins's reasons for having no recollection and since no evidence rebuts her contentions, the State Bar has failed to meet its burden to show clear and convincing evidence that Ms. Watkins's testimony amounts to a finding of moral turpitude.
Conclusion		
☐ Neither Ms. Watkins's conduct nor her testimony at the hearing justify a finding of moral turpitude.		

PT: SELECTED ANSWER 1

To: Tia Lucci

From: Applicant

Subject: In the Matter of Abigail Watkins

Date: July 24, 2018

Brief

Issues Presented:

1. The conduct underlying the Watkins' plea agreement does not justify a finding of moral turpitude.

2. Watkins' testimony at the hearing does not justify a finding of moral turpitude

I. The conduct underlying Abigail Watkins' pleas does not justify a finding of moral turpitude, because at the time of the August 16 stock purchase she did not remember being told about the merger and thus she was with excuse at the time of the violation to which she pled guilty.

The State Bar must show cause to charge Abigail Watkins with willfully committing acts involving moral turpitude within the meaning of Business and Professions Code section 6101. Chadwick v. State Bar heard by the Columbia Supreme Court (1989)

is controlling. The concept of moral turpitude escapes precise definition. For Rules of Professional Responsibility, it has been described as an act of baseness, vileness or depravity in the private and social duties that a man owes to his fellowmen, or to society in general, contrary to the accepted and customary rule of right and duty between man and woman (Chadwick). The court in Chadwick summarized this definition and interpreted it as meeting "any crime or misconduct without excuse," noting that the meaning and test is the same whether the dishonest or immoral act is felony, misdemeanor or no crime at all. Furthermore, the concept of excuse as it relates to conduct is tested as of the time of the violation to which an individual has pled guilty, not whether they had excuse afterwards. In addition, though a defendant does not necessarily concede that the factual basis of a plea justifies ethical discipline, a court may nevertheless review the factual basis underlying the plea to determine if the conduct amounts to moral turpitude.

In Chadwick v. State Bar, Chadwick pled guilty to the misdemeanor of insider trading and related conduct (i.e. the illegal purchase of stock options based on insider information). After Chadwick engaged in the insider trading, he was contacted by the SEC, and after consulting with counsel he cooperated with the SEC's investigation and admitted to relying on insider trading when he bought the stock options in question. Chadwick then argued to the court that his willingness to comply with the SEC investigation showed "excuse" for his violation such that it did not rise to the level of moral turpitude. The Court rejected this argument, because this action took place *after* he had gone through with the insider trading, and since the concept of excuse relates to the insider trading conduct itself, he was not excused. Based on this, the court adopted the Review Department's finding that the underlying insider trading amounted to moral turpitude.

Watkins' case is strikingly similar to that of Chadwick's, but bears an important distinction because of Watkins' lack of awareness of the wrongness of her actions at the time she bought the Fort Stock. Like Chadwick, Watkins admitted in her plea agreement to the purchase of equity securities based on material, nonpublic information, here concerning the merger between Silicon and Fort. Also like Chadwick, Watkins promptly cooperated with the SEC investigation of her, as she quickly admitted to her actions the first time the SEC contacted her with respect to the August 16 transaction.

However unlike Chadwick, Watkins was not aware that she was engaging in insider trading at the time that she bought the security. In that case, Chadwick did not present any evidence and there were no surrounding circumstances to show that he had committed the insider trading inadvertently and that he was otherwise innocent. Here, though Watkins conceded in the plea agreement that the conversation between her and Darmond took place and that Darmond told her about the merger, she also maintains within the plea agreement that at the time of the purchase she was not aware of the planned merger. This is supported by her testimony before the hearing department of the State Bar court, where she admits that she believes Darmond's recollection of events, but she also was on Percocet at the time, which affected her energy levels and memory abilities.

Accordingly, at the time of the violation, i.e. August 16, she did not act 'contrary to the customary rule of right and duty between man and woman' because at the time of her crime, she had the excuse that she was unaware and did not remember being told about the merger, and but for her lack of memory she would not have gone through with the trade. Watkins testified that she had long been planning on buying the stock, and that because of recent public excitement over the stock, particularly by two major brokerage firms and also the technology message boards, she was encouraged to finally go through with the purchase. All of this was public information, and trading on public gossip about a possible merger does not amount to moral turpitude. That she inadvertently committed insider trading was thus also not a crime of moral turpitude, but an unfortunate outcome and side effect of her Percocet prescription.

This is true even though Watkins followed through with the request of the phone order in gathering the patent files. Watkins' testimony shows that she was hazy as to the particulars of the phone call, including the request for the patent files, and it was not even until a follow up phone call from J&H the next day that she knew where to send the files to.

Because at the time of the August 16 purchase, Watkins was by her own admission 'distracted in her thinking' because of the Percocet and the pain, and thus was unaware that she had been informed of nonpublic material information regarding the Fort-Silicon merger, she was 'with excuse' at the time of the violation, and her conduct underlying her plea agreement does not rise to moral turpitude. As such, she should not be disbarred or suspended on this basis.

II. Watkins' testimony at the hearing does not justify a finding of moral turpitude because her testified to belief that she was not aware of being told about the merger at the time of her August 16 purchase, while maybe mistaken, was honest, and the record does not show any other clear and convincing evidence that Watkins engaged in lack of candor.

When an attorney pleads guilty to a crime, the State Bar looks to the appropriate discipline under section 6102(a) of the Business and Professions Code, and this turns on whether the attorney has committed an act of moral turpitude (Salas). Any determination of moral turpitude by the State Bar must be found by clear and convincing evidence, including a determination that the attorney's testimony lacks candor (Salas). While testifying falsely before the Review Department is considered lack of candor giving rise to a finding of moral turpitude, the Review Department of the State Bar in the matter of Harold Salas stated that an honest, if mistaken belief in innocence is not a lack of candor, as lack of candor cannot be founded merely on different memory of events. Moreover, applying the standard of proof by clear and convincing evidence means reasonable doubts must be resolved in favor of the accused attorney, and if equally reasonable inferences may be drawn from a proven fact, i.e. it is equally likely that the respondent is telling the truth versus lying, the inference to innocence must be chosen and the State Bar has not met its burden of establishing clear and convincing evidence of culpability (Salas).

In Salas, the respondent pled guilty to the various felonies related to his conduct wherein the respondent-attorney Salas partnered with Anna Bash, the owner/operator of Chekov Legal Services, and violated the law by fees with her (a non-lawyer) in exchange for case referrals. However, he also lawfully partnered with Bash in certain aspects, as he also employed her for $5,000 a month to market his practice to the Russian community and to provide him secretarial services. At issue during his testimony before the Review Department was a certain $10,000 he had paid to Bash. The plea agreement was silent as to what the $10,000 represented. Salas insisted it was lawful payment of 2 months of Bash's salary as a secretary. Bash testified and insisted that the $10,000 represented an illegal referral fee. There, the Review Department of the State Bar court overturned the lower State Bar Court's finding that the conflicting evidence sufficiently proved that Salas had to be lying and holding him liable for disciplinary action based on this 'lie.' The Review Department noted that because in this situation Salas truly did not have any real reason to lie, the plea agreement was silent as to this issue (i.e. Salas's testimony did not conflict with his plea agreement), and the only other evidence was conflicting testimonial evidence, equal inferences could be drawn as to whether Salas was lying or telling the truth. Thus, the State Bar Court had not met its burden of providing clear and convincing evidence of lack of candor and thus moral turpitude.

Watkins' case again bears striking resemblance to the case law. Watkins' insistence that when she purchased her August 16 stock she did not remember that Darmond had told her about the Fort-Silicon merger was an honest, if mistaken, belief in her own innocence, and on its own that is not a lack of candor. She and Darmond merely have different memories of the event, but the fact that Watkins is testifying the exact same recollection that she told the SEC when they first confronted her, supports the finding that she subjectively and honestly believes that at the time, she lacked awareness of the merger. In her testimony, Watkins does not insist that she was not in fact told about the merger. She merely testifies to her memory of the events, stating that while she cannot agree that it happened, she also cannot deny that it happened - this is an honest statement of her beliefs. While, unlike with Salas, here Watkins does have a modicum of incentive to lie, as it would prevent her from being disbarred, this should in no way be dispositive or controlling. What is controlling is the veracity of her belief, which as discussed above, was sincere. Moreover, Watkins, like Salas, is not testifying in conflict with her plea agreement, and her statements are consistent with her plea agreement factual basis statement that on August 16 she was not aware that she knew about the merger. Thus, while contradiction with a plea agreement does raise severe doubts as to candor, such a contradiction is not present here.

Based on the facts and testimony at hand, equally reasonable inferences can be drawn from the proven fact that she had a conversation with Darmond and then bought shares on August 16. Thus, all reasonable doubts must be resolved in favor of Watkins, meaning that any doubts that the Percocet did not actually inhibit her memory so that she could not remember her phone conversation must be resolved in favor of believing Watkins' statement on this matter. Thus, an inference must be drawn as to Watkins' innocence.

Because the State Bar has not met its burden of establishing clear and convincing evidence of culpability, Watkins' testimony at the hearing does not justify a finding of moral turpitude.

PT: SELECTED ANSWER 2

To: Tia Lucci

From: Applicant

Subject: In the Matter of Abigail Watkins

Date: July 24, 2018

In the Matter of ABIGAIL WATKINS, a Member of the State Bar

Brief for Ms. Watkins

Argument

I. The conduct underlying Ms. Watkins' plea does not justify a finding of moral turpitude.

The conduct underlying Ms. Watkins' guilty plea does not justify a finding of moral turpitude because Ms. Watkin's act, while criminal, has a valid excuse.

In *Chadwick v. State Bar* (Co. S. Ct. 1989), the court stated that under, "the Rules of Professional Responsibility, moral turpitude has been described as an act of baseness, vileness or depravity in the private and social duties that [one] owes to his fellowmen, or to society in general," which is "contrary to the accepted and customary rule of right and duty between [people]." While the court then offered a summary definition, targeting "any crime or misconduct without <u>excuse</u>," it then noted that the key component in a finding of moral turpitude is not whether the act is criminal, but rather whether the act is dishonest or immoral. *Id.* (stating that the "meaning and test is the same whether the dishonest or immoral act is a felony, misdemeanor, or no crime at all.") Finally, the *Chadwick* court recognized that the act of entering a guilty plea does not automatically concede that the factual basis for the plea would justify ethical discipline based on those facts, but retained the discretion to review the factual basis underlying the plea to determine whether the conduct it describes warrants a finding of moral turpitude. *Chadwick*, at 3.

Significantly, the court in *In re the Matter of Harold Salas, a Member of the State Bar (Rev. Dept. St. Bar Ct. 2001),* noted that "it is equally likely that Respondent is telling the truth about controverted facts, the State Bar has not met its burden of establishing clear and convincing evidence of culpability."

<u>Ms. Watkins' Act Has an Excuse</u>

Ms. Watkins pled guilty to a single felony count of insider trading, but she should not be subject to a finding of moral turpitude because she did not know about the merger at the time of her stock purchase due to her use of prescription medication. Ms. Watkins' plea was for felony insider trading, while the Respondent in *Chadwick* pled guilty to a misdemeanor count of insider trading–yet, these cases should be treated differently. As the court noted in *Chadwick*, an act of moral turpitude is "crime or misconduct *without excuse*". *Id.* (emphasis added).

In July 2015, just a month before the alleged misconduct, Ms. Watkins underwent surgery for a tear to her rotator cuff. As a result of that surgery and through recovery she suffered, in her own words "considerable pain and limited mobility." *Hearing in the Matter of Abigail Watkins* (Case No. 18-SF-1023).   Ms. Watkins was prescribed medication, Percocet and Ambien, to help her deal with the pain and to sleep.   Ms. Watkins testified that the Percocet "had some side effects," and that her "memory from the surgery in July until September," after the alleged misconduct, "is very poor." Significantly, during that time, Ms. Watkins was "very distracted by the pain and the medications," all while trying to keep up a strenuous full-time work schedule.

The facts in *Chadwick* indicate that the attorney in that case committed misconduct by trading on inside information from a bank officer of a company set to acquire another.   The facts do not state the relationship between the attorney in that case and the source of the information, but that relationship is relevant in this case.   Here, Ms. Watkins was told of the merger by Samantha Darmond, with whom she had previously worked, and assumed that the reason Ms. Darmond, the target company Fort Software's (Fort's) in house counsel, asked Ms. Watkins to prepare and send patents to another firm was that that firm would be Fort's new intellectual property representative.   As the company's previous intellectual property representative, it would be reasonable for Ms. Watkins to believe that she would need to forward patent information on the company to another firm for purposes other than a merger if she was not told or did not hear or understand anything about the merger.

The court in *Chadwick* further held that cooperation of a Respondent with a criminal investigation does not excuse the Respondent's earlier moral turpitude, if any. *Chadwick*, at 3.   While this may be true, in this case the circumstances surrounding Ms. Watkins' cooperation with the SEC indicate the sincerity of her excuse– Ms. Watkins was surprised by the call from the SEC, and maintained that she did not recollect being told about the merger by Ms. Darmond on August 16.   The fact that Ms. Watkins maintained that she did not recollect being told about the merger rather than flatly denying being told makes it more likely that she was seriously affected by the pain and medication of post-surgery recovery during the period in question.

Ms. Watkin's purchase of stock was based on her own, independent feelings toward and valuations of Fort, not on the mention of a merger. While it is true that her valuations were based on boards and recommendations that in turn were influenced by rumors of a merger, her reliance on such boards and recommendations is not a dishonest act. In short, this is not the kind of base, vile, or depraved act at issue in *Chadwick*, but rather was an action with an excuse – Ms. Watkins may have been *told* about the merger, but she did not *know* about the merger.

II. Ms. Watkins' testimony at the hearing does not justify a finding of moral turpitude.

In *In the Matter of Harold Salas*, the Review Department of the State Bar Court held that, to justify a finding of moral turpitude based on testimony in a State Bar hearing, the State Bar must "support by clear and convincing evidence that" the Respondent has testified falsely. *In the Matter of Harold Salas, a Member of the State Bar* (Rev. Dept. St. Bar Ct. 2001). Further, the State Bar bears the burden of proof with respect to moral turpitude. *Id.* This burden of proof by clear and convincing evidence extends to a determination that a witness has testified falsely. *Id.* This means that reasonable doubts about whether an attorney testifies truthfully in a disciplinary hearing must be "resolved in favor of the accused attorney." *See id.*

The *Salas* court specifically noted that a Respondent's "honest if mistaken belief in his innocence does not signal a lack of candor," and, significantly, "a lack of candor should not be founded merely on [the Respondent's] different memory of events." *Id.* Here, Ms. Watkins is either telling the truth that she did not hear any information about the merger, or her testimony constituted just such an honest and mistaken belief. Ms. Watkins has maintained throughout the SEC and state bar proceedings that her memory of the time period in question is extremely poor. That testimony is buttressed by the fact that she was prescribed a potent pain killer during that time.

The court in *Salas* noted the difference between hearing testimony that contradicts a plea agreement and one which argues on a point the agreement is silent on. *Id.* In that case, the Respondent maintained at a disciplinary hearing the innocence of a particular transaction, while admitting culpability for other, similar actions. In comparison, Ms. Watkins did not testify in conflict with the plea agreement, which states that she was told about the merger on August 16. Rather, she testified that she does not recall being told about the merger, and that it is her recollection that she purchased Fort stock without knowledge of the merger. It is entirely possible that in a pained and medicated state, Ms. Watkins was told about the merger but did not hear or understand the information. As a result, Ms. Watkins is not contradicting the plea agreement, just as the respondent in *Salas*.

Ultimately, under *Salas*, if "it is equally likely that Respondent is telling the truth about controverted facts, the State Bar has not met its burden of establishing clear and convincing evidence of culpability." *Id.* Here, the State has shown that the medication did not cause Ms. Watkins on its own to commit a crime, and that if Ms. Watkins had continually taken her medication she would have finished it before August 16. The State is arguing that Ms. Watkin's August 16 purchase was based on insider information, and that her receipt of that information was not affected by her medication. But it is equally likely, as Ms. Watkins has testified that she did not remember being told about the merger when testifying, and that she did not hear or understand the information when told about the merger on August 16.

In conclusion, Ms. Watkins' conduct and testimony do not justify a finding of moral turpitude.

DEMONSTRATION 5

PEOPLE v. RAYMOND

February 2019

California
Bar
Examination

Performance Test INSTRUCTIONS
AND FILE

PEOPLE v. RAYMOND

PEOPLE v. RAYMOND

INSTRUCTIONS

1. This performance test is designed to evaluate your ability to handle a select number of legal authorities in the context of a factual problem involving a client.

2. The problem is set in the fictional State of Columbia, one of the United States.

3. You will have two sets of materials with which to work: a File and a Library.

4. The File contains factual materials about your case. The first document is a memorandum containing the instructions for the tasks you are to complete.

5. The Library contains the legal authorities needed to complete the tasks. The case reports may be real, modified, or written solely for the purpose of this performance test. If the cases appear familiar to you, do not assume that they are precisely the same as you have read before. Read each thoroughly, as if it were new to you. You should assume that cases were decided in the jurisdictions and on the dates shown. In citing cases from the Library, you may use abbreviations and omit page citations.

6. You should concentrate on the materials provided, but you should also bring to bear on the problem your general knowledge of the law. What you have learned in law school and elsewhere provides the general background for analyzing the problem; the File and Library provide the specific materials with which you must work.

7. This performance test is designed to be completed in 90 minutes. Although there are no parameters on how to apportion that 90 minutes, you should allow yourself sufficient time to thoroughly review the materials and organize your planned response. Since the time allotted for this session of the examination includes two (2) essay questions in addition to this performance test, time management is essential.

8. Your response will be graded on its compliance with instructions and on its content, thoroughness, and organization.

CRUZ COUNTY DISTRICT ATTORNEY'S OFFICE

65 N. Hammer Ave, 6th Floor

Dead Horse, Columbia

<u>MEMORANDUM</u>

TO: Applicant

FROM: Barbara Sattler, Deputy District Attorney

RE: State v. Henry Raymond, Defendant, and Oscar Raymond,

          the Bond Poster/Surety, Real Party in Interest

DATE: February 26, 2019

Our office recently sought forfeiture of a $45,000 cash bond posted to release Henry Raymond, a criminal defendant, because he did not appear for the trial. At the forfeiture hearing, Oscar Raymond, the surety, raised arguments why the bond should be exonerated -- in other words, returned to the surety -- despite the non-appearance. Oscar Raymond is the son of the defendant Henry Raymond.

The trial court offered each side the opportunity to brief the court concerning the issues. Please draft a Brief In Support of Forfeiture of the Bond demonstrating why forfeiture is appropriate and why exoneration is not justified.

TRANSCRIPT OF BOND FORFEITURE HEARING
Honorable Beth Jones, Presiding

THE COURT: The next case is The State of Columbia, Plaintiff, versus Henry Raymond, Defendant, Bond in the Amount of $45,000, and Oscar Raymond, the Bond Poster and Surety, Case number CR - 20180016.   This is a Bond Forfeiture Proceeding concerning an appearance bond.   Ms. Sattler, I see you are here for the People.   Ms. Urias, are you here on behalf of Oscar Raymond, the surety?

MS. URIAS: Yes, your honor.

THE COURT: Ms. Sattler, do you want to explain the facts and the grounds for forfeiture?

PEOPLE: Yes.   Thank you, your honor.   The Defendant, Henry Raymond, was arrested and booked on February 13, 2018, on felony charges of unlawful possession of a narcotic drug, unlawful possession of a narcotic drug for sale, and possession of drug paraphernalia.   An interim complaint on those charges was sworn out on that same date.   It included the information that the offenses involved about 44 grams of cocaine and admissions by Defendant that he was selling cocaine.   At the initial appearance, the Magistrate held Defendant without bond.   The grand jury returned an indictment against Defendant on February 23, 2018, on felony counts of possession of a narcotic drug for sale and possession of drug paraphernalia, including an allegation of exceeding the threshold amount of cocaine.   On February 27, 2018, Defendant appeared for his arraignment.   On March 13, 2018, the trial court conducted a hearing on defense counsel's motion to set conditions of release. The Pretrial Services report indicated that Defendant had no prior convictions.   He stated that his permanent residence was in the neighboring State of Franklin, but he provided no references or sources for verification of this information.   The trial court set a $45,000 cash bond requirement.   On March 15, 2018, Mr. Oscar Raymond posted the $45,000 cash bond and Defendant was released from Cruz County Superior Court hold.

THE COURT: Sorry to interrupt, Ms. Sattler. My understanding is that the surety, Mr. Oscar Raymond, is the son of Defendant Henry Raymond?

PEOPLE: Yes, your honor.

THE COURT: Okay. Please continue.

PEOPLE: Thank you, your honor. On March 23, 2018, at a pretrial conference, Defendant's counsel told the trial court that Defendant's bond had been posted and that Defendant had fled. The trial court noted in the Minute entry that "defense counsel bears the responsibility for arranging Defendant's return." A trial date was set for October 22, 2018. At a pretrial conference, the trial date was postponed by the trial judge until January 30, 2019. On January 30, 2019 trial began, and Defendant failed to appear. A jury was selected and impaneled, opening statements were made, two witnesses testified, and several items of evidence were admitted. On the second day of trial, January 31, Defendant again failed to appear. Several more witnesses testified and additional items of evidence were admitted. The State then rested, and defense counsel made a motion for judgment of acquittal. The trial court granted the motion, acquitting Defendant and ending the trial. Defense counsel moved to exonerate the bond. The trial court denied the motion, however, and ordered, I quote: "that this matter be referred to the Superior Court Hearing Office for the commencement of bond forfeiture proceedings, based upon Defendant's failure to appear for his trial." The State seeks forfeiture of the bond for failure to comply with the bond conditions, your honor.

THE COURT: Okay, unless you have anything more, Ms. Sattler . . . .

PEOPLE: No, that's it, your honor.

THE COURT: . . . then go ahead, Ms. Urias, and explain why, in face of the nonappearance and proper notice, the bond should be exonerated.

MS. URIAS: Thank you, your honor. Assuming for the moment that the People have made out a prima facie case for forfeiture, there are two reasons why the bond must be exonerated. First, the bond may be exonerated due to mandatory statutory grounds. Defendant was acquitted, and Columbia Rules of Criminal Procedure provide for mandatory exoneration in such a situation. It isn't discretionary. Second, the facts of this case justify the exercise of your discretion to exonerate the bond for several reasons, your honor . . .

THE COURT: . . . I got it. Why does the acquittal exonerate the bond?

MS. URIAS: At the close of the People's case in the *in absentia* trial proceeding, the defense moved for and received a judgment of acquittal. According to Columbia Rule of Criminal Procedure 13(d)(1), when there is no further need for an appearance bond, exoneration is mandatory. The rule does not allow discretion with regard to exoneration if there is no further need for an appearance bond, as the statute says "shall." Similarly, Columbia Rule of Criminal Procedure 13(d)(2) requires that when a prosecution is dismissed, the defendant shall be released on those charges and the bond exonerated. That rule must be construed to signify any dismissal of a case on its merits. It would be sheer absurdity to conclude that an appearance bond is exonerated on dismissal but not on acquittal. We believe the holding of *People v. Weinberger*, applied here, requires exoneration.

THE COURT: Ms. Sattler, do you have a response?

PEOPLE: Your honor, the statute Ms. Urias cites pertains to pretrial events and doesn't require mandatory exoneration in this case. The primary reason for an appearance bond is to have the defendant appear for trial, and Defendant didn't show up. The trial court found that Defendant's acquittal was because Defendant's absence made identification impossible. The finding was, I quote: "There is no substantial evidence to warrant a conviction, based upon insufficient evidence of the identity of the Defendant."

THE COURT: Ms. Urias, you said there were other reasons for exoneration.

MS. URIAS: Yes, your honor, Oscar made good faith efforts to ensure his father's appearance at trial. We would like to have him briefly testify, your honor.

THE COURT: Okay Mr. Raymond, come have a seat in the witness chair. The courtroom clerk will swear in the Witness.

THE COURT: Go ahead, Ms. Urias, you may question your witness.

BY MS. URIAS:

Q: Could you state your name and address for the record?

A: Oscar Raymond, 3898 West 14th Street, Twin Oaks, Columbia.

Q: When you arranged bail for your father, did you get a chance to speak to him?

A: Yes.

Q: Did you ask him whether he intended to appear at trial?

A: No.

Q: Why not?

A: I don't know. I guess I figured that he would appear.

Q: After you posted bail, what happened?

A: My dad came home and, according to my sister, he stayed around for a few weeks. One day, he said he was going to visit my aunt, his sister, who lives across town. My sister asked him if he was going to skip bail. He said, no, that he planned to fight the charges. Then he disappeared. I called my aunt, and she said he left her house after an hour. I didn't know what else I could do.

Q: Have you ever posted bail for anyone before?

A: Never.

MS. URIAS: That is all that I have, your honor.

THE COURT: Ms. Sattler, do you have questions for the witness?

MS. SATTLER: A few, your honor.

BY THE PEOPLE:

Q: You didn't live with your father did you, Mr. Raymond?

A: No, I didn't.

Q: In fact, he hasn't been much of a presence in your life, has he?

A: No, not really.

Q: How often did you see your father?

A: Not often. He hasn't been around much. He doesn't really have many ties here except for my sister, my aunt and me. And none of us really see him very much.

Q: You've been financially independent from him for a number of years, haven't you?

A: Yes, I moved out right after graduating from high school and have supported myself since then.

Q: You make a pretty good living, don't you?

A: I guess so. I work as a software engineer and I make about $120,000 per year.

Q: Was posting the $45,000 bond a financial hardship for you?

A: It would hurt to lose it, but I have quite a bit saved up to help my sister with her college education.

Q: When you posted the bond, were you aware that your father may have been involved in unlawful activities?

A: Yes, I was aware.

Q: You were aware, then, that there was a decent chance he would flee rather than face trial?

A: I didn't really think much about it, but I suppose that's true too. I didn't see that I had much choice, though. It was my dad.

Q: Oscar, did you make any effort to find out where your dad was and to contact his defense counsel or the prosecutor so that he would appear for trial?

A: No.

Q: Before you signed the appearance bond agreement, your read it very carefully, didn't you?

A: Yeah, I guess so.

Q: And you understood that by signing the agreement both you and your father were responsible for your father's appearances in court, didn't you?

A: Yeah.

Q: And you also understood that if you or your father failed in that responsibility you would lose all of the money you put up, right?

A: Yeah. I knew how it worked, and I knew that if he didn't show up for any of the stuff he was supposed to show up for that I would end up losing the money, but I didn't have any way to find him and make him show up.

THE PEOPLE: Your honor, I have no further questions.

THE COURT: Redirect, Ms. Urias?

MS. URIAS: Nothing, your honor.

THE COURT: Under the circumstances, I'm going to take this under advisement. I would like both sides to do some research and submit a brief on each of the reasons raised by Oscar Raymond as to why the bond should be exonerated.

THE PEOPLE: Thank you, your honor. We would appreciate it.

MS. URIAS: Thank you, your honor.

February 2019

California
Bar
Examination

Performance Test

LIBRARY

PEOPLE v. RAYMOND

LIBRARY

PEOPLE v. NATIONWIDE SURETY INSURANCE COMPANY
Columbia Supreme Court (2006)

Nationwide Surety Insurance Company (Nationwide Surety) appeals from the trial court's order denying its motion to vacate forfeiture and exonerate the bail bond it posted for Robert Roger. The bond was forfeited when Roger did not appear at his preliminary hearing.

FACTS

Roger was arrested for a drug-related offense. Nationwide Surety posted a $20,000 bail bond for him the same day, after Roger presented a Columbia driver's license, social security card, and other documents. Roger was ordered to return for his preliminary hearing. However, immediately following execution of the bond, Roger fled. He did not appear for the preliminary hearing, and Nationwide Surety's bond was then ordered forfeited.

BACKGROUND RELATING TO BAIL BOND STATUTES

While bail bond proceedings occur in connection with criminal prosecutions, they are independent from and collateral to the prosecutions and are civil in nature. The object of bail and its forfeiture is to insure the attendance of the accused and his obedience to the orders and judgment of the court. Nevertheless, the bail bond is a contract between the poster of the bond (the surety) and the government whereby the surety acts as a guarantor of the defendant's appearance in court under the risk of forfeiture of the bond. When there is a breach of this contract, the bond agreement should be enforced. The scope of the surety's risk is defined by the terms of the bond agreement and applicable statutes. The forfeiture or exoneration of the bail bond is entirely a statutory procedure, and forfeiture proceedings are governed entirely by the special statutes applicable thereto. Thus forfeiture proceedings, even though instituted in criminal matters, are simply a streamlined substitute for a civil suit resulting from a breach of contract.

Consistent with long-standing notions such as "equity abhors a forfeiture," the rules calling for bond forfeiture must be strictly construed in favor of the surety to avoid the harsh results of a forfeiture. However, nonappearance for trial creates a presumption of forfeiture. Once there has been a demonstration that by failing to appear the defendant has not complied with the terms of the bond agreement, the surety bears the burden of coming forward with a request for relief from forfeiture and making the necessary showing, by competent evidence, of a legally recognized justification for the failure to appear, either because the statute mandates exoneration or because it should be exonerated in whole or in part in the sound discretion of the court.

Rules of Criminal Procedure, Rule 13, specifically concerns the procedure applicable to forfeiture of bail bonds, which occurs when the defendant whose appearance in court is assured by the bond fails to appear.

If the surety surrenders the accused to the sheriff of the county in which the prosecution is pending, or delivers an affidavit to the sheriff stating that the defendant is incarcerated in this or another jurisdiction, and the sheriff reports the surrender or status to the court, the court shall vacate any order of forfeiture and exonerate the bond. Rules of Criminal Procedure, Rule 13(d), provides that the court shall exonerate an appearance bond in the event of pretrial dismissal or when other pretrial circumstances ranging from death of the defendant to diversion preclude further need for an appearance bond. Rules of Criminal Procedure, Rule 13(e), provides that in all other instances, "the decision whether or not to exonerate a bond shall be within the sound discretion of the court."

Respondent contends the bail should remain forfeited because Nationwide Surety should have known Roger was a flight risk. It is true that generally parties in contract disputes are held to bear the risk concerning events of which they knew or should have known. Just how Nationwide Surety should have known that Roger was a flight risk, however, is not demonstrated by the respondent. Roger presented a Columbia driver's license, a social security card, and other documents that showed his ties to the community. While these may have been fraudulent documents, there has been no showing that Nationwide Surety had any reasonable suspicion that Roger would flee when it posted the bail bond. We are convinced that Nationwide Surety cannot be faulted. Nationwide Surety acted in the good faith belief that Roger would appear.

For all of the above stated reasons, the order denying appellant's motion to vacate forfeiture is reversed.

PEOPLE v. SAINTLY BAIL BONDS
Columbia Court of Appeals (2008)

Saintly Bail Bonds (the surety) posted a $55,000 appearance bond for criminal defendant Jerry Marshall after he was indicted on a drug charge in April 2003. When the defendant failed to appear at a pretrial conference in July, his attorney told the judge the defendant was in the custody of the Department of Corrections of the State of Franklin. The judge nonetheless set a trial date and ordered the state to prepare a writ of habeas corpus and arrange for the defendant to be transported to Pima County for a pre-trial conference. When the state was unable to secure the defendant's appearance through the writ, the judge ordered the $55,000 bond forfeited. The surety appealed. We affirm.

The surety argues the defendant did not fail to appear on his own volition and that the surety cannot be held responsible for failing to produce the defendant. In short, according to the surety, "it is anyone's fault but the Bond Poster's that the defendant has technically, if at all, violated the release conditions." We disagree.

It is well settled in this jurisdiction that a surety assumes the risk of a defendant's failure to appear. To alleviate that risk, a surety should exercise care in ascertaining the defendant's circumstances and community ties before executing an appearance bond, much as a trial court must do before determining a defendant's release conditions. Although the surety claims it was not aware and had no reason to be aware that the Franklin Department of Corrections might be interested in defendant at the time it posted the bond, the record demonstrates that the surety could have easily acquired that information by simply contacting jail personnel. And, because we know of no authority that imposes a duty on the state to seek out a surety and furnish it information about a criminal defendant, we do not accept the surety's argument that someone else was to blame. To the contrary, no one but the surety had any duty to ascertain the wisdom or folly of contracting with the defendant to post a bond that would secure his appearance in court.

The *Nationwide Surety* case does not require a different conclusion. In that case, there was no reason for the surety to know that the defendant was a flight risk.

Nor do we accept the surety's argument that the trial court abused its discretion by rejecting the surety's explanation for the defendant's failure to appear. Once there has been a determination that a defendant failed to appear or otherwise comply with the terms of the appearance bond, except where a statute specifically requires exoneration, the decision to order an appearance bond forfeited or to remit in whole or in part lies essentially in the discretion of the trial court. A trial court may consider all of the relevant circumstances, including the following list of factors that Columbia courts have frequently delineated:

-- The defendant's willfulness in violating the order to appear;

-- Whether the surety is a commercial entity (noncommercial sureties are often given more latitude concerning return of some or all of the bond);

-- The effort and expense expended by the surety in trying to locate and apprehend the defendant to insure the return of the fugitive (lack of effort by the surety to locate the defendant's return justifies forfeiture, as it is necessary to provide an incentive to the surety to take active and reasonable steps to recapture a fugitive defendant);

-- The costs, inconvenience and prejudice suffered by the State, if any, because of the absence of defendant;

-- The public's interest in ensuring a defendant's appearance.

Here, there is no indication that the defendant made any effort to attend the scheduled court conference. Defense counsel never asserted that the defendant had expressed any desire to abide by his promise to appear. Indeed, nothing in the record suggests that the defendant had made any effort even to contact his defense counsel. Nor has the surety demonstrated that it expended any effort or expense in attempting to arrange for his appearance.

The trial court's decision to forfeit the bond was not an abuse of discretion. Because the defendant failed to make any effort to appear at trial, he must be considered to have willfully violated the terms of the appearance bond. In addition, because the surety, a commercial entity, expended no effort or expense to produce the defendant, there is no need to protect the incentives of sureties generally to post bonds, and forfeiture serves the purpose of providing proper incentives to sureties to live up to their obligations to ensure that the defendant adheres to the terms and conditions of the bond.

Affirmed.

PEOPLE v. WEINBERGER

Columbia Court of Appeals (2003)

FACTS AND PROCEDURAL BACKGROUND

Appellant Weinberger was arrested and charged with possession of marijuana for sale. He appeared before a magistrate for his initial appearance and bond was set at $30,000. Appellant and others were subsequently indicted for possession of marijuana for sale. Appellant posted the $30,000 cash bond through his agent and was ordered released from custody on that date. Subsequently, after appellant had failed to appear at a pretrial conference, a bench warrant was issued for appellant's arrest, but no motion was made to forfeit the bond. On the same date the warrant was issued, several motions were argued to the court, including motions to suppress evidence. The court took the matter under advisement for two days and then granted the motion to suppress. The state moved to dismiss the case against appellant, which was granted with prejudice. Shortly after, appellant moved to exonerate his bond. At the bond forfeiture hearing, the hearing officer ruled it irrelevant that the indictment against appellant had been dismissed and ordered the subject bond forfeited.

BOND FORFEITURE

Appellant contends that because the indictment against him was dismissed with prejudice prior to trial and prior to the bonds being forfeited, he is entitled by law to have his bond exonerated. It is well established that the termination of a prosecution before forfeiture of an appearance bond terminates a surety's liability on the bond. Additionally, appellants rely on Rule 13(d) of the Columbia Rules of Criminal Procedure to support this conclusion. According to its terms, Rule 13 "shall govern the procedure to be followed in cases between arraignment and trial."

Columbia Rules of Criminal Procedure, Rule 13(d) - Exoneration of Bond, Dismissal of Prosecution, provides:

(1) Exoneration of Appearance Bond: At any time before violation that the court finds that there is no further need for an appearance bond, it shall exonerate the appearance bond and order the return of any security deposit.

(2) Release of Defendant - Exoneration of Bond: When a prosecution is dismissed, the defendant shall be released from custody, unless he is in custody on some other charge, and any appearance bond exonerated.

The primary purpose of an appearance bond is to ensure the defendant's presence at the time of trial. When, as here, the charges are dismissed prior to trial, the primary purpose for the bond no longer exists, and from that point forward there is no further need for the appearance bond. This is why Rule 13(d) indicates that if the charges are dismissed or that there otherwise is no longer a reason for the appearance bond the appearance bond shall be exonerated.

Rule 13(d), by stating that the bond shall be exonerated if "at any time *before violation* there is no further need for an appearance bond" (emphasis added), envisions that there is no requirement to exonerate the bond if a violation of the bond terms took place prior to the dismissal. But the fact remains that in this case the main purpose of the appearance bond, to ensure the defendant's presence at trial, ceased at the dismissal. The State was not prejudiced by the non-appearance of appellant at one pretrial conference, which is the only possible violation of the bond terms. If there was a violation, it was for only a matter of hours. The appellant's presence was not required for any other event prior to dismissal, and the issue of forfeiture was not raised by the State, perhaps because the State anticipated filing a motion to dismiss the charges. Given these facts, Rule 13(d), which requires exoneration of the bond when a prosecution is dismissed, dictates the result.

The order of the court commissioner is vacated and the trial court is directed to enter an order exonerating appellant's bond.

Practice California Performance Test:
Step-by-Step Demonstration 5

People v. Raymond (Cal. Feb. 2019)

[Roadmap modeled on the computer.]

Step 1.	Scan the instructions, the file table of contents, and the library table of contents (1 minute)

Instructions

You should have already thoroughly read the instruction page once. When you are completing a PT, look for three important details: the jurisdiction (usually in paragraph two), the contents of the packet (usually in paragraph three), and any specific weighting information, which, if supplied, would be noted at the bottom of the instructions. Take a second to skim the rest of the instructions to ensure no changes were made in the standard instructions.

Raymond Instructions

1. The problem is set in the State of Columbia.
2. The packet contains a file and a library.
3. No special weighting information is included.

File Table of Contents

You are trying to get a general feel for what the case is about, how many pages of facts there are, and the type of documents you will be working with.

Raymond Observations

Since the case name is <u>People v. Raymond</u>, you know that the State and one individual, not two individuals, are the parties. The types of cases labeled like this are usually criminal cases or cases involving a criminal defendant. The file contains eight pages of facts.

- The first file document is a memorandum from Barbara Sattler, a Deputy District Attorney, the person directing us on our task. This memorandum informs us that we are working on behalf of the State in relation to a criminal case.
- The second file document is a transcript of a bond forfeiture hearing. This gives us an idea that the criminal issue involves a bond hearing, likely related to the defendant in the case.

Library Table of Contents

You are still trying to get a general feel for what the case is about, and you need to quickly determine the type of law you will be working with. You want to make a note of what and how many statutes and/or cases are included. You also want to note the jurisdiction/court of each case; this will help you begin to form a picture of the task and will help you determine whether the cases are binding or merely persuasive authority.

Raymond Library

The library includes three cases. The first case is from the Columbia Supreme Court, which is binding, as we are in that jurisdiction. The next two cases are from the Columbia Court of Appeals, so they are still in the proper jurisdiction. All three cases are named beginning <u>People v.</u>, before adding the name of the defendant; therefore all three likely involve a criminal defendant, making them similar to our case.

PEOPLE v. RAYMOND

INSTRUCTIONS

1. This performance test is designed to evaluate your ability to handle a select number of legal authorities in the context of a factual problem involving a client.

2. The problem is set in the fictional State of Columbia, one of the United States.

3. You will have two sets of materials with which to work: a File and a Library.

4. The File contains factual materials about your case. The first document is a memorandum containing the instructions for the tasks you are to complete.

5. The Library contains the legal authorities needed to complete the tasks. The case reports may be real, modified, or written solely for the purpose of this performance test. If the cases appear familiar to you, do not assume that they are precisely the same as you have read before. Read each thoroughly, as if it were new to you. You should assume that cases were decided in the jurisdictions and on the dates shown. In citing cases from the Library, you may use abbreviations and omit page citations.

6. You should concentrate on the materials provided, but you should also bring to bear on the problem your general knowledge of the law. What you have learned in law school and elsewhere provides the general background for analyzing the problem; the File and Library provide the specific materials with which you must work.

7. This performance test is designed to be completed in 90 minutes. Although there are no parameters on how to apportion that 90 minutes, you should allow yourself sufficient time to thoroughly review the materials and organize your planned response. Since the time allotted for this session of the examination includes two (2) essay questions in addition to this performance test, time management is essential.

8. Your response will be graded on its compliance with instructions and on its content, thoroughness, and organization.

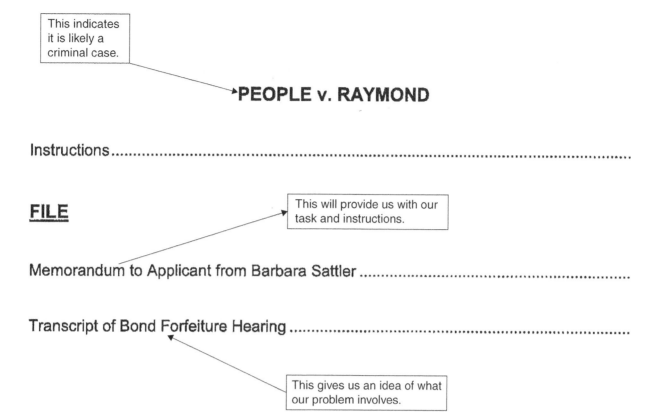

This indicates it is likely a criminal case.

►PEOPLE v. RAYMOND

Instructions...

FILE

This will provide us with our task and instructions.

Memorandum to Applicant from Barbara Sattler ....

Transcript of Bond Forfeiture Hearing ....

This gives us an idea of what our problem involves.

PEOPLE v. RAYMOND

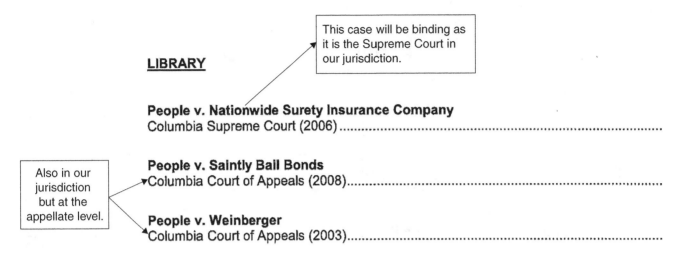

LIBRARY

This case will be binding as it is the Supreme Court in our jurisdiction.

People v. Nationwide Surety Insurance Company
Columbia Supreme Court (2006) ....

Also in our jurisdiction but at the appellate level.

People v. Saintly Bail Bonds
Columbia Court of Appeals (2008)...

People v. Weinberger
Columbia Court of Appeals (2003)...

<table>
<tr><td>Step 2.</td><td>Read the task memo (and format memo, if provided, and identify the macrostructure for your answer) (7–10 minutes)</td></tr>
</table>

Task Memo

This is the most important document in the packet so slow down and read it very carefully. Follow all directions exactly. Your goal is to identify three key pieces of information:

1. Information about your client: Who is your client? What is your client's legal issue? What is your client's goal?
2. Specific information about the task: What is the task? Who is the audience? Is there more than one task assigned? Are there directions about things to include and exclude?
3. The macrostructure of your answer: Can you start your roadmap?

Raymond Task Information

- **Client info:** As we suspected, this case involves a criminal defendant, Henry Raymond. We represent the State of Columbia in the Cruz County District Attorney's Office with regard to a bond for the defendant.
- **Task info:** We are asked to draft a Brief in Support of Forfeiture of the Bond that demonstrates why forfeiture is appropriate and why exoneration is not justified. The defendant did not appear for trial, so we are now trying to seek forfeiture of a $45,000 cash bond that was posted to release the defendant. The defendant's son is arguing that the bond should be exonerated.
- **Task structure:** Our brief should break down the task into two parts: (1) why the forfeiture is appropriate, and (2) why exoneration is not justified. Whenever the task structure has an "and" in it you should consider breaking those two parts down into separate sections in the brief, each with its own heading. The library will most likely supply more guidance regarding the overall structure.

CRUZ COUNTY DISTRICT ATTORNEY'S OFFICE

65 N. Hammer Ave, 6th Floor

Dead Horse, Columbia

MEMORANDUM

TO:	Applicant
FROM:	Barbara Sattler, <u>Deputy District Attorney</u>
RE:	State v. Henry Raymond, Defendant, and Oscar Raymond, the <u>Bond Poster/Surety</u>, Real Party in Interest
DATE:	February 26, 2019

> We will be working on the side of the State.

> Tells us what the problem involves.

DA's office

Our office recently sought forfeiture of a $45,000 cash bond posted to release Henry Raymond, a criminal defendant, because he did not appear for the trial. At the forfeiture hearing, Oscar Raymond, the surety, raised arguments why the bond should be

Parties and issue

exonerated -- in other words, returned to the surety -- despite the non-appearance. Oscar Raymond is the son of the defendant Henry Raymond.

The trial court offered each side the opportunity to brief the court concerning the issues.

Task

Please draft a Brief In Support of Forfeiture of the Bond demonstrating ① why forfeiture is appropriate and ② why exoneration is not justified.

> It is most likely that the library will give us rules to help with the remaining structure.

| Step 3. | **Start roadmap (time included in steps 2–7)** |

Roadmap

Having a well-planned roadmap is the key to writing a passing performance test. We can start our roadmap using the macrostructure from the task memo and add to it as we gather more information. We recommend that you to make a note at the top of the roadmap listing all essential information, including the client and opposing party, the client's goal, task specifics concerning included or excluded parts, the tone and vocabulary, any weighting of tasks, and a time goal for when you want to start writing your answer. Your time goal will vary depending on which approach you employ to organize your answer. If your written answer is already done because you input the headings and complete rules, etc., directly into your computer as you organized, you will need less time. If you need to write your answer in its entirety because you organized by creating a full shorthand roadmap on paper, you will need more time.

> *Important note:* When roadmapping on the computer, type the rules you know you will use directly into the appropriate section after briefing, but create a skeleton roadmap of the macrostructure on paper as well. Only write as much as you need to guide you in properly drafting your answer. **This performance test demonstration will show you how each part would look if you were typing it in on the computer as you organized it.**

Raymond Roadmap

From the task memo, we know we will be drafting a persuasive brief for the judge. The macrostructure will consist of the two issues we have identified: (1) why forfeiture is appropriate and (2) why exoneration is not justified. For now, set up the format, introduction, a heading for the fact section, an argument section with an introduction (or part of it), the two issues we will address, and the conclusion heading. We will fill in more later, after we read the library.

To: Barbara Sattler, Deputy District Attorney
From: Applicant
Re: State v. Henry Raymond, Defendant, and Oscar Raymond, the Bond Poster/Surety, Real Party in Interest
Date: February 26, 2019

Ms. Sattler,

Pursuant to your request, below is a Brief in Support of Forfeiture of the Bond demonstrating why forfeiture is appropriate and why exoneration is not justified. The arguments should convince the judge that the $45,000 cash bond should not be returned to the surety, but rather forfeited because the defendant, Henry Raymond, failed to appear for the trial. Please let me know if you need any additional help with the Raymond case.

Applicant

BRIEF IN SUPPORT OF FORFEITURE OF THE BOND

<u>FACTS</u>

(Since the task memo didn't tell us to omit a statement of facts, a brief one should be included.)

<u>ARGUMENT</u>

FORFEITURE OF RAYMOND'S BOND POSTED TO RELEASE HIM FROM JAIL IS APPROPRIATE BECAUSE . . . (need to fill in later)

EXONERATION OF RAYMOND'S BOND WHEN HE DID NOT APPEAR FOR HIS TRIAL IS NOT JUSTIFIED BECAUSE . . . (need to fill in later)

For the foregoing reasons, the bond should not be exonerated but rather forfeited.

| Step 4. | **Skim the client file/facts (2 minutes)** |

Skim the Client File/Facts

We know that this case involves a criminal defendant and his son, who posted a cash bond for the defendant's release. We also know that the defendant was released on the bond and did not appear for trial. Thus, the State argues that the bond should be forfeited, while the defendant's son, who posted the bond, argues that it should be exonerated and returned.

Raymond File Skim

Below is our quick take-away from the skim of the facts:

- **Transcript**: This comes from the bond forfeiture proceeding. Ms. Sattler is representing the People, and Ms. Urias is representing Oscar Raymond. Oscar, the son, posted the bond of $45,000, and the defendant, Henry Raymond, was released. Raymond did not appear at some point. Ms. Urias argued that the bond should be exonerated for two reasons: (1) on mandatory statutory grounds, because the defendant was acquitted, and (2) because the judge has discretion to exonerate the bond. Ms. Sattler argued that mandatory statutory grounds don't apply. Ms. Urias stated another reason for exoneration as well: Oscar made good faith efforts to ensure his father appeared.

- **Our assessment from the skim of the facts:** We will definitely need to review the facts in more detail later to parse out each side's specific reasons and arguments. You should have noted, however, the two arguments and reasons Ms. Urias gave for why the bond should be exonerated; these were in the first paragraph on one of the pages and so they should be easily noticeable even on a quick skim of the first and last sentences on the page. These two reasons help clarify a structure for your response and also indicate that the case law will likely talk about mandatory versus discretionary exoneration, a topic we now know to look for in the library. Note also that the court ends by saying that each side should address in a brief each of the reasons that Oscar raises to argue that the bond should be exonerated. We have two reasons above, and we should read his few pages of testimony, quickly but in more depth, looking for other reasons. Our quick read reveals no reasons other than the two that Ms. Urias pointed out and his failed attempts to find his father.

TRANSCRIPT OF BOND FORFEITURE HEARING
Honorable Beth Jones, Presiding

THE COURT: The next case is The State of Columbia, Plaintiff, versus Henry Raymond, Defendant, Bond in the Amount of $45,000, and Oscar Raymond, the Bond Poster and Surety, Case number CR - 20180016. This is a Bond Forfeiture Proceeding concerning an appearance bond. Ms. Sattler, I see you are here for the People. Ms. Urias, are you here on behalf of Oscar Raymond, the surety?

MS. URIAS: Yes, your honor.

THE COURT: Ms. Sattler, do you want to explain the facts and the grounds for forfeiture?

PEOPLE: Yes. Thank you, your honor. The Defendant, Henry Raymond, was arrested and booked on February 13, 2018, on felony charges of unlawful possession of a narcotic drug, unlawful possession of a narcotic drug for sale, and possession of drug paraphernalia. An interim complaint on those charges was sworn out on that same date. It included the information that the offenses involved about 44 grams of cocaine and admissions by Defendant that he was selling cocaine. At the initial appearance, the Magistrate held Defendant without bond. The grand jury returned an indictment against Defendant on February 23, 2018, on felony counts of possession of a narcotic drug for sale and possession of drug paraphernalia, including an allegation of exceeding the threshold amount of cocaine. On February 27, 2018, Defendant appeared for his arraignment. On March 13, 2018, the trial court conducted a hearing on defense counsel's motion to set conditions of release. The Pretrial Services report indicated that Defendant had no prior convictions. He stated that his permanent residence was in the neighboring State of Franklin, but he provided no references or sources for verification of this information. The trial court set a $45,000 cash bond requirement. On March 15, 2018, Mr. Oscar Raymond posted the $45,000 cash bond and Defendant was released from Cruz County Superior Court hold.

[Margin note: The parties/ counsel and issue]

[Margin note: For now just skim the beginning and end of each paragraph.]

> Explains why both the son and defendant are involved.

THE COURT: Sorry to interrupt, Ms. Sattler. My understanding is that the surety, Mr. Oscar Raymond, is the son of Defendant Henry Raymond?

PEOPLE: Yes, your honor.

THE COURT: Okay. Please continue.

PEOPLE: Thank you, your honor. On March 23, 2018, at a pretrial conference, Defendant's counsel told the trial court that Defendant's bond had been posted and that Defendant had fled. The trial court noted in the Minute entry that "defense counsel bears the responsibility for arranging Defendant's return." A trial date was set for October 22, 2018. At a pretrial conference, the trial date was postponed by the trial judge until January 30, 2019. On January 30, 2019 trial began, and Defendant failed to

> Again just skimming the beginning and end.

appear. A jury was selected and impaneled, opening statements were made, two witnesses testified, and several items of evidence were admitted. On the second day of trial, January 31, Defendant again failed to appear. Several more witnesses testified and additional items of evidence were admitted. The State then rested, and defense counsel made a motion for judgment of acquittal. The trial court granted the motion, acquitting Defendant and ending the trial. Defense counsel moved to exonerate the bond. The trial court denied the motion, however, and ordered, I quote: "that this matter be referred to the Superior Court Hearing Office for the commencement of bond forfeiture proceedings, based upon Defendant's failure to appear for his trial." The State seeks forfeiture of the bond for failure to comply with the bond conditions, your honor.

THE COURT: Okay, unless you have anything more, Ms. Sattler . . . .

PEOPLE: No, that's it, your honor.

THE COURT: . . . then go ahead, Ms. Urias, and explain why, in face of the nonappearance and proper notice, the bond should be exonerated.

> Note this informs us she will be giving us reasons that will be important for the structure.

MS. URIAS: Thank you, your honor. Assuming for the moment that the People have made out a prima facie case for forfeiture, there are two reasons why the bond must be exonerated. First, the bond may be exonerated due to mandatory statutory grounds. Defendant was acquitted, and Columbia Rules of Criminal Procedure provide for mandatory exoneration in such a situation. It isn't discretionary. Second, the facts of this case justify the exercise of your discretion to exonerate the bond for several reasons, your honor . . .

> This gives us two reasons to help structure our argument — we need to argue these do not justify exoneration.

THE COURT: . . . I got it. Why does the acquittal exonerate the bond?

MS. URIAS: At the close of the People's case in the *in absentia* trial proceeding, the defense moved for and received a judgment of acquittal. According to Columbia Rule of Criminal Procedure 13(d)(1), when there is no further need for an appearance bond, exoneration is mandatory. The rule does not allow discretion with regard to exoneration if there is no further need for an appearance bond, as the statute says "shall." Similarly, Columbia Rule of Criminal Procedure 13(d)(2) requires that when a prosecution is dismissed, the defendant shall be released on those charges and the bond exonerated. That rule must be construed to signify any dismissal of a case on its merits. It would be sheer absurdity to conclude that an appearance bond is exonerated on dismissal but not on acquittal. We believe the holding of *People v. Weinberger*, applied here, requires exoneration.

> We will need to distinguish this case — it is in our library and from the court of appeals.

THE COURT: Ms. Sattler, do you have a response?

PEOPLE: Your honor, the statute Ms. Urias cites pertains to pretrial events and doesn't require mandatory exoneration in this case. The primary reason for an appearance bond is to have the defendant appear for trial, and Defendant didn't show up. The trial court found that Defendant's acquittal was because Defendant's absence made identification impossible. The finding was, I quote: "There is no substantial evidence to warrant a conviction, based upon insufficient evidence of the identity of the Defendant."

THE COURT: Ms. Urias, you said there were <u>other reasons for exoneration</u>.

MS. URIAS: Yes, your honor, <u>Oscar made good faith efforts to ensure his father's</u> <u>appearance at trial</u>. We would like to have him briefly testify, your honor.

THE COURT: Okay Mr. Raymond, come have a seat in the witness chair. The courtroom clerk will swear in the Witness.

THE COURT: Go ahead, Ms. Urias, you may question your witness.

BY MS. URIAS:

Q: Could you state your name and address for the record?

> Note that now Oscar is testifying.

A: <u>Oscar Raymond</u>, 3898 West 14th Street, Twin Oaks, Columbia.

Q: When you arranged bail for your father, did you get a chance to speak to him?

A: Yes.

Q: Did you ask him whether he intended to appear at trial?

A: No.

Q: Why not?

A: I don't know. I guess I figured that he would appear.

Q: After you posted bail, what happened?

A: My dad came home and, according to my sister, he stayed around for a few weeks. One day, he said he was going to visit my aunt, his sister, who lives across town. My sister asked him if he was going to skip bail. He said, no, that he planned to fight the charges. Then he disappeared. I called my aunt, and she said he left her house after an hour. I didn't know what else I could do.

Q: Have you ever posted bail for anyone before?

A: Never.

MS. URIAS: That is all that I have, your honor.

THE COURT: Ms. Sattler, do you have questions for the witness?

MS. SATTLER: A few, your honor.

BY THE PEOPLE:

> Now the state is asking him questions on cross-examination.

Q: You didn't live with your father did you, Mr. Raymond?

A: No, I didn't.

Q: In fact, he hasn't been much of a presence in your life, has he?

A: No, not really.

Q: How often did you see your father?

A: Not often. He hasn't been around much. He doesn't really have many ties here except for my sister, my aunt and me. And none of us really see him very much.

Q: You've been financially independent from him for a number of years, haven't you?

A: Yes, I moved out right after graduating from high school and have supported myself since then.

Q: You make a pretty good living, don't you?

A: I guess so. I work as a software engineer and I make about $120,000 per year.

Q: Was posting the $45,000 bond a financial hardship for you?

A: It would hurt to lose it, but I have quite a bit saved up to help my sister with her college education.

Q: When you posted the bond, were you aware that your father may have been involved in unlawful activities?

A: Yes, I was aware.

Q: You were aware, then, that there was a decent chance he would flee rather than face trial?

A: I didn't really think much about it, but I suppose that's true too. I didn't see that I had much choice, though. It was my dad.

Q: Oscar, did you make any effort to find out where your dad was and to contact his defense counsel or the prosecutor so that he would appear for trial?

A: No.

Again, just skimming the beginning and end of the page here since no paragraphs.

Q: Before you signed the appearance bond agreement, your read it very carefully, didn't you?

A: Yeah, I guess so.

Q: And you understood that by signing the agreement both you and your father were responsible for your father's appearances in court, didn't you?

A: Yeah.

Q: And you also understood that if you or your father failed in that responsibility you would lose all of the money you put up, right?

A: Yeah. I knew how it worked, and I knew that if he didn't show up for any of the stuff he was supposed to show up for that I would end up losing the money, but I didn't have any way to find him and make him show up.

THE PEOPLE: Your honor, I have no further questions.

THE COURT: Redirect, Ms. Urias?

MS. URIAS: Nothing, your honor.

THE COURT: Under the circumstances, I'm going to take this under advisement. I would like both sides to do some research and submit a brief on each of the reasons raised by Oscar Raymond as to why the bond should be exonerated.

THE PEOPLE: Thank you, your honor. We would appreciate it.

MS. URIAS: Thank you, your honor.

> We will need to read all of his reasons in more detail. Since we already have some reasons, we can read his few pages of testimony in more detail here to get all of the reasons now, before reading the library. This might take a few more minutes, but then your read of the library will be more productive, since you will know what you are looking for.

This is how your answer should look at this point if you are adding in details as you organize your answer:

To: Barbara Sattler, Deputy District Attorney

From: Applicant

Re: State v. Henry Raymond, Defendant, and Oscar Raymond, the Bond Poster/Surety, Real Party in Interest

Date: February 26, 2019

Ms. Sattler,

Pursuant to your request, below is a Brief in Support of Forfeiture of the Bond demonstrating why forfeiture is appropriate and why exoneration is not justified. The arguments should convince the judge that the $45,000 cash bond should not be returned to the surety, but rather forfeited because the defendant, Henry Raymond, failed to appear for the trial. Please let me know if you need any additional help with the Raymond case.

Applicant

BRIEF IN SUPPORT OF FORFEITURE OF THE BOND

<u>FACTS</u>

(Although you have skimmed the facts, it is best to do this section after you have read the library and the file thoroughly.)

<u>ARGUMENT</u>

FORFEITURE OF RAYMOND'S BOND POSTED TO RELEASE HIM FROM JAIL IS APPROPRIATE BECAUSE . . . (need to fill in later)

EXONERATION OF RAYMOND'S BOND WHEN HE DID NOT APPEAR FOR HIS TRIAL IS NOT JUSTIFIED BECAUSE . . . (need to fill in later)

<u>Mandatory Exoneration</u> (This might be able to go above, too, and maybe both main headings tie together, although it is not clear yet.)

Mr. Raymond will argue this should apply because he was exonerated, but we need to show how it does not. (The file mentioned something about pretrial issues, which might help us when reading the library.)

<u>Court's Discretion on Exoneration</u>

Mr. Raymond will argue that the court has the discretion to exonerate the bond and should, because he tried to find his father and was unable to do so. (We need to argue against this.)

For the foregoing reasons, the bond should not be exonerated but rather forfeited.

Step 5.	**Actively read the library and synthesize rules (20–30 minutes)**

[Since we are inputting headings, rules, case reasoning, etc., directly into our answer as we go through each step, we need more time here than if we were roadmapping on scratch paper.]

Read the Library and Deconstruct and Synthesize Rules as Needed

Looking for the rules you can use to solve the problem posed and any analysis that can be borrowed from the cases. Depending on the task, we may need to synthesize cases or identify which rule among competing rules should be adopted. To most efficiently assess the library, read the materials in the order presented, since most often the rules are provided in the same order that they will be used to solve the problem, given the task macrostructure. Book brief the cases and add information to the roadmap as you go. Annotate your cases with notes so you don't waste time rewriting sentences into your roadmap. Determine how best to use any statutes. Each case in the library was included because it is likely needed to solve the problem, so it is up to you to determine how each can best be used. We typically note at the top of each case where it will be used in our answer and whether it is favorable or not for our client by writing a plus or minus sign at the top. Continue to look for clues as to how you should structure your answer.

Raymond Cases

The library contains three cases, a large number for a performance test, but they are all relatively short. We know we need to find rules about mandatory exoneration and factual situations or rules about when the court has discretion to grant exoneration and what circumstances give rise to such a finding. Further, since this is a persuasive task, we must look for reasoning that will bolster our argument that the bond should not be exonerated but rather forfeited. Thus, we will need to distinguish any unfavorable case law.

- <u>People v. Nationwide:</u> This case is binding, as it is in the Columbia Supreme Court (our jurisdiction). It involves a surety company that posted a bond for defendant (D). D failed to appear at his preliminary hearing, and the court ordered the bond forfeited. The Columbia Supreme Court reversed the decision in favor of the surety, reasoning that the surety had no reason to know that D would flee and thus should not be faulted. This case provides the rules for mandatory and discretionary exoneration, which should be added to your roadmap.

- <u>People v. Saintly Bail Bonds</u>: This is not a Columbia Supreme Court case, but it is in our jurisdiction. It also involves a surety that posted a bond for a defendant (D) who failed to appear. But here the court affirmed the forfeiture of the bond because the surety had made no effort to secure D's appearance and it could have determined where D was by contacting jail personnel. This case focuses on exoneration under the court's discretion and provides factors the court in our case will look at. (These factors should be included on your roadmap.)

- <u>People v. Weinberger</u>: This case, also in our jurisdiction, involves a defendant (D) and his agent, who posted his bond. The prosecution dismissed the case before D was set to appear, so the court exonerated his bond. This case provides rules for when exoneration is mandatory. (These rules should also be included on your roadmap.)

Goes to rules about mandatory and discretionary exoneration.

For surety so (—) for us; need to distinguish.

PEOPLE v. NATIONWIDE SURETY INSURANCE COMPANY

Columbia Supreme Court (2006)

Binding case

Nationwide Surety Insurance Company (Nationwide Surety) appeals from the trial court's order denying its motion to vacate forfeiture and exonerate the bail bond it posted for Robert Roger. The bond was forfeited when Roger did not appear at his preliminary hearing.

T. Ct. for People

Not all cases label the parts, but it is a bonus when they do.

FACTS

Roger was arrested for a drug-related offense. Nationwide Surety posted a $20,000 bail bond for him the same day, after Roger presented a Columbia driver's license, social security card, and other documents. Roger was ordered to return for his preliminary hearing. However, immediately following execution of the bond, Roger fled. He did not appear for the preliminary hearing, and Nationwide Surety's bond was then ordered forfeited.

BACKGROUND RELATING TO BAIL BOND STATUTES

While bail bond proceedings occur in connection with criminal prosecutions, they are independent from and collateral to the prosecutions and are civil in nature.

Policy

The object of bail and its forfeiture is to insure the attendance of the accused and his obedience to the orders and judgment of the court. Nevertheless, the bail bond is a contract between the poster of the bond (the surety) and the government whereby the surety acts as a guarantor of the

Rule

defendant's appearance in court under the risk of forfeiture of the bond. When

Rule

there is a breach of this contract, the bond agreement should be enforced. The

Scope of risk

scope of the surety's risk is defined by the terms of the bond agreement and applicable statutes. The forfeiture or exoneration of the bail bond is entirely a statutory procedure, and forfeiture proceedings are governed entirely by the special statutes applicable thereto. Thus forfeiture proceedings, even though instituted in criminal matters, are simply a streamlined substitute for a civil suit resulting from a breach of contract.

Interpretation of rules

Burden of proof

Consistent with long-standing notions such as "equity abhors a forfeiture," the rules calling for bond forfeiture must be strictly construed in favor of the surety to avoid the harsh results of a forfeiture. However, nonappearance for trial creates a presumption of forfeiture. Once there has been a demonstration that by failing to appear the defendant has not complied with the terms of the bond agreement, the surety bears the burden of coming forward with a request for relief from forfeiture and making the necessary showing, by competent evidence, of a legally recognized justification for the failure to appear, either because ① the statute mandates exoneration or because ② it should be exonerated in whole or in part in the sound discretion of the court.

Rule

Two reasons surety can use to justify noncompliance by D.

Rules of Criminal Procedure, Rule 13, specifically concerns the procedure applicable to forfeiture of bail bonds, which occurs when the defendant whose appearance in court is assured by the bond fails to appear.

Rule 13: to exonerate a bond

If the surety surrenders the accused to the sheriff of the county in which the prosecution is pending, or delivers an affidavit to the sheriff stating that the defendant is incarcerated in this or another jurisdiction, and the sheriff reports the surrender or status to the court, the court shall vacate any order of forfeiture and exonerate the bond. Rules of Criminal Procedure, Rule 13(d), provides that the court shall exonerate an appearance bond in the event of pretrial dismissal or when other pretrial circumstances ranging from death of the defendant to diversion preclude further need for an appearance bond. Rules of Criminal Procedure, Rule 13(e), provides that in all other instances, "the decision whether or not to exonerate a bond shall be within the sound discretion of the court."

Rule 13(d): mandatory

Rule 13(e): ct. discretion

State argues

Reasoning (for surety)

Reasoning (for surety)

Respondent contends the bail should remain forfeited because Nationwide Surety should have known Roger was a flight risk. It is true that generally parties in contract disputes are held to bear the risk concerning events of which they knew or should have known. Just how Nationwide Surety should have known that Roger was a flight risk, however, is not demonstrated by the respondent. Roger presented a Columbia driver's license, a social security card, and other documents that showed his ties to the community. While these may have been fraudulent documents, there has been no showing that Nationwide Surety had any reasonable suspicion that Roger would flee when it posted the bail bond. We are convinced that Nationwide Surety cannot be faulted. Nationwide Surety acted in the good faith belief that Roger would appear.

Contract rule

For all of the above stated reasons, the order denying appellant's motion to vacate forfeiture is reversed.

For surety

347

Goes to ct. discretion to exonerate.

For state, so (+) for us; analogize.

PEOPLE v. SAINTLY BAIL BONDS
Columbia Court of Appeals (2008)

Same jx

Facts

Saintly Bail Bonds (the surety) posted a $55,000 appearance bond for criminal defendant Jerry Marshall after he was indicted on a drug charge in April 2003. When the defendant failed to appear at a pretrial conference in July, his attorney told the judge the defendant was in the custody of the Department of Corrections of the State of Franklin. The judge nonetheless set a trial date and ordered the state to prepare a writ of habeas corpus and arrange for the defendant to be transported to Pima County for a pre-trial conference. When the state was unable to secure the defendant's appearance through the writ, the judge ordered the $55,000 bond forfeited. The surety appealed. We affirm.

T. Ct. for State; Aff'd

Surety argues

The surety argues the defendant did not fail to appear on his own volition and that the surety cannot be held responsible for failing to produce the defendant. In short, according to the surety, "it is anyone's fault but the Bond Poster's that the defendant has technically, if at all, violated the release conditions." We disagree.

Rules

It is well settled in this jurisdiction that a surety assumes the risk of a defendant's failure to appear. To alleviate that risk, a surety should exercise care in ascertaining the defendant's circumstances and community ties before executing an appearance bond, much as a trial court must do before determining a defendant's release conditions. Although the surety claims it was not aware and had no reason to be aware that the Franklin Department of Corrections might be interested in defendant at the time it posted the bond, the record demonstrates that the surety could have easily acquired that information by simply contacting jail personnel. And, because we know of no authority that imposes a duty on the state to seek out a surety and furnish it information about a criminal defendant, we do not accept the surety's argument that someone else was to blame. To the contrary, no one but the surety had any duty to ascertain the wisdom or folly of contracting with the defendant to post a bond that would secure his appearance in court.

Surety argues

Reasoning (for State)

Reasoning (for State)

Nationwide distinguished.	The *Nationwide Surety* case does not require a different conclusion. In that case, there was no reason for the surety to know that the defendant was a flight risk.

Nor do we accept the surety's argument that the trial court abused its discretion by rejecting the surety's explanation for the defendant's failure to appear.

Rule: ct. discretion	Once there has been a determination that a defendant failed to appear or otherwise comply with the terms of the appearance bond, except where a statute specifically requires exoneration, the decision to order an appearance bond forfeited or to remit in whole or in part lies essentially in the discretion of the trial court.

A trial court may consider all of the relevant circumstances, including the following list of factors that Columbia courts have frequently delineated:

Factors ct. considers in exonerating bond.	-- The defendant's willfulness in violating the order to appear;
	-- Whether the surety is a commercial entity (noncommercial sureties are often given more latitude concerning return of some or all of the bond);
	-- The effort and expense expended by the surety in trying to locate and apprehend the defendant to insure the return of the fugitive (lack of effort by the surety to locate the defendant's return justifies forfeiture, as it is necessary to provide an incentive to the surety to take active and reasonable steps to recapture a fugitive defendant);
	-- The costs, inconvenience and prejudice suffered by the State, if any, because of the absence of defendant;
	-- The public's interest in ensuring a defendant's appearance.

Reasoning (for State)

Here, there is no indication that the defendant made any effort to attend the scheduled court conference. Defense counsel never asserted that the defendant had expressed any desire to abide by his promise to appear. Indeed, nothing in the record suggests that the defendant had made any effort even to contact his defense counsel. Nor has the surety demonstrated that it expended any effort or expense in attempting to arrange for his appearance.

The trial court's decision to forfeit the bond was not an abuse of discretion. Because the defendant failed to make any effort to appear at trial, he must be considered to have willfully violated the terms of the appearance bond. In addition, because the surety, a commercial entity, expended no effort or expense to produce the defendant, there is no need to protect the incentives of sureties generally to post bonds, and forfeiture serves the purpose of providing proper incentives to sureties to live up to their obligations to ensure that the defendant adheres to the terms and conditions of the bond.

Affirmed.

For State (for forfeiture)

Goes to rules on mandatory exoneration

For surety, so (—) for us and thus need to distinguish.

PEOPLE v. WEINBERGER

Columbia Court of Appeals (2003)

Same jx

FACTS AND PROCEDURAL BACKGROUND

Facts

Appellant Weinberger was arrested and charged with possession of marijuana for sale. He appeared before a magistrate for his initial appearance and bond was set at $30,000. Appellant and others were subsequently indicted for possession of marijuana for sale. Appellant posted the $30,000 cash bond through his agent and was ordered released from custody on that date. Subsequently, after appellant had failed to appear at a pretrial conference, a bench warrant was issued for appellant's arrest, but no motion was made to forfeit the bond. On the same date the warrant was issued, several motions were argued to the court, including motions to suppress evidence. The court took the matter under advisement for two days and then granted the motion to suppress. The state moved to dismiss the case against appellant, which was granted with prejudice. Shortly after, appellant moved to exonerate his bond. At the bond forfeiture hearing, the hearing officer ruled it irrelevant that the indictment against appellant had been dismissed and ordered the subject bond forfeited.

T. Ct.: bond forfeited

BOND FORFEITURE

Surety argues

Appellant contends that because the indictment against him was dismissed with prejudice prior to trial and prior to the bonds being forfeited, he is entitled by law to have his bond exonerated. It is well established that the termination of a prosecution before forfeiture of an appearance bond terminates a surety's liability on the bond. Additionally, appellants rely on Rule 13(d) of the

Rule

Columbia Rules of Criminal Procedure to support this conclusion. According to its terms, Rule 13 "shall govern the procedure to be followed in cases between arraignment and trial."

Columbia Rules of Criminal Procedure, Rule 13(d) - Exoneration of Bond, Dismissal of Prosecution, provides:

Rule 13(d) on exoneration

(1) Exoneration of Appearance Bond: At any time <u>before violation</u> that the court finds that there is <u>no further need for an appearance</u> bond, it <u>shall exonerate the appearance bond</u> and order the return of any security deposit.

(2) Release of Defendant - Exoneration of Bond: <u>When a prosecution is dismissed</u>, the defendant shall be released from custody, unless he is in custody on some other charge, and any <u>appearance bond exonerated</u>.

Mandatory exoneration

Purpose of bond/ policy

<u>The primary purpose of an appearance bond is to ensure the defendant's presence at the time of trial.</u> <u>When, as here, the charges are dismissed prior to trial, the primary purpose for the bond no longer exists, and from that point forward there is no further need for the appearance bond.</u> This is why Rule 13(d) indicates that <u>if the charges are dismissed or that there otherwise is no longer a reason for the appearance bond the appearance bond shall be exonerated.</u>

Rule / reason for exoneration

Rule 13(d)

Rule 13(d), by stating that the bond shall be exonerated if "at any time *before violation* there is no further need for an appearance bond" (emphasis added), envisions that <u>there is no requirement to exonerate the bond if a violation</u> of the bond terms took place prior to the dismissal. But the fact remains that in this case the main purpose of the appearance bond, to ensure the defendant's presence at trial, ceased at the dismissal. <u>The State was not prejudiced by the non-appearance</u> of appellant at one pretrial conference, which is the only possible violation of the bond terms. If there was a violation, it was for only a matter of hours. The <u>appellant's presence was not required for any other event prior to dismissal</u>, and the <u>issue of forfeiture was not raised by the State</u>, perhaps because the State anticipated filing a motion to dismiss the charges. Given these facts, Rule 13(d), which requires exoneration of the bond when a prosecution is dismissed, dictates the result.

Rule

Reasoning (for surety)

The order of the court commissioner is vacated and the <u>trial court is directed to enter an order exonerating appellant's bond.</u>

For surety

Now that you have briefed the cases, if you are inputting your rules as you go through the steps, you can update your brief by adding in or reorganizing (if necessary) the headings to organize the issues and include the rules. Essentially, using this approach, you will be writing your performance test response as you go through each step.

To: Barbara Sattler, Deputy District Attorney
From: Applicant
Re: State v. Henry Raymond, Defendant, and Oscar Raymond, the Bond Poster/Surety, Real Party in Interest
Date: February 26, 2019

Ms. Sattler,

Pursuant to your request, below is a Brief in Support of Forfeiture of the Bond demonstrating why forfeiture is appropriate and why exoneration is not justified. The arguments should convince the judge that the $45,000 cash bond should not be returned to the surety, but rather forfeited because the defendant, Henry Raymond, failed to appear for the trial. Please let me know if you need any additional help with the Raymond case.

Applicant

BRIEF IN SUPPORT OF FORFEITURE OF THE BOND
FACTS

(Although you have skimmed the facts, it is best to do this section after you have read the library and completed a thorough read of the file.)

(Note: Time permitting, you can always add a brief section on procedural history. Otherwise, just include the procedural history at the end of your facts. Either option is acceptable.)

ARGUMENT

FORFEITURE OF RAYMOND'S BOND POSTED TO RELEASE HIM FROM JAIL IS APPROPRIATE BECAUSE . . . (need to fill in later)

The object of bail and its forfeiture is to insure the attendance of the accused and his obedience to the orders and judgment of the court. Nationwide and Weinberger.

The surety acts as a guarantor of the defendant's appearance in court under the risk of forfeiture of the bond. Nationwide. When there is a breach of contract, the bond agreement should be enforced. Nationwide. The scope of the surety's risk is defined by the terms of the bond agreement and applicable statutes. Nationwide.

Nonappearance for trial creates a presumption of forfeiture. Nationwide.

Once there has been a demonstration that by failing to appear the defendant has not complied with the terms of the bond agreement, the surety bears the burden of coming forward with a request for relief from forfeiture and making the necessary showing, by competent evidence, of a legally recognized justification for the failure to appear, either because (1) the statute mandates exoneration, or (2) because it should be exonerated in whole or in part in the sound discretion of the court. Nationwide.

In Nationwide, the defendant did not appear for his preliminary hearing and thus the trial court ordered the bond Nationwide posted forfeited. The Columbia Supreme Court vacated the lower court's order because it found that the surety had no reason to know that defendant would flee and thus should not be faulted for defendant's failure to appear. The court found that the defendant presented Nationwide (the surety) with his driver's license, a social security card, and other documents, and thus Nationwide acted in good faith when posting the bond for defendant to appear. Nationwide.

EXONERATION OF RAYMOND'S BOND WHEN HE DID NOT APPEAR FOR HIS TRIAL IS NOT JUSTIFIED BECAUSE . . . (need to fill in later)

<u>Mandatory Exoneration</u> (This might be able to go above, too, and maybe both main headings tie together, but it is not clear yet.)

If the surety surrenders the accused to the sheriff of the county in which the prosecution is pending, or delivers an affidavit to the sheriff stating that the defendant is incarcerated in this or another jurisdiction, and the sheriff reports the surrender or status to the court, the court shall vacate any order of forfeiture and exonerate the bond. <u>Nationwide.</u>

Criminal Procedure Rule 13(d) provides that the court shall exonerate an appearance bond in the event of pretrial dismissal or when other pretrial circumstances ranging from death of the defendant to diversion preclude further need for an appearance bond. <u>Nationwide.</u>

Termination of a prosecution before forfeiture of an appearance bond terminates a surety's liability on the bond. <u>Weinberger.</u>

Under Rule 13(d), at any time before violation that the court finds there is no further need for an appearance bond, it shall exonerate the appearance bond and order the return of any security deposit. <u>Weinberger.</u>

Under Rule 13(d), when a prosecution is dismissed, any appearance bond shall be exonerated. <u>Weinberger.</u>

In <u>Weinberger</u>, the State dismissed the case against the defendant before he was set to appear. Further, the State was not prejudiced at all by a non-appearance. Thus, the court ordered that the defendant's bond be exonerated. <u>Weinberger.</u>

(Mr. Raymond will argue this should apply because he was exonerated, but we need to show how it does not. The file mentioned something about pretrial issues, which might help us when reading the library.)

Court's Discretion on Exoneration

Criminal Procedure Rule 13(e) provides that in all other instances not discussed above under mandatory exoneration, the decision of whether to exonerate a bond shall be within the sound discretion of the court. <u>Nationwide</u> and <u>Saintly Bail Bonds.</u>

In determining whether to exonerate a bond, a trial court may consider all of the relevant circumstances as well as factors including: (1) the defendant's willfulness in violating the order to appear, (2) whether the surety is a commercial entity, (3) the effort and expense expended by the surety in trying to locate and apprehend the defendant to insure his appearance, (4) the costs, inconvenience, and prejudice suffered by the State due to defendant's absence, and (5) the public's interest. <u>Saintly Bail Bonds.</u>

In <u>Saintly Bail Bonds</u>, the court found for the State and forfeited Saintly Bail Bond's bond when defendant did not appear for court. While the defendant was in jail at the time of the appearance, the court found that the surety was a commercial entity that made no effort or expense to arrange for the defendant's appearance and didn't even attempt to contact his counsel. Thus, the court ordered the bond forfeited. <u>Saintly Bail Bonds.</u>

Mr. Raymond will argue that the court has the discretion to exonerate the bond and should because he tried to find his father and was unable to do so. (We need to argue against this.)

For the foregoing reasons, the bond should not be exonerated but rather forfeited.

Step 6. **Actively read the client file facts (15–20 minutes)**

[We are inputting facts and analysis directly into our answer as we go through each step, so this step will require extra time, as compared to roadmapping on scratch paper.]

Client File/Case Facts

Now that we know from the library the rules governing this situation and have determined how we will structure our argument, we must look for legally significant facts to apply to the rules to solve the problem. We want to look for helpful facts, harmful facts, and any missing facts, if pertinent to the task assigned. Add the legally significant facts into your roadmap as you go or input them into your answer in complete sentences if you are organizing your performance test in that manner.

Transcript of Bond Forfeiture Hearing

You know you are looking in the file for facts similar to or distinguishable from the facts in the library cases regarding whether the bond should be exonerated or not; look for facts in the cases that go to both mandatory and/or discretionary exoneration (the factors, in particular). Even when roadmapping on your computer as you read the file, using shorthand on paper first is a good idea; note the points and then enter useful sentences, keeping in mind that you are limited by time and should only include relevant, legally significant facts.

Background Facts

- Defendant Henry Raymond (D) was arrested/booked/indicted for drug-related felonies.
- Initially the magistrate held D without bond.
- D appeared for his arraignment.
- Defense counsel sought D's release.
- D resided in Franklin (neighboring state); no references or sources for verification here.
- D had no prior convictions.
- D's son, Oscar Raymond, posted a bond for $45,000 for D's release.
- Defense counsel bore the burden for D's appearance.
- Trial date was postponed, and D failed to appear for trial, but the trial began without him.
- State rested its case, defense counsel motioned for acquittal, and the court acquitted D, ending the trial. Note the timing: this was AFTER D failed to appear.

Defense Arguments

- Defense counsel moved to exonerate the bond; the court denied the motion and referred the matter to the Hearing Office for bond forfeiture proceedings.
- Defense counsel argues the bond should be exonerated because exoneration is (1) mandatory because D was acquitted, and (2) the court has discretion to do so.
- D argues Rule 13(d)(1): exoneration mandatory because no further need for appearance. (That rule was in the cases, so it's already in your roadmap.)
- D says rule does not allow discretion for exoneration: says "shall." (You need to verify rule and try to distinguish or argue against this.)
- D also argues Rule 13(d)(2) requires that when a case is dismissed, bond should be exonerated. (Recall timing issues with cases and try to argue that here.)
- D argues <u>Weinberger</u> applies. (So you need to distinguish this.)

People Arguments

- D's arguments pertain to pretrial events, so mandatory exoneration does not apply here.
- Primary reason for an appearance bond is to have D appear for trial.
- Reason for acquittal was because D's absence made identification impossible.

Defense's Further Arguments/Questioning of Oscar (Surety)

- Surety, Oscar (O), made good faith efforts to ensure his father's appearance.
- He didn't ask his father whether he would appear, but he figured he would.

- He did have the chance to speak with his father.
- D said he was going to visit his sister; she asked if he was going to skip bail and he said no, but then D disappeared.
- O called his aunt and didn't know what else to do.

People Questioning of Oscar (Surety)

- O didn't live with D.
- O says D hasn't had much of a presence in his life.
- D didn't have many ties in location and wasn't around much.
- O was financially independent from D since right after high school.
- O is a software engineer and makes about $120,000/year.
- O said it would hurt to lose $45,000, but he has quite a bit saved up to help his sister with her education.
- O was aware D may have been involved in unlawful activities.
- O didn't think much about D possibly fleeing, but he supposed it was true that there had been a decent chance he would. O said he had to post it anyway, as it was for his dad.
- O made no efforts to find D.
- O read the bond agreement carefully and knew he was responsible for D's appearance and would lose the money if D didn't show.
- O didn't have a way to find D and make him show up.

Our Assessment of the Detailed Facts

Now that you have the rules and organization input into your answer, you can line up facts with each rule or part of the argument in the brief. As you read the cases, annotate and highlight the pertinent facts listed above. Pay attention to facts similar to the <u>Saintly Bail Bonds</u> case, which found for the People, and note the facts you need to distinguish the cases, <u>Nationwide</u> and <u>Weinberger</u>, that found for the surety. Once you input these facts into your answer it should be close to done, since you have been writing it as you go through each step.

TRANSCRIPT OF BOND FORFEITURE HEARING
Honorable Beth Jones, Presiding

THE COURT: The next case is The State of Columbia, Plaintiff, versus Henry Raymond, Defendant, Bond in the Amount of $45,000, and Oscar Raymond, the Bond Poster and Surety, Case number CR - 20180016. This is a Bond Forfeiture Proceeding concerning an appearance bond. Ms. Sattler, I see you are here for the People. Ms. Urias, are you here on behalf of Oscar Raymond, the surety?

The parties/ counsel and issue

Pay attention to who is speaking and who they are.

MS. URIAS: Yes, your honor.

THE COURT: Ms. Sattler, do you want to explain the facts and the grounds for forfeiture?

PEOPLE: Yes. Thank you, your honor. The Defendant, Henry Raymond, was arrested and booked on February 13, 2018, on felony charges of unlawful possession of a narcotic drug, unlawful possession of a narcotic drug for sale, and possession of drug paraphernalia. An interim complaint on those charges was sworn out on that same date. It included the information that the offenses involved about 44 grams of cocaine and admissions by Defendant that he was selling cocaine. At the initial appearance, the Magistrate held Defendant without bond. The grand jury returned an indictment against Defendant on February 23, 2018, on felony counts of possession of a narcotic drug for sale and possession of drug paraphernalia, including an allegation of exceeding the threshold amount of cocaine. On February 27, 2018, Defendant appeared for his arraignment. On March 13, 2018, the trial court conducted a hearing on defense counsel's motion to set conditions of release. The Pretrial Services report indicated that Defendant had no prior convictions. He stated that his permanent residence was in the neighboring State of Franklin, but he provided no references or sources for verification of this information. The trial court set a $45,000 cash bond requirement. On March 15, 2018, Mr. Oscar Raymond posted the $45,000 cash bond and Defendant was released from Cruz County Superior Court hold.

D's charges

Hearing for bond

Bond posted

Explains why both the son and defendant are involved.	**THE COURT:** Sorry to interrupt, Ms. Sattler. My understanding is that the surety, Mr. Oscar Raymond, is the son of Defendant Henry Raymond?

PEOPLE: Yes, your honor.

THE COURT: Okay. Please continue.

Burden for appearance	**PEOPLE:** Thank you, your honor. On March 23, 2018, at a pretrial conference, Defendant's counsel told the trial court that Defendant's bond had been posted and that Defendant had fled. The trial court noted in the Minute entry that "defense counsel bears the responsibility for arranging Defendant's return." A trial date was set for
Trial D and D's absence	October 22, 2018. At a pretrial conference, the trial date was postponed by the trial judge until January 30, 2019. On January 30, 2019 trial began, and Defendant failed to appear. A jury was selected and impaneled, opening statements were made, two witnesses testified, and several items of evidence were admitted. On the second day of trial, January 31, Defendant again failed to appear. Several more witnesses testified and additional items of evidence were admitted. The State then rested, and defense
D acquitted; note timing: AFTER non-appearance.	counsel made a motion for judgment of acquittal. The trial court granted the motion, acquitting Defendant and ending the trial. Defense counsel moved to exonerate the bond. The trial court denied the motion, however, and ordered, I quote: "that this matter be referred to the Superior Court Hearing Office for the commencement of bond forfeiture proceedings, based upon Defendant's failure to appear for his trial." The State
Bond hearing	seeks forfeiture of the bond for failure to comply with the bond conditions, your honor.

THE COURT: Okay, unless you have anything more, Ms. Sattler . . . .

PEOPLE: No, that's it, your honor.

THE COURT: . . . then go ahead, Ms. Urias, and explain why, in face of the nonappearance and proper notice, the bond should be exonerated.

Note: This informs us she will be giving us reasons that will be important for the structure.

MS. URIAS: Thank you, your honor. Assuming for the moment that the People have made out a prima facie case for forfeiture, there are two reasons why the bond must be exonerated. (First,) the bond may be exonerated due to mandatory statutory grounds. Defendant was acquitted, and Columbia Rules of Criminal Procedure provide for mandatory exoneration in such a situation. It isn't discretionary. (Second,) the facts of this case justify the exercise of your discretion to exonerate the bond for several reasons, your honor . . .

> This gives us two reasons, which will help structure our argument: we need to argue that these do not justify exoneration.

> Note: Both of these options were discussed in the cases, so the rules are already in your structure.

THE COURT: . . . I got it. Why does the acquittal exonerate the bond?

MS. URIAS: At the close of the People's case in the *in absentia* trial proceeding, the defense moved for and received a judgment of acquittal. According to Columbia Rule of Criminal Procedure 13(d)(1), when there is no further need for an appearance bond, exoneration is mandatory. The rule does not allow discretion with regard to exoneration if there is no further need for an appearance bond, as the statute says "shall." Similarly, Columbia Rule of Criminal Procedure 13(d)(2) requires that when a prosecution is dismissed, the defendant shall be released on those charges and the bond exonerated. That rule must be construed to signify any dismissal of a case on its merits. It would be sheer absurdity to conclude that an appearance bond is exonerated on dismissal but not on acquittal. We believe the holding of *People v. Weinberger*, applied here, requires exoneration.

> Double check rules here and try to argue against this.

> D argues

> We will need to distinguish this case; it is in our library and from the court of appeals.

THE COURT: Ms. Sattler, do you have a response?

> Now switching to our arguments

PEOPLE: Your honor, the statute Ms. Urias cites pertains to pretrial events and doesn't require mandatory exoneration in this case. The primary reason for an appearance bond is to have the defendant appear for trial, and Defendant didn't show up. The trial court found that Defendant's acquittal was because Defendant's absence made identification impossible. The finding was, I quote: "There is no substantial evidence to warrant a conviction, based upon insufficient evidence of the identity of the Defendant."

> Reason for acquittal

THE COURT: Ms. Urias, you said there were other reasons for exoneration.   D argues

MS. URIAS: Yes, your honor, Oscar made good faith efforts to ensure his father's appearance at trial. We would like to have him briefly testify, your honor.

THE COURT: Okay Mr. Raymond, come have a seat in the witness chair. The courtroom clerk will swear in the Witness.

THE COURT: Go ahead, Ms. Urias, you may question your witness.

BY MS. URIAS:

Q: Could you state your name and address for the record?

Note that now Oscar is testifying.

A: Oscar Raymond, 3898 West 14th Street, Twin Oaks, Columbia.

Q: When you arranged bail for your father, did you get a chance to speak to him?

A: Yes.

Q: Did you ask him whether he intended to appear at trial?

A: No.

Q: Why not?

A: I don't know. I guess I figured that he would appear.

Q: After you posted bail, what happened?

A: My dad came home and, according to my sister, he <u>stayed around for a few weeks</u>. One day, he <u>said he was going to visit my aunt, his sister</u>, who lives across town. My sister asked him if he was going to skip bail. He said, no, that he planned to fight the charges. <u>Then he disappeared.</u> <u>I called my aunt</u>, and she said he left her house after an hour. <u>I didn't know what else I could do.</u>

D flees

O's efforts after D flees: didn't do much.

Q: Have you <u>ever posted bail for anyone</u> before?

A: <u>Never</u>.

MS. URIAS: That is all that I have, your honor.

THE COURT: Ms. Sattler, do you have questions for the witness?

MS. SATTLER: A few, your honor.

BY THE PEOPLE:

Now the state is asking him questions on cross-examination.

Q: You <u>didn't live with your father did you</u>, Mr. Raymond?

A: <u>No</u>, I didn't.

O talks about relationship with D: not close.

Q: In fact, he <u>hasn't been much of a presence in your life</u>, has he?

A: <u>No, not really</u>.

Q: <u>How often did you see your father?</u>

A: <u>Not often</u>. He <u>hasn't been around much</u>. He <u>doesn't really have many ties here</u> except for my sister, my aunt and me. And none of us really see him very much.

Q: You've been <u>financially independent from him</u> for a number of years, haven't you?

A: <u>Yes, I moved out right after graduating from high school</u> and have supported myself since then.

Q: You make a pretty good living, don't you?

A: I guess so. I work as a <u>software engineer and I make about $120,000 per year.</u>

Q: Was posting the <u>$45,000 bond a financial hardship</u> for you?

O hardship (not that much of one)

A: It <u>would hurt to lose it,</u> but I have <u>quite a bit saved up to help my sister with her college education.</u>

Q: When you posted the bond, were you <u>aware that your father may have been involved in unlawful activities</u>?

O's awareness

A: <u>Yes, I was aware.</u>

Q: You were <u>aware, then, that there was a decent chance he would flee</u> rather than face trial?

O agrees chance D might flee.

A: I didn't really think much about it, but I suppose that's true too. I <u>didn't see that I had much choice, though. It was my dad.</u>

O's efforts to find D.

Q: <u>Oscar, did you make any effort to find out where your dad was and to contact his defense counsel or the prosecutor so that he would appear for trial?</u>

A: <u>No.</u>

Q: Before you signed the appearance bond agreement, your read it very carefully, didn't you?

A: Yeah, I guess so.

Q: And you understood that by signing the agreement both you and your father were responsible for your father's appearances in court, didn't you?

A: Yeah.

Q: And you also understood that if you or your father failed in that responsibility you would lose all of the money you put up, right?

A: Yeah. I knew how it worked, and I knew that if he didn't show up for any of the stuff he was supposed to show up for that I would end up losing the money, but I didn't have any way to find him and make him show up.

THE PEOPLE: Your honor, I have no further questions.

THE COURT: Redirect, Ms. Urias?

MS. URIAS: Nothing, your honor.

THE COURT: Under the circumstances, I'm going to take this under advisement. I would like both sides to do some research and submit a brief on each of the reasons raised by Oscar Raymond as to why the bond should be exonerated.

THE PEOPLE: Thank you, your honor. We would appreciate it.

MS. URIAS: Thank you, your honor.

Now we need to match these facts to the rules we input from the library for our brief.

To: Barbara Sattler, Deputy District Attorney
From: Applicant
Re: State v. Henry Raymond, Defendant, and Oscar Raymond, the Bond Poster/Surety, Real Party in Interest
Date: February 26, 2019

Ms. Sattler,

Pursuant to your request, below is a Brief in Support of Forfeiture of the Bond demonstrating why forfeiture is appropriate and why exoneration is not justified. The arguments should convince the judge that the $45,000 cash bond should not be returned to the surety, but rather forfeited because the defendant, Henry Raymond, failed to appear for the trial. Please let me know if you need any additional help with the Raymond case.

Applicant

BRIEF IN SUPPORT OF FORFEITURE OF THE BOND

FACTS

The Defendant Henry Raymond was arrested/booked/indicted for drug-related felonies. Initially the magistrate held defendant without bond, and defendant appeared for his arraignment. After his arraignment, defense counsel sought defendant's release with a bond. Defendant indicated he resided in the neighboring state of Franklin, but no references or sources were presented to verify this information. It was also noted that defendant had no prior convictions. The court then allowed defendant's son, Oscar Raymond, to post a bond for $45,000 for defendant's release. It was noted that defense counsel bore the burden for defendant's appearance. Thereafter, defendant failed to appear for trial, but trial still began with witness testimony and other evidence being admitted. The People then rested its case and defense counsel motioned for acquittal. The court then acquitted defendant and ended the trial noting that there was insufficient evidence to identify defendant without his presence. The surety, Oscar, then sought return of the $45,000 bond. The court denied the motion and referred the matter to the Hearing Office for bond forfeiture proceedings.

At the bond forfeiture hearing, the defense counsel argued that exoneration was mandatory and also within the court's discretion. The People argued that exoneration was not mandatory and that the court should not exonerate the bond. The argument below will demonstrate why forfeiture is appropriate and why exoneration is not justified.

ARGUMENT

FORFEITURE OF RAYMOND'S BOND POSTED TO RELEASE HIM FROM JAIL IS APPROPRIATE BECAUSE HE FAILED TO APPEAR FOR TRIAL, WHICH WAS THE PRIMARY PURPOSE OF THE BOND

The object of bail and its forfeiture is to insure the attendance of the accused and his obedience to the orders and judgment of the court. Nationwide and Weinberger.

The surety acts as a guarantor of the defendant's appearance in court under the risk of forfeiture of the bond. Nationwide. When there is a breach of contract, the bond agreement should be enforced. Nationwide. The scope of the surety's risk is defined by the terms of the bond agreement and applicable statutes. Nationwide. Further, nonappearance for trial creates a presumption of forfeiture. Nationwide.

Here, defendant's son, Oscar, the surety, posted a $45,000 bond for defendant's release. The bond agreement indicated that defense counsel and the surety were responsible for defendant's appearance. Oscar testified at the bond hearing that he carefully read the agreement and knew he was responsible for defendant's appearance. He also testified that he knew he would lose the money if defendant did not appear for trial. Moreover, he admitted that he knew there was a chance that defendant would flee and not appear, which is exactly what occurred. Since defendant did not appear for trial, there is a presumption of forfeiture.

Once there has been a demonstration that by failing to appear the defendant has not complied with the terms of the bond agreement, the surety bears the burden of coming forward with a request for relief from forfeiture and making the necessary showing, by competent evidence, of a legally recognized justification for the failure to appear, either because (1) the statute mandates exoneration, or (2) because it should be exonerated in whole or in part in the sound discretion of the court. Nationwide.

In Nationwide, the defendant did not appear for his preliminary hearing and thus the trial court ordered the bond Nationwide posted forfeited. The Columbia Supreme Court vacated the lower court's order because it found that the surety had no reason to know that defendant would flee and thus should not be faulted for defendant's failure to appear. The court found that the defendant presented Nationwide (the surety) with his driver's license, a social security card, and other documents and thus Nationwide acted in good faith when posting the bond for defendant to appear. Nationwide. (LEAVING THIS HERE FOR NOW BUT LATER MAY NEED TO MOVE THIS TO ANOTHER SECTION WHEN REVIEWING ENTIRE DOCUMENT OR MIGHT INCORPORATE THESE ARGUMENTS ELSEWHERE AND DELETE THIS LATER.)

EXONERATION OF RAYMOND'S BOND WHEN HE DID NOT APPEAR FOR HIS TRIAL IS NOT JUSTIFIED BECAUSE EXONERATION IS NOT MANDATORY AND THE COURT SHOULD NOT EXONERATE THE BOND WHILE EXERCISING ITS DISCRETION

Mandatory Exoneration

There are few situations in which mandatory exoneration applies.

First, if the surety surrenders the accused to the sheriff of the county in which the prosecution is pending, or delivers an affidavit to the sheriff stating that the defendant is incarcerated in this or another jurisdiction, and the sheriff reports the surrender or status to the court, the court shall vacate any order of forfeiture and exonerate the bond. Nationwide.

Here, Oscar, the surety, never surrendered the accused to the sheriff or delivered an affidavit that he was incarcerated. Thus, this mandatory exoneration rule does not apply to the facts of this case.

Second, Criminal Procedure Rule 13(d) provides that the court shall exonerate an appearance bond in the event of pretrial dismissal or when other pretrial circumstances ranging from death of the defendant to diversion preclude further need for an appearance bond. Nationwide.

Under Rule 13(d) at any time before violation that the court finds there is no further need for an appearance bond, it shall exonerate the appearance bond and order the return of any security deposit. Weinberger.

At the bond forfeiture hearing, defense counsel argued that under Rule 13(d)(1) exoneration was mandatory because there was no further need for appearance. However, this argument is flawed because it fails to consider the actual language of the statute, with "pretrial" being the operative word. Defense counsel's arguments pertain to "pretrial" events, so mandatory exoneration does not apply here. As discussed above, the primary reason for an appearance bond is to have the defendant appear for trial. Here, the reason for acquittal was because defendant's absence at trial made identification impossible.

Further, Rule 13 focuses on the court exonerating the bond at any time "before" violation. Here, defendant violated the bond by not appearing for trial. Thus, the court did not find that there was no need for appearance before the violation. Rather, defendant's violation occurred first by his failing to appear for trial.

The third situation giving rise to mandatory exoneration occurs under Rule 13(d)(2), which states that when a prosecution is dismissed, any appearance bond shall be exonerated. Weinberger. Thus, termination of a prosecution before forfeiture of an appearance bond terminates a surety's liability on the bond. Weinberger.

In Weinberger, the State dismissed the case against the defendant before he was set to appear. Further, the State was not prejudiced at all by a non-appearance. Thus, the court ordered that the defendant's bond be exonerated. Weinberger. At the bond forfeiture hearing, defense counsel argued that Weinberger should apply here and that Rule 13(d)(2) requires exoneration because the case was dismissed. However, this case is distinguishable because here the case was dismissed after, not before, defendant was set to appear. Further, here the State was prejudiced as the main reason for dismissal was because the defendant was not present to be identified. Thus, the facts are contrary to those in Weinberger and require a different result.

Taking into consideration all situations in which mandatory exoneration shall apply, there are no circumstances or facts in this case that meet the requirements for exoneration.

Discretionary Exoneration
Criminal Procedure Rule 13(e) provides that in all other instances not discussed above under mandatory exoneration, the decision of whether to exonerate a bond shall be within the sound discretion of the court. Nationwide and Saintly Bail Bonds.

In determining whether to exonerate a bond, a trial court may consider all of the relevant circumstances as well as factors including: (1) the defendant's willfulness in violating the order to appear, (2) whether the surety is a commercial entity, (3) the effort and expense expended by the surety in trying to locate and apprehend the defendant to insure his appearance, (4) the costs, inconvenience, and prejudice suffered by the State due to defendant's absence, and (5) the public's interest. Saintly Bail Bonds.

In Saintly Bail Bonds, the court found for the State and forfeited Saintly Bail Bonds's bond when defendant did not appear for court. While the defendant was in jail at the time of the appearance, the court found that the surety was a commercial entity that made no effort or expense to arrange for the defendant's appearance and didn't even attempt to contact his counsel. Thus, the court ordered the bond forfeited. Saintly Bail Bonds.

(1) *Defendant's willfulness*
Here, defendant knew he had a trial date set and deliberately did not appear. Unlike Saintly Bail Bonds, the defendant here was not in jail but rather free and able to appear but chose not to. Thus, this factor weighs in favor of the State.

(2) *Surety status*
Here, the surety is Oscar, the defendant's son, who is not a commercial entity. However, Oscar admitted at the bond hearing that the loss of the money would not create a financial hardship on him as he has other money saved up and makes about $120,000 per year. Further, he carefully read the bond agreement and understood that if his father did not appear that he would lose the money. He also admitted that he knew there was a decent chance that his father would not appear. Thus, this factor should not be weighed in favor of the surety.

(3) *Surety effort and expense*
Here, similar to the lack of effort on the part of the surety in Saintly Bail Bonds, Oscar admitted that he did not expend any effort to locate his father or ensure that he appeared at trial, other than asking his aunt about it. He had the chance to speak with his father and didn't ask him if he would appear. Further, given Oscar's income and the fact that the trial date was delayed, he could have spent some money to find his father in an effort to secure his appearance that would have cost less than $45,000. Thus, this factor also weighs against Oscar and in favor of the State as it did in Saintly Bail Bonds.

Further, unlike Nationwide, where the court found that the surety had no reason to know that defendant would flee and thus should not be faulted for defendant's failure to appear, here Oscar admitted that his father was not around much, they did not see each other often, his father did not have ties to the area or family, and that there was a decent chance he would not appear. Also, unlike Nationwide, where the defendant presented his driver's license, a social security card, and other documents such that the court found Nationwide acted in good faith when posting the bond for defendant to appear, here Oscar did not require anything from his father and in fact was aware he may been involved in unlawful activity. Thus, this factor weighs against Oscar and in favor of the State.

(4) *Hardship to the State*

Here, unlike the lack of prejudice to the State in <u>Weinberger</u>, defendant's failure to appear did prejudice the State since it was unable to prove identity due to the defendant being absent. Also, the State expended money and effort and time into the trial as the trial began and was not dismissed at any pretrial stage. Thus, this factor also weighs in favor of the State.

(5) *Public interest*

The public interest in ensuring that appearance bond agreements are strictly enforced and that defendants appear at trial is great. Without such appearances, there is a risk that criminals may go free due to lack of identification or for other reasons if they flee rather than allow the justice system to administer a fair trial with the accused. Further, the public has an interest in ensuring that the court system is fiscally efficient, and trials are speedy and timely, which cannot occur when defendants go missing. Thus, this factor also favors the State.

As all factors weigh in favor of the State, this court should not exonerate the bond.

CONCLUSION

For the foregoing reasons, the bond should not be exonerated but rather forfeited.

Step 7.	Reread the task memo and refine your roadmap to solve the problem posed (5 minutes)

Reread the Task Memo, See the Big Picture, and Solve the Problem

Before you start writing, always take a moment to ensure you are solving the problem posed and haven't gotten off track while going through the documents. Reread the task memo to refocus on precisely what you've been asked to do. Make sure that you are clear on your client's goal, plan to use the appropriate tone and vocabulary in your response, and follow all directions in the task memo. Consider your presentation's organization to ensure your response is clear and easy to follow. Lastly, consider the complexity of the various sections and components of your answer to assess how you think the grader will allocate points and devise a plan to spend your time accordingly.

Raymond

After rereading the task memo, be sure that you are writing a persuasive brief that covers both mandatory and discretionary exoneration. Since you are not told to omit any parts of the brief, you should have a short "facts" section prior to your argument. Also end with a brief conclusion.

Step 8.	Write an answer that solves the problem posed (about 45 minutes)

Since you have been writing your answer the entire time as you went through each step, this should be mostly, if not completely, finished. Spend your remaining time rereading your answer and making sure that everything is cohesive, written in complete sentences, and flows as it should. You can also use any additional time to bolster your introduction, making sure you address the person who initially requested the information, if you didn't already do so. Add in a conclusion, if you haven't already done so, and add any facts you may have only summarized earlier to save time.

SAMPLE ANSWER FOR RAYMOND

To: Barbara Sattler, Deputy District Attorney
From: Applicant
Re: State v. Henry Raymond, Defendant, and Oscar Raymond, the Bond Poster/Surety, Real
Party in Interest
Date: February 26, 2019

Ms. Sattler,

Pursuant to your request, below is a Brief in Support of Forfeiture of the Bond demonstrating why forfeiture is appropriate and why exoneration is not justified. The arguments should convince the judge that the $45,000 cash bond should not be returned to the surety, but rather forfeited because the defendant, Henry Raymond, failed to appear for the trial. Please let me know if you need any additional help with the Raymond case.

Applicant

BRIEF IN SUPPORT OF FORFEITURE OF THE BOND

FACTS

The Defendant Henry Raymond was arrested/booked/indicted for drug-related felonies. Initially the magistrate held defendant without bond and defendant appeared for his arraignment. After his arraignment, defense counsel sought defendant's release with a bond. Defendant indicated he resided in the neighboring state of Franklin, but no references or sources were presented to verify this information. It was also noted that defendant had no prior convictions. The court then allowed defendant's son, Oscar Raymond, to post a bond for $45,000 for defendant's release. It was noted that defense counsel bore the burden for defendant's appearance. Thereafter, defendant failed to appear for trial, but trial still began with witness testimony and other evidence being admitted. The People then rested its case and defense counsel motioned for acquittal. The court then acquitted defendant and ended the trial noting that there was insufficient evidence to identify defendant without his presence. The surety, Oscar, then sought return of the $45,000 bond. The court denied the motion and referred the matter to the Hearing Office for bond forfeiture proceedings. At the bond forfeiture hearing, the defense counsel argued that exoneration was mandatory and also within the court's discretion. The People argued that exoneration was not mandatory and that the court should not exonerate the bond. The arguments below will demonstrate why forfeiture is appropriate and why exoneration is not justified.

ARGUMENT

FORFEITURE OF RAYMOND'S BOND POSTED TO RELEASE HIM FROM JAIL IS APPROPRIATE BECAUSE HE FAILED TO APPEAR FOR TRIAL, WHICH WAS THE PRIMARY PURPOSE OF THE BOND

The object of bail and its forfeiture is to insure the attendance of the accused and his obedience to the orders and judgment of the court. <u>Nationwide</u> and <u>Weinberger.</u>

The surety acts as a guarantor of the defendant's appearance in court under the risk of forfeiture of the bond. <u>Nationwide.</u> When there is a breach of contract, the bond agreement should be enforced. <u>Nationwide.</u> The scope of the surety's risk is defined by the terms of the bond agreement and applicable statutes. <u>Nationwide.</u> Further, nonappearance for trial creates a presumption of forfeiture. <u>Nationwide.</u>

Here, defendant's son, Oscar, the surety, posted a $45,000 bond for defendant's release. The bond agreement indicated that defense counsel and the surety were responsible for defendant's appearance. Oscar testified at the bond hearing that he carefully read the agreement and knew he was responsible for defendant's appearance. He also testified that he knew he would lose the money if defendant did not appear for trial. Moreover, he admitted that he knew there was a chance that defendant would flee and not appear, which is exactly what occurred. Since defendant did not appear for trial, there is a presumption of forfeiture.

Once there has been a demonstration that by failing to appear the defendant has not complied with the terms of the bond agreement, the surety bears the burden of coming forward with a request for relief from forfeiture and making the necessary showing, by competent evidence, of a legally recognized justification for the failure to appear, either because (1) the statute mandates exoneration, or (2) because it should be exonerated in whole or in part in the sound discretion of the court. Nationwide.

The surety argues that both mandatory and discretionary exoneration apply. Both will be addressed below.

EXONERATION OF RAYMOND'S BOND WHEN HE DID NOT APPEAR FOR HIS TRIAL IS NOT JUSTIFIED BECAUSE EXONERATION IS NOT MANDATORY AND THE COURT SHOULD NOT EXONERATE THE BOND WHILE EXERCISING ITS DISCRETION

Mandatory Exoneration

| This is the second part the task memo asks about: why exoneration is not justified. |

There are few situations in which mandatory exoneration applies.

| Use subheadings for the types of exoneration. |

First, if the surety surrenders the accused to the sheriff of the county in which the prosecution is pending, or delivers an affidavit to the sheriff stating that the defendant is incarcerated in this or another jurisdiction, and the sheriff reports the surrender or status to the court, the court shall vacate any order of forfeiture and exonerate the bond. Nationwide.

| Signal words, like first, second, and third, help the grader follow your argument. |

Here, Oscar, the surety, never surrendered the accused to the sheriff or delivered an affidavit that he was incarcerated. Thus, this mandatory exoneration rule does not apply to the facts of this case.

Second, Criminal Procedure Rule 13(d) provides that the court shall exonerate an appearance bond in the event of pretrial dismissal or when other pretrial circumstances ranging from death of the defendant to diversion preclude further need for an appearance bond. Nationwide.

| Be sure to use the arguments that both counsel made at the hearing, too; those are easy points to earn. |

Under Rule 13(d) at any time before violation that the court finds there is no further need for an appearance bond, it shall exonerate the appearance bond and order the return of any security deposit. Weinberger.

At the bond forfeiture hearing, defense counsel argued that under Rule 13(d)(1), exoneration was mandatory because there was no further need for appearance. However, this argument is flawed because it fails to consider the actual language of the statute, "pretrial" being the operative word. Defense counsel's arguments pertain to "pretrial" events so mandatory exoneration does not apply here. As discussed above, the primary reason for an appearance bond is to have the defendant appear for trial. Here, the reason for acquittal was because defendant's absence at trial made identification impossible.

Further, Rule 13 focuses on the court exonerating the bond at any time "before" violation. Here, defendant violated the bond by not appearing for trial. Thus, the court did not find that there was no need for appearance before the violation. Rather, defendant's violation occurred first by his failing to appear for trial.

The third situation giving rise to mandatory exoneration occurs under Rule 13(d)(2), which states that when a prosecution is dismissed, any appearance bond shall be exonerated. Weinberger. Thus, termination of a prosecution before forfeiture of an appearance bond terminates a surety's liability on the bond. Weinberger.

| Try to compare the facts of your case to some of the key facts of the precedent cases from the library; distinguish unfavorable facts/holdings. |

In <u>Weinberger</u>, the State dismissed the case against the defendant before he was set to appear. Further, the State was not prejudiced at all by a non-appearance. Thus, the court ordered that the defendant's bond be exonerated. <u>Weinberger.</u> At the bond forfeiture hearing, defense counsel argued that <u>Weinberger</u> should apply here and that Rule 13(d)(2) requires exoneration because the case was dismissed. However, this case is distinguishable because here the case was dismissed after, not before, defendant was set to appear. Further, here the State was prejudiced as the main reason for dismissal was because the defendant was not present to be identified. Thus, the facts are contrary to those in <u>Weinberger</u> and require a different result. Taking into consideration all situations in which mandatory exoneration shall apply, there are no circumstances or facts in this case that meet the requirements for exoneration.

Discretionary Exoneration
Criminal Procedure Rule 13(e) provides that in all other instances not discussed above under mandatory exoneration, the decision of whether to exonerate a bond shall be within the sound discretion of the court. <u>Nationwide</u> and <u>Saintly Bail Bonds.</u>

In determining whether to exonerate a bond, a trial court may consider all of the relevant circumstances as well as factors including: (1) the defendant's willfulness in violating the order to appear, (2) whether the surety is a commercial entity, (3) the effort and expense expended by the surety in trying to locate and apprehend the defendant to insure his appearance, (4) the costs, inconvenience, and prejudice suffered by the State due to defendant's absence, and (5) the public's interest. <u>Saintly Bail Bonds.</u>

In <u>Saintly Bail Bonds</u>, the court found for the State and forfeited Saintly Bail Bonds's bond when defendant did not appear for court. While the defendant was in jail at the time of the appearance, the court found that the surety was a commercial entity that made no effort or expense to arrange for the defendant's appearance and didn't even attempt to contact his counsel. Thus, the court ordered the bond forfeited. <u>Saintly Bail Bonds.</u>

(1) *Defendant's willfulness*
Here, defendant knew he had a trial date set and deliberately did not appear. Unlike <u>Saintly Bail Bonds,</u> the defendant here was not in jail but rather free and able to appear but chose not to. Thus, this factor weighs in favor of the State.

(2) *Surety status*
Here, the surety is Oscar, the defendant's son, who is not a commercial entity. However, Oscar admitted at the bond hearing that the loss of the money would not create a financial hardship on him as he has other money saved up and makes about $120,000 per year. Further, he carefully read the bond agreement and understood that if his father did not appear that he would lose the money. He also admitted that he knew there was a decent chance that his father would not appear. Thus, this factor should not be weighed in favor of the surety.

(3) *Surety effort and expense*
Here, similar to the lack of effort on the part of the surety in <u>Saintly Bail Bonds</u>, Oscar admitted that he did not expend any effort to locate his father or ensure that he appeared at trial, other than asking his aunt about it. He had the chance to speak with his father and didn't ask him if he would appear. Further, given Oscar's income and the fact that the trial date was delayed, he could have spent some money to find his father in an effort to secure his appearance that would have cost less than $45,000. Thus, this factor also weighs against Oscar and in favor of the State as it did in <u>Saintly Bail Bonds</u>.

Further, unlike <u>Nationwide</u>, where the court found that the surety had no reason to know that defendant would flee and thus should not be faulted for defendant's failure to appear, here Oscar admitted that his father was not around much, they did not see each other often, his father did not have ties to the area or family, and that there was a decent chance he would not appear. Also, unlike <u>Nationwide</u>, where the defendant presented his driver's

---

Margin notes:

> List factors first and then go through each one.

> Separate each factor with its own heading; it will be easier to follow, and it ensures you address each factor.

> Use as many pertinent facts as you can when analyzing these factors.

> Use cases and facts of the cases to compare on some of the most fact-heavy factors.

license, a social security card, and other documents such that the court found Nationwide acted in good faith when posting the bond for defendant to appear, here Oscar did not require anything from his father and in fact was aware he may been involved in unlawful activity. Thus, this factor weighs against Oscar and in favor of the State.

(4) *Hardship to the State*

Here, unlike the lack of prejudice to the State in <u>Weinberger</u>, defendant's failure to appear did prejudice the State since it was unable to prove identity due to the defendant to being absent. Also, the State expended money and effort and time into the trial as the trial began and was not dismissed at any pretrial stage. Thus, this factor also weighs in favor of the State.

(5) *Public interest*

The public interest in ensuring that appearance bond agreements are strictly enforced and that defendants appear at trial is great. Without such appearances, there is a risk that criminals may go free due to lack of identification or other reasons if they flee rather than allow the justice system to administer a fair trial with the accused. Further, the public has an interest in ensuring that the court system is fiscally efficient, and trials are speedy and timely, which cannot occur when defendants go missing. Thus, this factor also favors the State.

As all factors weigh in favor of the State, this court should not exonerate the bond.

CONCLUSION

The facts here do not give rise to any of the statutes that require mandatory exoneration. Nor do the facts give rise to discretionary exoneration as the factors all weigh in favor of the State. Thus, the bond should not be exonerated but rather forfeited.

> Add a quick conclusion to recap your analysis.

Self-Assessment Grid: Raymond

Persuasive Brief

Overall organization and presentation

- ☐ An introduction to the requester that you have written the brief as requested
- ☐ Organized like a persuasive brief with headings and a conclusion
- ☐ Persuasive tone and formal vocabulary since writing to the court
- ☐ Organized/presented in the format requested with two separate issues addressed separately (mandatory and discretionary exoneration)
- ☐ Appropriately used headings to persuade and guide grader (brief persuasive style headings recommended for main point headings)
- ☐ Properly cited to rules in the cases
- ☐ Presented rule/rule explanation before analysis
- ☐ Analogized/distinguished cases where helpful and appropriate
- ☐ Used all pertinent facts well
- ☐ Followed all directions in task memo

Rules (from library)	Rule Explanation (library case facts)	Analysis (our case facts)
Introduction		

Briefly describe the task you have been asked to complete for the requestor. Then set up the brief argument format based on the two issues you need to address.

Facts

- ☐ D was arrested/booked/indicted for drug-related felonies.
- ☐ Initially the magistrate held D without bond.
- ☐ D appeared for his arraignment.
- ☐ Defense counsel sought D's release.
- ☐ D resided in Franklin (neighboring state), but no references or sources to verify.
- ☐ D had no prior convictions.
- ☐ D's son, Oscar Raymond, posted a bond for $45,000 for D's release.
- ☐ Defense counsel bore the burden for D's appearance.
- ☐ Trial date was postponed; D failed to appear for trial, but trial still began.
- ☐ State rested its case. Defense counsel motioned for acquittal, and court acquitted D and ended the trial, stating identification of D not possible.

Argument

Forfeiture of bond is appropriate.

☐ The object of bail and its forfeiture is to insure the attendance of the accused and his obedience to the orders and judgment of the court. <u>Nationwide/ Weinberger</u> ☐ The surety acts as a guarantor of the defendant's appearance in court under the risk of forfeiture of the bond. <u>Nationwide</u> ☐ When there is a breach of contract, the bond agreement should be enforced. <u>Nationwide</u> ☐ The scope of the surety's risk is defined by the terms of the bond agreement and applicable statutes. <u>Nationwide</u> ☐ Nonappearance for trial creates a presumption of forfeiture. <u>Nationwide</u> ☐ Once D has not complied with the bond agreement, the surety bears the burden of showing the failure to appear because (1) the statute mandates exoneration, or (2) it should be exonerated in the sound discretion of the court. <u>Nationwide</u>		☐ D's son, Oscar, the surety, posted a $45,000 bond for defendant's release. ☐ The bond agreement indicated that defense counsel and the surety were responsible for defendant's appearance. ☐ O testified at the bond hearing that he carefully read the agreement and knew he was responsible for defendant's appearance. ☐ O testified that he knew he would lose the money if defendant did not appear for trial. ☐ O knew there was a chance that D would flee and not appear. ☐ D failed to appear at trial. ☐ Surety argues that both mandatory and discretionary exoneration apply.

Argument		
Exoneration is not justified: (1) Mandatory exoneration.		
☐ (1) If the surety surrenders the accused to the sheriff of the county in which the prosecution is pending, or delivers an affidavit to the sheriff stating that the defendant is incarcerated in this or another jurisdiction, and the sheriff reports the surrender or status to the court, the court shall vacate any order of forfeiture and exonerate the bond. <u>Nationwide</u> ☐ (2) Rule 13(d) provides that the court shall exonerate an appearance bond in the event of pretrial dismissal or when other pretrial circumstances ranging from death of the defendant to diversion preclude further need for an appearance bond. <u>Nationwide</u> ☐ Under Rule 13(d) at any time before violation that the court finds there is no further need for an appearance bond, it shall exonerate the appearance bond and order the return of any security deposit. <u>Weinberger</u> ☐ (3) When a prosecution is dismissed, any appearance bond shall be exonerated. <u>Weinberger</u> ☐ Termination of a prosecution before forfeiture of an appearance bond terminates a surety's liability on the bond. <u>Weinberger</u>	☐ In <u>Weinberger</u>, the State dismissed the case against the defendant before he was set to appear. ☐ The State was not prejudiced at all by a non-appearance. <u>Weinberger</u> ☐ The court ordered that the defendant's bond be exonerated. <u>Weinberger</u>	☐ (1) O never surrendered the accused to the sheriff or delivered an affidavit that he was incarcerated. ☐ (2) Defense counsel's arguments pertain to "pretrial" events so mandatory exoneration does not apply here. ☐ The reason for acquittal was because defendant's absence at trial made identification impossible. ☐ D violated the bond by not appearing for trial; the court did not find that there was no need for appearance before the violation; D's violation occurred first by his failing to appear for trial. ☐ (3) Here the case was dismissed after, not before, defendant was set to appear. ☐ Here the State was prejudiced as the main reason for dismissal was because the defendant was not present to be identified.
Exoneration is not justified: (1) Discretionary exoneration.		
☐ Rule 13(e) provides that in all other instances, the decision of whether to exonerate a bond shall be within the sound discretion of the court. <u>Nationwide/Saintly Bail Bonds</u> ☐ A court may consider factors (1) the D's willfulness in violating the order to appear, (2) whether the surety is a commercial entity, (3) the effort and expense expended by the surety in trying to locate and apprehend the defendant to insure his appearance, (4) the costs, inconvenience, and prejudice suffered by the State due to D's absence, and (5) the public's interest. <u>Saintly Bail Bonds</u>	☐ In <u>Saintly Bail Bonds</u>, the court found for the State and forfeited the bond when D did not appear for court. ☐ Although D was in jail, the court found that the surety was a commercial entity that made no effort or expense to arrange for D's appearance and didn't attempt to contact his counsel. <u>Saintly Bail Bonds</u> ☐ In <u>Nationwide</u>, the court found that the surety had no reason to know that D would flee and thus should not be faulted for D's failure to appear.	☐ (1) D knew he had a trial date set and deliberately did not appear. ☐ (2) Surety is Oscar, the D's son, who is not a commercial entity. ☐ (2) O admitted at the bond hearing that the loss of the money would not create a financial hardship on him as he has other money saved up and makes about $120,000 per year. ☐ (2) O carefully read the bond agreement and understood that if his father did not appear he would lose the money. ☐ (2) O knew there was a decent chance that his father would not appear. ☐ (3) O did not expend any effort to locate his father or ensure he appeared at trial, other than asking his aunt about it. ☐ (3) O's father was not around much, they did not see each other often, and his father did not have ties to the area or family. ☐ (3) O did not require anything from his father and was aware he was involved in unlawful activity. ☐ (4) D's failure to appear prejudiced the State since it was unable to prove identity due to the absence of D.

Argument		
	☐ In <u>Nationwide</u>, D presented his driver's license, a social security card, and other documents such that the court found Nationwide acted in good faith when posting the bond for D. ☐ There was no prejudice to the State in <u>Weinberger.</u>	☐ (4) The State expended money and effort and time into the trial, as the trial began and was not dismissed at any pretrial stage. ☐ (5) The public interest requires ensuring that appearance bond agreements are strictly enforced. ☐ (5) The risk is that criminals who flee may go free due to lack of identification or for other reasons.
Conclusion		

☐ Neither mandatory nor discretionary exoneration is appropriate.

PT: SELECTED ANSWER 1

```
-----------------------------------------------------------------x
```

THE STATE OF COLUMBIA,   :

    Plaintiff,   :

                                   Case number CR-0180016

    v.   :

HENRY RAYMOND, Defendant and   :

OSCAR RAYMOND, Bond Poster and Surety   :

```
-----------------------------------------------------------------x
```

The State of Columbia's Brief In Support of Forfeiture of the Bond

The State of Columbia ("_Plaintiff_") respectfully submits this Brief in support of forfeiture of that certain appearance bond in the amount of $45,000 (the "_Bond_") which had been posted by Oscar Raymond (the "_Surety_") on behalf of his father Henry Raymond ("_Defendant_").

PRELIMINARY STATEMENT

The entire purpose of the Bond was to ensure that Defendant appeared at his criminal trial. Surety - Defendant's own son - knowingly and voluntarily chose and agreed to act as Surety and, as such, he was responsible for ensuring his father's appearance at trial.   Defendant never showed up for multiple pre-trial proceedings, and then never showed up at his trial. Defendant unjustly benefited from his violations of court orders because he was acquitted at trial only because his failure to appear allowed him to shield his identity from evidence at trial.

This is exactly the type of case for which the Surety's Bond should be forfeited. Surety breached his obligations under the Bond and indeed acted in complete disregard of his responsibilities, having taken no action whatsoever to secure his father's appearance at trial. Under these circumstances, the law requires forfeiture of the Bond. See Argument Point I below.

On oral argument for this matter, Surety argued that exoneration of the Bond is required by Columbia Rule of Criminal Procedure 13(d)(1) and/or (2). We show below that those arguments are meritless, as nothing within either of those rules mandates or permits exoneration of the Bond. See Argument Points II.A and II.B below.

The law does permit exoneration of the Bond in the Court's discretion, but we show below that any such discretion should not be exercised based upon the facts of this case, as applied to the relevant factors which the Columbia Supreme Court has ruled should be applied in connection with the discretionary determination. See Point II.C below.

FACTS

A. Defendant's Arrest, Indictment, Trial and Acquittal

In February 2018, Defendant was arrested, booked and indicted on felony counts of possession of a narcotic drug for sale and possession of drug paraphernalia, including an allegation of exceeding the threshold amount of cocaine. On February 27, 2018, Defendant appeared for his arraignment --- but this was the last appearance Defendant ever would make in the case.

On March 13, 2018, the trial court conducted a hearing on defense counsel's motion to set conditions of release. Defendant stated that his permanent residence was in the neighboring State of Franklin, but he provided no references or sources for verification of this information. The trial court set a $45,000 cash bond requirement.

On March 15, 2018, the aforementioned bond was posted by Surety, who is Defendant's son. As a result, Defendant was released from Cruz County Superior Court hold.

On March 23, 2018, at a pretrial conference, Defendant's counsel told the trial court that Defendant's bond had been posted and that Defendant had fled. The trial court noted in the Minute entry that "defense counsel bears the responsibility for arranging Defendant's return." A trial date was set for October 22, 2018, and later postponed by the trial judge until January 30, 2019.

On January 30, 2019, trial began, and Defendant failed to appear. A jury was selected and impaneled, opening statements were made, two witnesses testified and several items of evidence were admitted. The State then rested, and defense counsel made a motion for judgment of acquittal. The trial court granted the motion, acquitting Defendant and ending the trial. Importantly, the trial court found that Defendant's acquittal was because Defendant's absence made identification impossible. The court specifically found that "There is no substantial evidence to warrant a conviction, based upon insufficient evidence of the identity of the Defendant."

B. The Surety's Lack of Knowledge, Effort and/or Diligence.

At a hearing before this Court, the Surety testified in a way making clear that he exercised little if any effort and/or diligence in causing his father to appear at trial. Indeed, among his testimony, Surety admitted the following in open Court (see transcript):

  (1) Surety never asked his father if he intended to appear at trial

  (2) Surety made little to no effort to locate his father: all he did was call his aunt who said that Defendant had left her house; Surety took no further action to locate Defendant;

(3) Surety and Defendant had little to no relationship such that Surety never had good cause to believe that he would have any contact with Defendant sufficient to cause his appearance;

(4) Surety was aware of the fact that Defendant had few if any ties to the community, and he was rarely seen;

(5) Forfeiture of the security bond would not cause hardship upon Surety because Surety has "quite a bit saved up";

(6) Surety was aware that his father may have been involved in unlawful activities;

(7) Surety made no effort to find out where Defendant was so that he would appear at trial;

(8) Surety read and understood the appearance bond agreement he entered, and understood the consequence of Defendant's failure to appear.

PROCEDURAL HISTORY

Following Defendant's acquittal, Defendant's counsel moved to exonerate the bond. The trial court denied the motion and ordered that "this matter be referred to the Superior Court Hearing Office for the commencement of bond forfeiture proceedings, based upon Defendant's failure to appear for his trial." Oral argument was conducted, and each party was offered the opportunity to brief the court concerning the issues.

ARGUMENT

For the reasons set forth below, forfeiture of the Bond is appropriate and exoneration is not justified.

POINT I

THE BOND SHOULD BE FORFEITED BECAUSE DEFENDANT FAILED TO APPEAR AT TRIAL

As the Columbia Supreme Court made clear in People v. Nationwide Surety Insurance Company (2006), "The object of bail and its forfeiture is to insure the attendance of the accused and his obedience to the orders and judgment of the court." Further, "[i]t is well settled in this jurisdiction that a surety assumes the risk of a defendant's failure to appear." People v Saintly Bail Bonds, Columbia Court of Appeals (2008). Moreover, "nonappearance for trial creates a presumption of forfeiture." *People v. Nationwide Surety Ins. Co.* (Columbia Supreme Court 2006).

Here, it is undisputed that Defendant failed to appear at trial as required by the Bond. Moreover, Defendant unjustly benefited by his failure to appear because it was a direct result of his failure to appear that he received an acquittal. The Surety breached its agreement and the Bond should be forfeited.

POINT II

THE SURETY'S ARGUMENTS ARE MERITLESS

A

A. Columbia Rule of Criminal Procedure 13(d)(1) does not mandate or permit exoneration.

At oral argument, counsel for Surety argued that Columbia Rule of Criminal Procedure 13(d)(1) mandates exoneration. That is a false statement of law. As set forth below, Rule 13(d)(1) by its own terms, and as interpreted by the Courts, is inapplicable to this case.

Rule 13(d)(1) specifically provides that "At any time before violation that the court finds that there is no further need for an appearance bond, it shall exonerate the appearance bond." (emphasis added). By its own terms, this statute is inapplicable on its face because Defendant violated the terms of the Bond by failing to appear in Court. Rule 13(d)(1) only applies to a Defendant who complied by making scheduled court appearances... that is not the case here. The statute only applies to release of Bonds "before violations" and in this case we are dealing with a situation that occurred "after the violation." The Surety's reliance upon this Rule is completely misplaced. See, e.g., *People v. Nationwide Surety Ins. Co.* (Columbia Supreme Court 2006) ("Rule 13(d) provides that the court shall exonerate an appearance bond <u>in the event of pretrial dismissal or when other pretrial circumstances</u> ranging from death of the defendant to diversion preclude further need for an appearance bond." (emphasis added). *People v. Weinberger* (Columbia Court of Appeals, 2003) ("Rule 13(d) . . . envisions that there is no requirement to exonerate the bond if a violation of the bond terms took place <u>prior to the dismissal</u>.") (emphasis added).

B. <u>Columbia Rule of Criminal Procedure 13(d)(2) does not mandate or permit exoneration.</u>

At oral argument, counsel for Surety next argued that Rule 13(d)(2) mandates exoneration, but even the most cursory examination of the statute and surrounding case law shows that this Rule is also inapplicable to this case. The Rule provides that "When a prosecution is dismissed, the defendant shall be released from custody, unless he is in custody on some other charge, and any appearance bond exonerated."

First, this rule by its own terms provides for releasing a defendant from custody, and does not apply to a situation where the defendant has fled without an appearance.

Moreover, courts have made crystal clear that this Rule only applies to pre-trial proceedings, and not to trial proceedings as is the situation in the case at bar.

At oral argument, Surety claimed that *People v. Weinberger* (Columbia Court of Appeals, 2003) supported Surety's position, but a review of the case shows nothing of the sort. To the contrary, the case supports the State's position that the Bond should be released because, as noted, Rule 13(d) only applies to pre-trial proceedings. For example, the Weinberger Court reviewed a case where an indictment was dismissed with prejudice "prior to trial." The Court focused extensively on this fact in concluding that a bond should be released; for example explaining that "The primary purpose of an appearance bond is to ensure the defendant's presence at the time of trial. <u>When, as here, the charges are dismissed prior to trial,</u> the primary purpose of the bond no longer exists, and from that point forward there is no further need for the appearance bond." (emphasis added). The Court further explained that "the main purpose of the appearance bond [is] to ensure the defendant's presence at trial." That very purpose was not satisfied here. Appearance at trial did not occur, the terms of the Bond were therefore violated, and the Bond should be forfeited. There is nothing in the statute or surrounding case law to the contrary.

To the extent Surety seeks to rely on any of the facts in People v. Weinberger, they are further distinguishable because the Court's holding in *Weinberger*, by which an bond was exonerated, was done not only before trial, but also under a fact pattern where the defendant's non-appearance was non-prejudicial to the prosecution's case. See e.g. Weinberger ("The State was not prejudiced by the non-appearance of appellant at one pretrial conference, which is the only possible violation of the bond terms."). That lack of prejudice in *Weinberger* is a far cry from the facts of this case --- where the Trial Court itself recognized that the Defendant's case was dismissed as a direct result of his non-appearance.

C. <u>The Facts Do Not Support the Court's Exercise of Discretion to Exonerate the Bond.</u>

For the reasons set forth above, contrary to Surety's contention at oral argument, there is nothing in the statutory framework and/or surrounding case law that requires exoneration of the Bond. Surety's next and final argument was that the Court should exonerate the Bond in its discretion.

It is true that the Court has discretion to exonerate a Bond. See Rules of Criminal Procedure 13(e) ("the decision whether or not to exonerate a bond shall be within the sound discretion of the court"); see also e.g. *People v. Saintly Bail Bonds* (Columbia Court of Appeals 2008) ("Once there has been a determination that a defendant failed to appear or otherwise comply with the terms of the appearance bond, except where a statute specifically requires exoneration, the decision to order an appearance bond forfeited or to remit in whole or in part lies essentially in the discretion of the trial court." The *Saintly Bail* case then goes on to list the following factors to be considered by a court in deciding whether or not to exercise its discretion and, as set forth below, those factors do NOT justify exoneration on the facts of this case:

   - Factor 1: defendant's willfulness in violating the order to appear: here, Defendant willfully violated the Court's order and failed to appear at multiple hearings, including without limitation a failure to appear at trial;

   - Factor 2: whether the surety is a commercial entity: here, the Surety is not a commercial entity; provided, however, the Surety specifically testified at trial that forfeiture of the bond would NOT create an economic hardship upon him; as such, any presumption of favorable treatment towards a non-commercial entity should not be adhered to;

   - Factor 3: effort and expense expended by the Surety in trying to locate and apprehend the defendant: here, Surety by his own admission made no effort at all to locate Defendant, who was his own father. In this respect, the Saintly Bail Bonds court further explained that "It is well settled in this jurisdiction that a surety assumes the risk of a defendant's failure to appear."

   - Factor 4: the costs, inconvenience and prejudice suffered by the State: here, the State suffered severe prejudice by virtue of expending large sums of money on pretrial and trial proceedings, only to lose based on the Defendant's failure to appear by virtue of having fled notwithstanding the Bond

- Factor 5: the public's interest in ensuring a defendant's appearance: here, the public has great interest in ensuring Defendant's appearance... due to his failure to appear there is a potential drug dealer back on the streets who evaded justice.

A closer look at the facts of the Saintly Bail Bonds case renders it beyond doubt that the Court should not exonerate the Bond in its discretion. In the Saintly Bail Bonds case, the Columbia Court of Appeals found that the trial court did NOT abuse its discretion in refusing to exonerate a bond under a circumstance where the defendant did not appear at trial only because the defendant was incarcerated in another jail. The surety in that case therefore had a much stronger argument than does the Surety in this case as to the circumstance for the non-appearance: the surety in Saintly Bail Bonds couldn't secure the defendant's appearance because the defendant was incarcerated elsewhere; the Surety in this case was unable to secure his own father's appearance because his father fled to evade the law.

CONCLUSION

For the reasons set forth above, forfeiture of the Bond is appropriate and exoneration is not justified.

Respectfully submitted,

_____

Counsel for the State of Columbia

PT: SELECTED ANSWER 2

State of Columbia v. Henry Raymond and Oscar Raymond

Case Number CR - 20180016

Brief in Support of Forfeiture of the Bond

Facts and Issue Before the Court

Henry Raymond (**HR**) was arrested for various drug-related offenses. Oscar Raymond (**OR**), the son of HR, posted a $45,000 bond for HR. HR failed to appear at his trial on January 30, 2019 and January 31, 2019. Following the State's case, the defense moved for a judgment of acquittal, which was granted. Any further relevant facts are set out with particularity in the arguments below. The issue that the court must decide is whether to order that the bond be forfeited on account of HR's failure to appear at trial.

Overview of the Law and Procedure

The primary purpose of an appearance bond is to ensure the defendant's presence at the time of trial (People v. Weinberger) (**Weinberger**). As equity abhors a forfeiture, the law is strictly construed in favor of the surety. However, nonappearance at trial creates a presumption of forfeiture. The burden is then on the surety to establish a case for relief from forfeiture, either because this is mandatory under statute or because the court should so exercise its discretion (People v. Nationwide Surety Insurance Company) (**Nationwide**).

Rule 13(d) - Mandatory Exoneration

The law applicable to the mandatory exoneration of bail bonds is derived from Rules 13(d) and 13(e) of the Columbia Rules of Civil Procedure, which govern "the procedure to be followed in cases between arraignment and trial".

Rule 13(d) provides for mandatory exoneration of an appearance bond. It states that, "at any time before violation that the court finds that there is no further need for an appearance bond, it shall exonerate the appearance bond and order the return of any security deposit" (Rule 13(d)(1)). Additionally, Rule 13(d) further provides that "when a prosecution is dismissed, the defendant shall be released from custody, unless he is in custody on some other charge, and any appearance bond exonerated" (Rule 13(d)(2)).

As such, Rule 13(d) establishes two situations in which exoneration is mandatory: first, when, before violation, the court finds that there is no further need for an appearance bond; and second, when a prosecution is dismissed.

Rule 13(e) - Discretionary Exoneration

Under Rule 13(e), in all instances other than those in Rule 13(d), "the decision whether or not to exonerate a bond shall be within the sound discretion of the court" (Nationwide).

This Brief In Support of Forfeiture of the Bond will argue that mandatory exoneration does not apply, and that discretionary exoneration should not be ordered by this court in this case.

Mandatory Exoneration Does Not Apply

First, it is submitted that this case should be treated as falling outside Rule 13(d) altogether, and therefore that mandatory exoneration cannot apply.

Rule 13(d), by its terms, states that it shall "govern the procedure to be followed in cases between arraignment and trial".

As described above, this case in fact proceeded to trial and indeed to judgment on January 31, 2019. As a matter of statutory interpretation, this clearly takes the case outside of Rule 13(d).

Defense counsel argued in the bond forfeiture hearing (**Hearing**) that, as a matter of policy, an equivalent rule to 13(d) should apply following trial, as there should not be a distinction between dismissal and acquittal.

With respect, we find this argument to be absurd as it would fundamentally undermine the existence and purpose of appearance bonds. As outlined above, the purpose of an appearance bond is to ensure that the defendant appears at trial (Nationwide). Defense counsel's argument would mean the surety would recover its bond whenever the defendant was ultimately acquitted, regardless of whether the defendant appeared at trial. This greatly reduces the incentive on the surety to ensure that the accused is present at trial, which is not in the interests of justice and is unfair to the victims of crime.

Additionally, it creates a greater risk of guilty defendants evading justice because of their nonappearance. In the present case, the court found that "there is no substantial evidence to warrant a conviction, based upon insufficient evidence of the identity of the Defendant". This compounds the problem: the surety may become indifferent as to whether the defendant appears at trial, since a nonappearance may increase the likelihood of an acquittal, in which case the surety would be entitled to exoneration. In our opinion, this cannot be in the interests of promoting the integrity of the criminal justice system.

If the court disagrees and finds that Rule 13(d) does apply, there are two situations in which exoneration of the bond is mandatory. We submit that neither of these applies in this case.

Rule 13(d)(1): Before Violation, No Further Need

Rule 13(d)(1) provides that, where at any time before violation that the court finds that there is no further need for an appearance bond, it shall exonerate the appearance bond and order the return of any security deposit.

The Court of Appeals in Weinberger gave guidance on the application of the "before violation" and "no further need" requirements in that case. There, the defendant failed to appear at a pretrial conference, but charges were dismissed on the same day before trial could commence. The Court of Appeal ultimately held that the fact that the violation occurred prior to the pretrial conference did not prevent mandatory exoneration. The Court of Appeals, in construing the "before violation" requirement and the requirement of "no further need", found it relevant that:

- the main purpose of the bond is to ensure the defendant's presence at trial, and this ceased after the dismissal;

- the State was not prejudiced by the non-appearance of the defendant;

- any violation was only for a matter of hours;

- the defendant's presence was not required for any other event prior to dismissal; and

- the issue of forfeiture was not raised by the State.

We therefore argue that Weinberger should be distinguished in this case for the following reasons:

- the need to ensure the defendant appeared at trial does not disappear when there is no dismissal of the charges;

- the non-appearance of the defendant was highly prejudicial to the state; in fact, it was the reason for the acquittal of HR in this case;

- the violation was substantial and for longer than a matter of hours: the first date on which HR was found to have fled was March 23, 2018, so the defendant has been in violation for over a year;

- the defendant's presence was required at multiple occasions: the two pretrial conferences, on the initial trial date in October 2018 and the postponed trial date on January 2019; and

- the State has raised the issue of forfeiture.

Rule 13(d)(2): Dismissal of Prosecution

Under Rule 13(d)(2), the bond must be exonerated when a prosecution is dismissed. Here, there was no dismissal: the trial went ahead and HR was acquitted. We have submitted above why, in our opinion, the court should uphold the distinction between dismissal of prosecution and an acquittal and should not extend mandatory exoneration to acquittals. Finally, as a matter of the plain wording of Rule 13(d)(2), mandatory exoneration does not apply for an acquittal.

Discretionary Exoneration Should Not Be Ordered

As discussed above, under Rule 13(e), the court may exercise its discretion to exonerate the bond. We set out below why the court should not order exoneration in this case.

Factors to be considered by the court

According to the case law, the following factors are relevant to the court's exercise of its discretion under Rule 13(e):

- Whether the surety knew, or should have known, that the defendant was a flight risk (Nationwide);

- Whether the surety acted in the good faith belief that the defendant would appear (Nationwide);

- The defendant's willingness in violating the order to appear (People v. Saintly Bail Bonds) (**Saintly**);

- Whether the surety is a commercial entity (Saintly);

- The effort and expense expended by the surety trying to apprehend the defendant (Saintly);

- The cost, inconvenience and prejudice suffered by the State due to the defendant's absence (Saintly); and

- The public interest in ensuring a defendant's appearance (Saintly).

<u>Application of factors</u>

- *Whether the surety knew, or should have known, that the defendant was a flight risk*

At the Hearing, OR stated that he did not ask his father whether or not he planned to appear at trial. He also stated that his father did not have "many ties" to the community and that none of his family sees much of his father. Finally, OR admitted, when asked that he supposed it was true, that he was aware that there was a "decent chance" that his father would flee.

- *Whether the surety acted in the good faith belief that the defendant would appear*

As mentioned above, OR admitted, when asked that he supposed it was true, that he was aware that there was a "decent chance" that his father would flee. In addition, OR states that he "didn't have much choice" about posting the bond, indicating that he was not motivated by a good faith belief that the defendant would appear, but rather out of familial obligation.

- *The defendant's willingness in violating the order to appear*

OR has provided no evidence that the violation was involuntary; as discussed above, the burden is on OR to rebut the presumption of forfeiture arising from nonappearance.

- *Whether the surety is a commercial entity*

OR is not a commercial entity. However, OR is employed and makes a good living as a software engineer, earning $120,000 per year. The loss of the $45,000 bond would not be a significant hardship as OR notes that he has sufficient savings.

- *The effort and expense expended by the surety trying to apprehend the defendant*

OR has provided no evidence that he has expended either effort or expense to apprehend HR. As the court explains in Saintly, this is a relevant factor because it encourages the surety to take action and reasonable steps to recapture an absent defendant. OR admits that he has taken no steps to contact his father despite clearly understanding the terms of the agreement and that by signing he would "lose all of the money" he put up.

- *The cost, inconvenience and prejudice suffered by the State due to the defendant's absence*

This factor weighs heavily in favor of the State. As explained at the hearing, the court has endured the cost and waste of time and resources of (1) two pretrial conferences and (2) two wasted days of trial, at which a jury was impaneled, witnesses testified and evidence was admitted. Finally, as mentioned above, the acquittal itself was a result of HR's nonappearance. This amounts to significant prejudice to the State.

- *The public interest in ensuring a defendant's appearance*

Again, the public interest in favor of ensuring HR's appearance at trial is strong and is the basis of the need for appearance bonds. In this case, HR was charged with dealing cocaine, a serious offense for which the public has an interest in securing justice.

Conclusion

In conclusion, we argue that:

1. The present case should be treated as falling outside of the rules under Rule 13(d) regarding mandatory exoneration as this case went to trial, and did not end in a dismissal, and further there are strong policy reasons for not extending the remit of Rule 13(d) to acquittals;

2. Alternatively, if the court finds that this case does fall within Rule 13, exoneration is not mandatory in this case because the need for the appearance bond continued long after the initial violation by HR, and again the scope of mandatory exoneration should not be extended to acquittals; and

3. Finally, the court should not exercise its discretion to exonerate the bond, in particular because of the significant cost, inconvenience and prejudice suffered by the State due to HR's absence.

PART III *EXTRA PRACTICE APPENDIX*

INTRODUCTION

When students struggle with performance tests, the problem is almost always a result of either:

- Improperly decoding the task memo information, which results in a poorly organized and/or non-responsive answer, and/or
- Difficulty working with the library, which results in going over on time and/or inappropriately using the law provided.

Either will lead to a failing score.

> ***Important Note:*** The practice materials used in this section are redacted from the old three-hour version of the California Performance Tests. They are good for practicing your skills because they include format memos and an array of tasks that California has assigned in past PTs, and their libraries contain more complicated rule structures. Essentially, these older tests provide excellent practice materials, even though they present more difficult tasks and rules and may be more difficult overall than those you will encounter on the 90-minute PT. Since these materials are not equivalent in length to current 90-minute PTs, however, do not focus on timing when working with them.

How to Use This Appendix: This appendix is designed to give you extra practice and guidance in decoding task memos and working with libraries, allowing you to efficiently target the particular skill or skills that are problematic for you. Since few students have trouble pulling facts out of client files and appropriately using them in their answers, we have eliminated the case file facts from these exercises. In their place you will find brief factual summaries that provide the key information you would identify in a skim of the facts. Practicing this way allows you to hone the more challenging skills in the least amount of time.

Each task memo and library appears first in an unannotated version for you to work through, followed by an annotated version that will allow you to compare your assessment with a sample. The extra practice libraries correspond to the task memos, so you can deconstruct the task memo(s) to identify the macro structure of your answer, read the factual summary for the library, and then book brief the corresponding library, adding the rules into your roadmap.

- **Task Memo:** Use the task memo examples to practice decoding the directions contained in the task memos and internal format memos (where supplied). For each task memo, start a roadmap by identifying an appropriate response macrostructure. Try to visualize what a finished answer should look like, given the specific instructions. Compare your roadmap organization to the sample provided.
- **Library:** For the libraries, practice book briefing to identify the rules you can use to solve the problem posed in the task memos, deconstruct each rule into its elements, and identify how you would structure your response. The key here is to make sure that you are properly extracting rules and reasoning from the library cases to use in your answer. Another important skill is deconstructing rules properly. Thus, after each set of cases, we provide annotated demonstrations of book briefs, a deconstruction of the rules contained in each case, an assessment of the importance of each rule, and suggestions on how the rule would best be formatted and used in the response. For context, read the factual summaries before briefing the cases. Compare your case briefs and roadmap to the samples.

Approach for Extra Practice: Use the following practice approach to target problem areas. For students who already feel comfortable with PTs (especially timing), you can do multiple PTs using the approach in Phase 1 below, which is akin to issue spotting and outlining practice essays instead of writing them out in full.

- **Phase 1— Organize only:** Organize and roadmap a PT (task memo, fact skim, and library), then check your roadmap against a sample answer or grading point sheet. Repeat the process with two more PTs. If the skills are still challenging, repeat this process until you consistently achieve your desired response or score for your PTs that are graded.
- **Phase 2— Organize and assess, then write:** Organize and roadmap another PT, completing all phases of the step-by step approach. Glance at a sample answer or grading point sheet to check your organization. Make adjustments if needed. Write a composed response from your roadmap. Afterwards, fully self-assess your performance. Repeat this process until your responses meet your goals.

- **Phase 3 — Complete PTs under timed conditions**.
- **Phase 4**: Once you feel comfortable with PTs, you can continue to practice doing complete, timed PTs or practice PTs using Phase 1 above, which allows you to gain PT pattern recognition experience and to cover the most ground in the least amount of time.

Practice Tip: For additional targeted practice using this technique, older practice MPTs are freely available on the NCBE website.

TASK MEMO: SPOTLIGHT ON TASK AND INTERNAL FORMAT MEMOS

Task 1— Estate of Keefe

This performance test task memo assigns a somewhat unusual task and includes a corresponding internal format memo clarifying how the response should be formatted. The task focuses entirely on analyzing and assessing the client facts, so it does not correspond to the library.

Task 2 — Estate of Keefe

This example uses the same factual scenario as Task 1, but it assigns a more typical task; the corresponding internal format memo provides additional guidance in formatting the response. After organizing using the task memo, read the factual summary and brief the library cases to complete the roadmap.

Task 3 — Snyder v. Regents

This test presents another commonly assigned task. After organizing from the task memo, read the factual summary and brief the library cases to complete the roadmap.

TASK 1:

ESTATE OF KEEFE

McIntyre, Yost and Amrein, LLP

MEMORANDUM

TO: Applicant

FROM: Gretchen Pronko

DATE: February 26, 2002

Our client, Mason Finch, is the former caretaker of decedent, Sandra Keefe, who promised to leave him a life estate in certain real and personal property in exchange for Mr. Finch's agreement to care for her. We recently filed a complaint on behalf of Mr. Finch, asserting a simple cause of action against the administrator of Ms. Keefe's estate for specific performance of an oral contract. Defendant has filed a motion for summary judgment.

The file contains a number of documents and some relevant cases you will need to review in order to perform the following task:

Draft declarations for all witnesses whose testimony will be useful in establishing that there are disputed issues of fact and in supporting our arguments. Don't take time to write out headings or other boilerplate language. Our client, the witnesses interviewed by our investigator, and the friend contacted by our client (see Mr. Finch's letter on this subject in the file) have all agreed to sign declarations if you think their testimony will help.

In performing this assignment, please comply with the Internal Memorandum regarding Oppositions to Motions for Summary Judgment.

McIntyre, Yost and Amrein, LLP

INTERNAL MEMORANDUM

TO: Associates

FROM: Myron Taylor

RE: Oppositions to Motions for Summary Judgment DECLARATIONS

All facts asserted in opposition to motions for summary judgment must be supported by admissible evidence established in declarations or by judicial notice.

Declarations must:
- Be limited to facts relevant to the motion for summary judgment.
- Include only admissible evidence that the declarant could testify to if called as a witness.
- Be concise and direct statements of facts; a declaration should not be a summary of everything the declarant knows.
- Be drafted before the memorandum of points and authorities; then, the statements of undisputed and disputed facts and argument can cite to the declarations by paragraph number, and need not repeat all of the facts.

McIntyre, Yost and Amrein, LLP

MEMORANDUM

TO: Applicant
FROM: Gretchen Pronko
DATE: February 26, 2002

Our client, Mason Finch, is the former caretaker of decedent, Sandra Keefe, who promised to leave him a life estate in certain real and personal property in exchange for Mr. Finch's agreement to care for her. We recently filed a complaint on behalf of Mr. Finch, asserting a simple cause of action against the administrator of Ms. Keefe's estate for specific performance of an oral contract. Defendant has filed a motion for summary judgment.

The file contains a number of documents and some relevant cases you will need to review in order to perform the following task:

> Pay attention to what you can avoid: this helps save time.

> This is your task.

Draft declarations for all witnesses whose testimony will be useful in establishing that there are disputed issues of fact and in supporting our arguments. Don't take time to write out headings or other boilerplate language. Our client, the witnesses interviewed by our investigator, and the friend contacted by our client (see Mr. Finch's letter on this subject in the file) have all agreed to sign declarations if you think their testimony will help.

> They are most likely referring you to this letter to find facts necessary to complete this task.

> Here they tell you which people you will need to complete declarations for.

In performing this assignment, please comply with the Internal Memorandum regarding Oppositions to Motions for Summary Judgment.

> This informs you that there are further directions to follow as to how to organize the declaration, which is always helpful.

McIntyre, Yost and Amrein, LLP

INTERNAL MEMORANDUM

TO: Associates

FROM: Myron Taylor

RE: Oppositions to Motions for Summary Judgment DECLARATIONS

All facts asserted in opposition to motions for summary judgment must be supported by admissible evidence established in declarations or by judicial notice.

Declarations must:

- Be limited to facts relevant to the motion for summary judgment.
- Include only admissible evidence that the declarant could testify to if called as a witness.
- Be concise and direct statements of facts; a declaration should not be a summary of everything the declarant knows.
- Be drafted before the memorandum of points and authorities; then, the statements of undisputed and disputed facts and argument can cite to the declarations by paragraph number, and need not repeat all of the facts.

> This tells you that your declarations should not be paragraphs but rather only concise statements of facts that a witness could testify to in court.

EXAMPLE 1 STRUCTURE (DECLARATIONS)

Declaration of Witness 1 (you would name the witness)

> Do each witness separately with a heading so the grader can easily see it.

I, (insert witness name), declare as follows:

> It is a good idea to start with the basics, like which side the party is on and how they are involved.

1. I am on the (insert plaintiff or defendant) in this action.
2. I am (insert what they do for a living or some other fact from the file that is relevant to the case at hand).
3. Insert more facts for each sentence.

Declaration of Witness 2 (you would name the witness)

You would complete declarations in this format for all the listed witnesses you were told would agree to sign declarations.

Example of how one declaration with facts (this is only an example using some facts, as opposed to all facts that you would use) would look:

Declaration of Witness 1, Mason Finch

I, Mason Finch, declare as follows:

1. I am the plaintiff in this action.
2. I have worked as a licensed Marriage, Family and Children's Counselor for 12 years.
3. I met Mabel and Sandra Keefe 12 years ago through an agreement where I would manage their office building in exchange for 50% discount in office rent.
4. Full rent of the office was $500, so half rent was $250 per month.
5. I spent approximately 1½ hours per week on office building management duties including taking calls, showing units, collecting rents, repairs, etc.
6. During this time I was earning between $40 and $85 per hour as a counselor, with the amount increasing over time.
7. My daughter Megan and I developed a close friendship with Mabel and Sandra including dinners and trips and I considered them a second family.
8. In 1994 Mabel Keefe had a stroke and Sandra asked me to cut back my MFCC practice to care for Mabel in the afternoons and prepare dinner in the evening for both Mabel and Sandra. In exchange, Megan and I moved into their converted garage apartment rent free and the office space was rent free.
9. The reduction in my work hours resulted in a $1,000 monthly loss, even with the free rent.

> Notice how these are concise and factual, not paragraphs and not arguments.

TASK 2:

ESTATE OF KEEFE

McIntyre, Yost and Amrein, LLP

MEMORANDUM

TO: Applicant
FROM: Gretchen Pronko
DATE: February 26, 2002

Our client, Mason Finch, is the former caretaker of decedent, Sandra Keefe, who promised to leave him a life estate in certain real and personal property in exchange for Mr. Finch's agreement to care for her. We recently filed a complaint on behalf of Mr. Finch, asserting a simple cause of action against the administrator of Ms. Keefe's estate for specific performance of an oral contract. Defendant has filed a motion for summary judgment.

The file contains a number of documents and some relevant cases you will need to review in order to perform the following task:

Draft only sections III and IV of a Memorandum of Points and Authorities in Opposition to Motion for Summary Judgment.

In performing this assignment, please comply with the Internal Memorandum regarding Oppositions to Motions for Summary Judgment.

McIntyre, Yost and Amrein, LLP

INTERNAL MEMORANDUM

TO: Associates

FROM: Myron Taylor

RE: Oppositions to Motions for Summary Judgment

MEMORANDUM OF POINTS AND AUTHORITIES

The Memorandum of Points and Authorities in Opposition to Motion for Summary Judgment consists of five different sections, as follows:

Section I.   Introduction: This consists of a concise one-paragraph summary of the nature of the underlying case, the basis for the summary judgment motion, and the basis for the opposition.

Section II.   Response to Moving Party's Statement of Undisputed Facts: This is in two-column format. In the first column we restate the alleged Undisputed Facts. In the second column, we respond with "Agree" or "Disagree," indicating whether we agree or disagree that the fact alleged to be undisputed is in fact undisputed.

Section III.   Responsive Party's Statement of Disputed Facts: This is a two-column section identical in format to the Moving Party's Statement of Undisputed Facts (Section II of their Memorandum). In the first column, we state those facts we believe are disputed. The second column lists citations to evidence that establish these facts.

Section IV.   Response to Moving Party's Arguments: In this section, we draft arguments that respond point by point to the arguments made in the moving party's Memorandum of Points and Authorities in Support of Motion for Summary Judgment. In support of our arguments, we cite to our Disputed Facts by the number assigned in Section III, and to relevant cases to support our legal assertions. We also make any additional arguments that support the position that there are triable issues of fact or that there are legal issues precluding entry of judgment as a matter of law.

Section V.   Conclusion: This is a brief statement asking the court to find in our favor.

McIntyre, Yost and Amrein, LLP

MEMORANDUM

TO: Applicant

FROM: Gretchen Pronko

DATE: February 26, 2002

Our client, Mason Finch, is the former caretaker of decedent, Sandra Keefe, who promised to leave him a life estate in certain real and personal property in exchange for Mr. Finch's agreement to care for her. We recently filed a complaint on behalf of Mr. Finch, asserting a simple cause of action against the administrator of Ms. Keefe's estate for specific performance of an oral contract. Defendant has filed a motion for summary judgment.

The file contains a number of documents and some relevant cases you will need to review in order to perform the following task:

> This is your task.

> This tells us that we only need to draft specific sections, so make a note of that now.

Draft only sections III and IV of a Memorandum of Points and Authorities in Opposition to Motion for Summary Judgment.

In performing this assignment, please comply with the Internal Memorandum regarding Oppositions to Motions for Summary Judgment.

> This informs us that there will be further directions on how to format the task requested.

McIntyre, Yost and Amrein, LLP

INTERNAL MEMORANDUM

TO: Associates

FROM: Myron Taylor

RE: Oppositions to Motions for Summary Judgment

MEMORANDUM OF POINTS AND AUTHORITIES

The Memorandum of Points and Authorities in Opposition to Motion for Summary Judgment consists of five different sections, as follows:

Section I.   Introduction: This consists of a concise one-paragraph summary of the nature of the underlying case, the basis for the summary judgment motion, and the basis for the opposition.

Read the instructions carefully. Here, the internal memo gives you details about all five sections of the memorandum, but the task only asks you to include two of those five sections. So three of the sections are unnecessary and simply test your ability to follow the instructions.

Section II.   Response to Moving Party's Statement of Undisputed Facts: This is in two-column format. In the first column we restate the alleged Undisputed Facts. In the second column, we respond with "Agree" or "Disagree," indicating whether we agree or disagree that the fact alleged to be undisputed is in fact undisputed.

Pay attention to the format required.

Section III.   Responsive Party's Statement of Disputed Facts: This is a two-column section identical in format to the Moving Party's Statement of Undisputed Facts (Section II of their Memorandum). In the first column, we state those facts we believe are disputed. The second column lists citations to evidence that establish these facts.

These are the only two sections you need to prepare drafts for.

This informs you as to what you need in each column, both of which seem to be factual and thus will be found in the file.

This tells us we need law (which we will get from the library) as well as facts.

Section IV.   Response to Moving Party's Arguments: In this section, we draft arguments that respond point by point to the arguments made in the moving party's Memorandum of Points and Authorities in Support of Motion for Summary Judgment. In support of our arguments, we cite to our Disputed Facts by the number assigned in Section III, and to relevant cases to support our legal assertions. We also make any additional arguments that support the position that there are triable issues of fact or that there are legal issues precluding entry of judgment as a matter of law.

We would find their arguments in the file as well to respond to.

Make sure you make some additional arguments too.

Section V.   Conclusion: This is a brief statement asking the court to find in our favor.

EXAMPLE 2 STRUCTURE

MEMORANDUM OF POINTS AND AUTHORITIES

III.   RESPONSIVE PARTY'S STATEMENT OF DISPUTED FACTS

Disputed Facts	Citation to Evidence
1. Here you would list a disputed fact.	Declaration of witness 1 ¶ 12
2. List another disputed fact.	Declaration of witness 3 ¶ 2
3. And so on.	Declaration of witness 4 ¶ 5

> Note the two column format as requested; use headings to show "disputed facts" and "citations" as this forces you to properly add the correct components.

> Remember the first task you organized (with the same factual scenario). The citations here would be to the witness declarations you completed in task 1. When the examiners give you multiple tasks they often have one refer to the other.

Example of how Section III would be organized with actual facts:

Disputed Facts	Citations
1. Defendant did not spend significant time with the decedent before her death, rather in her final 6 months he spent a few hours 2-3 times a week visiting her.	Declaration of Grant Keefe ¶4 Declaration of Tori Phillips ¶3
2. Decedent did not feel she had more than provided adequate compensation for the services plaintiff provided.	Declaration of Mason Finch ¶16 Declaration of Mildred Fowler ¶6, ¶7
3. Decedent did not indicate she would not leave a will, rather she told plaintiff she would instruct her attorney to draft one.	Declaration of Mason Finch ¶16 Declaration of Mildred Fowler ¶7

IV. RESPONSE TO MOVING PARTY'S ARGUMENTS

In this section, you have to respond point by point to the moving party's Memorandum of Points and Authorities in Support of Motion for Summary Judgment. Where would you find this Memorandum of theirs? In the file as it is not law but factual. So you need to go through the memorandum in the file to see what arguments they made point by point and respond to each of them. The directions further tell you how to cite to your response. Accordingly, we cite to our Disputed Facts by the number assigned in Section III, and to relevant cases to support our legal assertions. The directions also state that you can make additional arguments here as well.

Example of how Section IV might be organized:

> You would find these statements in the file in their memorandum and respond to each point they argue.

Moving Party's Statement 1: Plaintiff's Claim Based on an Oral Contract to Make a Will is Sufficient as there is Evidence from the Declarations of the Oral Agreement.

Response to moving party's argument: Defendant asserts that the non-existence of a writing proves that decedent never promised to make a will with provisions in favor of plaintiff and therefore no oral or written contract ever existed. Mr. Finch (this would be one of the witnesses that you cited to above in Section III) has always maintained that he received oral promises from decedent for a life estate in the house. (Finch Disputed Fact 2, Evidence 4 ¶ 5.) Ms. Fowler (another witness that would be in your above section III) also supports this contention of Mr. Finch as to his claim to the life estate. (Fowler Disputed Fact 3, Evidence 3 ¶ 2.)

Some of the moving party's arguments would be based on law and you would cite to law in response to their argument and cite the case or statute from the library that is relevant to their argument and then follow that with facts from a witness that corroborates the law cited. For example, if a moving party's argument was about an action not being barred by a statute of limitations because it was filed within a certain time period, your response would include the rule from the library about the statute of limitations followed by facts from your disputed facts about the timing the claim was filed.

> Organization tip: If you are ever assigned two tasks in a performance test, you should first think about which section would be easiest to complete first. Compare these last two task examples (based on the same factual scenario). Assume the declarations are the first task; it is easier to do those at the end after you have done your argument portion in the memorandum since you will go through the file in detail last. Thus, adding in facts for a declaration would make sense to complete last even if you are placing that first in your answer if that was the first task assigned. So when you organize your argument section, any fact that you use and include in your argument would then be one you would cut and paste and insert into your disputed fact section. To save time you could add in facts to go to the declarations as you complete your argument and then label them with the proper citation as you go.

TASK 3:
SNYDER v. REGENTS

POLACEK & SCHEIER
5700 North Prospect, Suite 2600
Springville, Columbia

MEMORANDUM

TO: Applicant

FROM: R.J. Morrison

DATE: February 28, 2008

Re: **Snyder v. Regents of the University of Columbia**

We have been retained by Dr. Norm Snyder to represent him in claims arising from his removal as Chairperson of the Department of Medicine at the University of Columbia. The Regents of the University terminated him as head of the Department following his very vocal and public opposition to the relocation of the Medical School from its current location here in Springville to Palatine, some 20 miles away. The termination is to become effective almost a month from today. He will retain his professorship after his termination as Chair.

Dr. Snyder wishes to pursue injunctive relief to stop his termination, if possible. Please write me an objective memorandum in which you analyze the likelihood of obtaining a preliminary injunction based on retaliatory employer action in violation of Dr. Snyder's First Amendment right to free speech under the State of Columbia Constitution. For tactical reasons, we are going to rely on the Columbia State Constitution rather than the United States Constitution. We will do so because the Columbia State Constitution is more protective of public employee First Amendment rights. Since the facts will be woven throughout your memorandum, limit your statement of facts to a brief one-paragraph summary.

POLACEK & SCHEIER
5700 North Prospect, Suite 2600
Springville, Columbia

MEMORANDUM

TO: Applicant
FROM: R.J. Morrison
DATE: February 28, 2008
Re: **Snyder v. Regents of the University of Columbia**

> Tells you who your client is and why he hired you. Sounds like there might be a free speech issue related to his termination.

We have been retained by Dr. Norm Snyder to represent him in claims arising from his removal as Chairperson of the Department of Medicine at the University of Columbia. The Regents of the University terminated him as head of the Department following his very vocal and public opposition to the relocation of the Medical School from its current location here in Springville to Palatine, some 20 miles away. The termination is to become effective almost a month from today. He will retain his professorship after his termination as Chair.

> Client's goal

> Your task

> Predictable based on first paragraph above.

Dr. Snyder wishes to pursue injunctive relief to stop his termination, if possible. Please write me an objective memorandum in which you analyze the likelihood of obtaining a preliminary injunction based on retaliatory employer action in violation of Dr. Snyder's First Amendment right to free speech under the State of Columbia Constitution. For tactical reasons, we are going to rely on the Columbia State Constitution rather than the United States Constitution. We will do so because the Columbia State Constitution is more protective of public employee First Amendment rights. Since the facts will be woven throughout your memorandum, limit your statement of facts to a brief one-paragraph summary.

> Tells you source of law and why to use this law.

> Make a note of this now.

EXAMPLE 3 STRUCTURE (Objective Memorandum)

Memorandum

To: R.J. Morrison

From: Applicant

Re: Snyder v. Regents of University of Columbia

Date: February 28, 2008

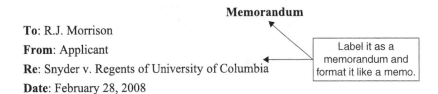

Label it as a memorandum and format it like a memo.

I.   Statement of Facts

Dr. Snyder is the Chairperson of the Dept. of Medicine at the University of Columbia. He has worked the last 20 years building up the Dept. of Medicine. The School of Medicine is considering moving its location 20 miles away from its current location, which Dr. Snyder opposes. Dr. Snyder's reasons for opposing the move include separation of facilities from the research facilities and the medical school, citizens of Columbia not getting their monies' worth because the bonds will take 40 years to pay off, and the lack of public transportation to the medical center, which is 20 miles away. Dr. Snyder proposed splitting some faculty in each location and voiced his concerns to the faculty in a report and wrote a letter to the editor of the Star Bulletin complaining about the relocation plans. In his letter, he referred readers to visit his report on his UC website. Community activists are using Dr. Snyder's letter in their support to prevent the move too. Nonetheless, the Regents voted to move the campus and the day after sent Dr. Snyder a termination letter as Chairperson, but maintained his tenure status. Dr. Snyder is now seeking advice on a possible preliminary injunction.

> Since they tell you to do a brief one-paragraph statement of facts be sure to do exactly that and label it, since you are writing a memo.

> Use broad relevant facts that tell the story.

> End by stating what relief the client is seeking.

II.   Discussion

Preliminary Injunction

Start the discussion section with a recitation of the rule at issue. Here, the client seeks a preliminary injunction. Even though you should know the basic rule for permanent injunction and already have a general idea of the elements, typically the exact rule elements will come from a statute or case in the library. For now, know there will be several subsections.

> Main rule for the cause of action the client is seeking.

III. Conclusion

LIBRARY: SPOTLIGHT ON BOOK BRIEFING

Library 1 — Estate of Keefe

The task assigned in Task 2, Estate of Keefe, is to prepare a Motion of Points and Authorities in Opposition to Motion for Summary Judgment. As in most cases, after reading the task memo, you would skim the facts to find key information before briefing the cases. Here, when you skim the facts, you will be looking for your opponent's main arguments in their summary judgment motion (included in the client file), since your job is to refute their arguments. This assignment and search provide the macrostructure for your response. The opposing party's three arguments/statements in their motion were:

1. Plaintiff's claim based on an oral contract to make a will must fail because there is no evidence to establish the existence of an oral contract.
2. Even if an oral contract exists, it cannot be enforced because it is not in writing.
3. This action is barred by the statute of limitations because it was filed more than two years after decedent's death.

Library 2 — Snyder v. Regents

After reading the task memo, a skim of the facts in this PT reveals more factual details about Dr. Snyder's opposition to the Medical School relocation and his corresponding activities speaking out against it. He wrote a letter to the editor that was published, sparking public outcry, and in an interview, for which the transcript is provided, he explained the reasons for his opposition to the proposed move. Once you have briefed the cases, you return to the case file to find the specific facts to analogize and distinguish the cases. After you finish briefing the cases and comparing your briefed cases to the annotated cases, you should review the rule deconstruction and organizational approach to how you would organize your task for Snyder in the samples provided after the annotated library.

LIBRARY 1:

ESTATE OF KEEFE

ESTATE OF KEEFE

LIBRARY

TABLE OF CONTENTS

RIGANTI v. McELHINNEY
Court of Appeal of Columbia (1967)

This is an action for quasi-specific performance of an oral contract between plaintiffs and one James R. Trissel, now deceased, wherein plaintiffs agreed to look after Trissel's improved real property, collect the rents, and account to him for same, and to care for Trissel so long as he lived, and show respect and obedience toward him as children toward a father. For this service, attention, and care, Trissel agreed plaintiffs should have free rent of the living quarters on his property that they then occupied, and that on his death he would leave them a part of his property by his will. Although plaintiffs carried out their part of the agreement, decedent failed to provide for them in his will.

The court rendered judgment in favor of plaintiffs. Defendant, Muriel McElhinney, niece of Trissel and the residuary devisee and legatee under the will, has appealed.

The judgment decrees, *inter alia*, that plaintiffs have quasi-specific performance of an oral agreement with Trissel; that plaintiffs are the sole and only beneficial and equitable owners of the improved real property here in question; that defendant has no right, title, interest, or estate whatsoever in and to said real property or the rents, issues, and profits therefrom, and that she and her heirs, representatives, transferees, or assigns, and each of them, is permanently restrained and enjoined from claiming or asserting any right, title, interest, claim, or estate whatsoever in, to, or over said real property.

Defendant pled the statute of frauds as embodied in Probate Code section 150 and the statute of limitations. But even though the agreement is oral, sufficient facts may be shown to take the case out of the statute of frauds.

Where a contract is within the statute of frauds, as it is here, the mere rendition of services is not usually such a part performance of a verbal agreement as will relieve the contract from the operation of the statute. If the services are of such a peculiar character, however, that it is impossible to estimate their value by any pecuniary standard, and it is evident that the parties did not intend to measure them by any such standard, and if the plaintiff, after the performance of the services, could not be restored to the situation in which he was before the rendition of the services, it is such a part performance of the verbal agreement as will remove the contract from the rule. Equity, where other objections are not present, will decree specific performance. But in such cases the reason for the interposition of equity is quite obvious. The plaintiff has rendered services of extraordinary and exceptional character, such service as in contemplation of the parties was not to be compensated for in money, and as in contemplation of law, cannot be compensated for in money; therefore, by no action at law could a plaintiff be restored to his original position. It would be in the nature of a fraud upon him to deny him any relief, and, the law failing by reason of its universality, equity, to promote justice, makes good its imperfections.

Applying these principles to the facts as found by the trial court, we conclude the judgment must be affirmed.

Plaintiffs had been living in Trissel's downstairs duplex at 623 South Catalina Avenue for a little more than five years when the oral agreement here in question was entered into. They had ample time and opportunity to get well acquainted and had apparently developed confidence and respect for each other. Trissel was without immediate family except for a son with whom his relations were not friendly and with whom he seldom communicated. His health was not good and he faced surgery. He was then 62 years of age. In these circumstances Trissel no doubt felt alone in the world and in need of "a family" who would take an interest in him and look after his needs and welfare, and treat him like a father. It seems that over the next two years plaintiffs gave Trissel the care and attention he needed and wanted and served him as though they were members of his family. He recognized this by referring to plaintiffs as "his kids" and stating to a friend that they were closer to him than the members of his own family had ever been. These services and this type of devotion for the rest of Trissel's life were of such a peculiar character that it was impossible to estimate their value by any pecuniary standard. Furthermore, it is evident that the parties did not intend to measure the value of these services by any such standard, for if they had so intended they could have fixed a fee therefor just as they had agreed that free rent would compensate for plaintiffs' taking care of Trissel's rental units and the collection of the rentals.

Having special skills as a mechanic and in certain trades of the building industry, Wade Riganti could have improved his station in life by leaving Trissel's living accommodations and "walking away" from his and his wife's obligations under their agreement with Trissel. But they did not do that. They honored their commitment with Trissel. As a result, plaintiffs, after the performance of their services, could not be restored to the situation in which they were before the rendition of the services. The failure therefore of Trissel to leave his will as agreed works a fraud upon plaintiffs and serves to remove the oral agreement from the statute of frauds. Equity then steps in, as it did in this case, and decrees what we call "quasi-specific" performance to avoid the perpetration of a fraud upon plaintiffs and unjust enrichment of defendant. Of course, equitable relief should not be granted where it would work a gross injustice upon innocent third parties. No such problem is presented in the case at bench, for the trial court drew the conclusion, *inter alia*, that plaintiffs were entitled to quasi-specific performance "to avoid . . . unjust enrichment of defendant."

There is no merit in defendant's suggestion that plaintiffs failed to show that the consideration rendered by them was adequate. It sufficiently appears that there was adequate consideration for the contract, for the extent of the consideration is to be measured by the breadth of the undertaking rather than by the eventuality. Plaintiffs might have had to serve and nurse Trissel for many years. Each party to the agreement knowingly stood to lose or gain by that contingency.

We can also dispose of the statute of limitations argument. An action for quasi-specific performance accrues on the death of the person who breached the agreement. Where quasi-specific performance by declaration of a constructive trust on real property is sought on the basis of an oral agreement pursuant to which that property was to have been left by will, a four-year period applies rather than the two-year period of limitation generally applicable to contracts not in writing.

The judgment is affirmed.

KENNEDY v. BANK OF COLUMBIA
Court of Appeal of Columbia (1965)

This appeal originated in an action brought by plaintiff against the Bank of Columbia National Trust & Savings Association, as executor of the will of Thomas J. McDermott, deceased (hereinafter referred to as executor). The complaint contained a single cause of action for quasi-specific performance of an alleged oral contract between plaintiff and decedent, by which decedent agreed to devise and bequeath his property to plaintiff by his will as compensation for personal services rendered and to impose a constructive trust upon the property. Executor filed a motion for summary judgment. The motion was granted, and judgment was entered.

The allegations of the complaint upon which plaintiff's case must stand or fall are these: On or about May 1, 1941, decedent offered to employ plaintiff in his home as a domestic servant and as an assistant in his retail gasoline station business, and orally promised that, if she would perform services for him and his family and would remain at Bakersfield and assist him in building up his business, he would execute an irrevocable will leaving her his entire estate; prior to May 1, 1941, plaintiff was a healthy woman and used her time to care for her own household and to earn money working at various tasks; plaintiff accepted decedent's offer of employment and worked for him substantially all of the time from May 1, 1941 until about June 15, 1953, at which time decedent orally informed her that he was retiring from business and he would no longer need her services, but that a will theretofore made by him in her favor would remain irrevocable.

Further, plaintiff alleged that, in order to fulfill her portion of said oral agreement between the parties, she gave up most of her own social life, opportunities to move to other cities with her husband, and opportunities to work for other persons so as to assist her husband in accumulating savings and property of their own. In general, plaintiff alleged, in reliance upon the oral agreement of decedent to leave all of his property to her by will upon his death, she put aside most of her personal pleasures, comforts, and affairs, and forsook many of her friends while she was performing services as housekeeper and assistant to decedent in his business.

Plaintiff alleged that in doing all of these things she was acting in reliance upon the promise of decedent to make her beneficiary of his will, and upon his promise that he would not change said will. Had it not been for such oral promises plaintiff would not have performed said services without receiving compensation therefor, which plaintiff did not receive, and were it not for said promises plaintiff would not have altered her way of life in the manner in which she did.

Plaintiff further alleged that the nature of her services and contributions was such that compensation therefor may not be measured, nor would compensation for services rendered be fair and reasonable under the circumstances; nor was it the intent of the parties that compensation be measured except by the total value of decedent's estate. Plaintiff alleged that she has no adequate or speedy remedy at law.

Executor filed a motion for summary judgment on the ground that the alleged contract is oral and unenforceable under our statute of frauds, section 150 of the Probate Code. The principal concern on this appeal is whether plaintiff has alleged evidence sufficient to demonstrate that triable issues of fact exist in this action.

In order to enforce an oral contract to bequeath or devise property in equity by quasi-specific performance, it must be shown that the contract is definite and certain, the consideration adequate, the contract is founded on good morals and not against public policy, the character of the services is such that a money payment would not furnish adequate compensation to the plaintiff, there is such a change in the plaintiff's condition and relations in reliance on the contract that a refusal to complete the contract would be a fraud upon him, and the remedy asked for is not harsh, oppressive, or unjust to innocent third parties.

The doctrine of estoppel, which lifts an agreement to make a will out of the operation of the statute of frauds, is based on either of two grounds. It has been applied where an unconscionable injury would result from denying enforcement after one party has been induced to make a detrimental change of position in reliance upon the oral agreement. It has also been applied where unjust enrichment would result if the party who has received the benefits of the performance of the other were allowed to invoke the statute.

Courts have found a detrimental change of position where there is a family relationship or close friendship, and the decedent has turned to the plaintiff for care, solace, comfort, and companionship. Oftentimes, at the decedent's supplication, the plaintiff has moved from an established home, leaving an established position or business in his or her hometown or state, to make a residence in the home of the decedent far from friends and family, and devoting himself or herself with dedicated care to the needs of the decedent, sometimes until the death of the decedent. Where the services rendered by the plaintiff consisted in nursing and caring for a person enfeebled and suffering from a horrible disease, requiring constant and unceasing watchfulness, harrowing to the mind, destructive to the peace and comfort of the one performing the services, and possibly injurious to the health, it has been held that it is impossible to estimate their value by any pecuniary standard; and where it is evident that the decedent did not intend so to measure them, it is out of the power of any court, after the performance of such services, to restore the plaintiff to the situation in which he was before the contract was made or to compensate him therefor in damages.

Plaintiff in this case has not submitted evidence sufficient to create triable issues as to either ground. The best description of the nature of the services that plaintiff can make is that she acted as a domestic servant and as an assistant in the retail gasoline station business operated by decedent. The services of both a domestic servant and a gasoline station assistant may be adequately compensated for in money. Such services are neither peculiar, nor exceptional, nor unique. They are performed for wages by thousands of employees similarly situated. It is not alleged that plaintiff made her home with decedent; or that she occupied a close or continuing familial relationship with him; or that she attended to his personal needs; or that she nursed him through any illness; or that she did anything that was "harrowing to the mind" or "destructive to her peace and comfort" or "injurious to her health" for which money cannot compensate. The allegation in the complaint that the nature of the services was such that compensation therefor may not be measured is a mere conclusion.

The allegations of the declaration that plaintiff gave up her social life, opportunities to move to other cities and to work for other persons, opportunities to assist her husband in accumulating savings and property of their own, and that she put aside most of her personal pleasures and forsook many of her friends are not sufficient.

Nor does the declaration establish sufficient facts to show that decedent or anyone else will be unjustly enriched if the purported oral contract is not enforced. There are no allegations that services rendered to decedent, either in his household as a domestic servant or in his service station business, substantially contributed to the value of the business or to the assets that comprise the estate. No unjust enrichment results, or may be implied, from mere allegations that plaintiff performed services of an impersonal nature for decedent.

We conclude that there are no triable issues of fact as to the inapplicability of the statute of frauds. The grant of the motion for summary judgment is affirmed.

HORSTMANN v. SHELDON
Court of Appeal of Columbia (1962)

Plaintiff, Ella Horstmann, brought this action to establish a trust in real and personal property held in the estate of her deceased mother, Bertha Horstmann. The complaint alleged that "on numerous occasions during the approximately 20 years before decedent's death, decedent urged plaintiff to reside with decedent and care for decedent; that decedent offered if plaintiff would so reside with and care for decedent and not undertake to obtain regular gainful employment outside the home of decedent, decedent would provide a home for plaintiff during the lifetime of decedent and would by a will leave the home of decedent, including the real property upon which it was situated and the furniture and furnishings therein, to plaintiff." The complaint further alleged that "plaintiff accepted each of decedent's offers and proposals and did all things required to be done in compliance therewith; that in connection therewith plaintiff refrained from undertaking any general employment outside the home and resided with decedent and cared for her and for her property for many years up to the time of the death of decedent; that during all of the aforesaid period of time decedent reiterated the aforesaid promises on numerous occasions." Plaintiff further alleged that she received no compensation for her services, and that decedent breached the alleged agreement by her will naming her brother-in-law, defendant George Sheldon, sole devisee and legatee of decedent's entire estate and the executor of her will.

The answer denied the existence of the contract and affirmatively asserted that plaintiff had been entirely supported by decedent during her lifetime.

At trial, plaintiff testified consistent with her complaint. In addition, several witnesses testified to extensive personal services rendered by plaintiff to decedent, including nursing and personal care, cooking, housework, serving meals, gardening, cutting wood, house repairs, and a multitude of other duties and responsibilities relating to the premises where the parties lived.

The trial court found the existence of the contract as alleged by plaintiff, and that plaintiff had fully performed her part of the bargain but that decedent had not performed her part of the agreement. The judgment imposed a trust upon the home property for the lifetime of plaintiff and also allowed her the life use of certain personal property.

The chief contention of defendant on appeal is that the evidence is insufficient to support the judgment. The record, however, is replete with evidence to support the making of the agreement between plaintiff and decedent and the full performance of the contract by plaintiff. Under long established rules it is not for this court to review the evidence and determine its weight and sufficiency. Where, as here, there is substantial evidence in the record to support the judgment, it will not be disturbed on appeal in the absence of some error requiring reversal on other grounds.

Defendant also urged that plaintiff filed no claim against decedent's estate and therefore the complaint does not state a cause of action. There is no merit in this contention, however. Plaintiff's suit here is not one for the recovery of damages for breach of contract, nor in quantum meruit for the value of her services. Plaintiff's suit is in equity for the purpose of enforcing her contract by having defendant declared trustee of the described property for plaintiff's benefit. She seeks no relief at law but only in equity, and under such a pleading no claim against the estate of the decedent need be filed.

Another question presented by this appeal is whether our statute of frauds, Probate Code section 150, bars the enforcement of plaintiff's contract. We conclude that it does not.

The doctrine of estoppel to assert the statute of frauds has been consistently applied by the courts of this state to prevent fraud that would result from refusal to enforce oral contracts in certain circumstances. Such fraud may contribute to the unconscionable injury that would result from denying enforcement of the contract after one party has been induced by the other seriously to change his position in reliance on the contract, or in the unjust enrichment that would result if a party who has received the benefits of the other's performance were allowed to rely upon the statute.

At the time of trial, plaintiff was 63 years of age. The understanding or agreement between plaintiff and decedent commenced about 1926, and from that date to the date of decedent's death plaintiff had been engaged in the performance of her part of the bargain. As the trial court found, many of the years of her youth and all of the years of her maturity were spent in the care and maintenance of decedent. The agreement was breached at a time when plaintiff was approaching the later years of her life. It can hardly be said that to permit this would not result in unconscionable injury to plaintiff. Having made this finding, we need not address the second prong.

If plaintiff is not permitted to pursue her remedy in a court of equity, she would be relegated to an action at law for damages for the breach of her contract, or left to pursue her quasi-contractual remedy for the value of services rendered. Neither is adequate for the breach of a contract to leave property by will in exchange for services of a peculiar nature involving the assumption or continuation of a close family relationship.

The judgment is affirmed.

ESTATE OF KEEFE

LIBRARY

TABLE OF CONTENTS

Compare these annotated book briefed cases with your book briefs to see if you properly extracted the correct information.

Goes to Task: response to moving party's arguments, all 3 of their statements.

When you determine if the case is favorable to your client or not make a notation at the top here so you know whether to analogize or distinguish it later.

Always note the court and jx to see if it is a binding case.

RIGANTI v. McELHINNEY

Court of Appeal of Columbia (1967)

+ for us

Same COA as the client in our task memo.

Similar to our client from the task memo.

This is an action for quasi-specific performance of an oral contract between plaintiffs and one James R. Trissel, now deceased, wherein plaintiffs agreed to look after Trissel's improved real property, collect the rents, and account to him for same, and to care for Trissel so long as he lived, and show respect and obedience toward him as children toward a father. For this service, attention, and care, Trissel agreed plaintiffs should have free rent of the living quarters on his property that they then occupied, and that on his death he would leave them a part of his property by his will. Although plaintiffs carried out their part of the agreement, decedent failed to provide for them in his will.

T. Ct. for P

The court rendered judgment in favor of plaintiffs. Defendant, Muriel McElhinney, niece of Trissel and the residuary devisee and legatee under the will, has appealed.

The judgment decrees, *inter alia*, that plaintiffs have quasi-specific performance of an oral agreement with Trissel; that plaintiffs are the sole and only beneficial and equitable owners of the improved real property here in question; that defendant has no right, title, interest, or estate whatsoever in and to said real property or the rents, issues, and profits therefrom, and that she and her heirs, representatives, transferees, or assigns, and each of them, is permanently restrained and enjoined from claiming or asserting any right, title, interest, claim, or estate whatsoever in, to, or over said real property.

D argues

Defendant pled the statute of frauds as embodied in Probate Code section 150 and the statute of limitations. But even though the agreement is oral, sufficient facts may be shown to take the case out of the statute of frauds.

All a rule about removing an oral contract from the SOF requirement.

Where a contract is within the statute of frauds, as it is here, the mere rendition of services is not usually such a part performance of a verbal agreement as will relieve the contract from the operation of the statute. If the services are of such a peculiar character, however, that it is impossible to estimate their value by any pecuniary standard, and it is evident that the parties did not intend to measure them by any such standard, and if the plaintiff, after the performance of the services, could not be restored to the situation in which he was before the rendition of the services, it is such a part performance of the verbal agreement as will remove the contract from the rule. Equity, where other objections are not present, will decree specific performance. But in such cases the reason for the interposition of equity is quite obvious. The plaintiff has rendered services of extraordinary and exceptional character, such service as in contemplation of the parties was not to be compensated for in money, and as in contemplation of law, cannot be compensated for in money; therefore, by no action at law could a plaintiff be restored to his original position. It would be in the nature of a fraud upon him to deny him any relief, and, the law failing by reason of its universality, equity, to promote justice, makes good its imperfections.

> Reason for the rule.

Applying these principles to the facts as found by the trial court, we conclude the judgment must be affirmed.

> For P – good for us – at this time go to the top of your case and add a + to remind you it is positive for us (so you will want to analogize the facts in this case to the facts of our case).

> All reasoning why the court found the SOF would not bar this oral contract.

Plaintiffs had been living in Trissel's downstairs duplex at 623 South Catalina Avenue for a little more than five years when the oral agreement here in question was entered into. They had ample time and opportunity to get well acquainted and had apparently developed confidence and respect for each other. Trissel was without immediate family except for a son with whom his relations were not friendly and with whom he seldom communicated. His health was not good and he faced surgery. He was then 62 years of age. In these circumstances Trissel no doubt felt alone in the world and in need of "a family" who would take an interest in him and look after his needs and welfare, and treat him like a father. It seems that over the next two years plaintiffs gave Trissel the care and attention he needed and wanted and served him as though they were members of his family. He recognized this by referring to plaintiffs as "his kids" and stating to a friend that they were closer to him than the members of his own family had ever been. These services and this type of devotion for the rest of Trissel's life were of such a peculiar character that it was impossible to estimate their value by any pecuniary standard. Furthermore, it is evident that the parties did not intend to measure the value of these services by any such standard, for if they had so intended they could have fixed a fee therefor just as they had agreed that free rent would compensate for plaintiffs' taking care of Trissel's rental units and the collection of the rentals.

Reasoning continued.

Having special skills as a mechanic and in certain trades of the building industry, Wade Riganti could have improved his station in life by leaving Trissel's living accommodations and "walking away" from his and his wife's obligations under their agreement with Trissel. But they did not do that. They honored their commitment with Trissel. As a result, plaintiffs, after the performance of their services, could not be restored to the situation in which they were before the rendition of the services. The failure therefore of Trissel to leave his will as agreed works a fraud upon plaintiffs and serves to remove the oral agreement from the statute of frauds. Equity then steps in, as it did in this case, and decrees what we call "quasi-specific" performance to avoid the perpetration of a fraud upon plaintiffs and unjust enrichment of defendant. Of course,

Another related rule.

equitable relief should not be granted where it would work a gross injustice upon innocent third parties. No such problem is presented in the case at bench, for the trial court drew the conclusion, *inter alia*, that plaintiffs were entitled to quasi-specific performance "to avoid . . . unjust enrichment of defendant."

There is no merit in defendant's suggestion that plaintiffs failed to show that the consideration rendered by them was adequate. It sufficiently appears that there was

Consideration ok, but not really the issue here.

adequate consideration for the contract, for the extent of the consideration is to be measured by the breadth of the undertaking rather than by the eventuality. Plaintiffs might have had to serve and nurse Trissel for many years. Each party to the agreement knowingly stood to lose or gain by that contingency.

We can also dispose of the statute of limitations argument. An action for quasi-specific performance accrues on the death of the person who breached the agreement.

SOL rule used here.

Where quasi-specific performance by declaration of a constructive trust on real property is sought on the basis of an oral agreement pursuant to which that property was to have been left by will, a four-year period applies rather than the two-year period of limitation generally applicable to contracts not in writing.

The judgment is affirmed. **Again for P.**

Goes to Task: response
to moving party's
arguments, statement 2.

Always note the court
and jx to see if it is a
binding case; same
as last case but 2
years older.

KENNEDY v. BANK OF COLUMBIA

Court of Appeal of Columbia (1965)

For D so (-) for our client
(need to distinguish).

This appeal originated in an action brought by plaintiff against the Bank of Columbia National Trust & Savings Association, as executor of the will of Thomas J. McDermott, deceased (hereinafter referred to as executor). The complaint contained a single cause of action for quasi-specific performance of an alleged oral contract between plaintiff and decedent, by which decedent agreed to devise and bequeath his property to plaintiff by his will as compensation for personal services rendered and to impose a constructive trust upon the property. Executor filed a motion for summary judgment. The motion was granted, and judgment was entered. T. Ct. for D

Same COA
as P from the
task memo.

Similar to
our P in
task memo.

The allegations of the complaint upon which plaintiff's case must stand or fall are these: On or about May 1, 1941, decedent offered to employ plaintiff in his home as a domestic servant and as an assistant in his retail gasoline station business, and orally promised that, if she would perform services for him and his family and would remain at Bakersfield and assist him in building up his business, he would execute an irrevocable will leaving her his entire estate; prior to May 1, 1941, plaintiff was a healthy woman and used her time to care for her own household and to earn money working at various tasks; plaintiff accepted decedent's offer of employment and worked for him substantially all of the time from May 1, 1941 until about June 15, 1953, at which time decedent orally informed her that he was retiring from business and he would no longer need her services, but that a will theretofore made by him in her favor would remain irrevocable.

Facts

P argues

Further, plaintiff alleged that, in order to fulfill her portion of said oral agreement between the parties, she gave up most of her own social life, opportunities to move to other cities with her husband, and opportunities to work for other persons so as to assist her husband in accumulating savings and property of their own. In general, plaintiff alleged, in reliance upon the oral agreement of decedent to leave all of his property to her by will upon his death, she put aside most of her personal pleasures, comforts, and affairs, and forsook many of her friends while she was performing services as housekeeper and assistant to decedent in his business.

Plaintiff alleged that in doing all of these things she was acting in reliance upon the promise of decedent to make her beneficiary of his will, and upon his promise that he would not change said will. Had it not been for such oral promises plaintiff would not have performed said services without receiving compensation therefor, which plaintiff did not receive, and were it not for said promises plaintiff would not have altered her way of life in the manner in which she did.

> P also argues

Plaintiff further alleged that the nature of her services and contributions was such that compensation therefor may not be measured, nor would compensation for services rendered be fair and reasonable under the circumstances; nor was it the intent of the parties that compensation be measured except by the total value of decedent's estate. Plaintiff alleged that she has no adequate or speedy remedy at law.

> Issue

Executor filed a motion for summary judgment on the ground that the alleged contract is oral and unenforceable under our statute of frauds, section 150 of the Probate Code. The principal concern on this appeal is whether plaintiff has alleged evidence sufficient to demonstrate that triable issues of fact exist in this action.

> All rule: mostly similar to last case but not worded exactly the same.

In order to enforce an oral contract to bequeath or devise property in equity by quasi-specific performance, it must be shown that the contract is definite and certain, the consideration adequate, the contract is founded on good morals and not against public policy, the character of the services is such that a money payment would not furnish adequate compensation to the plaintiff, there is such a change in the plaintiff's condition and relations in reliance on the contract that a refusal to complete the contract would be a fraud upon him, and the remedy asked for is not harsh, oppressive, or unjust to innocent third parties.

> Two ways to remove oral K from SOF based on estoppel.

The doctrine of estoppel, which lifts an agreement to make a will out of the operation of the statute of frauds, is based on either of two grounds. It has been applied where ① an unconscionable injury would result from denying enforcement after one party has been induced to make a detrimental change of position in reliance upon the oral agreement. It has also been applied ② where unjust enrichment would result if the party who has received the benefits of the performance of the other were allowed to invoke the statute.

Courts have found a detrimental change of position where there is a family relationship or close friendship, and the decedent has turned to the plaintiff for care, solace, comfort, and companionship. Oftentimes, at the decedent's supplication, the plaintiff has moved from an established home, leaving an established position or business in his or her hometown or state, to make a residence in the home of the decedent far from friends and family, and devoting himself or herself with dedicated care to the needs of the decedent, sometimes until the death of the decedent.

Where the services rendered by the plaintiff consisted in nursing and caring for a person enfeebled and suffering from a horrible disease, requiring constant and unceasing watchfulness, harrowing to the mind, destructive to the peace and comfort of the one performing the services, and possibly injurious to the health, it has been held that it is impossible to estimate their value by any pecuniary standard; and where it is evident that the decedent did not intend so to measure them, it is out of the power of any court, after the performance of such services, to restore the plaintiff to the situation in which he was before the contract was made or to compensate him therefor in damages.

Plaintiff in this case has not submitted evidence sufficient to create triable issues as to either ground. The best description of the nature of the services that plaintiff can make is that she acted as a domestic servant and as an assistant in the retail gasoline station business operated by decedent. The services of both a domestic servant and a gasoline station assistant may be adequately compensated for in money. Such services are neither peculiar, nor exceptional, nor unique. They are performed for wages by thousands of employees similarly situated. It is not alleged that plaintiff made her home with decedent; or that she occupied a close or continuing familial relationship with him; or that she attended to his personal needs; or that she nursed him through any illness; or that she did anything that was "harrowing to the mind" or "destructive to her peace and comfort" or "injurious to her health" for which money cannot compensate. The allegation in the complaint that the nature of the services was such that compensation therefor may not be measured is a mere conclusion.

The allegations of the declaration that plaintiff gave up her social life, opportunities to move to other cities and to work for other persons, opportunities to assist her husband in accumulating savings and property of their own, and that she put aside most of her personal pleasures and forsook many of her friends are not sufficient.

| Reason no unjust enrichment |

Nor does the declaration establish sufficient facts to show that decedent or anyone else will be unjustly enriched if the purported oral contract is not enforced. There are no allegations that services rendered to decedent, either in his household as a domestic servant or in his service station business, substantially contributed to the value of the business or to the assets that comprise the estate. No unjust enrichment results, or may be implied, from mere allegations that plaintiff performed services of an impersonal nature for decedent.

We conclude that there are no triable issues of fact as to the inapplicability of the statute of frauds. The grant of the motion for summary judgment is affirmed. | Aff'd for D |

Goes to Task: response to moving party's arguments, statement 2.

Same court as last two cases and earlier in time than both.

HORSTMANN v. SHELDON

Court of Appeal of Columbia (1962)

+ for us

COA: slightly different from last two cases and our P in the task memo.

P alleges these facts.

Plaintiff, Ella Horstmann, brought this action <u>to establish a trust in real and personal property held in the estate</u> of her deceased mother, Bertha Horstmann. The complaint alleged that "on numerous occasions during the approximately <u>20 years</u> before decedent's death, <u>decedent urged plaintiff to reside with decedent and care for</u> decedent; that decedent offered if plaintiff would so reside with and care for decedent and <u>not undertake to obtain regular gainful employment outside the home</u> of decedent, decedent would provide a home for plaintiff during the lifetime of <u>decedent</u> and <u>would by a will leave the home of decedent, including the real property upon which it was situated</u> and the furniture and furnishings therein, to plaintiff." The complaint further alleged that "<u>plaintiff accepted each of decedent's offers</u> and proposals and did all things required to be done in compliance therewith; that in connection therewith plaintiff <u>refrained from undertaking any general employment</u> outside the home and resided with decedent and cared for her and for her property for many years up to the time of the death of decedent; that during all of the aforesaid period of time decedent reiterated the aforesaid promises on numerous occasions." Plaintiff further alleged that she <u>received no compensation</u> for her services, and that decedent breached the alleged agreement by her will <u>naming her brother-in-law</u>, defendant George Sheldon, <u>sole devisee</u> and legatee of decedent's entire estate and the executor of her will.

D's answer

The <u>answer denied the existence of the contract</u> and affirmatively asserted that <u>plaintiff had been entirely supported by decedent during her lifetime.</u>

Facts about what P did for D.

At trial, plaintiff testified consistent with her complaint. In addition, <u>several witnesses testified to extensive personal services rendered by plaintiff to decedent</u>, including nursing and personal care, cooking, housework, serving meals, gardening, <u>cutting wood, house repairs, and a multitude of other duties and responsibilities</u> relating to the premises where the parties lived.

The trial court found the existence of the contract as alleged by plaintiff, and that plaintiff had fully performed her part of the bargain but that decedent had not performed

T. Ct. for P

her part of the agreement.   The judgment imposed a trust upon the home property for the lifetime of plaintiff and also allowed her the life use of certain personal property.

The chief contention of defendant on appeal is that the evidence is insufficient to support the judgment.   The record, however, is replete with evidence to support the making of the agreement between plaintiff and decedent and the full performance of the contract by plaintiff.   Under long established rules it is not for this court to review the evidence and determine its weight and sufficiency.   Where, as here, there is substantial evidence in the record to support the judgment, it will not be disturbed on appeal in the absence of some error requiring reversal on other grounds.

Reasoning ct. found for P.

Defendant also urged that plaintiff filed no claim against decedent's estate and therefore the complaint does not state a cause of action.   There is no merit in this contention, however.   Plaintiff's suit here is not one for the recovery of damages for breach of contract, nor in quantum meruit for the value of her services.   Plaintiff's suit is in equity for the purpose of enforcing her contract by having defendant declared trustee of the described property for plaintiff's benefit.   She seeks no relief at law but only in equity, and under such a pleading no claim against the estate of the decedent need be filed.

More reasoning.

Another issue: SOF

Another question presented by this appeal is whether our statute of frauds, Probate Code section 150, bars the enforcement of plaintiff's contract.   We conclude that it does not.

Same rule as in past cases.

> The doctrine of estoppel to assert the statute of frauds has been consistently applied by the courts of this state to prevent fraud that would result from refusal to enforce oral contracts in certain circumstances.   Such fraud may contribute to the unconscionable injury that would result from denying enforcement of the contract after one party has been induced by the other seriously to change his position in reliance on the contract, or in the unjust enrichment that would result if a party who has received the benefits of the other's performance were allowed to rely upon the statute.

Reasoning

At the time of trial, plaintiff was 63 years of age.   The understanding or agreement between plaintiff and decedent commenced about 1926, and from that date to the date of decedent's death plaintiff had been engaged in the performance of her part of the bargain.   As the trial court found, many of the years of her youth and all of the years of her maturity were spent in the care and maintenance of decedent.   The

Reasoning

agreement was breached at a time when plaintiff was approaching the later years of her life. It can hardly be said that to permit this would not result in unconscionable injury to plaintiff. Having made this finding, we need not address the second prong.

If plaintiff is not permitted to pursue her remedy in a court of equity, she would be relegated to an action at law for damages for the breach of her contract, or left to pursue her quasi-contractual remedy for the value of services rendered. Neither is adequate for the breach of a contract to leave property by will in exchange for services of a peculiar nature involving the assumption or continuation of a close family relationship.

Reason this is the proper remedy.

The judgment is affirmed.

> For P: good for our case.

Estate of Keefe Rule Deconstruction Examples

Riganti v. McElhinney rules

EXAMPLE 1:

Applies to point 2 in your response to the moving party's argument:

Where a contract is within the statute of frauds, the mere rendition of services is not usually such a part performance of a verbal agreement as will relieve the contract from the operation of the statute. If the services are of such a peculiar character, however, that it is impossible to estimate their value by any pecuniary standard, and it is evident that the parties did not intend to measure them by any such standard, and if the plaintiff, after the performance of the services, could not be restored to the situation in which he was before the rendition of the services, it is such a part performance of the verbal agreement as will remove the contract from the rule.

Deconstruct this rule as follows after stating the overall rule upfront:

- Rendition of services does not always equal performance for SOF to not apply
- Services can amount to performance so the SOF does not apply when:
    - Services are peculiar
    - Services are impossible to estimate the value by any pecuniary standard
    - Parties did not intend to measure the services by any pecuniary standard
    - P cannot be restored to the position he was originally in

Format: Each element will be analyzed separately here in separate paragraphs—time permitting add headings for each too.

EXAMPLE 2:

Applies to point 3 in your response to the moving party's argument:

Equitable relief should not be granted where it would work a gross injustice upon innocent third parties.

Deconstruct this rule as follows after stating the overall rule upfront:

- Gross injustice
- Innocent third party

Format: Go through each part of the rule but no need for headings or separate paragraphs as it is a minor rule.

EXAMPLE 3:

Applies to point 3 in your response to the moving party's argument:

Where quasi-specific performance by declaration of a constructive trust on real property is sought on the basis of an oral agreement pursuant to which that property was to have been left by will, a four-year period applies rather than the two-year period of limitation generally applicable to contracts not in writing.

Deconstruct this rule as follows after stating the overall rule upfront:

- ○ Quasi-specific performance via constructive trust is sought
- ○ Based on an oral agreement
- ○ To leave property in a will
- ○ Four year statute of limitations applies

Format: **Go through each part of the rule but no need for headings or separate paragraphs as it is a minor rule.**

> **Kennedy v. Bank of Columbia rules**

EXAMPLE 4:

Applies to point 2 in your response to the moving party's argument:

The doctrine of estoppel, which lifts an agreement to make a will out of the operation of the statute of frauds, is based on either of two grounds. It has been applied where an unconscionable injury would result from denying enforcement after one party has been induced to make a detrimental change of position in reliance upon the oral agreement. It has also been applied where unjust enrichment would result if the party who has received the benefits of the performance of the other were allowed to invoke the statute.

Deconstruct this rule as follows after stating the overall rule upfront:

There are two grounds that lift an agreement to make a will out of the operation of the statute of frauds under the doctrine of estoppel.

(1) Unconscionable injury

> The SOF will not apply when unconscionable injury would result from denying enforcement after one party has been induced to make a detrimental change of position in reliance upon the oral agreement.

Deconstruct this rule as follows after stating the overall rule upfront:

- o Unconscionable injury
- o One party induced
- o That party (induced) made a detrimental change
- o In reliance on
- o The oral agreement

(2) Unjust enrichment

The SOF will not apply when unjust enrichment would result if the party who has received the benefits of the performance of the other were allowed to invoke the statute.

Deconstruct this rule as follows after stating the overall rule upfront:

- o Unjust enrichment (would result from)
- o The party that received the benefits of performance

<u>Format:</u> **Each ground will receive a heading; the elements under each ground will be analyzed separately here but do not need separate headings or paragraphs.**

> **Horstmann v. Sheldon rules**

The same rules are given in <u>Horstmann</u> as in the above cases so no need to deconstruct again (this case just provided more reasoning as to how the above estoppel rules apply).

<u>Rule Deconstruction tip:</u> Most cases involve the same rules, but the latter cases usually explain a part of the prior case rules in more depth, provide an additional rule related to those rules, or provide additional analysis on rules already provided. Also note that the rules in the cases don't always go under the various parts of the task in the order they are presented (see above how some rules in prior cases go to point 3 while later rules/cases go to point 2).

LIBRARY 2:
SNYDER v. REGENTS

SNYDER v. REGENTS OF THE UNIVERSITY OF COLUMBIA

LIBRARY

Elkins v. Hamel

Columbia Supreme Court (2007)

This is an action brought pursuant to Columbia Civil Rights Code ' 1983 by two City of Tunbridge police officers against Steve Hamel, the City of Tunbridge police chief, alleging a violation of their First Amendment rights under the Columbia Constitution. In their complaint, plaintiffs Kenneth Elkins and George Chanel assert they have been illegally disciplined by Chief Hamel for exercising their rights to free speech. Plaintiff Elkins asserts he has been disciplined by a fifteen day suspension, and plaintiff Chanel asserts he has been disciplined by a one day suspension. They sought a preliminary injunction. Plaintiffs requested rescission of their suspensions. They further sought injunctive relief restraining and enjoining the defendant from further discipline or threat of discipline for the exercise of their rights to free speech. The request for injunctive relief was denied, and this appeal followed.

The verified complaint sets forth the following facts: On February 16, 2006, Glenda Oliver wrote a column in the *Tunbridge Journal* addressing several issues "concerning her perception of racism in the state court criminal system." The complaint notes: "Ms. Oliver's comments included her questioning the justice involved in the sentencing of a young African-American male on drug charges since no other African-Americans were involved in the young man's sentencing, including the jury, judge and attorneys involved." The column concluded with Ms. Oliver's e-mail address, which was provided for the public to contact her with comments.

On the next day, plaintiff Elkins sent an e-mail from his personal account at his home to several officers of the Tunbridge Police Department (TPD) and the editorial departments of the *Tunbridge Journal* and the *Tunbridge Metro News*. On February 19, 2006, plaintiff Chanel sent an e-mail from his personal account at his residence to Ms. Oliver in response to her column. The complaint states: "Chanel commented that Ms. Oliver's article was racist in tone, and stated his belief that the young man referred to in her article was not sentenced because of his race." Ms. Oliver responded by e-mail to Chanel's e-mail. Chanel sent this e-mail to Elkins and TPD officer David Ernst. On February 22, 2006 Elkins sent an e-mail from his TPD account at his home to the e-mail accounts of Chanel, Ernst and Ms. Oliver. The complaint states: "The e-mail contained comments in response to Ms. Oliver's article regarding her allegations of racism in the state court system." On February 24, 2006, Elkins' comments that had been sent to the newspapers' editorial boards were published in both papers. On March 13, 2006, Chief Hamel instituted discipline in the form of a one day suspension without pay for Chanel and a fifteen day suspension without pay for Elkins.

We review the decision to deny a motion for a preliminary injunction for abuse of discretion. In order to obtain a preliminary injunction, a party must demonstrate the following: (1) a substantial likelihood of prevailing on the merits; (2) irreparable harm in the absence of the injunction; (3) the threatened harm outweighs any damage the injunction may cause to the party opposing it; and (4) the injunction, if issued, will not be adverse to the public interest.

Substantial Likelihood of Success on the Merits

Plaintiffs are correct that public employees retain their First Amendment rights under the Columbia Constitution. However, in the public employment context, a public employer may impose some restraints on job-related speech of public employees that would be plainly unconstitutional if applied to the public at large. This is particularly true of police officers. Because police departments function as paramilitary organizations charged with maintaining public safety and order, police departments are given more latitude in their decisions regarding discipline and personnel regulations than an ordinary government employer.

To determine whether a public employer's actions impermissibly infringe on free speech rights, this court has followed the *Boyer* test enunciated by this Court.[a] The test is as follows: (1) Does the speech in question involve a matter of public concern? If so, (2) we must weigh the employee's interest in the expression against the government employer's interest in regulating the speech of its employees so that it can carry on an efficient and effective workplace. If the employee prevails on both these questions, we proceed to the remaining two steps. In step (3), the employee must show the speech was a substantial factor driving the challenged governmental action. If the employee succeeds, in step (4) the employer, in order to prevail, must in turn show that it would have taken the same action against the employee even in the absence of the protected speech.

Whether an employee's speech addresses a matter of public concern must be determined by the content, form, and context of a given statement, as revealed by the whole record. In evaluating the nature of an employee's speech in a retaliatory discipline or discharge case, we have articulated that when an employee speaks as an employee upon matters only of personal interest the speech is not protected. To judge whether particular speech relates merely to internal workplace issues, courts must conduct a case by case inquiry, looking to the content, form, and context of the speech, which includes scrutinizing whether the speaker's purpose was to bring an issue to the public's attention or to air a personal grievance. An employee's speech must not merely relate generally to a subject matter that is of public interest, but must sufficiently inform the issue as to be helpful to the public in evaluating the conduct of government. That is, we look beyond the general topic of the speech to evaluate more specifically what was said on the topic.

---

[a] The language of the Columbia Constitution's First Amendment is identical to that of the U.S. Constitution. Historically, this Court has interpreted these words more expansively than the U.S. Supreme Court. As such, we choose not to follow the recent U.S. Supreme Court opinion in *Garcetti v. Ceballos* (2006).

Because Plaintiffs' letters concerned the integrity of the police department's operations, though arguably touching upon internal workplace issues, the speech addressed matters of public concern.   Therefore, Plaintiffs satisfied the first prong of the *Boyer* analysis.

Once a court determines that the Plaintiffs' speech involves a matter of public concern, the *Boyer* balancing test requires a court to weigh the interest of a public employee in commenting on such matters against the interest of the employer in promoting the efficiency of its services.   We balance these interests by weighing the following factors: (1) whether the speech would or did create problems in maintaining discipline or harmony among coworkers; (2) whether the employment relationship is one in which personal loyalty and confidence are necessary; (3) whether the speech impeded the employee's ability to perform his responsibilities; (4) the time, place, and manner of the speech; and (5) whether the matter was one on which debate was vital to informed decision-making.

While possible disruption of the employer's operations does not satisfy the *Boyer* test, the government need not wait for speech actually to disrupt core operations before taking action.   The matters noted by the defendant at the hearing, i.e., the disruption of the prosecution of criminal cases and the disruption of personnel matters, were deemed by the trial court to tip the balance in favor of the employer.   Thus, Plaintiffs were unable to show a likelihood of success on the merits.

Irreparable Harm

We have held that the loss of First Amendment freedoms, for even minimal periods of time, unquestionably constitutes irreparable harm.   Nevertheless, we also must note that to show irreparable harm, the party seeking injunctive relief must at least demonstrate that there exists some cognizable danger of recurrent violation of its legal rights.   Here, the legal foundation for "irreparable harm" is an underlying violation of the Plaintiffs' constitutional rights. But, it is evident that the trial court was unable to conclude that such violations occurred or were occurring, and found that Plaintiffs did not demonstrate that they would have suffered irreparable harm if injunctive relief was not granted. We agree.

Furthermore, in the employment context, courts are loathe to grant preliminary injunctions because injuries often associated with employment discharge or discipline, such as damage to reputation, financial distress, and difficulty finding other employment, do not constitute irreparable harm. Plaintiffs wrongfully discharged from employment generally may be made whole by monetary damages after a full trial on the merits, such as in this case.

Balancing of harms

The moving party has the burden of showing that the threatened injury to the moving party outweighs the injury to the other party. The standard is easy to understand in common sense terms even if the expression is imperfect: the judge should grant or deny preliminary relief with the possibility in mind that an error might cause irreparable loss to either party. Consequently the judge should attempt to estimate the magnitude of that loss on each side and also the risk of error. That is, in deciding whether to grant or deny a preliminary injunction the court must choose the course of action that will minimize the costs of being mistaken. If the judge grants the preliminary injunction to a plaintiff who it later turns out is not entitled to any judicial relief - whose legal rights have not been violated - the judge commits a mistake whose gravity is measured by the irreparable harm, if any, that the injunction causes to the defendant while it is in effect. If the judge denies the preliminary injunction to a plaintiff who it later turns out is entitled to judicial relief, the judge commits a mistake whose gravity is measured by the irreparable harm, if any, that the denial of the preliminary injunction does to the plaintiff. The court below found the potential harm to the efficient and smooth operation of the police department to outweigh the prospective minimal First Amendment deprivation to be suffered by the plaintiffs. We do not disagree.

Not Adverse to the Public Interest

The moving party must demonstrate that the injunction, if issued, is not adverse to the public interest. This court has recognized that the public has a strong interest in the vindication of an individual's constitutional rights, particularly in encouraging the free flow of information and ideas under the First Amendment. On the other hand, in cases such as this, the public has an interest in the efficient and dependable operation of law enforcement agencies. The court below did not reach this issue. We need not either. In the absence of a showing of substantial likelihood of success on the merits, the court below did not err in denying Plaintiffs' motion for preliminary injunction.

Affirmed.

Harlan v. Yarnell

Columbia Supreme Court (2002)

Defendants, two state university officials, appeal from the superior court's finding of a violation of Plaintiff's First Amendment rights under the Columbia Constitution and awarding him damages. We affirm.

Background

Plaintiff Myron Harlan is a tenured faculty member at Columbia State University ("CSU"). He was appointed as an assistant professor in the Department of Accounting in 1989. His field is taxation. Beginning in 1995, Dr. Harlan sought to revoke the tenure of a colleague (Dr. William Mosser) on grounds of plagiarism and copyright violations, emotional abuse of students, abuse and harassment of staff, misuse of state funds, receipt of kickbacks from a publisher in return for adopting textbooks, and other charges. Administrators at CSU allegedly threatened Dr. Harlan with adverse employment-related actions unless his charges against Dr. Mosser were dropped. These threatened actions included termination of the Masters of Accounting (M.S.) degree program in which Dr. Harlan taught, assignment to teach courses outside his area of expertise, transfer to another department, and eventual termination due to overstaffing if the graduate program were eliminated.

Ultimately, a special university committee recommended that Dr. Mosser's tenure be retained, but it did so without considering evidence beyond the initial charges and without interviewing Dr. Harlan. In July 1996, Dr. Carlson became the Dean of the College of Business, and, after learning of the more than six years of divisiveness and dysfunction within the Department of Accounting, he proposed transferring Dr. Harlan out of the Department. In the summer of 1997, Dr. Harlan was transferred involuntarily from the Department of Accounting into the Department of Management, in which he claims he is not qualified to teach any courses, thereby resulting in a diminished ability to attract research funds, publish scholarship, receive salary increases, teach summer tax classes, and obtain reimbursement for professional dues and journal subscriptions. As we discuss in depth later, Dr. Harlan aired his professional concerns about being removed from the Department of Accounting to Dean Carlson several times before he was transferred. Dr. Harlan contends that he was notified in May 1998 that he could only teach two classes, both in tax, in the Department of Accounting in any given year. He further contends that adjunct staff and temporary faculty have been hired to teach the courses he normally teaches.

In response to the transfer, Dr. Harlan filed a grievance. Eventually, the Provost denied the grievance.

Dr. Harlan filed suit alleging that his transfer to the Department of Management was in retaliation for his public allegations against Dr. Mosser. He was awarded damages and injunctive relief following a jury trial. This appeal followed.

Discussion

Dr. Harlan's Columbia Constitution First Amendment claim rested on the assertion that state actors may not condition public employment on a basis that infringes the employee's constitutionally protected interest in freedom of expression and cannot retaliate against an employee for exercising his constitutionally protected right of free speech. In considering this type of claim, it is essential to identify the speech which resulted in the alleged retaliation. Here, Dr. Harlan's Aspeech@ consisted of his statements in support of administrative revocation of tenure of Dr. Mosser and his statements refusing to withdraw his support for an investigation despite the university's opposition.

The four-part test for evaluating a Columbia constitutional claim for First Amendment retaliation is stated in *Boyer*. The test is as follows: (1) whether the speech is protected, i.e., on a matter of public concern; (2) whether the employee's interest in commenting on matters of public concern outweighs the government employer's interest in promoting efficient government services. If the employee prevails on both these questions, step (3) requires the employee to demonstrate that his speech was a substantial or motivating factor in the adverse employment action. If the employee so demonstrates, step (4) considers whether the government employer has proven that it would have taken the same adverse employment action, even in the absence of the protected speech.

The trial court properly found that speech which discloses any evidence of corruption, impropriety, or other malfeasance on the part of state officials, in terms of content, clearly concerns matters of public importance. In deciding whether an employee's speech touches on a matter of public concern, or constitutes a personal grievance, courts look at the "content, form and context of a given statement, as revealed by the whole record." *Boyer.* They also consider the motive of the speaker B was the speech calculated to redress personal grievances or did it have a broader public purpose? Here, Dr. Harlan attempted to bring his concerns about Dr. Mosser to the CSU Administration, and stated in response to threats that if the charges were withdrawn, he would personally refile them. He wrote memos to the Provost about the lack of investigation that generated the recommendation that Dr. Mosser's tenure not be revoked and requested an investigation of the alleged threats made against him. The speech in this case fairly relates to charges at a public university that plainly would be of interest to the public, e.g., plagiarism and copyright violations, emotional abuse of students, abuse and harassment of staff, misuse of state funds, receipt of kickbacks from a publisher in return for adopting textbooks, and a claimed inadequate investigation of the allegations and alleged retaliation against the person who made the allegations.

Dean Carlson contended that Dr. Harlan merely sought to establish internal order in the Department of Accounting, not bring to light governmental wrongdoing. Of course, speech relating to an internal department dispute will normally be classified as a personal grievance outside of public concern. Dr. Harlan testified that while he knew that filing tenure revocation charges against Dr. Mosser would be divisive in the short run, in the long run it would lead to greater harmony in the Department because most of the problems were attributable to that issue. The fact that Dr. Harlan might receive an incidental benefit of what he perceived as improved working conditions does not transform his speech into purely personal grievances. Moreover, speech which touches on matters of public concern does not lose protection merely because some personal concerns are included. The trial court properly concluded that Dr. Harlan's speech related to matters of public concern.

As to the second step, the trial court balanced Dr. Harlan's right to speak out about this matter with the interests of his employer. In engaging in this balancing, courts consider the following factors: (1) whether the speech would or did create problems in maintaining discipline or harmony among coworkers; (2) whether the employment relationship is one in which personal loyalty and confidence are necessary; (3) whether the speech impeded the employee's ability to perform his responsibilities; (4) the time, place, and manner of the speech; and (5) whether the matter was one on which debate was vital to informed decision-making.

In weighing factor one, the trial court found that Dr. Harlan's speech contributed to disharmony among coworkers. Its inquiry properly did not stop there. In a democratic society, healthy levels of dissent and debate are essential to the vitality of institutions. In particular, an academic institution strives to foster critical thinking skills in its students and does so in part by modeling the give and take of debate within the institution itself. Thus, the court must consider the ability of the employer to do its essential work without undue disruption in its operations despite the exercise of free speech rights of its employees. Defendants were unable to convince the court that the disharmony caused disruption in teaching, research or administration at the school, nor were Defendants able to demonstrate long-term morale or discipline problems caused by the speech.

The second factor goes to the essence of the specific employer-employee relationship in question. For example, an executive depends upon the loyalty and confidence of her administrative assistant. Similarly, a political appointee must rely upon the loyalty of her aides. The trial court found here that the nature of the relationship between a professor in a department and his superiors did not necessitate loyalty and confidence.

The third factor speaks for itself. Here, the court found that Dr. Harlan's speech had no effect on his ability to perform his duties as a professor. He continued to teach classes, hold office hours, serve on faculty committees, and participate in outside activities such as conferences and symposia.

The court also considered the time, place and manner of Dr. Harlan's speech. It is noteworthy that Dr. Harlan's speech occurred through proper channels. He filed charges according to university protocols. He spoke with colleagues privately and in faculty or committee meetings. He aired his concerns directly with the Dean of the College. He then filed a grievance. This is not to say that more public forums for expression of opinions are never appropriate, but Dr. Harlan followed authorized procedures and appealed to appropriate authorities.

The next factor considers whether the matter was one on which debate was vital to informed decision-making. The allegations addressed a matter of public concern, not mere public interest, because they involve charges of wrongdoing and malfeasance. Thus, debate was essential to potentially avoid the alleged ongoing wrongdoing.

The third step of the *Boyer* test requires the employee to demonstrate that his speech was a substantial or motivating factor in the adverse employment action. There is no question here that the employer's motivation for transferring Dr. Harlan was his speech.

The fourth step considers whether the government employer has proven that it would have taken the same adverse employment action, even in the absence of the protected speech. Dean Carlson testified that "every expression of the reason for Dean Carlson's transfer of Dr. Harlan in August 1997 involved an attempt to resolve once and for all six years of divisiveness and dysfunction within the Department." We recognize that Dean Carlson testified that there were a variety of reasons (other than the content of Dr. Harlan's protected speech) for the transfer: (1) getting the Department of Accounting back on track after 8 to 9 years of divisiveness between the Accounting faculty and the Tax and Law faculty, (2) getting the Department to focus on the upcoming 150-hour requirement for accounting professionals, (3) increasing the productivity of the non-tenured faculty, and (4) finding a suitable fit between Dr. Harlan's non-accounting and interdisciplinary Ph.D. and the Department of Management. In examining the record before us, however, we are not persuaded that the court erred in finding that CSU would not have transferred Dr. Harlan in the absence of his speech.

Affirmed.

SNYDER v. REGENTS OF THE UNIVERSITY OF COLUMBIA

LIBRARY

> Goes to COA elements — preliminary injunction and free speech employment rules within such a COA — both asked about in task.

> (—) for us so need to distinguish our client (P) from these Ps.

> Note the ct. and jx– binding.

Elkins v. Hamel

Columbia Supreme Court (2007)

[Parties] This is an <u>action brought</u> pursuant to Columbia Civil Rights Code ' 1983 <u>by two City of Tunbridge police officers against Steve Hamel, the City of Tunbridge police chief</u>, alleging a <u>violation of their First Amendment rights</u> under the Columbia Constitution. In their complaint, <u>plaintiffs Kenneth Elkins and George Chanel assert they have been illegally disciplined by Chief Hamel for exercising their rights to free speech</u>. Plaintiff Elkins asserts he has been disciplined by a fifteen day suspension, and plaintiff Chanel asserts he has been disciplined by a one day suspension. <u>They sought a preliminary injunction.</u> Plaintiffs <u>requested rescission of their suspensions.</u> They further sought injunctive relief restraining and enjoining the defendant from further discipline or threat of discipline for the exercise of their rights to free speech. The <u>request for injunctive relief was denied, and this appeal followed.</u>

[Ps argue]

[COA]

[T. Ct. for D; Ps appeal]

[Facts] The verified complaint sets forth the following facts: On February 16, 2006, Glenda Oliver wrote a column in the *Tunbridge Journal* addressing several issues "concerning her perception of racism in the state court criminal system." The complaint notes: "Ms. Oliver's comments included her questioning the justice involved in the sentencing of a young African-American male on drug charges since no other African-Americans were involved in the young man's sentencing, including the jury, judge and attorneys involved." The column concluded with Ms. Oliver's e-mail address, which was provided for the public to contact her with comments.

On the next day, plaintiff Elkins sent an e-mail from his personal account at his home to several officers of the Tunbridge Police Department (TPD) and the editorial departments of the *Tunbridge Journal* and the *Tunbridge Metro News*. On February 19, 2006, plaintiff Chanel sent an e-mail from his personal account at his residence to Ms. Oliver in

Facts continued

response to her column. The complaint states: "Chanel commented that Ms. Oliver's article was racist in tone, and stated his belief that the young man referred to in her article was not sentenced because of his race." Ms. Oliver responded by e-mail to Chanel's e-mail. Chanel sent this e-mail to Elkins and TPD officer David Ernst. On February 22, 2006 Elkins sent an e-mail from his TPD account at his home to the e-mail accounts of Chanel, Ernst and Ms. Oliver. The complaint states: "The e-mail contained comments in response to Ms. Oliver's article regarding her allegations of racism in the state court system." On February 24, 2006, Elkins' comments that had been sent to the newspapers' editorial boards were published in both papers. On March 13, 2006, Chief Hamel instituted discipline in the form of a one day suspension without pay for Chanel and a fifteen day suspension without pay for Elkins.

Discipline

Rule

We review the decision to deny a motion for a preliminary injunction for abuse of discretion. In order to obtain a preliminary injunction, a party must demonstrate the following: (1) a substantial likelihood of prevailing on the merits; (2) irreparable harm in the absence of the injunction; (3) the threatened harm outweighs any damage the injunction may cause to the party opposing it; and (4) the injunction, if issued, will not be adverse to the public interest.

Std. of review

Substantial Likelihood of Success on the Merits

Element 1: easy to follow with headings; this should give you an idea of how to organize your headings in your memo.

Rule

Plaintiffs are correct that public employees retain their First Amendment rights under the Columbia Constitution. However, in the public employment context, a public employer may impose some restraints on job-related speech of public employees that would be plainly unconstitutional if applied to the public at large. This is particularly true of police officers. Because police departments function as paramilitary organizations charged with maintaining public safety and order, police departments are given more latitude in their decisions regarding discipline and personnel regulations than an ordinary government employer.

Reasoning

Boyer test rule	To determine whether a public employer's actions impermissibly infringe on free speech rights, this court has followed <u>the *Boyer* test</u> enunciated by this Court.[a] The test is as follows: (1) Does the speech in question involve a matter of public concern? <u>If so,</u> (2) we must weigh the employee's interest in the expression against the government employer's interest in regulating the speech of its employees so that it can carry on an efficient and effective workplace. <u>If the employee prevails on both these questions, we proceed to the remaining two steps.</u> In step (3), the employee must show the speech was a substantial factor driving the challenged governmental action. If the employee succeeds, in step (4) the employer, in order to prevail, must in turn show that it would have taken the same action against the employee even in the absence of the protected speech.

Rule: public concern (goes to factor 1 of the Boyer test).	<u>Whether an employee's speech addresses a matter of public concern must be determined by the content, form, and context of a given statement, as revealed by the whole record.</u> In evaluating the nature of an employee's speech in a retaliatory discipline or discharge case, we have articulated that <u>when an employee speaks as an employee upon matters only of personal interest the speech is not protected.</u> To judge <u>whether particular speech relates merely to internal workplace issues, courts must conduct a case by case inquiry, looking to the content, form, and context of the speech, which includes scrutinizing whether the speaker's purpose was to bring an issue to the public's attention or to air a personal grievance.</u> <u>An employee's speech must not merely relate generally to a subject matter that is of public interest, but must sufficiently inform the issue as to be helpful to the public in evaluating the conduct of government.</u> That is, we look beyond the general topic of the speech to evaluate more specifically what was said on the topic.	Another rule Another rule

---

[a] The language of the Columbia Constitution's First Amendment is identical to that of the U.S. Constitution. Historically, this Court has interpreted these words more expansively than the U.S. Supreme Court. As such, we choose not to follow the recent U.S. Supreme Court opinion in *Garcetti v. Ceballos* (2006).

Reason factor 1 of Boyer test met.	Because Plaintiffs' letters concerned the integrity of the police department's operations, though arguably touching upon internal workplace issues, the speech addressed matters of public concern. Therefore, Plaintiffs satisfied the first prong of the *Boyer* analysis.

Factor 2 of Boyer test	Once a court determines that the Plaintiffs' speech involves a matter of public concern, the *Boyer* balancing test requires a court to weigh the interest of a public employee in commenting on such matters against the interest of the employer in promoting the efficiency of its services. We balance these interests by weighing the following factors:
Another factor test that goes to factor 2 of the Boyer test.	(1) whether the speech would or did create problems in maintaining discipline or harmony among coworkers; (2) whether the employment relationship is one in which personal loyalty and confidence are necessary; (3) whether the speech impeded the employee's ability to perform his responsibilities; (4) the time, place, and manner of the speech; and (5) whether the matter was one on which debate was vital to informed decision-making.

Reasoning (for D)	While possible disruption of the employer's operations does not satisfy the *Boyer* test, the government need not wait for speech actually to disrupt core operations before taking action. The matters noted by the defendant at the hearing, i.e., the disruption of the prosecution of criminal cases and the disruption of personnel matters, were deemed by the trial court to tip the balance in favor of the employer. Thus, Plaintiffs were unable to show a likelihood of success on the merits.

Irreparable Harm	Element 2 for preliminary injunction

Ps did not meet element 1 to preliminary injunction.

Rule	We have held that the loss of First Amendment freedoms, for even minimal periods of time, unquestionably constitutes irreparable harm. Nevertheless, we also must note that to show irreparable harm, the party seeking injunctive relief must at least demonstrate that there exists some cognizable danger of recurrent violation of its legal rights. Here, the legal foundation for "irreparable harm" is an underlying violation of the Plaintiffs' constitutional rights. But, it is evident that the trial court was unable to

Reasoning (for D)	conclude that such violations occurred or were occurring, and found that <u>Plaintiffs did not demonstrate that they would have suffered irreparable harm if injunctive relief was not granted. We agree.</u>

More reasoning	Furthermore, in the employment context, courts are loathe to grant preliminary injunctions because injuries often associated with employment discharge or discipline, <u>such as damage to reputation, financial distress, and difficulty finding other employment, do not constitute irreparable harm.</u> Plaintiffs wrongfully discharged from employment generally may be made whole by monetary damages after a full trial on the merits, such as in this case.

<u>Balancing of harms</u> | Element 3 for preliminary injunction |

Rule/ burden	The moving party has the burden of showing that the threatened injury to the moving party outweighs the injury to the other party. The standard is easy to understand in

common sense terms even if the expression is imperfect: the judge should grant or deny preliminary relief with the possibility in mind that an error might cause irreparable loss to either party. Consequently the judge should attempt to estimate the magnitude of that loss on each side and also the risk of error. That is, in deciding whether to grant or deny a preliminary injunction the court must choose the course of action that will minimize the costs of being mistaken. If the judge grants the preliminary injunction to a plaintiff who it later turns out is not entitled to any judicial relief - whose legal rights have not been violated - the judge commits a mistake whose gravity is measured by the irreparable harm, if any, that the injunction causes to the defendant while it is in effect. If the judge denies the preliminary injunction to a plaintiff who it later turns out is entitled to judicial relief, the judge commits a mistake whose gravity is measured by the irreparable harm, if any, that the denial of the preliminary injunction does to the plaintiff. <u>The court below found the potential harm to the efficient and smooth operation of the police</u>

Reasoning (for D)	<u>department to outweigh the prospective minimal First Amendment deprivation to be suffered by the plaintiffs. We do not disagree.</u>

Not Adverse to the Public Interest

Element 4 for
preliminary injunction

Rule/
burden

The moving party must demonstrate that the injunction, if issued, is not adverse to the public interest. This court has recognized that the public has a strong interest in the vindication of an individual's constitutional rights, particularly in encouraging the free flow of information and ideas under the First Amendment. On the other hand, in cases such as this, the public has an interest in the efficient and dependable operation of law enforcement agencies. The court below did not reach this issue. We need not either. In the absence of a showing of substantial likelihood of success on the merits, the court below did not err in denying Plaintiffs' motion for preliminary injunction.

This
element
not
analyzed.

Affirmed.

For D

Goes to the free speech issue (needed to prove element 1 for preliminary injunction).

+ for us so analogize our facts to this case

Note the ct. and jx: binding (older case than last case).

Harlan v. Yarnell

Columbia Supreme Court (2002)

Parties and issue

Defendants, two state university officials, appeal from the superior court's finding of a violation of Plaintiff's First Amendment rights under the Columbia Constitution and awarding him damages. We affirm.   For P

Background

Facts

Plaintiff Myron Harlan is a tenured faculty member at Columbia State University ("CSU"). He was appointed as an assistant professor in the Department of Accounting in 1989. His field is taxation. Beginning in 1995, Dr. Harlan sought to revoke the tenure of a colleague (Dr. William Mosser) on grounds of plagiarism and copyright violations, emotional abuse of students, abuse and harassment of staff, misuse of state funds, receipt of kickbacks from a publisher in return for adopting textbooks, and other charges. Administrators at CSU allegedly threatened Dr. Harlan with adverse employment-related actions unless his charges against Dr. Mosser were dropped. These threatened actions included termination of the Masters of Accounting (M.S.) degree program in which Dr. Harlan taught, assignment to teach courses outside his area of expertise, transfer to another department, and eventual termination due to overstaffing if the graduate program were eliminated.

Ultimately, a special university committee recommended that Dr. Mosser's tenure be retained, but it did so without considering evidence beyond the initial charges and without interviewing Dr. Harlan. In July 1996, Dr. Carlson became the Dean of the College of Business, and, after learning of the more than six years of divisiveness and dysfunction within the Department of Accounting, he proposed transferring Dr. Harlan out of the Department. In the summer of 1997, Dr. Harlan was transferred involuntarily from the Department of Accounting into the Department of Management, in which he claims he is not qualified to teach any courses, thereby resulting in a diminished ability

Action against P/ harm to P

to attract research funds, publish scholarship, receive salary increases, teach summer tax classes, and obtain reimbursement for professional dues and journal subscriptions. As we discuss in depth later, Dr. Harlan aired his professional concerns about being removed from the Department of Accounting to Dean Carlson several times before he was transferred. Dr. Harlan contends that he was notified in May 1998 that he could only teach two classes, both in tax, in the Department of Accounting in any given year. He further contends that adjunct staff and temporary faculty have been hired to teach the courses he normally teaches.

> P argues these harms.

In response to the transfer, Dr. Harlan filed a grievance. Eventually, the Provost denied the grievance.

> T. Ct. for P

Dr. Harlan filed suit alleging that his transfer to the Department of Management was in retaliation for his public allegations against Dr. Mosser. He was awarded damages and injunctive relief following a jury trial. This appeal followed.

Discussion

> Rule

Dr. Harlan's Columbia Constitution First Amendment claim rested on the assertion that state actors may not condition public employment on a basis that infringes the employee's constitutionally protected interest in freedom of expression and cannot retaliate against an employee for exercising his constitutionally protected right of free speech. In considering this type of claim, it is essential to identify the speech which resulted in the alleged retaliation. Here, Dr. Harlan's "speech" consisted of

> Speech at issue

his statements in support of administrative revocation of tenure of Dr. Mosser and his statements refusing to withdraw his support for an investigation despite the university's opposition.

> Rule: same test as in last case.

The four-part test for evaluating a Columbia constitutional claim for First Amendment retaliation is stated in *Boyer*. The test is as follows: (1) whether the speech is protected, i.e., on a matter of public concern; (2) whether the employee's interest in commenting

Boyer test continued

on matters of public concern outweighs the government employer's interest in promoting efficient government services. If the employee prevails on both these questions, step (3) requires the employee to demonstrate that his speech was a substantial or motivating factor in the adverse employment action. If the employee so demonstrates, step (4) considers whether the government employer has proven that it would have taken the same adverse employment action, even in the absence of the protected speech.

Part 1 of Boyer test

Rules

Rule

The trial court properly found that speech which discloses any evidence of corruption, impropriety, or other malfeasance on the part of state officials, in terms of content, clearly concerns matters of public importance. In deciding whether an employee's speech touches on a matter of public concern, or constitutes a personal grievance, courts look at the "content, form and context of a given statement, as revealed by the whole record." *Boyer.* They also consider the motive of the speaker - was the speech calculated to redress personal grievances or did it have a broader public purpose?

Reasoning in public interest

Here, Dr. Harlan attempted to bring his concerns about Dr. Mosser to the CSU Administration, and stated in response to threats that if the charges were withdrawn, he would personally refile them. He wrote memos to the Provost about the lack of investigation that generated the recommendation that Dr. Mosser's tenure not be revoked and requested an investigation of the alleged threats made against him. The speech in this case fairly relates to charges at a public university that plainly would be of interest to the public, e.g., plagiarism and copyright violations, emotional abuse of students, abuse and harassment of staff, misuse of state funds, receipt of kickbacks from a publisher in return for adopting textbooks, and a claimed inadequate investigation of the allegations and alleged retaliation against the person who made the allegations.

D argues

Dean Carlson contended that Dr. Harlan merely sought to establish internal order in the Department of Accounting, not bring to light governmental wrongdoing. Of course, speech relating to an internal department dispute will normally be classified as a

P argues	personal grievance outside of public concern. Dr. Harlan testified that while he knew that filing tenure revocation charges against Dr. Mosser would be divisive in the short run, in the long run it would lead to greater harmony in the Department because most of the problems were attributable to that issue. The fact that Dr. Harlan might receive an
Reasoning	incidental benefit of what he perceived as improved working conditions does not transform his speech into purely personal grievances. Moreover, speech which touches on matters of public concern does not lose protection merely because some personal concerns are included. The trial court properly concluded that Dr. Harlan's speech related to matters of public concern.

Part 2 of Boyer test

Factor test that goes to part 2 of Boyer; same as in last case.	As to the second step, the trial court balanced Dr. Harlan's right to speak out about this matter with the interests of his employer. In engaging in this balancing, courts consider the following factors: (1) whether the speech would or did create problems in maintaining discipline or harmony among coworkers; (2) whether the employment relationship is one in which personal loyalty and confidence are necessary; (3) whether the speech impeded the employee's ability to perform his responsibilities; (4) the time, place, and manner of the speech; and (5) whether the matter was one on which debate was vital to informed decision-making.

Reasoning (for P) for factor 1	In weighing factor one, the trial court found that Dr. Harlan's speech contributed to disharmony among coworkers. Its inquiry properly did not stop there. In a democratic society, healthy levels of dissent and debate are essential to the vitality of institutions. In particular, an academic institution strives to foster critical thinking skills in its students and does so in part by modeling the give and take of debate within the institution itself. Thus, the court must consider the ability of the employer to do its essential work without undue disruption in its operations despite the exercise of free speech rights of its employees. Defendants were unable to convince the court that the disharmony caused disruption in teaching, research or administration at the school, nor were Defendants able to demonstrate long-term morale or discipline problems caused by the speech.

| Reasoning (for P) for factor 2 | The second factor goes to the essence of the specific employer-employee relationship in question. For example, an executive depends upon the loyalty and confidence of her administrative assistant. Similarly, a political appointee must rely upon the loyalty of her aides. The trial court found here that the nature of the relationship between a professor in a department and his superiors did not necessitate loyalty and confidence. |

| Reasoning (for P) for factor 3 | The third factor speaks for itself. Here, the court found that Dr. Harlan's speech had no effect on his ability to perform his duties as a professor. He continued to teach classes, hold office hours, serve on faculty committees, and participate in outside activities such as conferences and symposia. |

| Reasoning (for P) for factor 4 | The court also considered the time, place and manner of Dr. Harlan's speech. It is noteworthy that Dr. Harlan's speech occurred through proper channels. He filed charges according to university protocols. He spoke with colleagues privately and in faculty or committee meetings. He aired his concerns directly with the Dean of the College. He then filed a grievance. This is not to say that more public forums for expression of opinions are never appropriate, but Dr. Harlan followed authorized procedures and appealed to appropriate authorities. |

| Reasoning (for P) for factor 5 | The next factor considers whether the matter was one on which debate was vital to informed decision-making. The allegations addressed a matter of public concern, not mere public interest, because they involve charges of wrongdoing and malfeasance. Thus, debate was essential to potentially avoid the alleged ongoing wrongdoing. |

The third step of the *Boyer* test requires the employee to demonstrate that his speech was a substantial or motivating factor in the adverse employment action. There is no question here that the employer's motivation for transferring Dr. Harlan was his speech.

| Part 3 of Boyer test |

Reasoning (for P)

The fourth step considers whether the government employer has proven that it would have taken the same adverse employment action, even in the absence of the protected

| Part 4 of Boyer test |

speech. Dean Carlson testified that "every expression of the reason for Dean Carlson's transfer of Dr. Harlan in August 1997 involved an attempt to resolve once and for all six years of divisiveness and dysfunction within the Department." We recognize that Dean Carlson testified that there were a <u>variety of reasons</u> (other than the content of Dr. Harlan's protected speech) <u>for the transfer</u>: (1) getting the Department of Accounting back on track after 8 to 9 years of divisiveness between the Accounting faculty and the Tax and Law faculty, (2) getting the Department to focus on the upcoming 150-hour requirement for accounting professionals, (3) increasing the productivity of the non-tenured faculty, and (4) finding a suitable fit between Dr. Harlan's non-accounting and interdisciplinary Ph.D. and the Department of Management. <u>In examining the record</u>

Reasoning <u>before us, however, we are not persuaded that the court erred in finding that CSU would not have transferred Dr. Harlan in the absence of his speech.</u>

<u>Affirmed.</u> For P

Snyder v. Regents Rule Deconstruction Examples

Elkins v. Hamel rules

EXAMPLE 1:

Applies to the preliminary injunction task:

In order to obtain a preliminary injunction, a party must demonstrate the following: (1) a substantial likelihood of prevailing on the merits; (2) irreparable harm in the absence of the injunction; (3) the threatened harm outweighs any damage the injunction may cause to the party opposing it; and(4) the injunction, if issued, will not be adverse to the public interest.

Deconstruct this rule as follows after stating the overall rule upfront:

(1) Substantial likelihood of prevailing on the merits

(2) Irreparable harm

(3) Balancing of interests

(4) Adverse to the public interest

Format: Analyze the elements separately with headings and separate paragraphs for each element.

EXAMPLE 2:

Applies to the speech related issues (necessary to analyze for the first element of preliminary injunction — likelihood of prevailing on the merits):

To determine whether a public employer's actions impermissibly infringe on free speech rights, the Boyer test is analyzed: (1) Does the speech in question involve a matter of public concern? If so, (2) we must weigh the employee's interest in the expression against the government employer's interest in regulating the speech of its employees so that it can carry on an efficient and effective workplace. If the employee prevails on both these questions, proceed to the remaining two steps. In step (3), the employee must show the speech was a substantial factor driving the challenged governmental action. If the employee succeeds, in step (4) the employer, in order to prevail, must in turn show that it would have taken the same action against the employee even in the absence of the protected speech.

Deconstruct this rule as follows after stating the overall rule upfront:

    (1) Public concern

If yes, then go to (2)

    (2) Balance interests

If (1) and (2) are met in the employee's favor, go to (3)

    (3) Speech was a substantial factor

If yes to (3), go to (4)

    (4) Employer would have taken same action

<u>Format:</u> **Analyze the test elements separately and clearly, preferably with headings and separate paragraphs — ensuring that make sure you properly indent the headings since this test/rule belongs to one element of another rule.**

<u>EXAMPLE 3:</u>

Applies to the speech-related issues (necessary to analyze for the first element of preliminary injunction — likelihood of prevailing on the merits):

Courts balance these interests (factor 2 above) by weighing the following factors: (1) whether the speech would or did create problems in maintaining discipline or harmony among coworkers; (2) whether the employment relationship is one in which personal loyalty and confidence are necessary; (3) whether the speech impeded the employee's ability to perform his responsibilities; (4) the time, place, and manner of the speech; and (5) whether the matter was one on which debate was vital to informed decision-making.

Deconstruct this rule as follows after stating the overall rule upfront:

(a) Discipline or harmony among coworkers
(b) Employment relationship
(c) Employee's ability to perform
(d) Time, place, and manner of the speech
(e) Debate vital to informed decision-making

<u>Format:</u> **Analyze the factors separately (preferably with separate paragraphs), but due to timing and lack of facts (you will determine this after reading the file), you may not use headings for sub-sub rules such as these.**

The last three deconstructed rules would appear as follows on the performance test (you need to deconstruct the rules and combine and organize them properly):

Preliminary Injunction

(1) Substantial likelihood of prevailing on the merits

Here the merits would be free speech, so you need to go through free speech rules here as follows:

   (1) Public concern

If yes, then go to (2)

     (2) Balance interests
        (a) Discipline or harmony among coworkers
        (b) Employment relationship
        (c) Employee's ability to perform
        (d) Time, place, and manner of the speech
        (e) Debate vital to informed decision-making

If (1) and (2) are met in the employee's favor, go to (3)

     (3) Speech was a substantial factor

If yes to (3), go to (4)

     (4) Employer would have taken same action

(2) Irreparable harm

(3) Balancing of interests

(4) Adverse to the public interest

<u>Rule Deconstruction tip:</u> It is important that you have each factor test (whether it is the sub-test to an element or the sub-sub-test to a factor that is already the sub-test to another test) in the proper place for organization purposes. Also note that not all cases provide new rules (here the second case, <u>Harlan</u>, is not here since it just analyzed the same rules provided in the first case from a different perspective).

SAMPLE TASK 2 STRUCTURE (Objective Memorandum)

Memorandum

To: R.J. Morrison
From: Applicant
Re: Snyder v. Regents of University of Columbia
Date: February 28, 2008

> Label it as a memorandum and format it like a memo.

I.   Statement of Facts

> Since they tell you to do a brief one-paragraph statement of facts be sure to do exactly that and label it, since you are writing a memo.

Dr. Snyder is the Chairperson of the Dept. of Medicine at the University of Columbia. He has worked the last 20 years building up the Dept. of Medicine. The School of Medicine is considering moving its location 20 miles away from its current location, which Dr. Snyder opposes. Dr. Snyder's reasons for opposing the move include separation of facilities from the research facilities and the medical school, citizens of Columbia not getting their monies' worth because the bonds will take 40 years to pay off, and the lack of public transportation to the medical center, which is 20 miles away. Dr. Snyder proposed splitting some faculty in each location and voiced his concerns to the faculty in a report and wrote a letter to the editor of the Star Bulletin complaining about the relocation plans. In his letter, he referred readers to visit his report on his UC website. Community activists are using Dr. Snyder's letter in their support to prevent the move too. Nonetheless, the Regents voted to move the campus and the day after sent Dr. Snyder a termination letter as Chairperson, but maintained his tenure status. Dr. Snyder is now seeking advice on a possible preliminary injunction.

> Use broad relevant facts that tell the story.

> End by stating what relief the client is seeking.

II.   Discussion

Preliminary injunction

> Since they did not give you a particular format for the headings and since this PT has several headings due to numerous tests and tests within tests, simple headings will suffice.

> Main rule for the cause of action the client is seeking.

To obtain a preliminary injunction, a party must demonstrate that (1) he has a substantial likelihood of prevailing on the merits, (2) he will suffer irreparable harm in the absence of an injunction, (3) the threatened harm outweighs any damage the injunction may cause to the party opposing it, and (4) the injunction, if issued, will not be adverse to the public interest. <u>Elkins</u>.

1.   <u>Substantial likelihood of prevailing on the merits</u>

> Use headings for each element—easier for the grader to follow and best for memos.

Dr. Snyder must be able to show that he has a proper claim for infringement of his First Amendment rights under the Columbia State Constitution. In the public employment context, a public employer may impose some restraints on job-related speech of public employees that would be unconstitutional if applied to the public at large. Elkins.

In the first case, you will find rules for some of the elements, and each rule is provided in proper chronological order with the main elements above.

To determine whether a public employer's actions impermissibly infringe on free speech rights, the Columbia Supreme Court in Boyer adopted a four-part test. Elkins. The Boyer test requires the court to analyze the following: (1) Does the speech in question involve a matter of public concern? If so, (2) we must weigh the employee's interest in the expression against the government employer's interest in regulating the speech of its employees so that it can carry on an efficient and effective workplace. If the employee prevails on both these questions, we proceed to the remaining two steps. In step (3), the employee must show the speech was a substantial factor driving the challenged governmental action. If the employee succeeds, in step (4) the employer, in order to prevail, must in turn show that it would have taken the same action against the employee even in the absence of the protected speech. Elkins citing Boyer.

The first case cites another case that provides a test used just to analyze the first element of the main test; it is important that you organize where these rules go as you read the case, either on your paper or the computer.

(1) Matter of public concern

Indent and label the sub-issues so the grader can easily see that these are part of a bigger test above.

Whether an employee's speech addresses a matter of public concern must be determined by the content, form, and context of a given statement, as revealed by the whole record. Elkins. For discipline or discharge cases, when an employee speaks as an employee upon matters only of personal interest, the speech is not protected. Elkins.

Our mini-rule for our mini issue.

Analysis for this issue/ rule: you have to find facts in the file that align to public concern.

Here, Dr. Snyder's speech was not just a matter of personal interest as he was concerning with the community at large. In fact, he was concerned because the new location is 20 miles away from the current location and there is no public transportation to help people get there. Further, he was concerned that the citizens of Columbia might not get their monies' worth because the bonds would take 40 years to pay off. Finally, he was also concerned about isolating faculty in research from those in the medical school by having the medical center so far away from the research. Thus, considering the content of his speech in regard to the entire community and institution his speech was a matter of public concern. Further, in regard to the form of his speech, he wrote a report to the faculty and the school as well as a letter to the editor of the Star Bulletin, both of which are appropriate forums to voice concerns regarding the school and its move that will affect the community.

> This further breaks down the rule and requires further analysis.

The court in <u>Elkins</u> further stated that to evaluate whether particular speech relates merely to internal workplace issues, courts must conduct a case by case inquiry to see whether the speaker's purpose was to bring an issue to the public's attention or to air a personal grievance. Here, the University will allege that Dr. Snyder was angry because they rejected his proposal and thus sought a personal grievance. However, Dr. Snyder has disagreed with the University in the past and once outvoted he has always gone with the plan.

> This is the rule explanation followed by the comparison of the facts in our case.

In <u>Elkins</u>, the court found that the letters police wrote in response to an editorial about racism in the criminal system did concern the integrity of the police department's operations and thus were a matter of public concern. Similar to Elkins, here, Dr. Snyder's comments in response to a proposed move of a medical facility concerned the entire community and taxpayer money spent in bonds. Thus, his speech is also a matter of public concern.

> Now you need to move onto the next part of the test.

Since, Dr. Snyder's speech was a matter of public concern, the second part of the <u>Boyer</u> test must be analyzed: (2) weigh the employee's interest in the expression against the government employer's interest in regulating the speech of its employees so that it can carry on an efficient and effective workplace.

> Again, use a heading for the next part of the test.

(2) <u>Weigh the employee's interest against the employer's interest</u>

> Here it gets tricky if you aren't organized. The second case in the library gives you another 5-part test for one of the factors in the last test from the first case (which was also a new rule within the overall main rule for one of the main elements).

In engaging in this balancing, courts consider the following factors: (a) whether the speech would or did create problems in maintaining discipline or harmony among coworkers; (b) whether the employment relationship is one in which personal loyalty and confidence are necessary; (c) whether the speech impeded the employee's ability to perform his responsibilities; (d) the time, place, and manner of the speech; and (e) whether the matter was one on which debate was vital to informed decision-making. <u>Harlan</u>.

(a) Discipline or harmony among coworkers

> Note how this heading is even further indented to show it is an element within the prior bigger element/factor test.

In weighing the employee's interest against the employer's interest, the court will consider whether the speech would or did create problems in maintaining discipline or harmony among coworkers. Harlan. In Harlan, the court found that Dr. Harlan's speech contributed to disharmony among coworkers, but in a democratic society, healthy levels of dissent and debate are essential to the vitality of institutions. Similarly, here tension among faculty is possible if other professors felt intimidated by Dr. Snyder opposing the move and asking them to sign a petition, but they signed the petition voluntarily and could have declined.

> This is another rule explanation followed by a brief analysis of the facts in our case.

> Note that as the factors seem to go on and on the analysis for most of them is very short.

> Next you would quickly analyze the remaining factors in this test just as you did above and you would note that the analysis is quick and short here since there are not many facts to analyze.

(b) Employment relationship

(c) Employee's ability to perform

(d) Time, place, and manner of speech

(e) Debate vital to decision making

(3) <u>Employee must show the speech was a substantial factor</u>

(4) <u>The employer must show that it would have taken the same action even in the absence of the protected speech</u>

> You would still need to analyze the last two factors of the prior test as well, but since everything was already input into your roadmap you would be fine.

2. **Irreparable Harm**

3. **Balancing of Harms**

4. **Public Interest**

III.   **Conclusion**

> Finally you would analyze the last 3 elements for the main issue — preliminary injunction — and you would notice that none of these elements have separate tests within them and the analysis here is short compared to the first element. This is a reminder that not all elements or points within a brief are equally weighted, which is why creating a roadmap before writing is crucial to help you plan your time.

> Have an overall conclusion summarizing the main test and your conclusion.

Since Dr. Snyder is able to prove that he has a substantial likelihood of prevailing on the merits of his free speech claim, that he will suffer irreparable harm in the absence of an injunction, that the threatened harm to him outweighs any damage the injunction may cause to the University, and that the injunction will not be adverse to the public interest, Dr. Snyder should be able to obtain a preliminary injunction against the University. Therefore, he should be able to prevent them from removing him as the Chairperson for the Department of Medicine.